Outdoor Living
❖ The Ultimate Project Guide ❖

Outdoor Living
The Ultimate Project Guide

Published by Landauer Corporation
3100 NW 101st Street, Suite A
Urbandale, IA 50322
800-557-2144

CREDITS

Tom Carpenter
Creative Director

Mark Johanson
Book Products Development Manager

Dan Cary
Photo Production Editor

Chris Marshall
Editorial Coordinator

Steve Anderson
Senior Editorial Assistant

John English, Kam Ghaffari, Dave Griffin
Bill Hylton, Richard Steven
Authors & Project Designers

Jim Barret
Contributing Writer

Bill Nelson
Series Design, Art Direction and Production

Marti Naughton
Art Direction and Production

Mark Macemon
Lead Photographer

Kim Bailey, Ralph Karlen, Dan Cary, Walter Chandoha, William D. Adams
Photography

Craig Claeys, Jon Drigot, Bruce Kieffer, Bill Nelson
Illustrators

Jon Drigot
Contributing Project Designer

John Nadeau, Jon Hegge, Tom Deveny, Troy Johnson
Project Builders

Brad Classon, Carolyn Henry-Johanson, Kari Schwab
Production Assistance

Jennifer Weaverling, Heather Koshiol
Senior Book Development Coordinators

PHOTO CREDITS

Pages 10, 11
Hedberg Aggregates

Pages 13, 15, 59, 77, 78, 79, 80, 97, 98
Southern Pine Council

Pages 13, 21
Portland Cement Association

Pages 12, 14, 59
Keystone Retaining Wall Systems

Page 21
Brick Institute of America

Pages 11, 12, 14, 15, 77, 78, 98, 99, 151, 152
California Redwood Association

Pages 10, 11, 15, 45, 53, 54, 55, 56
Lilypons Water Gardens

Pages 13, 78
Jim Barrett

Pages 262, 269, 270
GardenStyles

ISBN 1-890621-80-3

Printed in China
10 9 8 7 6 5 4 3 2 1

Table of Contents

2 Yard & Garden Structures

3 Backyard Woodworking Projects

4 The Perfect Yard

Welcome to *Outdoor Living* and its *Ultimate Project Guide*

Outdoor living is a casual activity, and the projects we build for our yards reflect it. Generally, they are simpler than interior projects, and the standards by which we judge them aren't as high —building a cedar picnic table is a lot easier than building a cherry dining table, and if you make a few mistakes along the way no one is likely to notice or care.

So from a practical standpoint, outdoor building projects are very popular. But there is more to it than that. Whether it's an interlocking block retaining wall or a classic Adirondack chair for the deck, do-it-yourself projects for outdoor living are fun and gratifying.

In this book you will find nearly 1,000 beautiful, color photos of projects for outdoor living. A basic deck planter built with only portable power tools. A sophisticated gazebo that's as beautiful to look at as it is challenging to build. An in-ground garden pond with a playful fountain. And dozens upon dozens more Taken together, the yard upgrades and furnishings you'll find on these pages cover a huge range of complexities, purposes and lifestyles.

For your convenience, *Outdoor Living — The Ultimate Project Guide* is divided into four major parts, each with its own index at the very end of the book. It's like getting three books for the price of one

The first section, "Landscape Structures Decks," is packed with information and projects within the category that has come to be known as "Hardscaping." Featured projects include patios and walkways, fences and gates, landscape walls, and ponds. Each project is pictured in thorough detail from start to finish. Plus, you get plenty of helpful tips and building insights along the way. Also included in this major section is a spectacular 70-page primer on one of the most popular do-it-yourself projects today: building decks. From deck design to setting posts to laying decking, you'll be hard-pressed to find a deckbuilding question left unanswered.

The second part, "Yard Garden Structures," focuses on an array of beautiful and functional projects that will improve the quality of your outdoor living. Beginner and professional alike will discover the inside information on how to go about building several popular outdoor structures, including a cedar gazebo, an elegant arbor-and-trellis, a landscape bridge, a tool shed made from scratch and more. Plus, photos detail the construction of a kit-built shed and greenhouse.

You'll find the third major section of this book useful whether it's the height of summer or the dead of winter. "Backyard Woodworking Projects" is a collection of 4 carpentry and woodworking projects you can build in your workshop, garage or yard. Included among them are an Adirondack chair and a garden bench plan. Each project features step-by-step photographs, an exploded view drawing with details, a cutting list, a shopping list and detailed step-by-step instructions.

The fourth part, "The Perfect Yard," shows you how to create a showcase-quality yard without spending all your time doing back-breaking work. When you approach the challenge with a good plan (like the one outlined here), having a great yard is no longer a hassle. You'll come to understand the grasses you should be using for your particular growing situation, and learn how to control weeds, pests and diseases efficiently and without harming the environment. It's all about giving you time to do the projects you really enjoy instead of slaving away in the yard and then having time to sit back and appreciate it all

Your backyard is a treasure trove of possibilities for the imaginative and ambitious homeowner. With the projects in this book to guide and inspire you, you'll discover what multitudes before you have found out: When you're building projects for outdoor living, the sky really is the limit.

IMPORTANT NOTICE

For your safety, caution and good judgment should be used when following instructions described in this book. Take into consideration your level of skill and the safety precautions related to the tools and materials shown. Neither the publisher, nor any of its affiliates can assume responsibility for any damage to property or persons as a result of the misuse of the information provided. Consult your local building department for information on permits, codes, regulations and laws that may apply to your project.

Part 1
Landscape Structures & Decks

Introduction

For any homeowner, the backyard provides unique opportunities for recreation and relaxation. But for the handyman, outdoor space provides another important benefit: it is a place to design, to build and to put your skills and creativity on display.

Unlike your house, your yard is a very forgiving canvas for building projects: holes can be filled in; grass and small plants will grow back; and just about any structure can be easily removed and replaced with something you like better. For these reasons, many handymen and weekend remodelers especially enjoy working outdoors.

Although many backyard building projects involve more muscle than talent, it helps to know exactly what you need to do before you strip off the sod for your new patio or set the posts for your new deck. In this section, you'll find all the information you need to undertake today's most popular backyard building projects. In fact, *Part 1 — Landscape Structures & Decks* was planned and produced to focus solely on the building projects that homeowners are most interested in accomplishing.

The first section here is devoted to landscape construction projects: building patios, walkways, walls, fences, gates and garden ponds. Quite a number of building materials are used to make these structures, from cast concrete pavers to natural stone; from prefabricated fence panels to raw exterior lumber. For each project, you'll find a wealth of helpful information, along with beautiful full-color photographs that take you through each major step of the process. It's like watching a landscape contractor from start to finish as he completes a job—but without leaving the comfort of your favorite chair.

The second section here focuses on a backyard building project that's on just about every handyman's wish list or resume: building a deck. In these pages, you'll find all the basic information you need to build a simple deck, but much more.

Because most of us know enough about basic carpentry to design and build a basic square deck that has all the charm of a wooden pallet, our deck section aims a little higher. In it you'll see every detail and every painstaking step as we create a glorious, two-tier feature deck that quickly became the envy of the entire neighborhood where it was built. How-to instructions for the planning and layout, pouring foundation piers, building the undercarriage, laying the deck boards, and dressing out the deck with stairs, railings, fascia and even benches are all shown in exciting full-color detail. By the time you've finished reviewing this section, you'll have most of the knowledge and skills you need to build a unique deck that's the envy of *your* neighborhood.

Think ahead to your next backyard barbecue or party. Now imagine it taking place on your brand new paver patio or your spacious new deck. Remember slogging through the mud last summer to weed your garden or pick your tomatoes? Now imagine making the trek on a neat walkway made of natural stones, and perhaps stopping along the way to gaze into your new garden pond. There is almost no end to the satisfaction and payback you can obtain from even the simplest backyard building or landscaping project.

Ideas for Landscape Structures & Decks

On the following pages you'll find examples of a number of deck-building and landscape construction projects. They range from casual and simple to elaborate. In addition, each of the major sections of this book has a shorter gallery of completed projects to help spur your imagination when designing your own backyard building effort. While we did our best to choose a wide range of projects to help with your initial planning, you'll probably want to extend your search for inspiration beyond the pages of this book. You can visit your local library or bookstore and thumb through other printed material, or consult with designers or landscape architects for their thoughts. But perhaps the best way to generate ideas you know will work out well is simply to walk through your own neighborhood and take note of what your neighbors have done, looking for successes as well as projects that, for any number of reasons, didn't pan out.

A raised flower bed created with interlocking blocks cast from concrete provides a nice contrast to the warm wood deck tones in this emerging suburban neighborhood.

A figure-eight shaped garden pond and a planting bed add interest to an otherwise flat and ordinary lawn. The symmetrical shapes of these two structures introduce elements of nature to the backyard, while preserving the neatly clipped appearance favored by this homeowner.

Cobblestones and poured concrete join forces to create these elegant backyard steps — and complement the interlocking block retaining wall.

Exotic foliage thrives in this flexible-liner water garden, adding a taste of the tropics to a Midwestern backyard.

Interesting angles and well-placed railings allow this low-level deck to blend in perfectly in this rustic backyard setting. A little creativity and vision result in an original deck that picks up and keeps on going where rectangles and simple "L's" leave off.

RIGHT: A sturdy arbor-and-trellis creates a canopy of climbing plants and beautiful blossoms above a custom-built fence and gate.

BELOW: The austere brick facade of this contemporary house is softened by a gently meandering planting bed built with interlocking concrete blocks.

BOTTOM: Swimmers step down to the pool in style as they enjoy the graceful lines and easy access created by a well-designed deck.

Charm and grace are the two qualities that come to mind when passing by this lovely picket fence.

This floating deck proves that a good design is at home anywhere in your yard.

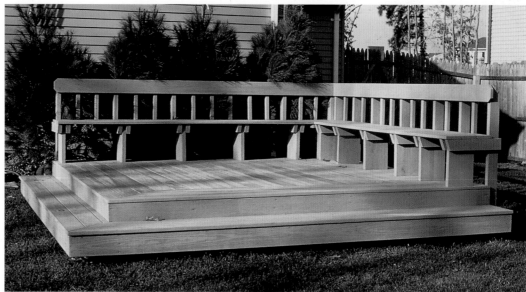

Tumbled pavers have the look and feel of an authentic cobblestone street in this spacious patio.

ABOVE: An urban retreat is established in a big-city backyard through the use of an efficient deck, a slatted privacy fence and some cleverly arranged potted plants.

RIGHT: A multi-media showcase can be put on display by carefully combining several backyard building materials, as these steps and adjoining wall demonstrate.

Garden ponds don't need to look artificial. Surrounding this flexible-liner pond with prairie grasses and natural flagstone lends an untamed feeling to the paver walkway and cast-paver coping stones that border most of the pond.

The feel of a Japanese garden is created more by the landscape structures than the plantings in this well-designed setting.

Natural stone, greenery and weathered wood are combined for an inviting effect in this lovely garden sanctuary.

Building Landscape Structures

Landscape Building Basics

Building landscape structures is not an exact science, as some forms of interior carpentry and woodworking are. The common step shared by most projects is quite simple: moving dirt. And even though there are do's and don't's related to digging, the basic ingredients are a sturdy shovel, a strong back, a wheelbarrow or garden cart, and a spot to dispose of any earth you remove from the project area.

Beyond digging, most landscape building projects also require you to do some sort of ground preparation: leveling off an excavation site, filling in low spots, and tamping down loose soil. Then a subbase, most often made from compactible gravel, is laid and tamped for most projects (exceptions being garden ponds and informal loose-fill walkways or patios laid over stable soil with good drainage). Landscape fabric should be layered into most landscape building projects to control weed growth and keep subbase or base materials from settling together.

Once the subbase is created, the individual projects diverge quickly into the unique steps they require.

Digging tools are required for just about any landscape construction project. A basic set includes: (A) a hoe for moving loose soil and mixing concrete; (B) a general-purpose spade; (C) a hand tamper; (D) a posthole digger; and (E) a wheelbarrow.

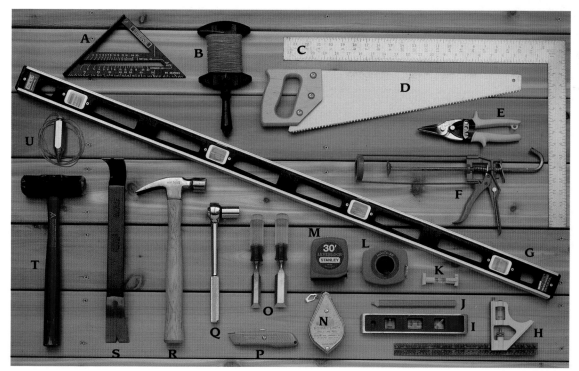

Hand tools are used in most landscape building projects, if only for layout and leveling. A basic set includes: (A) speed square; (B) mason's line; (C) framing square; (D) hand saw; (E) aviator snips; (F) caulk gun; (G) carpenter's level (4 ft.); (H) combination square; (I) spirit level; (J) pencil; (K) line level; (L) 50 ft. roll tape; (M) rigid tape measure; (N) chalkline; (O) wood chisels; (P) utility knife; (Q) socket wrench; (R) hammer; (S) flat pry bar; (T) hand maul; (U) plumb bob.

Coarse sand is used as a base material for setting pavers and natural stones, and as a base for flexible pond liners. Fine sand can also be purchased at most landscape materials centers, but it has little application in landscape construction.

Decorative rock, like the pink quartz above, is used in loose-fill walkways and patios, planting beds and as a border treatment. Styles vary by region. It is relatively expensive.

Compactible gravel is used as a subbase material in most landscape construction projects. Known in some regions as "Class V" or "Class II" (lower numbers denote smaller aggregate), it improves drainage and can be tamped to create a stable base.

Pea gravel is also used mostly as a drainage material but can be used successfully as a border treatment around plantings. It is not recommended for use as a loose fill for walkways or patios.

Trap rock is a slate-based aggregate used mostly to create dry wells and to provide drainage. It can be used for decorative purposes in some situations. It is not compactible.

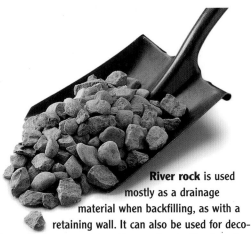

River rock is used mostly as a drainage material when backfilling, as with a retaining wall. It can also be used for decorative or loose-fill purposes. It is sold according to the diameter of the stones (3⁄8 in., 3⁄4 in., and 1½ in. are typical). As a general rule, use larger diameter stones for walkways and patios, and smaller diameter (or a combination of smaller and larger) for drainage fill. 1½ in. dia. river rock is shown above.

MATERIALS FOR LANDSCAPE CONSTRUCTION

Landscape fabric is a weather-resistant, semiporous fabric that inhibits weed growth, but allows water to pass through. It is frequently installed between layers of subbase and base material to keep the upper layer from settling down into the lower layer.

Landscape edging has several purposes in landscape construction. It is laid around planting beds to keep plantings segregated from the lawn. It is installed around patios and walkways to contain subbase and base materials. And it can be used as a decorative treatment to create visible barriers around landscape elements. Better quality edging is more rigid.

Rules for Building Outdoors

❑ **WATCH OUT FOR BURIED LINES.** Always contact your local public utilities to identify the location of buried power lines and gas lines before you dig. Utilities will provide line location identification as a free service.

❑ **RESEARCH BUILDING CODES.** Although building permits may not be required for many landscape projects, most municipalities enforce outdoor building restrictions. Allowable height of fences and walls, and minimum distance from city land and other property lines are two common areas subject to restrictions.

❑ **DISCUSS PLANS WITH YOUR NEIGHBORS.** Your outdoor building project will likely be within the field of vision of your neighbors. As a courtesy, share plans with neighbors and give them the chance to raise objections or concerns before you start working. As a rule, maintain a setback of at least 1 ft. from property lines.

❑ **BE AWARE OF WEATHER CONDITIONS.** Working outdoors can be highly strenuous, especially on hot, humid days. Avoid working in direct sunlight, drink plenty of water, and wear light-colored clothing (long pants and a long-sleeve shirt for protection). Work with a partner when possible. Don't work in threatening weather.

❑ **TAKE CARE OF POWER CORDS.** Extension cords are a danger and a nuisance. Keep them out of traffic areas. Always use exterior-rated extension cords with ground-fault circuit interruption (GFCI) protection.

RENTAL TOOLS FOR LANDSCAPE CONSTRUCTION

Sod kicker

Gas-powered auger

Plate vibrator (power tamper)

A sod kicker is a hand-powered blade that removes sod in usable strips that can be laid elsewhere in your yard. **A gas-powered auger** makes quick work of digging holes for fence posts or deck footings. Most require two people to operate. **A plate vibrator** (also called a power tamper or a jumping jack) provides greater compaction of subbase material than a hand tamper, with greater uniformity and less effort.

Patios & Walkways

Patios and walkways are the most prominent features in typical outdoor living spaces. They can be built in just about any size or shape with a wide range of building material options. Pavers and natural stone are the most popular materials for patios and walkways today because they're relatively easy to install and they can conform to the sizes and shapes that best fit in with your landscape design.

You can also build walkways and patios by creating a stable base, bordering it with landscape edging, and covering the area with loose fill, such as aggregate, mulch or bark. Loose-fill projects are the simplest to build but are limited mostly to more informal or rustic environments. Traditionally, patios and walkways have also been built with poured concrete. In some situations, poured concrete is a good landscape option, but working with it involves a multitude of specific masonry skills that are not shown in this book.

While precast concrete or brick pavers are sold in a vast assortment of shapes, sizes and colors (See pages 24 to 25), resourceful do-it-yourselfers sometimes prefer to cast their own concrete pavers in original shapes and sizes, using dry premixed concrete. To make your own pavers, simply construct a form from plywood or hardboard and fill it with concrete mixture (if you live in a colder climate, making pavers is a great winter project to prepare yourself for the spring building season). Another way to achieve the look of pavers or even natural stone is to stamp patterns into freshly poured concrete. Most concrete suppliers sell stamping tools that can impart the look of flagstone or pavers into the concrete.

The main challenges when building patios and walkways are choosing a design and materials that blend with your home and yard, then doing careful installation work to create a stable, weed-free subbase and a pleasing arrangement of the building materials.

Brick pavers are fired from natural clay and feature color variations that add to their decorative appeal. On larger surfaces they can be formed into nonsquare shapes with only minimal cutting.

Loose-fill walkways and patios are simple to create and have a natural appearance that blends in well in rustic or casual settings.

Stamped concrete gives the general appearance of pavers or natural stone, but at a fraction of the cost. The paver shapes and textures are stamped in with a stamping tool as soon as the fresh concrete has set up.

Cast your own pavers from concrete for unique walkways and patios. The lizard-shaped, custom-cast pavers above form interesting patterns when interlocked.

Flagstones are used to build very traditional patios and walkways that can fit in well in either a casual or a formal setting. The joints between stones usually are filled with a mixture of sand and mortar or cement to keep the stones in place.

Interlocking Pavers

Interlocking pavers have become an extremely popular surfacing material for patios, walks and driveways. They're relatively easy to install and, when set on a firm, properly prepared subbase, they'll hold up to foot traffic and heavy loads under a variety of weather conditions, without sinking, cracking, or shifting.

Set in sand, the pavers "flex" with changing temperatures, soil saturation levels, conditions and loads, rather than cracking as poured concrete patios some-

times will. Because of their high compressive strength, interlocking pavers are used for many commercial applications, such as public sidewalks and crosswalks, outdoor shopping malls, and even industrial equipment yards. Another advantage to building with sand-set interlocking pavers is that the individual units are easy to replace or reset, should the need arise.

About pavers

The two basic categories of pavers are brick pavers and concrete pavers. Brick pavers are fired in kilns from clay, and concrete pavers are cast in forms. Brick pavers tend to have more natural warmth and less of a hard, symmetrical appearance than concrete pavers, but they're more expensive. Concrete pavers are denser and generally available in a much wider range of sizes and shapes and are more common today.

Planning a paver patio or walkway

Plan the finished patio or walkway dimensions to avoid excess cutting of pavers. If you have the pavers on hand, lay out two rows on a flat surface (such as a driveway) to represent the width and length of the patio, providing the desired spacing between each unit. Take into account the width of any border pavers and

Anatomy of a Concrete Paver Structure

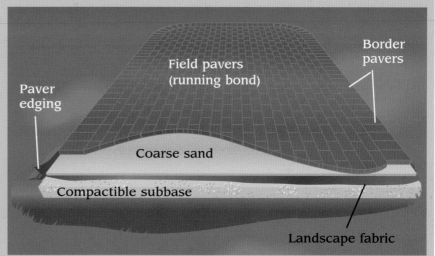

An interlocking paver patio or walkway consists of several different building materials layered together into the excavation area. After removing the sod and topsoil in the work area, a layer of compactible gravel is laid and tamped to 4 in. thick. Then, special paver edging is installed around the border of the project area. Landscape fabric is laid over the compactible gravel, a 1 in. layer of coarse sand is poured and leveled on top of the landscape fabric. The pavers are laid in pattern, starting at one corner, then filling in throughout the field area. Finally, a mixture of sand and mortar or Portland cement is swept into the gaps between pavers. When moistened with water, the mixture hardens to hold the pavers in place.

edging materials. Most concrete pavers have nubs on the sides that provide uniform 1/16 or 1/8 in. gaps that are filled with dry sand or a mixture of sand and mortar on Portland cement to lock the pavers in place. See the *Tip* on page 25 for information on estimating the number of pavers your project will require.

If building a patio that will adjoin your house, use the door threshold, stoop, or steps/stairs as your initial guideline for determining the final height and slope for your patio. Ideally, the transitional step-up from the patio surface to the door threshold or first step tread should be between 5 and 7½ in. You'll also need to plan for a slight slope (typically 1/8 in. per foot) when laying out your project. The slope should direct water runoff away from your house. In addition, a slight crown in the overall surface from side to side will help facilitate water runoff on both patios and walkways.

TOOLS FOR SETTING PAVERS

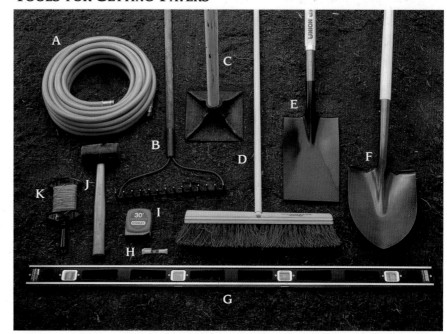

Tools for installing paver patios and walkways include: (A) a garden hose; (B) a garden rake; (C) a hand tamper; (D) a stiff-bristled push broom; (E) a square-nose spade; (F) a standard spade; (G) a carpenter's level; (H) a line level; (I) a tape measure; (J) a rubber mallet; and (K) a mason's line.

LAYOUT PATTERNS FOR RECTANGLE PAVERS

Running Bond

Standard Basketweave

Herringbone

Offset Basketweave

Running Stack

Two-to-one Basketweave

Offset diamond shapes can be combined into dozens of pattern variations, especially when combined with square pavers. An X-shaped repeating medallion pattern is indicated above, and a running diamond pattern below.

Cobblestones are noninterlocking square or rectangular pavers, typically antiqued using a tumbling process. The roundovers at the edges of the top surfaces create a quilted look when installed in groups.

Zig-zag shapes have a larger amount of interlocking surface area, and are best used in running bond types of patterns.

Estimating Paver Quantities

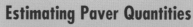

To estimate how many pavers you need to complete your project, the most accurate method is to arrange a handful of the pavers you'll be using into a small section of the pattern, then measure the total length and width of the section. Divide the measurements by the number of pavers it contains for an average per-unit length and width that allow for the gaps between pavers. Divide the planned width and length of the patio or walkway by the average unit dimensions and add 10% to the total for waste.

Split octagon with offset square ends can be combined to form any of the most common patterns. Note that the pavers are arranged in mirror-image pairs.

Paver patios

If the patio you plan to build will adjoin a house, use a door threshold or steps to determine the height of the patio closest to the house. Ideally, the transitional step up from the patio surface to the door threshold or first step tread should be between 5 and 7½ in. Patio surfaces should slope away from the building so that water drains away from the foundation, so the patio side closest to the house is the "high" side. You must establish and maintain a drainage slope across the patio surface from high side to low side as you build your patio.

Installing a paver patio

1 For square or rectangular patios, outline the patio area with wood stakes and mason's line **(See FIGURE A).** Attach the lines roughly 4 in. above ground level. Position the stakes about 2 ft. outside the planned patio area. Check the layout for square by measuring diagonally from corner to corner; the layout is square when the diagonals are equal.

2 Use a line level to level the mason's line on what will be the patio's high side first. Once the string is level, mark its height on the stake at either end **(See FIGURE B).** You'll be using this high side as a starting point and adjusting the remaining three string lines to it.

3 Use a carpenter's level to transfer level marks from the leveled string to an adjacent stake at one corner **(See FIGURE C).** Adjust the second string line to this mark, level the string with a line level, then mark the stake at the opposite end. Repeat this procedure at each corner until all strings are level with each other. The strings should barely touch one another where they intersect.

4 The patio should slope gradually so water drains away from buildings or follows the natural drainage pattern of your yard. The slope should be ⅛ in. per ft. At each low-end stake, measure and mark the amount of drop from the level mark and retie the strings at these marks **(See FIGURE D).** Adjust the intersecting

FIGURE A: Drive two stakes approximately 2 ft. outside each of the prospective four corners of the patio area. Attach mason's line between the stakes to mark the length and width of the patio. The points where the strings intersect between the stakes determines the actual corners of the patio.

Line level

FIGURE B: Level the mason's line on the high side of the layout using a line level. Mark its height on the stakes at each end. This level line serves as a reference to level the other three layout string lines.

string at the low end to this height. Leave the strings in place to serve as guides for excavating the patio area.

5 Clear the layout area of all plantings, large stones and other obstructions. If you're installing the patio in a grass yard, remove all sod within the patio area and 6 to 8 in. beyond the strings on each side **(See FIGURE E).** Save some of the sod for filling in any bare spots around the patio after it's installed.

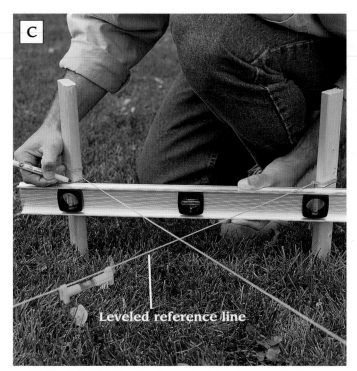

FIGURE C: Once one string line is exactly level, use it as a reference for leveling the rest of the strings, A carpenter's level can be used to transfer the height of the reference string line to adjacent string lines.

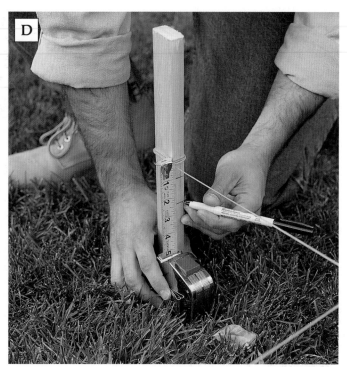

FIGURE D: Calculate how much the patio will drop on the low side and mark this distance below the level line marks on the low-side stakes. **NOTE: Here we moved the string up and out of the way of the level reference line to make marking easier.**

6 If the patio includes curved areas or rounded corners, lay out the curve with a garden hose, providing an 8-in. margin outside the actual curved edge of the patio **(See FIGURE F).** On bare ground, mark the location with spray paint or pieces of paper with nails stuck through them. If your patio will replace a section of lawn, use the hose as a guide and remove the grass with a sod kicker.

Preparing the base

7 Starting at one corner, excavate the entire site to a depth that will accommodate at least 4 in. of subbase material, 1 in. of sand and the thickness of the pavers (for example, if the pavers are 2½ in. thick, you'd excavate to a depth of 7½ in. below the finished patio surface). Use a spade to dig the sides of the excavation as straight as possible, following your excavation marks. Check excavation depth around the perimeter by measuring down from the strings with a tape measure or a story pole **(See FIGURE G).** Then remove the soil within the patio area with a shovel. Be sure the entire excavation area follows the drainage slope of the strings. *TIP: On larger patios, tie intermediate strings across the project site to provide more depth reference lines in the middle of the excavation.*

8 After excavating the site, use a long, straight 2 × 4 to check for low and high spots **(See FIGURE H).** Fill any low spots with compactible gravel subbase and tamp firmly with a hand tamper.

FIGURE E: Remove sod within the patio area plus 6 to 8 in. beyond the layout lines using a sod kicker. Roll several strips (green side in), and keep it moist and shaded for later use to patch in around the patio.

9 Spread an even layer of compactible gravel subbase into the project area. The depth of the subbase should be 4 in. plus ½ in. to allow for compaction. Compact the subbase material with a plate vibrator or hand tamper around the patio perimeter, then move in overlapping passes toward the center of the excavated area, overlapping each pass by 4 in. **(See FIGURE I).** After compacting, double-check the height of the subbase to the guide strings. The distance between the subbase and strings should be equal over the whole

FIGURE F: Use a garden hose to plot curved corners of the patio for excavation. The hose should lay 6 to 8 in. outside the actual curve to allow for excavation and patio edging.

FIGURE G: Use a scrap wood story pole as a depth reference as you excavate. The marks on the pole indicate the depth of the excavation below grade, plus the distance between ground level and the string lines.

FIGURE H: Check for high and low spots in the excavated area with a straight 2 × 4. Remove or fill areas as needed and tamp the ground firmly with a plate vibrator or hand tamper to create a solid base.

FIGURE I: Fill the excavation area with a 4½-in.-thick layer of compactible subbase and compact it with a plate vibrator or hand tamper.

excavation area and follow the drainage slope marked by the reference string lines.

10 Lay down strips of landscape fabric, overlapping each strip by 6 to 8 in. **(See FIGURE J).** The fabric will help control weed growth and separate the sand layer from the compactible gravel subbase. Without it, the sand would eventually settle into the subbase material and cause the pavers to sink.

11 Starting at the center of the patio, dry-lay a line of pavers in both directions to establish the actual size of the finished patio **(See FIGURE K).** Be sure to include border pavers. Leave the two lines of pavers in place to serve as reference guides for installing the edging.

12 Using your layout lines as guides, install paver edging around the patio perimeter. When installed, the L-shaped edging is designed to hold the sand base and border pavers in place. Lay a level

FIGURE J: Roll out landscape fabric to cover the entire patio area. Overlap the fabric strips at least 6 to 8 in.

FIGURE K: Lay a line of pavers in each direction to establish the actual length and width of the patio. Make sure to include border pavers, if applicable, and allow for joints between each paver.

FIGURE L: Align the edging with the layout string lines using a carpenter's level. The vertical ledges of the paver edging should be flush with the outer edges of the pavers.

FIGURE M: Tack sections edging with 10-in. galvanized landscape spikes to establish curves in the patio layout. Once the curves are determined, space the spikes every 12 to 18 in. to lock the edging in place.

against the layout lines and adjust the edging until it is directly below the lines. Adjust the pavers until they butt up against the edging **(See FIGURE L).**

13 Install the edging by driving 10-in. galvanized landscape spikes through the predrilled holes in the edging. Place spikes 18 to 24 in. apart for straight sections, 12 to 18 in. apart for curved sections, or as specified by the manufacturer **(See FIGURES M and N).** Trim sections of the edging flange so that the edging fits around obstructions like steps **(See FIGURE O).**

14 After the edging is installed, remove the stakes and reference lines. Lay down 1-in.-dia. pipes across the width of the patio, spacing them about 6 ft. apart, and lay a 1½-in.-dia. pipe across the center. Cover the patio area with a layer of sand **(See FIGURE P).** The pipes will serve as depth spacers for the sand base when it's leveled and smoothed. The wider center pipe will establish a gentle slope from the center of the patio to the sides (called crowning) so that water will not pool in the middle but shed to either side. Moisten the sand so it's wet but not soaked through.

FIGURE N: Anchor the straight sections of edging at each spike hole with 10-in. galvanized landscape spikes. Be careful that the edging doesn't shift out of alignment with the string layout lines.

FIGURE O: Trim the edging, if necessary, to fit around steps or other obstructions. Paver edging that you trim should be supported from behind to keep these border areas rigid.

FIGURE P: Lay spacer pipes across the patio area (widthwise) and cover the patio area with a layer of sand. Settle the sand by dampening it with water. The pipes serve as spacers to crown and even out the sand layer.

FIGURE Q: Screed the sand layer with a straight 2 × 4 using two pipes at a time as runners under the screed board. Then tamp the sand with a hand tamper to pack it firmly.

15 Set a straight 2 × 4 screed board across the sand that is long enough to rest on both the wider center spacer pipe and a narrower pipe. Shuffle it side to side along the two pipes in a sawing motion as you pull it toward you **(See FIGURE Q).** Continue screeding across sets of pipes, working from the center of the patio area outward until you've smoothed the whole patio. As you go, fill in any low spots and remove excess sand that builds up in front of the screed board.

Laying the pavers

16 Starting at one corner (nearest to the house or at the high end of the patio), lay the first border paver tight against the edging. Use a rubber mallet or hammer and short wood block to set the paver into the sand **(See FIGURE R).**

17 Lay a row of border pavers 2 to 3 ft. in each direction from the corner along the edging, and

FIGURE R: Set the first paver into one corner of the edging. Tap it lightly with a rubber mallet or a hammer and a block of wood to bed it into the sand base.

FIGURE S: Establish your paver pattern by laying a 2- to 3-ft. row of border pavers, then fill the border area in. Bed the pavers into the sand with a mallet and check the flatness of the paver surface with a level or straightedge.

fill in the space with field pavers following the paver pattern you choose **(See FIGURE S).** Tap the pavers in place, checking frequently with a level or straightedge to make sure all pavers are at the same height. As you encounter spacer pipes, remove them, filling in the grooves left behind with sand and lightly patting these areas smooth.

18 Continue laying the border and field pavers in 2- to 3-ft. sections diagonally across the patio area. As you work, measure from paver rows over to the edging to make sure the rows are lining up with one another. Compensate for inconsistencies by increasing or decreasing the joint width between pavers to bring a row back into alignment. When you get to the opposite end of the patio, adjust the edging, if needed, so it is snug against the pavers **(See FIGURE T).**

19 If your pattern requires you to cut only a few pavers, you can score and break them with a hand maul and brick set. If you have several dozen cuts to make or need to make angled cuts, rent a masonry saw (See *TIP,* above). These saws feature a water-cooled diamond-grit blade and a sliding carriage for

moving the paver into the blade. Some models include a miter guide attached to the carriage that enables you to make angled cuts. Simply align the paver cutting line with the saw blade and slide the movable saw carriage forward, easing the paver slowly into the blade.

20 When your patio design includes a curve, lay full-size border pavers into the curve first, then fill in the field with full pavers as close to the border curve as possible **(See FIGURE U).** If you're working into a tight radius, use half-pavers (cut across their width)

FIGURE T: Continue to add pavers until you reach the opposite end of the patio. If paver rows extend beyond the edging or come up short, shift the edging by removing and repositioning the stakes to avoid cutting border pavers.

FIGURE U: Lay the border pavers first in curved corners, then fill in the field area with full pavers as close to the curved border as possible. Field pavers that meet the border pavers at angles will have to be cut to fit.

FIGURE V: Mark full-size pavers that must be cut at angles by setting them over the empty spaces between border and field pavers and marking the angle. Allow for a ⅛-in. gap between border and cut pavers.

FIGURE W: Check the patio surface for flatness with a straight 2 × 4, and set high pavers deeper into the sand base with a mallet. In some cases, you'll need to remove low pavers, add sand and reset.

for the border to minimize large, pie-shaped gaps that would result from laying full-sized pavers. Shortening the pavers tightens their fit into the radius.

21 Set full-size pavers over the empty spaces between field pavers and border pavers, and draw angled reference lines (See FIGURE V). Subtract ⅛ in. and make a second angled line inside the first to mark your cutting line. Cut or score and break the pavers along the inside line and fit them into place.

22 Once all the pavers are laid, check for high or low spots by laying the screed board across the paver surface in several directions and look for gaps. Use a rubber mallet or a hammer and wood block to adjust uneven pavers by setting higher pavers deeper into the sand (See FIGURE W). Remove any pavers in low spots, add more sand and reset them.

FIGURE X: Fill gaps between the pavers by covering the patio with a layer of sand and sweeping it back and forth into the joints. Use a plate vibrator to settle the entire patio into the sand base and pack the sand into the joints.

FIGURE Y: Sweep loose sand off the patio and settle the sand in the joints by misting with a garden hose.

23 Spread an even ½-in. coat of dry sand over the entire paver surface. Sweep the sand thoroughly into the paver joints to fill them, adding more dry sand if necessary **(See FIGURE X).** Leave a ¼-in. layer of sand on top of the patio to act as a cushion for tamping the pavers with a plate vibrator. This will keep the vibrator from chipping the paver corners.

24 Tamp the pavers into the sand bed. Start around the outside perimeter and work toward the center. Make at least two passes to pack the sand firmly into the joints. If you notice joints settling, add more sand to refill them before making the next tamping pass. During this process, keep the tamper moving: if you stay in one place too long, you'll run the risk of creating uneven low spots by over-compacting the subbase.

25 Sweep up any loose sand, then mist the paver area, being careful not to dislodge sand from the joints **(See FIGURE Y).** Wait several days for the sand to settle and dry, then sweep in and wet additional sand to fill in any voids in the joints.

26 Fill in bare spots around the patio perimeter with topsoil, then cut strips of sod to cover the bare spots **(See FIGURE Z).** Press the sod firmly in place and soak it with water. Water the sod daily for two weeks so that it can establish new roots.

27 After the joints are fully packed with sand, the patio is ready for use. However, you may want to

FIGURE Z: Fill excavated areas behind the patio edging with topsoil and patch it in with sod strips. Press the sod firmly into place and water it every day for several weeks until it takes root.

coat the paver surface with concrete sealer, using a roller or garden sprayer. The sealer not only provides some protection against water penetration and weed growth; it also enhances the color of the pavers and provides a barrier against stains and dirt. Check the sand joints seasonally and replenish them with sand. Reset low pavers as needed.

Before

Flagstone

Flagstone patios and walkways provide a durable if slightly rough walking surface, but lend themselves well to natural or informal garden settings. Because of their relatively large size and weight, flagstones usually don't require the extensive base preparation of an interlocking paver patio. In many cases, you can lay the stones directly on stable, well-tamped soil, although a 2 in. bed of screeded sand will make it easier to place and level stones of varying thickness. If the soil is very soft or unstable (subject to severe frost heave), lay down a 2 to 4 in. layer of compactible gravel subbase material, and compact it with a hand tamper or plate vibrator.

About flagstones

"Flagstone" is a general term referring to any sedimentary rock that cleaves naturally into stepping stone shapes. The name derives from the obvious resem-

Buying Flagstones

Rockeries and landscape suppliers generally sell flagstones by the ton (in pallet lots) for large projects, or by the pound for smaller ones. The stones in any given lot will vary in size, shape, and thickness, making estimating difficult. To determine the amount of stone needed to cover your walk or patio area, your best bet is to rely on the experience of the supplier.

Flagstones used for patios and walks range from 1 to 2 in. thick (as opposed to thinner "veneer" flagstones, which range from ¼ to ¾ in. thick — the latter should not be used for patios or walks). Generally, a ton of 1- to-2 in.-thick, medium-density stones will cover approximately 120 square feet.

After determining the square footage of your patio, order 10% extra to allow for cutting, fitting and breakage. While dealers usually won't let you pick through the pile to choose the exact stones you want, you can look for pallets that contain a good mixture of sizes and shapes to save time cutting and fitting. Also, a good percentage of the stones should have at least one reasonably straight side for use as perimeter stones on square or rectangular patios and straight walks.

As with other patio materials, have the stones delivered as close to the site as possible. Have a helper on hand to move and place the larger stones.

In formal landscapes, where a more symmetrical patio is desired, use "gauged" stones. These are natural stones split to roughly the same thickness, then cut into rectangular shapes in random widths and lengths. Gauged-stone patios are generally easier to fit together, with straight, wet-mortared joints of an even width (typically ½ to ¾ in. wide). Alternatively, you can lay these stones without mortar joints, using the same procedures as you would for installing the interlocking paver patio described on pages 22 to 33.

---

blance to flag shapes exhibited by flagstones. Limestone, slate and quartzite are some of the most common rock types in the flagstone category — specific types vary according to geographic region. To be useful for creating walkways and patios, flagstones should be at least 1 in. thick, but at least 1½ to 2 in. is preferable. Because flagstones are split and cleaved into usable and manageable sizes (rather than cut), their shapes are slightly irregular, which contributes to their natural quality. When purchased at a landscape stone supplier, natural stones like flagstone are considerably more expensive than cast pavers.

Laying out flagstone structures

Laying stones for a flagstone patio or walkway is somewhat like putting together a jigsaw puzzle. You'll want to lay the stones in an eye-pleasing pattern, while at the same time fitting them together to minimize the number of cut stones needed. Generally, the thickest stones are laid around the perimeter, serving as a border to help keep the thinner field stones in place. The largest stones are sometimes placed near the center of the patio. Strive for a pattern that includes a good mixture of large and small stones, placed in a random pattern, with staggered joints. For the most part, the larger

stones are laid and leveled first, then the smaller stones are fitted in between the larger ones. This allows you to limit any cutting to the smaller stones.

Installing flagstones

Before laying in the base materials, you can experiment with different patterns to make best use of the stones. Starting at one corner or side, test-fit various stones to find the best pattern without having to make too many cuts. You don't need to dry-lay the entire patio or walkway, but you should at least play around with the shapes enough to develop a feel for how they naturally fit together. If you do dry-lay the entire arrangement, either number the stones before moving them or keep the dry-lay intact, transplanting the stones one-at-a-time into the actual work site. Another option is simply to take a photograph of the dry-lay and use it as a reference for recreating the arrangement in the work site. Strive to keep the joints between the stones from ½ in. to not more than 1½ in. wide.

Even medium-sized flagstones can weigh 100 pounds or more, so make sure to get plenty of help handling them. Doing careful planning and base preparation will minimize the number of times you need to handle each stone.

Flagstone patios

Before laying in the base materials for your patio, experiment with different patterns to make best use of the stones. Mark any stones that will need to be cut. Draw a rough sketch of the layout to show where the stones will be placed. You might also find it helpful to number the stones with a pencil or piece of chalk to indicate their location, then cross-reference these to your sketch. Remove and stack them in small piles outside the patio area, near where they will be laid.

Excavate the project area

1 If you're building a square or rectangular patio, lay out the patio outline with stakes and leveled strings as described in the paver patio project on pages 22-29. Be sure to adjust the strings to provide the proper 1/8-in.-drop-per-ft. slope to facilitate water runoff from the patio surface, especially if the patio will adjoin a building. If you're laying a free-form design such as the one shown in this project, drive stakes every 3 to 4 ft. around the perimeter to indicate the border. Prepare the project area by removing all obstacles and sod, then excavate to a depth that will accommodate the thickest flagstones plus 4 in. of compactible gravel sub-

base and 2 in. of sand **(See FIGURE A).** Run leveled strings across the excavation (from stake to stake) in several directions, and measure down from these to make sure the bottom of the excavation follows the intended slope of the finished patio. Then tamp it firmly with a hand tamper or plate vibrator.

Prepare the base

2 Install landscape edging around the patio border to contain the subbase, then pour and spread an even layer of compactible gravel subbase into the excavation (the back side of a garden rake works well for this). The depth of the material should be at least 4 in. plus 1/4 to 1/2 in. to allow for compaction. Compact the material with a hand tamper, or for larger areas, a rented plate vibrator **(See FIGURE B).**

3 Lay down a layer of landscape fabric over the compacted base, overlapping the edges of the fabric at least 6 to 8 in. **(See FIGURE C).** Trim the edges to leave a 6-in. overlap beyond the patio borders.

4 Spread a 2- to 3-in.-thick bed of coarse, dry sand into the excavation area. Level and smooth the sand with a 2 × 4 screed board **(See FIGURE D).**

How to install a flagstone patio

FIGURE A: Drive stakes to indicate the borders of the patio, then excavate deep enough for the subbase, sand and flagstones (around 8 in. for most projects).

FIGURE B: Fill the project area with a 4½-in.-thick layer of compactible subbase. Tamp it with a hand tamper or plate vibrator.

Then compact the sand with a hand tamper or plate vibrator. *TIP: For a more stable base, you can mix Portland cement into the sand before screeding (use one 90 lb. sack of dry Portland cement mix per 100 sq. ft. of patio surface). After laying the sand, spread the dry cement mix evenly onto the sand and blend it in with a rake or hoe.*

Lay the stones

5 Starting at one high side of the patio, lay all of the border stones around the patio perimeter. Avoid kneeling on the screeded sand bed — if you must do so, cut a 4 × 4 piece of plywood and use it as a kneeling board to help distribute your weight evenly **(See FIGURE E).** Use the thickest stones for the border, setting them a bit deeper than the rest to offset the extra thickness. Thicker, heavier border stones will help anchor the center (field) stones in place. Twist the stones slightly to bed them into the sand. Check the border stones with a level and adjust as needed to ensure that the desired drainage slope is maintained.

6 After the border stones are in place, arrange the stones to fill in the field area **(See FIGURE F).** Maintain a good mixture of large and small stones across the entire patio to create an even, attractive pattern. Strive to keep the joint width between the stones about ½ in. to 1½ in. Bed the stones into the sand with a rubber mallet or a hammer and wood block.

7 No matter how carefully you arrange the stones, some stones will need to be cut to fill in odd spaces. To cut the stones, mark the cutting lines with a pencil on both sides. Score the cutting line ⅛ in. deep with a circular saw fitted with a carborundum or diamond masonry blade. (You can use a hammer and brick set instead to score the stones.) Then tap back and forth along the score line with your hammer and brick set until the stone fractures **(See FIGURE G).**

8 After laying all the stones, recheck the entire surface to make sure the stones are reasonably close to the same height. Use a long 2 × 4 with a level attached to check for overall level and slope. Let the

FIGURE C: Cover the subbase with landscape fabric, overlapping the edges 6 to 8 in. Extend the fabric up the sides of the excavated area.

FIGURE D: Spread a 2-in. layer of sand over the landscape fabric and screed the sand flat with a straight 2 × 4. Be sure the surface follows the drainage slope of the patio.

FIGURE E: Set the border flagstones into place and twist them slightly to bed them into the sand base. Where possible, use the largest, thickest stones for the border. If you must work within the patio field area, kneel on plywood to keep from disturbing the sand base.

FIGURE F: Once you've positioned pavers around the patio border, fill in the field area. Let your larger stones dictate the layout and set them into the patio field area first. Then fill in remaining areas with smaller stones. Keep the width of the joints between stones to 1½ in. or less.

stones settle for a few days and then recheck the patio area for level and slope. If one or more stones have sunk lower than the rest, remove these and add more sand beneath **(See FIGURE H).** Remove sand under stones that are higher than the rest. Bed the stones firmly into the sand by tapping them with a rubber mallet or hammer and wood block. Be patient and do your best work at this dry-fit stage — this step is critical to the appearance of the finished patio.

Fill the joints

9 Fill the joints with dry mortar mix. To make the mortar, mix one part Portland cement to six parts coarse sand in a wheelbarrow or five-gallon bucket. Wet the entire patio surface by misting it with a hose, then allow the surfaces of the stones to dry. Pour the

dry-mortar mixture evenly over the patio surface and sweep it into the joints with a push broom **(See FIGURE I).** Compact the mortar into the joints with a 4-ft. length of 1 × 4, or a strip of plywood. (It's a good idea to wear gloves when you handle the mortar mix.) Repeat the process until the dry mortar is well-packed and flush with the stone surfaces. *NOTE: In colder climates where the ground freezes seasonally, use sand instead of mortar mix to fill the joints. Sweep sand into the joints and tamp it firmly.*

10 Mist the patio surface **(See FIGURE J)**, being careful not to wash the mortar from the joints. When the patio surface has dried out and the mortar has partially set (about one hour), repeat the joint-filling process, if necessary to fill any low spots. After all joints are flush, allow the mortar to set for several hours, then use a coarse, water-soaked rag or burlap sack and stiff bristle brush to clean off any excess mortar from the stone surfaces. Cover the entire patio with 4- or 6-mil plastic sheeting and allow the mortar to cure for at least two days. Do not walk on the patio during this time. After the mortar is fully cured, you can remove any remaining mortar stains from the stones by scrubbing with a light solution of one part muriatic acid to nine parts water (wear safety glasses, heavy rubber gloves and long sleeves).

JOINT OPTION: Ground cover

For a more natural looking patio, you can fill joints between the flagstones with topsoil, then plant grass or a low ground cover in the soil. Popular low ground covers for this purpose include dichondra, Scotch or Irish moss, baby tears, and woolly thyme, to name a few. Check with local nurseries for options that will be suitable for your climate.

FIGURE G: To cut stones, score along your cutting lines with a mason's chisel and hammer or with a circular saw and masonry blade set to ⅛ in. Tap along the score line until the stone breaks.

FIGURE H: Backfill with sand beneath low pavers. You may also need to remove some sand behind pavers that are higher than others. The goal is to create a flat flagstone surface overall.

FIGURE I: Sweep a dry mortar mixture of one part cement to six parts sand into the patio joints. Compact the joints with pieces of scrap wood.

FIGURE J: Set the joints by misting them with water. Fill any joints that settle with more mortar mix before the joints cure.

Loose Fill

Loose fill is used mostly for walkways, but can make a very effective patio material in the proper setting as well. Smaller aggregates, like river rock or quartz, are common loose-fill materials that are quite durable. But mulch, bark and other organic matter may be used instead. Organic matter will decompose eventually and require replenishing, but it is easy to work with, inexpensive, and has a natural warmth that cannot be achieved with stone.

To keep the loose fill confined to the project area, you'll need to install edging around the border of the project. There are several edging options to choose from, including those shown in the TIP on the next page. But one of the beauties of working with loose-fill is that you can improvise by using your creativity to employ other materials for edging. Rubble stone from your yard, reclaimed bricks, chunks of logs, and pieces of salvaged fence material are just a few possibilities.

While ease of installation and natural beauty are two big advantages to creating loose fill walkways and patios, perhaps the greatest advantage is that they conform easily to curves, serpentine shapes, and other non-linear forms — with no time-consuming cutting of pavers or flagstones. And if you decide to alter the layout of your landscape, a loose-fill walkway or patio is easy to relocate.

LOOSE FILL OPTIONS

Loose fill for landscaping projects can be created from just about any natural material. Smaller aggregates, mulch and bark are the most common, however. Examples shown above are: (A) crushed limestone; (B) ⅜ to ¾ in. dia. river rock; (C) cypress mulch and; (D) cedar bark chips.

TOOLS FOR BUILDING A LOOSE-FILL WALKWAY

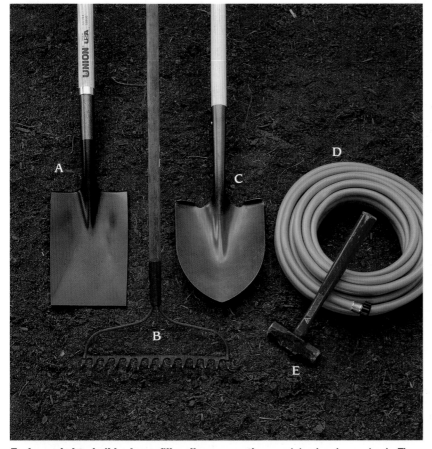

Tools needed to build a loose-fill walkway or patio are minimal and very simple. They include: (A) square-nose spade; (B) garden rake; (C) standard spade; (D) garden hose; and (E) hand maul for driving layout stakes.

Edging Options

Concrete pavers laid on their sides create stable edging that resists decay and adds a formal flavor to the pathway or patio, especially if there are other paver structures in the vicinity of the walkway or patio.

Landscape edging is the most common edging treatment for loose-fill walkways and patios. It is inexpensive and bends easily to follow curves. Avoid cheaper versions of this product that are flimsy and not designed to be staked in place.

Exterior lumber, such as cedar, redwood or pressure-treated pine makes excellent edging for straight borders.

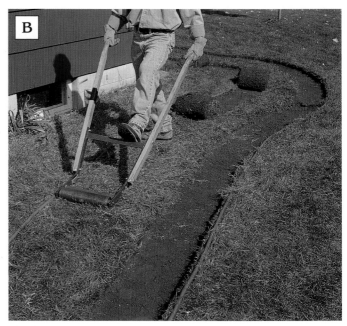

FIGURE A: Lay out curved walkways with lengths of garden hose or heavy rope. Keep the width of the walkway uniform, even around curves.

FIGURE B: Remove sod within the layout area using a rented sod kicker. Then excavate the walkway area to a depth of 3 to 4 in.

Loose-fill walkways

1 For straight walks, set up stakes and strings to outline the walkway area, as you would for a patio. For curved walks, lay out the area using a garden hose or rope **(See FIGURE A).** Be sure to include a margin on each side to allow for the width of the edging you'll install, if using heavier edging materials like pavers or pressure-treated wood.

2 If the walkway will cross a lawn, remove the sod with a sod cutter **(See FIGURE B).** On bare ground, remove all plantings and other obstacles within the walkway area (although you're better off designing the walkway to wind around them). Then, remove topsoil in the area to a depth of 3 to 4 in. below grade, and tamp the bottom of the excavation with a hand tamper or plate vibrator. If the soil is very loose or sandy, you may need to install a compactible gravel subbase, as you would for a paver patio.

3 Dig a shallow trench along the walkway edges for the edging material **(See FIGURE C).** The bottom of the edging should extend about 2 in. below the excavated area. The top of the edging should be about 1 in. above ground level to prevent soil from washing into the walkway, and ½ in. above the finished walk surface to contain the aggregates.

4 If you're using plastic edging, install it on both sides of the excavated walk area. Installation techniques will vary, depending on the brand of edging used. In

this case, we drove galvanized stakes through a flange on the strip to secure the edging **(See FIGURE D)**.

5 As you lay successive plastic edging strips end to end, connect the ends according to the manufacturer's instructions. Here, the ends of the edging are coupled together with short sections of tubing **(See FIGURE E).**

6 Lay down a strip of landscape fabric to keep the loose fill from migrating into the soil beneath, and to prevent weed growth in the walkway area **(See FIGURE F).** Overlap the ends of the fabric 6 to 8 in. and drape it up over the sides of the excavated area. On tight curves, pleat the fabric neatly and secure it with 16d galvanized nails, poked through the material and into the ground.

7 Fill in the walkway area with 3 to 4 in. of loose aggregate material and rake it smooth **(See FIGURE G).** We used river rock for this project, but several aggregate options are widely available (See page 37). The finished walkway surface should be ½ to 1 in. below the edging.

8 Trim off excess landscape fabric or plastic sheeting with a pair of scissors or a utility knife **(See FIGURE H).** Replace the aggregate to hide any exposed fabric or plastic. Replenish the loose fill with fresh material as it settles or deteriorates.

FIGURE C: With a square-nose spade, dig shallow trenches along the edges of the walkway to provide for the edging you choose. Plan for the top of the edging to be 1 in. above the level of the surrounding ground.

FIGURE D: Install the edging. For this project, we used rolled plastic landscape edging that is held in place with galvanized stakes. Drive the stakes through the edging and into the ground.

FIGURE E: Lock lengths of plastic edging together with couplings provided by the manufacturer. This edging uses short sections of tubing.

FIGURE F: Cover the bottom of the excavation with a landscape fabric as a weed barrier material.

FIGURE G: Fill the walkway with 3 or 4 in. of loose aggregate material and smooth it with a rake. For heavier aggregates like rock, have the load dumped close to the worksite to make filling the walkway easier.

FIGURE H: Trim away excess landscape fabric or plastic sheeting and hide the edges with more aggregate.

Water gardens

Not too many years ago, the only way a homeowner could have a natural-looking garden pond was to pour a concrete shell to hold the water. Such ponds were — and still are — expensive and labor-intensive to build. And, if they're not installed correctly, with careful attention paid to climate and soil conditions, they'll soon develop cracks, causing leaks.

However, with the advent of flexible plastic and rubber pond liners, even large, elaborate ponds are well within the building capabilities of the home handyman. The liners are durable, cheaper than concrete, easy to install, and they enable you to create a pond of practically any size or shape. You can also use the liners to build natural-looking streams or waterfalls leading to the pond. Depending on the quality and thickness of the liner, a properly installed pond can last 30 years or more.

Preformed rigid plastic or fiberglass pond shells are another option for do-it-yourself water garden construction. They work especially well in soft, sandy or unstable soil, where any shifting, slippage, or erosion may deform the original shape of the hole beneath a flexible liner. However, sizes and shapes of preformed shells are limited. Also, unless carefully disguised with stone edgings and border plantings, the shells can have an artificial look, and may not be the best choice for a "natural-looking" pond. Conversely, those with geometric shapes and straight sides (squares, rectangles, circles, hexagons, etc.) better lend themselves to formal landscapes, where you might want to use bricks, patio tiles or pavers as edging materials.

Rigid shell liners, made from plastic or fiberglass, are usually buried below grade. But the shell above rests on the patio surface, where it is a real attention-getter.

All the bells and whistles of water garden design are displayed in this fanciful water garden project, including a multi-level waterfall, a charming footbridge, well-chosen water plants and decorative accessories, and even livestock (goldfish) inhabiting the main pond area.

In more formal settings, symmetrical shapes convey a sense of order, as shown by this flexible-liner pond. Rigid shell liners can be used for the same effect.

Integrating your pond with its surroundings is key to a successful water garden project, as shown by this pond that's recessed into a tiled patio.

This flexible-liner pond with waterfall relies on irregular coping stones and an abundance of water plants to achieve an easygoing, natural look.

Flexible liner ponds

Installing flexible plastic or rubber pond liners is a quick and easy way to create a water garden. You simply outline the pond shape, dig the hole, install under-layment or a puncture-protection layer, lay in the liner to conform to the hole shape, fill the pond with water, then place stones (called *coping stones*) around the edges of the overhanging liner to make a border. Once you have all the materials on hand, you can easily build a modest garden pond in a single weekend. After the pond is installed, you can add a recirculating pump and filter to keep the water clear and healthy to support water plants and even livestock. You can give your pond a real custom flavor by adding a waterfall or a fountain.

Choosing a Liner

You have two basic choices in flexible pond liners: *PVC* plastic and *EPDM* (ethylene propylene diene monomer) or butyl rubber. Both types are designed to flex and stretch to conform to the pond shape, and are resistant to ultraviolet (UV) radiation and nontoxic to fish and water plants.

Rubber liners outlast plastic ones (especially in cold climates where alternate freezing and thawing will eventually make plastic liners brittle), but are costlier. Both types come in different grades, depending on the thickness and material composition. PVC liners come in 20-mil and 32-mil thicknesses. Relatively new on the market are "enhanced" PVC liners (called *PVCE* in catalogs) that have better resistance to tears, punctures and UV radiation than conventional liners of the same thickness. Both the price and manufacturer's warranty are a good indication of the liner life. The same holds true for rubber liners, which come in 30- to 45-mil thicknesses. Premium rubber liners come with a bonded geotextile backing material to better resist tears and punctures. These are easier to install and come with a lifetime warranty. You can also buy the backing material separately to use as an underlayment beneath conventional plastic and rubber liners.

Sizing the Liner

You can buy flexible pond liners in a variety of stock sizes, as well as by the running foot in various widths. Whether you go with a stock size liner, or buy the material by running foot, estimate the amount you need as follows:

Step 1: After selecting the site (choose a site that's away from leaf-dropping trees and shrubs, and gets at least a half-day of full sunshine), clear the area of plantings and other obstructions, then outline the pond shape with a garden hose or heavy rope. For square or rectangular ponds, set up strings and batter boards, as you would to outline a deck or patio. These measurements represent the water surface of the pond only, not taking into account the width of any coping stones or materials.

Step 2: Measure the maximum length and width of the pond, then calculate the smallest rectangle that will enclose the overall length and width. Then determine the maximum depth of the pond (18 to 24 in. is optimum for raising fish and most aquatic plants).

Step 3: To calculate the required liner size, double the maximum depth, then add this figure to the width and length of the pond. Next, add the average width of the coping stones (typically 12 in.) and double this figure. *Example:* The pond fits inside a 6 × 8 ft. rectangle and is 24 in. deep in the center. The minimum liner width would be: 6 ft. (pond width) + 4 ft.(twice pond depth) + 2 ft. (twice the width of the coping stones) for a total width of 12 ft. The minimum liner length would be 8 ft. + 4 ft. + 2 ft. for a total of 14 ft. For this pond, you would need a liner approximately 12 × 14 ft. If your pond will include a waterfall, the pond liner should be large enough to extend up over the waterfall lip and partially into the first catch basin behind it. Order extra material to line the falls or the stream.

IMPORTANT NOTICE: **Because ponds and pools are drowning hazards, many municipalities require that any yard containing a permanent water feature be completely fenced in. Check with your local building inspector before starting your water garden project.**

CROSS-SECTION OF A FLEXIBLE LINER POND

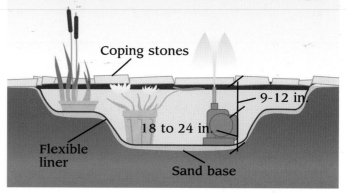

Coping stones

9-12 in.

18 to 24 in.

Flexible liner

Sand base

Flexible liner ponds in the 3 × 5 ft. to 4 × 6 ft. range should be 18 to 24 in. deep in the center to support water plants and livestock. A shallow shelf around the edge supports border plants, like cattails.

Installing a preformed shell liner

Installing a shell liner **(See Photo, page 45, top right)** is similar to installing a flexible liner in many ways. The soil should be free of stones, projecting roots and other sharp objects. Also, the excavation must be firmly tamped to prevent possible erosion from ground water that may create voids under the shell. If you're dealing with extremely loose or crumbly soil, or soils subject to frost heave or erosion from ground water, excavate the hole a bit larger to provide a firm, 4-in.-thick base of smooth pea gravel, topped by 2 to 3 in. of coarse sand, tamping firmly with a hand tamper.

To lay out the excavation area for a shell, place it on the ground, right-side up, then use a rope or garden hose and a plumb bob to transfer the outline of the pond shape to the ground beneath. Mark the outline with small stakes. Excavate the hole to conform to the shape of the pond shell, allowing an additional 2 to 3 in. around the sides and in the bottom for backfilling. Remove any stones, roots, or other sharp objects. Backfill the bottom of the hole, and other horizontal surfaces (such as ledges for plant shelves) with 2 to 3 in. of damp sand. Level the hole bottom. Test-fit the shell by setting it in into the hole. The shell rim should be about 1 in. above ground. Check the top of the shell for level with a 2 × 4 and carpenter's level. If necessary, lift out the shell and add or remove sand.

After you've leveled the shell, start filling the shell with water. As the water level rises, backfill around the shell with damp sand. Keep the sand even with the water level as it rises. After the pond is filled with water and the backfilling is complete, place coping stones or other coping materials around the pond perimeter to conceal the pond rim.

Installing a flexible liner pond

Test your soil before installing a flexible liner—if it's very sandy or silty, it may not be stable enough to support the liner. Either add a layer of compactible gravel, or choose a hard shell liner instead (See page 43).

Prepare the project area

1 Lay out your pond shape using an extension cord, garden hose or rope **(See FIGURE A)**. Remove sod within the layout lines and approximately 12 to 20 in. beyond them with a square-nosed spade. For large ponds (in excess of 50 sq. ft.), you may want to rent a sod kicker to make the job go more quickly. Level the area around the pond layout lines by removing or adding more dirt, and reestablish the layout lines as needed. *Note: When you design the shape of your pond, avoid sharp angles or too much symmetry in your layout. The more irregular and gentle the shape, the more natural the pond will look.*

2 Excavate within the layout lines to a depth of at least 9 in., sloping the sides of the hole about 20° from the edges of the excavation in toward the bottom. Check the hole depth by setting a carpenter's level on top of a long, straight 2 × 4. Lay the board across the excavation area in several directions, and measure

down from the board to the bottom of the hole with a tape measure **(See FIGURE B)**.

3 Lay out a deeper center area of the pond around the bottom of the excavation area, as you did in *Step 1*. The borders should be 9 to 12 in. in from the walls of the hole. Dig out this center area to 20 to 26 in. deep, measuring down from ground level. Slope the walls 20° in toward the bottom of the excavation **(See FIGURE C)**. The resulting pond excavation should be a tiered hole with a 9 to 12-in.-wide upper "shelf" for aquatic plants.

4 Remove any sharp stones or protruding roots in the sides and bottom of the excavation area to minimize the risk of puncturing the liner. Smooth the cleared area outside the pond's perimeter and add or remove soil as needed to bring it to level. Check for level with a level and straight 2 × 4 **(See FIGURE D)**.

5 Spread a ½- to 1-in. layer of sand around the bottom of the excavation and on the plant shelf. The sand layer serves as a protective cushion under the pond liner **(See FIGURE E)**. Dampen the sand and tamp lightly with a hand tamper. Pack damp sand into voids left by any rocks or debris you removed from the pond walls.

HOW TO INSTALL A FLEXIBLE LINER POND

FIGURE A: Lay out the pond shape with a length of extension cord, garden hose or rope. Keep the shape somewhat asymmetric with gently rounding curves.

FIGURE B: Check the depth of the initial excavation area with a carpenter's level and a straight length of 2 × 4. Measure the depth at multiple points along the board and across several directions.

Plant shelf

FIGURE C: Dig a smaller, 20 to 26-in.-deep section of the pond in the center of the first excavation area, leaving a 9 to 12 in.-wide plant shelf around the inside perimeter of the hole.

FIGURE D: Level off an area for coping stones around the edges of the pond excavation by adding or removing soil.

FIGURE E: Spread a layer of sand around the bottom of the hole and along the plant shelf. Dampen it and tamp lightly.

FIGURE F: Drape the pond liner over the pond excavation and press it into place so it conforms to the shape of the hole. Bricks or stones around the perimeter will help hold the liner in place.

FIGURE G: Fill the bottom of the excavation area with a 2-in. layer of clean pea gravel and smooth it with a rake or shovel. The gravel lends a natural look to the pond bottom and anchors potted aquatic plants.

FIGURE H: Fill the pond with water. Reposition the brick or stone liner hold-downs to allow the liner to shift and settle into its final shape.

FIGURE I: Trim extra liner away, allowing for a 9-in. overhang all around the pond rim.

Installing the flexible liner

6 Unfold the pond liner and place it in a sunny location for 15 to 20 minutes to warm it, which will help flatten it and make it more flexible. Drape the liner over the hole, overlapping it evenly on all sides of the excavation area. Press the liner down so it roughly conforms to the shape of the hole and lays flat in the bottom — don't worry about wrinkles at this point; these will be smoothed out when you fill the pond with water. Crease the liner neatly around the perimeter of the hole and weight down the liner edges temporarily with smooth bricks or stones, spaced 1 ft. apart to hold the liner in place **(See FIGURE F).**

7 Spread a 2-in. layer of clean pea gravel over the deeper center excavation area and smooth it with a shovel **(See FIGURE G).** The gravel will give the pond bottom a more natural appearance and help hold potted aquatic plants in place.

8 Fill the pond with water, and readjust the bricks or stones that are holding the liner in place as the pond fills and the liner settles into shape **(See FIGURE H).** Do not kneel or stand on the liner. To determine the volume of your pond before you fill it, see *TIP,* left. As the pond fills, smooth the liner to remove smaller wrinkles. Fold or pleat large wrinkles to make them less obvious. Fill the pond to within 2 in. of ground level, then remove the brick or stone weights. Let the liner settle for a day.

9 Trim the excess lining around the pond perimeter, leaving a 9-to 12-in. overhang **(See FIGURE I).** The overhang forms a watertight edge around the pond and will be concealed by the coping stone border.

Estimating pond volume

There are several good reasons for knowing your pond's water volume. First, it will help you choose the correct size pump and filter if you plan to add one. Second, this information will help you determine dosages of various pond treatments, like algaecides and aquatic plant fertilizers, should the need arise.

Shortly before you're ready to fill up the pond for the first time, turn on the garden hose and record how long it takes to fill a 5-gallon bucket. Adjust the flow rate so the bucket fills up within an amount of time easily divisible into one minute (for example, 120 seconds). Then determine the flow rate: (5 gallons at 120 seconds divided by 2 equals 2.5 gallons per minute). Without changing the flow rate, place the hose in the pond and keep track of how long it takes to fill it up (say 45 minutes). Then multiply the gallons per minute by the number of minutes (2.5 gallons per minute times 45 minutes equals 112.5 total gallons).

FIGURE J: Pin the liner overhang to the ground with 4-in. galvanized nails, spaced 12 to 18 in. apart.

FIGURE K: Dry-lay large, wide coping stones around the rim of the pond and fill in behind them with smaller stones. Overhang the front edges of the stones nearest the rim by 2 in.

10 Secure the liner overhang by driving 4-in. galvanized nails through it and into the ground about 3 to 4 in. in from the liner edge, spaced 12 to 18 in. apart **(See FIGURE J).** The nails will help hold the liner in place while you position the coping stones.

Lay the coping stone border

11 Dry-lay the coping stones around the pond perimeter so they overhang the pond by approximately 2 in. **(See FIGURE K).** For pointers on buying coping stones, see *TIP,* page 52. Try different coping stone arrangements until you find one that pleases you. For best drainage, identify the direction you want to direct water runoff and set the stone that's nearest that spot slightly lower than the rest of the coping stones. Use large, wide stones closest to the pond rim for stability, and fit smaller stones in between and behind the larger stones. Try to keep joint widths between stones to 2 in. or less. *Note: If you use flagstones, as we do for this project pond, it's relatively easy to cut them, should you need to. See page 39 for more information on cutting flagstones.*

12 While you can lay relatively large, flat stones directly over the liner without further anchoring, it's usually better to mortar the stones in place to keep them from slipping into the pond. Mix two parts sand to one part dry mortar in a wheelbarrow, using a shovel or hoe **(See FIGURE L).** *NOTE: Wear protective gloves when working with mortar.* Mist the mixture

FIGURE L: Prepare a mortar mix of two parts sand to one part dry mortar and mist with water. The mix should be just wet enough throughout to stick together and hold its shape. Lay a thick bed of the mortar mix around the perimeter of the pond to seat the coping stones. Try to keep the mortar at least 2 to 3 in. away from the edge of the pond.

FIGURE M: Spread a 2-in.-thick bed of mortar around the rim of the pond and set the coping stones into place. Pack mortar into the joints between stones.

TIP: Choosing coping stones

While you can use almost any type of rocks for coping stones, those with relatively smooth, flat surfaces and uniform thickness are the easiest to lay. Avoid stones with sharp edges that could puncture the liner. If you use field stones, make sure they have at least one relatively flat side, which should be placed flat-face down on the liner.

If you choose flagstone (as shown in this project), select stones that are at least 1 in. thick and at least 10 in. wide so they are able to overhang the pond edges by a few inches and hide the liner — without falling into the water. Consider building up several layers of flagstones, stacking them on top of one another and staggering the joints. Step each layer back slightly to help hold the stones in place.

FIGURE N: Smooth and brush away excess mortar from the joints with a damp paint brush. Work carefully to keep mortar from falling into the pond.

with water and mix it thoroughly — the mortar mix proportions are correct when you can form it into a ball in your palm and it retains the shape.

13 Spread a 2-in.-thick bed of mortar over the pond liner to within 2 in. of the pond rim. Set the coping stones into the mortar bed, twisting them slightly to seat them in the mortar **(See FIGURE M)**. If you are using large, flat stones, such as flagstones, angle them back from the pond rim to direct water runoff away from the pond. Pack the joints between the stones full with mortar, and extend the joints to within 2 in. of the pond rim.

14 Smooth the mortar joints and sweep away excess mortar with a paint brush dampened with water **(See FIGURE N)**. Allow the mortar to fully cure (about 5 to 7 days in dry weather). Scrub the stones and mortar edging with distilled white vinegar to neutralize the lime in the mortar. Rinse the stones with clean water and a sponge.

Filters, Fountains & Falls

In their most basic forms, small garden ponds can look quite plain — little more than a glorified mud puddle. It's adding your own unique details, like water plants, fountains and even waterfalls, that transform a basic pond into a unique landscape element.

Filtration systems. Most small garden ponds don't absolutely need a pump/filtration system once a biological balance has been achieved. But, if you want reasonably clear water for viewing fish and other aquatic life, it's a good idea to install one. A correctly sized pump and filter will also enable the pond to support a larger population of fish; for certain types, such as koi, filtration is essential.

Filters fall into two basic types: *mechanical* and *biological*. Both types clarify water by trapping particulate matter, such as floating algae, fish wastes and leftover fish food, dirt and organic matter, which cause cloudy water. Biological filters, and some mechanical ones, will also remove ammonia and other toxic chemicals.

Most homeowners with small backyard ponds (1,000 gallons or less) opt to install an in-pond mechanical filter with a matching pump. These employ a replaceable corrugated polyester cartridge (similar to those used in automobile oil filters) or a foam filter wrap. Other in-pond units combine the pump and filter in a single unit, and have replaceable filter pads. These filters are sized by maximum gallon capacity of the pond (for ponds up to 600 gallons, for example). Mechanical filters require frequent cleaning (every few days during the summer months), and high flow rates (larger pumps) to operate efficiently.

Water fountains are basically vertical attachments to recirculating pumps. Choose one with a spray pattern and water volume that's in proportion to your pond.

FILTERS & PUMPS

Submersible pumps are available in a wide range of sizes and with varying abilities to recirculate water for waterfalls and fountains. Some are sold with attachments for fountains. Read the package labeling carefully, and see the Tip on page 46 to determine which size pump your pond requires. The machine above is an external, biological filtration pump.

Waterfalls. Many garden ponds benefit by the addition of a waterfall. You can either buy a preformed watercourse, made of the same materials as preformed ponds, or use a flexible liner. Designs are as unique as the ponds into which they fall, and are largely a matter of personal taste. However, here are a few pointers to keep in mind:

• The most natural-looking waterfalls and streams consist of a series of two or more small catch basins or level areas connected by short cascades. For streams, a 1 to 2 in. drop per 10 feet is all that's required to make the water run downhill. This approach assures that some water will remain in the stream bed or catch basins when the pump is turned off.

• Use large, flat, overhanging rocks for the lip of the falls; this enables the water to fall directly into the pond with minimal water loss. A hollow area behind the falls amplifies the sound of splashing water as it falls into the pond.

• Placing small rocks and gravel in the streambed provides a more natural watercourse, and also helps protect the liner from the damaging effects of sunlight.

• As with ponds, the coping or edging stones along the bank can be mortared in place to prevent them from shifting and to help prevent leaks or runoff.

• If you're dealing with flat ground, use the soil excavated from the pond to build a mound or berm; use additional soil if necessary. Tamp the berm firmly to prevent erosion or slippage. On sloped sites, excavate flat steps or terraces for the pools or catch basins. Leave enough space to install coping stones. Dig the catch basins, leaving a 12-to 16-in. lip between them to form the connecting waterfalls. Install the liner over

Waterfalls help keep pond water healthy by creating aeration as the water flows and is reintroduced into the major pond basin. They're also beautiful and relaxing to watch and to listen to.

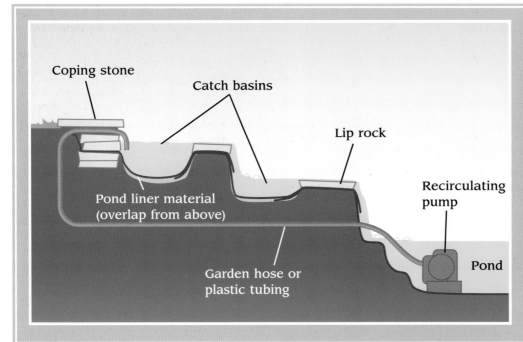

Coping stone

Catch basins

Lip rock

Recirculating pump

Pond liner material (overlap from above)

Garden hose or plastic tubing

Pond

Anatomy of a waterfall

You can build your own waterfall using scraps of pond liner material to create a waterflow channel. Build up a slope leading up and away from the pond, creating two or more basins. Line the waterway with the pond liner material, being sure to overlap pieces from above. Secure the liner pieces with coping stones, as you would for a flexible liner pond. Run a hose or tubing up from the main pond so the outlet is at the head of the falls.

the catch basins, following the same procedures as for a flexible liner pond. To finish the falls, install the pump and run the outlet tubing up alongside the falls to the top catch basin. Turn on the pump and make any final adjustments to the stones at the waterfall lip. If desired, you can bury the outlet tubing under a few inches of soil to help conceal it.

For a waterfall, you can buy a pump only, or a pump and filter. In all cases, you'll need to choose a pump that puts out enough water at the top of the falls to provide a pleasing cascade. Generally, if you've designed the falls to be in proportion to the pond, a pump that recirculates ½ to ⅔ of the pond's total water volume per hour should be sufficient to operate the falls. For larger cascades, choose a pump that can recirculate the entire gallonage of the pond in 1 hour.

A few words on electrical requirements: Make sure the pump you buy is designed for use in ponds. Submersible pumps should have waterproof cords; all pumps used outdoors or near water must be connected to a weatherproof GFCI outlet or have a GFCI breaker wired into the circuit. Electrical outlets for plug-in-pumps must be placed at least 6 ft. away from the water. Pump manufacturers usually offer cords of several different lengths to fit various situations. Check local electrical codes for additional requirements.

The waterfall above was created by piling rocks at one edge of this flexible liner pond, then running plastic tubing up from a recirculating pump submerged in the pond.

Fountains. Fountains fall into two basic categories—sprays and statuary. *Spray fountains* consist of a jet nozzle or ring (similar to garden sprinkler heads) attached to the outlet pipe of a submerged pump placed in the pond. You can choose from a variety of ornamental spray patterns. When added to the pond, sprays aerate the water, providing oxygen for fish and other pond life. When choosing a spray, make sure it is in proportion to the size of the pond. If the spray is too large, gusts of wind can blow water outside the perimeter of the pond; also the falling water will disrupt a large portion of the water surface, making it hard to grow water plants or view aquatic life beneath the water. Likewise, fountains with delicate or bell-shaped spray patterns must be placed in wind-free locations to avoid disrupting the pattern.

Spray fountains are relatively simple to install; for most backyard garden ponds, you'd buy the fountain head or nozzle, all the required fittings, and a matched submersible pump as a complete system. Some units can be fitted with a diverter valve to operate a second water feature, such as a waterfall or another fountain. If you're installing a custom fountain, seek advice from a knowledgeable pond dealer or installer in choosing components. In all cases, the submersible pump you choose should either have a top-mounted outlet or discharge, or include an elbow fitting that enables you to attach a vertical extension pipe and fittings for the spray head. The pump should also include a filter

screen or prefilter attached to the inlet to prevent the jet nozzles from clogging.

Statuary fountains are often sold as completely self-contained units that include the statue (also called the *ornament*), an integral pedestal and water reservoir, and in some cases, a base, or riser, beneath the reservoir bowl. Typically, a small submersible pump is housed inside the hollow pedestal below the water level of the reservoir and connects to the statue via a short length of flexible plastic tubing. The pump cord runs through the hollow statue base, hidden from view. Actual installation procedures will vary slightly, depending on the fountain style: To install, follow the directions that come with the unit. As with other water features that require pumps, the pump cord must be connected to a GFCI outlet or circuit.

Heavier statues (over 75 pounds, or so) will require a concrete footing installed beneath the pond liner or shell to support the weight of the statue—if the statue isn't supported by a firm footing, its weight may puncture or tear the flexible liner or eventually crack the rigid shell. Before installing the liner or shell, lay down a poured concrete footing in the statue location, about 4 to 6 in. thick, extending 3 to 4 in. beyond the statue base on all sides. For lighter statuary, firmly tamp the ground beneath the liner. In all cases, add an underlayment material both beneath and on top of the liner or shell to cushion the statue base and help prevent punctures of the pond liner.

A mixture of lillies, bog plants, floating plants and submerged plants keep the aquatic environment in balance in this pond.

Feature plants add color and a tropical flavor to any water garden.

Water lillies are the staples of aquatic plants. They're available in hundreds of varieties with flowers in dozens of rich colors.

Stocking Your Water Garden

While some people prefer a clear water pond without fish or aquatic plants, most pond builders opt to include one or both to add beauty and interest to the waterscape. While it's possible to have a pond with plants only, or one with fish only, it's usually best to have a good combination of both, along with scavengers such as snails, tadpoles, or freshwater clams or mussels. Ponds that include a diversity of aquatic life in correct proportions will achieve a natural biological balance, which will reduce the need for chemicals to control algae and the larvae of various insects, such as mosquitoes. Fish and plants also rely on each other to provide nutrients and oxygen necessary for their mutual survival.

Aquatic plants fall into four general categories: *Water lilies* come in hundreds of different varieties, but are generally subdivided into two main groups: *tropical* (for warm climates) and *hardy* (for moderate to cold climates). Lilies are typically planted in pots in the deep areas of the pond. In addition to having beautiful, showy flowers, their broad, floating leaves provide shade to help control water temperature for fish and cut down on algae growth during the hot summer months.

Bog plants include water iris, cattails, pickerel rush, and lotus, to name a few. These are also called *marginal plants* because they're grown in shallower water, on marginal plant shelves around the pond perimeter, or in bog gardens adjacent to the pond. Some bog plants have showy flowers, while others are grown for their interesting foliage. Bog plants help hide the liner around the pond margin, for a more natural appearance.

Floating plants, as the name implies, require no soil to grow. Their buoyant leaves keep them afloat as their dangling roots draw nutrients directly from the pond water. Popular species include water fern, water hyacinth, water lettuce, and duckweed. These plants, too, provide shade for fish and reduce algae growth, but must be selected carefully and thinned out periodically, as some types

Stocking ratios

To get started, you can follow this general formula for stocking the pond: These figures are based on a pond 18 to 24 in. deep, without a pump or filter. For each square yard of pond surface area, add:

• 12 in. of goldfish or koi (three 4-in.-long fish, for example.)

• One medium to large water lily (or enough lilies and/or floating plants to cover 50% to 60% of the total surface area).

• Two bunches of submerged plants (oxygenating grasses)

• Eight to ten large water snails or freshwater clams/mussels.

• One large tadpole or four small pollywogs

Planting aquatic plants

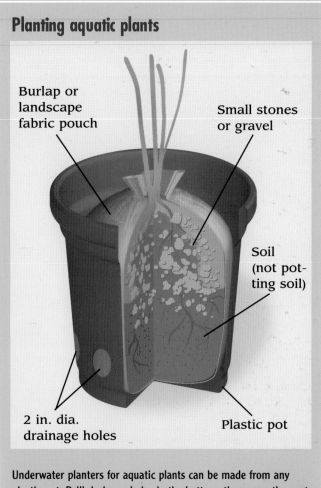

Burlap or landscape fabric pouch

Small stones or gravel

Soil (not potting soil)

2 in. dia. drainage holes

Plastic pot

Underwater planters for aquatic plants can be made from any plastic pot. Drill drainage holes in the bottom, then warp the root system of the plant in a burlap or landscape-fabric pouch filled soil at the bottom and rocks or gravel near the top. Tie the pouch closed around the base of the plant stems. To winter aquatic plants, cut the plants a few inches up the stem and leave them to rest in a cool area, such as a basement.

---

can completely cover the entire water surface in short order during their growing season.

Submerged plants, also called *oxygenating grasses,* grow completely underwater. Popular species include cabomba, anachris, ceratophyllum and vallisneria—the same types used in indoor aquariums. While they may not even be visible in the pond, submerged plants play a significant utilitarian role by providing oxygen for fish, and consuming nutrients (fish waste) that would otherwise promote algae growth. In larger ponds, submerged plants also provide a food source and spawning area for fish. Plant oxygenating grasses in pots to keep them anchored on the pond bottom; plastic bird netting secured over the leaves will prevent overgrazing by fish.

The most popular fish for ponds include goldfish, koi, and mosquito fish (the latter are small guppy-like fish, so named for their voracious appetite for mosquito larvae). All are cold-water fish (as opposed to tropical fish) because they adapt well to a wide variety of water temperatures. Tropical fish (such as those sold at pet stores) and game fish (trout, bass, catfish, bluegill, etc.) are generally not recommended for backyard ponds.

In addition to fish, you may want to add a few scavengers to the pond—water snails, tadpoles or pollywogs, and perhaps a few freshwater clams or mussels. Scavengers serve as the pond's "vacuum cleaner system," consuming fish waste, algae, and decaying plant matter, transforming these materials into nutrients for plants, and helping clarify the water. Pollywogs and tadpoles also hold a special fascination for children, as they eventually grow legs and turn into frogs.

The size and number of fish, plants, and other aquatic life you can grow in a pond depends on a variety of factors—available oxygen, sunlight and nutri-

ents, and the amount of water circulation and filtration provided by the pump and filter, if any. (The use of pumps and filters not only helps clarify the water, but enables you to support a larger population of fish and plants.) In all cases, no two ponds are exactly alike, so the process of establishing a good ecological balance will be a matter of trial and error.

Before stocking the pond, wait several days for the "free chlorine" in the tap water to dissipate. Then, test the water with a test kit, available from water garden catalogs, pond and swimming pool dealers and pet shops. Simple kits test for pH (acidity or alkalinity) and levels of chlorine; others may include tests for ammonia, chloramines, nitrates, and water hardness. Or, you can take a sample of the water to a local pool dealer. After the water is balanced, add the plants, then wait a week or two for them to get established and oxygenate the water before stocking the pond with livestock.

Wall Structures

Walls serve a multitude of purposes in landscape construction, including retaining walls that prevent erosion and level off slopes, short walls built in a frame configuration to create raised planting beds, freestanding garden walls that divide a yard and border walls that define the boundaries of your property. From a visual standpoint, walls are key elements to a landscape design. They introduce new textures, define space and create vertical lines for visual interest.

Most walls are built using natural stone or concrete-based products, but you can also use landscape timbers for ease of workability and a softer appearance. Interlocking concrete blocks have become a very popular building material for walls, especially retaining walls and planting beds that contain earth. These artificial products are now available in a range of sizes, shapes and colors to give you plenty of design options. Hollow-core concrete construction blocks can also be used for building landscape walls, but they lack the texture and ease of installation of interlocking blocks designed specifically for outdoor and garden building purposes. Natural stone, such as rubble stone or fieldstone, is used to build all types of landscape walls, both dry-laid and mortared.

Wall structures 3 ft. in height or shorter pose no particular building problems for the do-it-yourselfer. Taller walls, however, usually need to be designed by a qualified professional, such as a landscape architect or soils engineer. Regardless of whether they're used as retaining walls, walls over 3 ft. high generally require building permits and fully-developed structural drawings.

Many wall building projects will require excavation and grading of the building area. Especially if you're building a large retaining wall into a steep slope, look into hiring a contractor to perform the earth moving chores (or, if you're at all experienced with earth moving equipment you can rent a small front end loader or skid — but be sure to contact your local public utilities first to have them check for any buried cables or pipes in the work area).

COMMON TYPES OF WALL STRUCTURES

Interlocking concrete blocks are a very do-it-yourselfer friendly building material. They're generally cast with a flange on the lower back edge that slips behind the block beneath it, holding the wall together and creating a slight backwards slope that is intended to help the wall withstand the force of the earth pressing against. The retaining walls shown to the right demonstrate one of the best features of interlocking concrete blocks: they can easily be stacked to follow curves.

Landscape timbers are made from pine that is pressure-treated with rot-resisting chemicals. The 5 × 6 in. timbers to the right are joined together with pieces of steel rebar to form a planting bed or a shorter retaining wall.

Rough-hewn timbers are used to build posts and heavy-duty stringers that create support for the split-log vertical members in this unique retaining wall project. The posts and stringers are joined with half-lap joints reinforced with galvanized landscape spikes driven toe-nail style through the posts and into the stringers.

Raised planting beds break up flat lawns and help focus attention on your favorite feature plants. Interlocking concrete blocks represent an easy and effective solution to building planting beds.

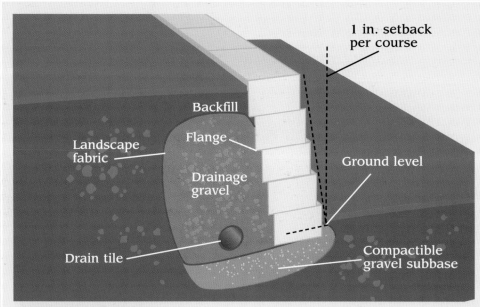

Interlocking block retaining walls

Interlocking concrete blocks are stacked in staggered courses, beginning with half of the first block below grade. Half-blocks are used at the ends of alternating courses. Blocks with flanges on the back lower edges are overlapped to tie the wall together. Some blocks are pinned together with nylon pins (called keys). Construction adhesive is applied between courses for extra holding power. A course of thin capstones can be installed at the top of the wall to conceal the gaps between interlocking blocks.

1 in. setback per course

Backfill

Flange

Landscape fabric

Ground level

Drainage gravel

Drain tile

Compactible gravel subbase

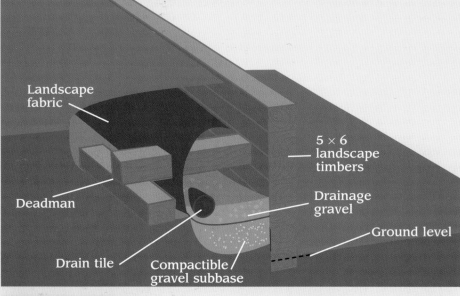

Timber retaining walls

Landscape timbers are stacked together, with the first timber course below grade. Subsequent courses are joined with landscape spikes or pieces of steel rebar. Weep holes for drainage are drilled in the lower courses, and sometimes created by leaving slight gaps at end joints between timbers. About ⅔ up the wall, a timber with an attached cross piece (called a deadman) is installed perpendicular to the wall every 4 to 6 ft. The deadmen anchor the wall to the hill. See Page 75.

Landscape fabric

Deadman

Drain tile

Compactible gravel subbase

5 × 6 landscape timbers

Drainage gravel

Ground level

Cut stone (ashlar) retaining walls

Cut sedimentary stones (sometimes called ashlar stones) are mortared together in courses. The first course is set below grade, sloping slightly from front to back. This creates a cant in the wall, allowing it to utilize gravity to counteract the pressure of the earth behind it. Longer stones are inserted in the deadman position, as with timber retaining walls. On the second or third course above grade, sections of 1 to 2 in. pipe are inserted into the gaps between stones every 6 to 8 ft. for drainage.

5° to 10° setback

Backfill

Landscape fabric

Deadman

Drainage gravel

Mortared cut stone

Ground level

Drain tile

Compactible gravel subbase

Retaining Walls

From a functional standpoint, retaining walls serve to prevent soil erosion on hillsides and to create usable flat spaces on sloping lots. If you're faced with a steep slope, it's often easier and more attractive to install a series of low terraced walls, rather than one tall one. Terracing provides space for a series of raised planting beds or walkways (See *Illustration,* right).

A slope doesn't necessarily have to be steep to benefit from the addition of a retaining wall. For example, low walls can be built simply to prevent water runoff from a gently sloping lawn onto a sidewalk or driveway. Low retaining walls can also serve as decorative boundary markers to discourage people and animals from cutting across your lawn area.

The basic site preparation, excavation, and installation of base and backfill materials are essentially the same for all types of retaining walls — regardless of building material. The wall footing consists of a trench filled with tamped compactible gravel. The excavated space behind the wall is covered with landscape fabric, then filled with coarse gravel or river rock; a perforated drain pipe at the base of the wall further promotes drainage. In poorly draining soil, you may also want to dig a swale on the uphill side of the wall, about 2 ft. back from and parallel to the wall. A swale is a shallow trench about 2 ft. wide and 6 to 8 in. deep designed to slow the flow of rushing water runoff and help direct it away from the wall.

The way you treat the retaining wall ends should depend on the angle and direction of the slope, the desired drainage patterns, and surrounding features on your property. To prevent soil erosion at each end of the wall, you may need to turn the wall back into the hillside or slope. The sidewalls can meet the front wall at a sharp 90° angle, or they can be curved back gently, or tapered back at a shallow angle. To reduce the number of blocks needed for the sidewalls, dig a stepped trench between the front wall and the top of the slope. Extend the sidewalls as far back as necessary to contain the slope or create the desired amount of flat space above the retaining wall.

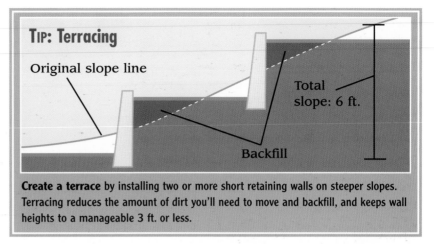

TIP: Terracing

Original slope line

Total slope: 6 ft.

Backfill

Create a terrace by installing two or more short retaining walls on steeper slopes. Terracing reduces the amount of dirt you'll need to move and backfill, and keeps wall heights to a manageable 3 ft. or less.

TOOLS & MATERIALS FOR BUILDING WALL STRUCTURES

Blocks with overlapping flanges

Blocks with nylon keys

Landscape timbers and interlocking concrete blocks can be used to make landscape walls for just about any purpose. Timbers range in size from 4×4 to 8×8 (5×6 is shown above). Interlocking blocks, sold in a range of sizes, styles and colors, are connected either with overlapping flanges or with nylon keys.

Tools for building landscape walls include: (A) rubber mallet; (B) hand maul; (C) 4-ft. level; (D) circular saw with masonry-cutting blade; (E) combination blade for cutting wood; (F) hand tamper; (G) spade; (H) 50-ft. roll tape; (I) tape measure; (J) caulk gun; and construction adhesive; (K) corded drill with spade bits and bit extender; (L) brickset; (M) mason's line.

Interlocking block

Today, most residential and commercial wall structures are made of interlocking concrete blocks.
Sometimes called gravity walls, these interlocking systems usually require no concrete footings, and can be
built without mortar.

The blocks come in many different sizes, textures
and colors. Correctly installed, interlocking block walls
are exceptionally durable and maintenance free. The
modular blocks require little skill to install. Some types
are solid, with predrilled holes in which you install
nylon or fiberglass connecting pins (keys) to lock the
courses together; others have hollow cores and built-in
flanges to hold them in place; the cores are filled with a
backfill material (crushed rock or gravel) to stabilize
the wall and promote drainage.

The blocks are designed with a built-in setback to
better resist soil and water pressure behind the wall.
Most types are also self-draining, so no weep holes are
required. They accommodate themselves to straight or
curved (serpentine) walls. Some block styles have
prescored grooves so you can easily cut them into half-
blocks with a hammer and masonry chisel or brickset
for corner applications. Other systems include decorative cap blocks to finish off the top of the wall.

Interlocking blocks come in a range of sizes and
shapes, but even the smallest weigh 40 to 60 pounds
each. The standard size blocks weigh from 80 to 120
pounds each. Most have roughly textured faces created
by cleaving off the front of each block after it's cast.
Some shapes are designed especially for use in curved
walls, but most will conform with curves easily. Most
manufacturers provide a range of color choices, but
styles and colors are limited by local supply.

Installing an interlocking block retaining wall

1 Remove sod from the wall project area with a sod kicker up to the top of the lawn slope **(See FIGURE A)**. Plan for the top of the retaining wall to sit even with the top of the slope. *NOTE: If the slope behind the wall rises more than 3 ft., you'll need to terrace the hill with two or more retaining walls (See terracing illustration, page 61).* If you plan on re-laying the sod later, roll it up (green side in) and keep it moist.

2 Set up stakes and a leveled mason's line to mark the excavation area. The trench must be wide enough to include the width of the blocks plus 12 to 14 in. for installing backfill and drain pipe behind the wall. Using the mason's line as a guide, dig a flat trench deep enough to accommodate 6 in. of compactible gravel subbase plus ½ the thickness of the first course of blocks **(See FIGURE B)**. Measure down from the string line to keep the bottom of the trench level. Once the trench is dug, remove the stakes and mason's line.

3 Fill the trench with 6 in. of compactible gravel subbase plus ½ in. to allow for compaction, then rake it smooth and compact it with a hand tamper **(See FIGURE C)**. The subbase serves as a footing beneath the block wall. Use a carpenter's level attached to a long, straight 2 × 4 to make sure the subbase remains level along the length of the trench.

FIGURE A: Remove sod from the project area up to the top of the hill slope, using a sod kicker or a square-nosed spade. If you plan to reuse the sod, roll it up and keep it moist.

FIGURE B: Mark the back of the excavation area with a mason's line and stakes. Dig a trench deep enough to contain 6 in. of subbase plus half the thickness of the first row of interlocking blocks.

FIGURE C: Fill the trench with 6½ in. of compactible gravel subbase and tamp it with a hand tamper. Check to be sure the subbase is level along the entire length.

FIGURE D: Set one block into the trench and mark its height with a leveled mason's line that runs the entire length of the wall. Lay the rest of the base course of blocks so their height aligns with the mason's line. Make adjustments to high blocks by tapping them with a rubber mallet.

4 Set a block into the trench at one end of the wall, then stake a mason's line so it is level and even with the top of the block, and runs the length of the wall. (The mason's line indicates the height of the first course of blocks.) Lay the first course (called the *base course*) into the trench, lining up the block faces, butting the front corners and making sure the block tops touch but do not move the mason's line. Add or remove subbase material beneath the blocks as needed to adjust their height. Check each block for level along the back edges and widthwise using a carpenter's level, and make fine adjustments by tapping the blocks with a rubber mallet **(See FIGURE D).** *NOTE: Some block manufacturers may suggest that you install the base course of blocks upside-down and backward, so that the flanged bottom edge of each block faces up along the front edge of the wall. This allows the block to rest flat on the subbase. Follow the manufacturer's instructions for proper block orientation on the base course.*

5 When you reach the end of the wall, cut a half block (widthwise) to fit into the corner, with the cut face facing frontwards **(See FIGURE E).** Then lay the base course of the end wall back into the hillside.

Cutting interlocking concrete blocks

Because most block walls are set in a running bond pattern, which results in staggered joints, you'll need to cut full blocks into half-blocks at wall ends and corners. Some manufacturers sell half blocks or right-angle corner blocks, but you can easily split full blocks in half with a brickset and hand maul. Some blocks have a shallow groove on the back face to make splitting easier. If the blocks you've purchased don't have these, use a circular saw equipped with a masonry blade to cut a ⅛-in.-deep groove along the top and back of the block. Then break the blocks by tapping along score lines. This will assure a clean, square cut, yielding usable left- and right-hand block sections.

6 Cut a length of landscape fabric wide enough to extend from the back edges of the blocks to the top of the excavation area, plus an extra 1 to 2 ft. that eventually will overlap and cover the rock backfill **(See FIGURE F).** Be sure that any seams between sheets of landscape fabric overlap by at least 6 to 8 in. The landscape fabric keeps soil from washing into the rock backfill material and potentially obstructing drainage.

7 Backfill the trench behind the blocks with a 3- to 4-in. layer of drainage rock to cover the landscape fabric in the trench bottom **(See FIGURE G).**

8 Designate one end of the trench to be the low end in order to establish a drainage slope that runs the full length of the wall. Water will pass from the surface of the hill down through the drainage rock backfill and into a perforated drain pipe that follows the trench. The pipe should lie on a slope that drops approximately 1 in. every 8 ft. to keep water from pooling behind the wall. Grade the drainage rock so it follows the proper slope to the low end of the trench, and lay flexible drain pipe (usually called *drain tile*) along the full length of the trench **(See FIGURE H).** Extend the pipe 1 or 2 ft. beyond the end of the wall or around it. This end should remain exposed and must be kept unobstructed so runoff water can drain away.

FIGURE E: Split a full-sized block in half to form the corner of the wall. The cut face should face forward.

FIGURE F: Spread landscape fabric into the trench so that it extends from the back of the blocks up the full height of the excavation. Allow 1 to 2 ft. extra along the top to fold back over the backfill material. If you need to use more than one continuous sheet of fabric, overlap the seams by at least 6 to 8 in.

FIGURE G: Backfill behind the base course of blocks with 3 to 4 in. of drainage rock, covering the landscape fabric on the bottom of the trench. Slope this rock layer 1 in. for every 8 ft. of wall length, down to the low side of the drainage trench.

FIGURE H: Lay perforated drain pipe (drain tile) in the trench. Extend the pipe 1 to 2 ft. beyond each end of the wall or wrap it around the wall so it faces the wall front. It will channel water away from the wall.

FIGURE I: Set the second course of block over the base course. The bottom back flange of each block should butt against the top back edge of the blocks below it. Stagger the joints from course to course.

FIGURE J: Cut and lay the corner blocks in the second course so they are staggered over the joints in the base course.

FIGURE K: Cover the drain pipe with drainage rock and continue backfilling in front of the landscape fabric and behind each additional course of blocks you lay. Tamp the backfill lightly with a hand tamper.

NOTE: *On long walls, you may have to lay additional courses of blocks at this stage and add more drainage rock backfill to establish the proper drainage slope for the drain pipe.*

9 Lay the second course of block, butting the bottom flanges of the blocks tightly against the top back edges of the base course **(See FIGURE I).** The pattern for laying block courses depends on the block design, but most interlocking blocks are laid in a running bond pattern, where each course offsets the course below it by ½ the block, creating staggered joints.

10 When you reach the end of the wall, place a full or partial corner block to form a staggered joint with the corner block beneath it **(See FIGURE J).** Lay the second course for the side wall.

11 Backfill the trench with more rock, being careful not to dislodge the landscape fabric or disturb the drain pipe **(See FIGURE K).** Fill the trench to a level about 2 in. below the top of the second course of blocks. Pack the rock backfill with a hand tamper.

12 Fold the extra landscape fabric over the rock backfill, then fill the rest of the trench up to the top of the second course of block with clean topsoil **(See FIGURE L).**

13 Install the top course of blocks (called cap blocks) by adhering the cap blocks to the course beneath with a heavy bead of construction adhesive to hold them in place **(See FIGURE M).**

14 Fill the rest of the trench in with clean, amended topsoil to a level 2 or 3 in. below the tops of the cap blocks **(See FIGURE N).**

15 Patch over the excavation area with the sod **(See FIGURE O)** or fill the trench to the top with topsoil and use it as a garden bed for plantings.

FIGURE L: Fold over the extra landscape fabric to cover the drainage rock backfill, then fill the trench with topsoil up to the top of the second block course.

FIGURE M: Bond the top row of blocks to the course below with a heavy bead of construction adhesive.

FIGURE N: Fold the extra landscape fabric over the rock backfill and up against the backs of the cap blocks. Cover the fabric with topsoil to within 2 in. of the top of the wall.

FIGURE O: Patch over the excavation area with the sod. Press the sod firmly into the soil and water it daily for two weeks or until it establishes roots.

This timber planting bed was built using the same basic techniques you'd use to build a timber retaining wall (See page 75). Positioned at the far end of the yard, it provides a pleasant barrier to street traffic visible from the patio at the opposite end of the yard.

Before

Landscape Timbers

Back in the 1950s, railroad ties became a popular building material for raised planters, retaining walls, garden borders, patio edgings, steps, and the like. As railroad tracks were being torn up across the country in favor of freeways, air travel, and other modern forms of transportation, the recycled ties were readily available at lumber yards and building suppliers, at relatively low prices compared to other dimensional lumber of the same size. In recent years, however, railroad ties have become scarce, and now they're often quite expensive when you can find them. Because the ties are typically treated with highly toxic creosote, are often embedded with gravel, nails and tar (hard on saw blades), and come in limited lengths,

most professional landscape contractors prefer cleaner pressure-treated landscape timbers in their stead. Common sizes for landscape timbers are 5 × 6 in., 6 × 6 in., 6 × 8 in. and up, in various lengths. We used 5 × 6 timbers for this project.

Whether you use railroad ties or landscape timbers for your project, the concept is still the same: you can build a sturdy raised planting bed (information on building a timber retaining wall can be found on page 75) without the need for stakes to hold the timbers in place. Low retainers, freestanding walls and planters (up to 2 ft. in height) can be built easily by most do-it-yourselfers. For taller structures, seek the advice of a landscape architect or designer.

Building a raised planting bed with timbers

Calculate the amount of lumber you'll need for your planting bed by first creating a scale drawing of the planter on graph paper. For larger timbers, like those in our project planter, you'll save money if you try to design your planter to make maximum use of standard lumber lengths. It's also a good idea to stake out a full-size layout of your planter in the project area before you buy materials and start building to see how its size and shape will impact your yard.

1 Clear the planter project area of obstructions, then cut the first course of treated-wood timbers to size with a chain saw or circular saw and lay them out on the ground in the desired planter shape. *NOTE: If you choose to cut thick timbers with a circular saw, you may need to make a pass on two or more sides of each timber to cut all the way through.* Use a framing square to square up the corners **(See FIGURE A).** Butt the ends of these timbers in a consistent pattern around the planter perimeter so that the joints between courses of timbers do not align.

2 If you're installing the planter in a lawn area, cut the sod along the inside and outside edges of the loose-laid timbers with a square-nose spade to mark the locations of the timbers **(See FIGURE B).** If the planter will be installed over bare ground, mark the timber layout with spray paint or markers.

3 Set the timbers out of the way of the layout lines, then remove the sod within the layout lines with a square-nosed spade or a sod kicker **(See FIGURE C).** For our project planter, we used 5 × 6 treated timbers. For timbers this size, dig a trench where you've removed sod about 5 in. deep.

4 Fill the trench with 2½ in. of compactible subbase material and tamp it down with the end of one of the timbers **(See FIGURE D).** Level the subbase. The subbase layer provides a solid footing beneath the timber walls of the planter and promotes water drainage. The remaining trench depth will allow the first course of timbers to be about half below grade, which will help lock them into place and stabilize the base of the planter.

5 Before you permanently install the timbers for the base course, use a heavy-duty portable drill and spade bit to drill ½-in.-dia. guide holes through each timber **(See FIGURE E).** *NOTE: You may need to use a drill bit extension in order to drill through the timber in one pass.* For timbers up to 8 ft., drill a hole about 6 in. in from each end and one in the center. For timbers 10 ft. or longer, drill four evenly-spaced holes. Anchor rods will be driven through these holes later.

6 Place one of the longest timbers into the trench and check it for level. Add or remove subbase material as needed to level the timber and adjust its height **(See FIGURE F).** This leveled timber becomes a reference for leveling the other base course timbers.

HOW TO BUILD A RAISED PLANTING BED WITH TIMBERS

FIGURE A: Cut the base course of timbers and lay them into the project area to outline the planter's shape. Butt the ends of the timbers in a consistent orientation — each successive course of timbers should be staggered over the joints of the course below.

FIGURE B: Mark the outline of the timbers by cutting through the sod with a square-nosed spade.

FIGURE C: Set the base course timbers out of the way and remove sod from within the spaded outlines. Then dig a 5-in.-deep trench following the planter layout.

FIGURE D: Fill the trench with 2 to 3 in. of compactible gravel subbase to form a footing beneath the base course of timbers. Pack it down with the end of a timber and level the subbase layer all around.

Drill bit extension

FIGURE E: Drill three or four ½-in.-dia. holes in each base course timber, starting approximately 6 in. in from either end, to create guide holes for reinforcing rod anchors. Attach a drill bit extension to the end of your spade bit to bore through thick timbers.

FIGURE F: Set a long timber into the trench and level it by adding or removing subbase material beneath it. This timber will be a reference for leveling the other base course timbers.

FIGURE G: Set the remaining base course timbers into the trench and level each timber to the reference timber with a level and straight 2 × 4. Measure diagonally across the planter from the reference timber.

FIGURE H: Check each planter corner for square with a carpenter's square. Cut 18-in.-long reinforcing rod (rebar) anchors and drive them flush with the tops of the base course timbers, using a hand maul.

FIGURE I: Cut the second course of timbers to length, keeping in mind that the end joints should be staggered with those of the base course. Then lay the timbers in position.

7 Set the remaining base course timbers into the trench and butt the ends together to match the arrangement used in *Step 1*. Set a level on top of a straight 2 × 4 and lay it diagonally from the leveled timber across the base course in several directions to make sure all timbers are level to the long reference timber **(See FIGURE G).** Add or remove subbase material to level the rest of the timbers.

8 Cut 18-in. lengths of ½-in.-dia. reinforcing rod (rebar) with a hacksaw or reciprocating saw to serve as anchors for holding the base course of timbers in place. Use a framing square to check for square corners, then drive the rebar rods through the holes and into the ground with a hand maul **(See FIGURE H).** The tops of the rods should be flush with the tops of the base timbers.

9 Cut and lay the second course of timbers, overlapping the joints of the first course at each corner **(See FIGURE I).** As you install successive courses, you'll alternate the corner joints to form the lap pattern shown **(See FIGURE L for more corner detail).**

10 Attach the timbers at the joints, about 3 in. from the ends of each timber with 10-in. galvanized landscape spikes. Drill pilot holes for the spikes with a

bit extension and a 5/16-in. spade bit, then drive the spikes into the timbers with a hand maul **(See FIGURE J).** Drive additional spikes 18 to 24 in. along the length of the timbers.

11 Drill 1/2-in. weep holes through the second course of timbers every 3 ft. around the planter. Start the holes midway up the width of each timber from inside the planter and bore outward at a downward angle. Aim for the exit hole to hit the joint between the two courses **(See FIGURE K).** *TIP: You could drill larger diameter weep holes and fit them with 1/2-in. PVC pipe "sleeves" glued in place with construction adhesive. Sleeves help prevent the wood around the weep holes from decaying.*

12 Cut and lay the remaining timber courses, overlapping the end joints and securing each course with landscape spikes **(See FIGURE L).**

13 Cut and attach full-width sheets of landscape fabric to the inside walls of the planter, with the top edges of the fabric positioned 2 to 3 in. below the top edges of the walls. The fabric forms a barrier to keep the soil inside the planter from seeping out between the timbers or clogging the weep holes. Staple the fabric in place with rows of 1/2-in. staples, spaced 8 to 10

FIGURE J: Attach the second course of timbers to the first with 10-in. galvanized landscape spikes driven through the timbers 2 or 3 in. in from the ends. Drill 5/16-in. pilot holes to make the spikes easier to drive and to prevent splitting the timbers.

FIGURE K: Bore 1/2-in. weep holes through the second course of timbers, starting the holes from the inside of the planter, midway up the width of each timber. Drill downward and outward at an angle, aiming for the exit holes to hit the joints between courses.

FIGURE L: Cut and lay the remaining courses of timbers, securing each course to the one below it with landscape spikes. Be sure to overlap end joints so they interlock.

FIGURE M: Staple a sheet of landscape fabric around the inside of the planter, starting 2 to 3 in. below the top edges of the walls. Run extra fabric across the bottom of the planter.

FIGURE N: Add a 4-in. layer of drainage rock or compactible gravel subbase across the bottom of the planter to promote drainage.

in. apart **(See FIGURE M)**. Run excess fabric across the bottom of the planter.

14 Add a 4-in. layer of drainage rock or compactible gravel subbase across the bottom of the planter to promote drainage **(See FIGURE N).**

15 Fill the planter with topsoil or planting mix **(See FIGURE O)**. Tamp the soil in 8-in.-deep layers with a hand tamper as you fill the planter to minimize settling once the planter is full. Otherwise you may need to add more soil seasonally. Finish the planter with water sealer or an exterior oil-based stain.

FIGURE O: Fill the planter with topsoil, tamping 8-in. layers as you go to help minimize further settling. Rake the top smooth.

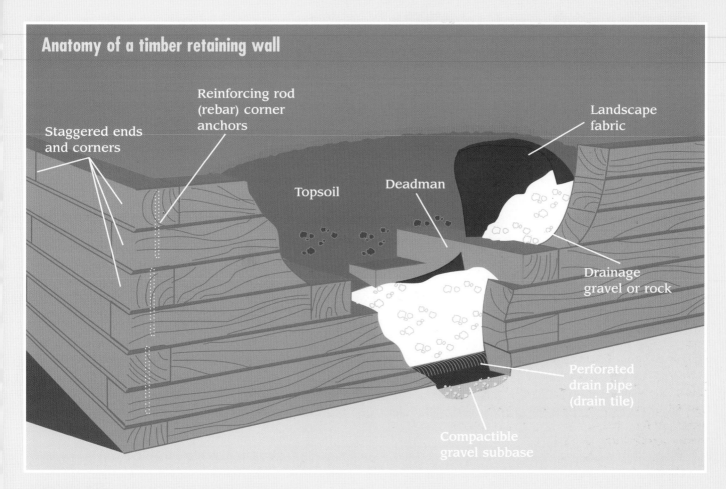

Anatomy of a timber retaining wall

Staggered ends and corners

Reinforcing rod (rebar) corner anchors

Topsoil

Deadman

Landscape fabric

Drainage gravel or rock

Perforated drain pipe (drain tile)

Compactible gravel subbase

VARIATION: Timber retaining wall

The information shown in the preceding project can easily be adapted to building a retaining wall from timbers. Timber retaining walls are less expensive to build than interlocking block walls but have a shorter life span and may look a bit "rustic" for many landscape designs. For walls up to 3 ft. high, use 5 × 6 or 6 × 6 pressure-treated timbers; taller walls may require larger-size timbers. Avoid using railroad ties as building materials, however, because they typically are soaked in creosote, which is harmful to vegetation.

Building basics

Foundation and drainage requirements are essentially the same as for interlocking block walls: The timber wall rests in a trench filled with a 6-in. layer of compactible gravel subbase, and the first course of timber sits half its thickness below grade. A perforated plastic drain pipe (drain tile) rests on the subbase and is set at a grade to facilitate water drainage. The wall is backfilled with river rock or coarse gravel. A layer of landscape fabric behind the rock backfill keeps soil from infiltrating the drainage materials.

The procedures for building timber retaining walls are similar to those for the raised planter on pages 66

to 70. The base-course timbers are anchored to the subbase with 18-in. lengths of ½-in. reinforcing rod, and 10-in. galvanized landscape spikes spaced every 2 ft. attach each course to the one beneath. Corner and end joints should be staggered. Set each course of timbers ½ in. behind the course beneath, so the wall forms a gradual backward angle (called "batter").

Reinforcing the wall

Timber retaining walls taller than 2 ft. require additional reinforcement. You have two basic reinforcement options: The most common is to install "deadmen" which consist of 3-ft.-long timbers extending horizontally from the face of the wall back into the slope, and attached to crosspieces of the same material with spikes (see the above illustration). Place the deadmen midway up the wall, spaced 4 to 6 ft. apart.

If there isn't enough space behind the wall to install deadmen, you can reinforce the wall from the front side by installing vertical anchor posts, cut from the same material used to build the wall. Space anchor posts 4 ft. apart, and set them below grade to a depth that equals ½ the height of the finished wall. It's a good practice to sink the bottoms of the posts in concrete. Stack the wall timbers flat against the backs of the anchor posts so the front face of the wall appears flush, rather than angling backward in batters.

Fences & Gates

Fences serve many purposes in your yard. They define boundaries, provide security and privacy, contain children and pets, serve as a windbreak, provide a backdrop or support for plantings, and more. Compared to solid masonry walls, fences are relatively easy and inexpensive to build. While installation can be done by one person, it's far easier if you enlist the aid of a helper.

Before you decide on a particular fence design or its location, check local building codes, city ordinances, and neighborhood covenants. These will dictate fence height, setbacks from property lines (or the street), and even the materials you can use to build the fence. For example, in residential areas, backyard boundary fences are typically limited to 6 feet; front yard fences, 3 to 4 feet in height. If you're building a boundary fence between your yard and your neighbor's you'll need to establish the exact location of the property line. Realize that you can't always rely on existing fences or other structures, or even on measuring the property yourself. If you have any questions as to where the property line is, hire a surveyor to establish it precisely. Also, it helps to discuss your plans with your neighbors (and ideally, enlist their help) to circumvent any future hard feelings or disputes regarding the fence. If in doubt, it's best to set the fence back at least 6 in. to 1 ft. from the property line.

Like any building project, building fence and gates requires requires careful construction work. But the fact is, most types of fences are much simpler to make than many other outdoor carpentry projects. The real key to a fence and gate project is in choosing the materials and style that best fit into your landscape. To get you started on the right foot, we've included a number of photos of successful fence and gate building projects in this chapter. Once you've selected a design and built your new fence, you'll find that of all the landscape building projects, adding fences and gates has perhaps the highest payback for the lowest investment of time and money.

Combine fence materials to create a unique fence that blends with your house style and follows the contours of your yard. Here, premilled fence pickets are attached to a framework of posts, stringers and skirt boards to manage a gentle slope in the yard with a fence that retains a consistent height throughout.

Prefabricated fence panels are suspended between fence posts to create a tall privacy fence that has the appearance of requiring much more work than actually went into it. Prefabricated panels are generally sold in 8 ft. lengths, in a range of styles, heights and materials (See page 79).

Stick-built fences can share design elements with prefabricated fence panels, but at the same time they offer greater flexibility. Because they're assembled on-site, one board at a time, they can be adapted easily to short runs (it's much easier to cut two stringers to length than to try and cut whole fence panels to length). And if your height requirements are non-standard (as with the 52-in.-high fence shown here), it's much easier to cut fence boards before attaching them than to trim panels and remove and relocate the lower stringer.

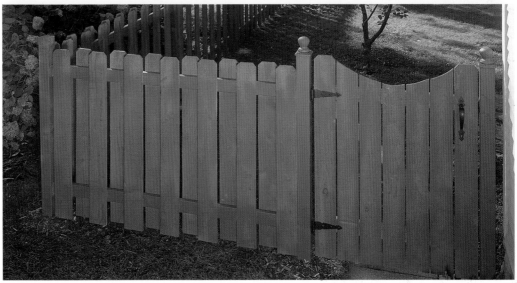

Pickets are often scalloped between fence posts to create a sense of flow and Country-style charm.

Tall privacy fences create a feeling of intimacy and have an added benefit as windbreaks.

Overhead structures, such as arbors and pergolas, enhance the character of fences and gates when the style and materials are complementary.

A decorative top treatment can transform a bulky, stockade-type fence into a landscape highlight.

A matching gate can be built simply by cutting down the same style prefabricated panels used for the fence. Try to plan the gate so you have at least a half-picket at each end. A diagonal cross-brace should be installed between the stringers on panels clad only one side.

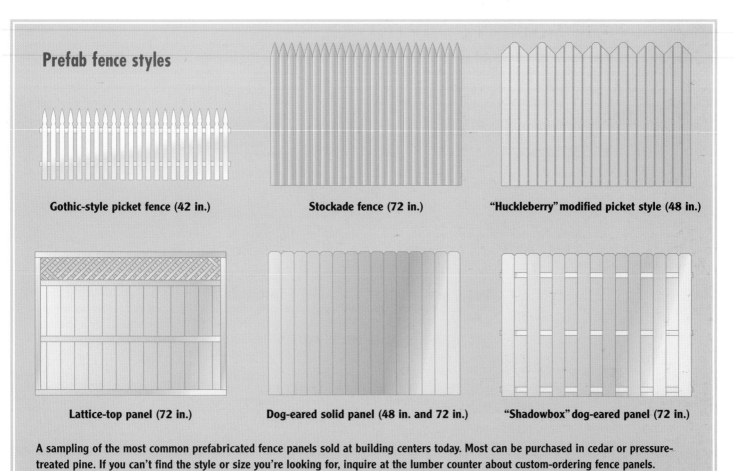

Prefab fence styles

Gothic-style picket fence (42 in.)

Stockade fence (72 in.)

"Huckleberry" modified picket style (48 in.)

Lattice-top panel (72 in.)

Dog-eared solid panel (48 in. and 72 in.)

"Shadowbox" dog-eared panel (72 in.)

A sampling of the most common prefabricated fence panels sold at building centers today. Most can be purchased in cedar or pressure-treated pine. If you can't find the style or size you're looking for, inquire at the lumber counter about custom-ordering fence panels.

Shadow-box style prefabricated fence panels are popular because they add privacy and wind-screening without the drawbacks of solid panels.

Classic picket fences can be purchased as prefabricated panels. There are many options for size, spacing and the shape of the picket finial.

Anatomy of a Fence

Fence post

Cap rail

Upper stringer

Siding
(Fence boards)

Lower stringer

Fences consist of posts that support at least two horizontal stringers. Generally, the posts are not more than 8 ft. apart. The fence boards, called the "siding," are attached to the stringers. Some fences include top treatments, such as a cap rail or lattice top, or post caps and finials

Setback distance

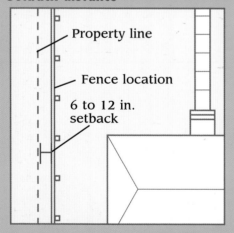

Property line

Fence location

6 to 12 in.
setback

Build fences at least 6 to 12 inches on your side of property lines. The buffer helps ensure that the structure is completely on your property, in the event the property line is not accurate or you veer away from the line during construction. If your fence or part of your fence is found to be on your neighbor's property, you may be ordered to remove and relocate the fence.

Post caps and finials give fence posts a decorative touch, and also protect the end grain of the posts from direct exposure to the elements. Choose caps or finials (or a combination of the two) that blend with the style and proportion of your fence and gate.

Fence Basics

The three basic components of a fence are posts, stringers (also called *rails*), and siding (the fence boards). Optional components include a cap rail, post caps or finials, and skirtboards between the bottom of the fence and the ground. When we think of fence siding materials, wood boards or pickets immediately come to mind, although a variety of other materials are commonly used, such as plywood, ornamental iron, steel, aluminum, chain link, welded wire, and vinyl plastics. All-vinyl fences have become a popular alternative to wood and imitate many popular wood designs, such as vertical board, picket, post-and-rail, lattice, and so on. These are often sold in kit form, which includes posts, prefabricated panels, and all the hardware/fasteners necessary to assemble them.

The framework. Typically, the framework of a fence consists of 4 × 4 posts and 2 × 4 top and bottom rails (either laid flat or on edge) to which you attach the siding (boards, pickets, plywood, wire, etc.). Although the posts and rails can be of redwood, cedar, or other naturally decay-resistant species, pressure-treated lumber is often used for these components, as it is typically less expensive. Even with pressure-treated wood, it's a good idea to treat all cut ends with a wood preservative, especially those that come in contact with the ground.

Attaching the stringers. Nailing or screwing the stringers to the posts provides a relatively weak attachment. Fence panel hangers (See page 82) will hold up better and are easy to use. For best results, cut dadoes into the posts for the stringers: Before setting the posts, lay them on a flat surface and mark the width and depth of the dadoes with a pencil and square. The dadoes should be no more than ½ in. deep, or they will weaken the post. When marking the dado locations, always measure down from the top of the post. After marking all posts, use a circular saw to make a series of ½-in.-deep saw cuts within the cutout area, then remove the waste with a hammer and wood chisel.

Gate hardware

Hardware required to install and operate gates includes hinges and a handle or handle/latch assembly. You may want to add closer hardware for gates that get heavy use. Because gates receive a lot of abuse, use the largest hinges that will fit your fence and gate framework, while still keeping within the aesthetics of the overall fence and gate design. Tall gates (5 ft. or taller) often employ a third hinge installed midway between the top and bottom hinges. Commonly, the screws supplied with prepackaged gate hinges and latches are too short to adequately secure them for heavy repeated use. So, substitute longer screws (of the same type) that extend at least ¾ the way into the gate posts and frame. See pages 90 to 91.

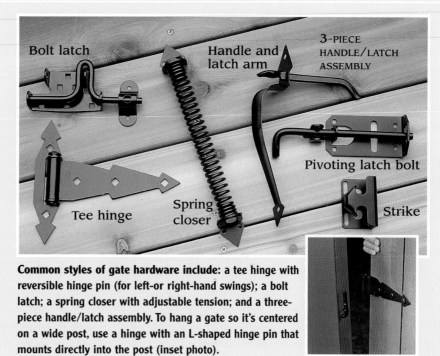

Common styles of gate hardware include: a tee hinge with reversible hinge pin (for left-or right-hand swings); a bolt latch; a spring closer with adjustable tension; and a three-piece handle/latch assembly. To hang a gate so it's centered on a wide post, use a hinge with an L-shaped hinge pin that mounts directly into the post (inset photo).

Applying wood preservative

Fences and gates (and any outdoor structure made from wood) will last longer if you apply a clear preservative, water repellent wood conditioner to all surfaces. Although these products provide some protection against decay, the primary reason for using them is to "stabilize" the wood to help prevent initial warping and splitting of fence boards and rails, due to changes in temperature and humidity. They also protect against ultraviolet (UV) radiation to keep wood looking "new" longer. However, these products will not keep the wood surface from weathering over time. CAUTION: Many wood preservatives are toxic; wear heavy gloves, goggles, long-sleeve shirt and a cartridge-type respirator (designed to filter mists and vapor) when applying these products. Read label precautions.

If you favor the look of a weathered fence, you can speed up the process and achieve an evenly weathered surface by applying a wood bleach. If not, your other options are to paint or stain the fence.

Stains are easier to apply than paint, especially on rough boards, but they will require more frequent

Finishing options for fences and gates include: staining with an exterior wood stain (often redwood); priming and painting; or clear-coating with clear wood sealer. If using pressure treated lumber, look for sealer designed for this material.

reapplication to maintain their appearance. Most top-quality "preservative-stains" contain a water repellent, UV inhibitors, and a mildew-cide, thus they can be applied directly to bare wood without need of a clear sealer/preservative. If using paint, make sure it contains mildew-cide. If you've already applied a wood preservative or water repellent, or if you've used green (unseasoned) redwood or cedar, wait at least 3 months before painting or staining the fence.

Options for attaching stringers to posts

Light duty

Medium duty

Heavy duty

After your posts are set, attach stringers (sometimes called rails) between the posts to support the fence siding. The quickest and cheapest method is simply to toe-nail the stringers to the posts with 8d galvanized common nails (left photo). But use this method only for very lightweight siding or fill material, such as lattice panels. For prefabricated fence panels, attach metal fence hangers (middle photo) to the posts, then fasten the stringers in the hanger hardware. For heavy siding and fences that are exposed to high wind, cut dadoes into the posts for the stringers (right photo).

Tools for building & installing fences & gates

Tools you'll need to build and install fences and gates include: (A) power miter saw; (B) circular saw; (C) posthole digger; (D) spade; (E) 4-ft. level; (F) post level; (G) mason's line; (H) framing square; (I) tape measure; (J) reciprocating saw; (K) jig saw; (L) drill/driver; (M) pencil; (N) hammer; (O) speed square.

Before

Stick-built fences

Unlike fences made with prefabricated fence panels, stick-built fences are created board-by-board at the building site. There are many good reasons why you may choose to stick-build your new fence rather than building it with panels: If your yard is sloped or hilly, you can adjust the length of each individual fence board to follow the terrain, while maintaining a level line on top. If your planned fence line is irregular or contains numerous short jogs, trying to cut full panels to length and fit them between posts can be very tricky. If you have a particular building material, size or fence style in mind, you can stick-build the exact fence you want. But another reason to stick-build your fence should not be to save money. If you calculate the per-foot cost of prefab panels versus the materials needed to make your own fence, you'll find that the panels usually come out cheaper. But the trade-off is that with panels, you don't have the ability to select each piece of stock, and you can easily end up with lower-grade building materials.

FIGURE A: Mark the borders of the fence with wood stakes and mason's line. Be sure the corners of the fence layout are square.

Building a wood fence

As shown, this project fence design employs 6-ft.-long posts set 5 ft. above ground, to support a shadowbox fence with a fence board height of 52 in.

Plotting the fence

1 Stake out the fence layout by driving stakes at the end or corner post locations, then stretching a mason's line between the stakes. Use a line level to level the line. At fence corner locations, square the corner string lines by using the "3-4-5" triangulation method. Measure off 3 ft. along one string line from the corner stake and 4 ft. off the adjacent string line from the stake. The lines are square to one another when a 5 ft. tape measure line intersects the 3- and 4-ft. string markings. Adjust the stakes and strings accordingly until the fence corners are square.

2 Locate the centers of intermediate posts by measuring along the string line in 6- to 8-ft. equal intervals. Use a plumb bob to transfer the post locations from the string to the ground. Mark the locations with stakes **(See FIGURE A).** *NOTE: When figuring the spans between posts, it's important to consider the width of the vertical fence boards you'll use, the spac-*

Options for digging postholes

Posthole digger

Gas-powered auger

If you have only a few post holes to dig, and the required hole depth does not exceed 30 in., use a hand-operated clamshell-type posthole digger (left). For deeper holes, or if you have a lot of holes to dig, rent a gas-powered auger (above) from a tool rental shop. Gas-powered augers come in one- and two-person models and save a considerable amount of time and labor. The model shown here uses the weight of the motor as a counterbalance to help withdraw the auger from the hole.

ing you plan to leave between the fence boards (at least ⅛ in.), and their arrangement on the stringers between the fence posts. Plan this now; otherwise you may have to rip-cut the width of one or more vertical fence boards later to get the fence board arrangement to fit between the posts. Once you've determined post locations, remove the strings.

Installing the posts

3 Dig the post holes, removing each stake as you go (See *TIP,* previous page). Check local building codes for required post depth in your area. This will determine the length of the posts you'll need to buy. As a general rule, plan to set about ⅓ of the total post length into the ground. Another guideline is to sink posts 2 ft. deep for a 5-ft.-tall fence; 2½ ft. for a 6-ft.-tall fence; and 3½ ft. for an 8-ft.-tall fence. The diameter of the hole should be about twice the diameter of the post. Make the post holes slightly larger at the bottom than at the top to form a bell shape that helps anchor the posts when you fill the hole with concrete.

4 Fill each post hole with 5 to 6 in. of compactible gravel subbase to provide drainage beneath the posts **(See FIGURE B).** Tamp it down with the end of a post or hand tamper.

5 Set one of the end or corner posts first. Lower the post into the hole and use a post level or two carpenter's levels held on adjacent sides of the post to plumb the post vertically. Be sure the overall aboveground length of the post is a few inches longer than planned finished height of the post. (The posts will get trimmed to final height later.) Attach temporary braces to the post on two adjacent sides to keep the post plumb while pouring the concrete footing **(See FIGURE C).** Each brace consists a 2 × 4 about 4 ft. long and tacked with a single pivot nail or screw to a stake that is driven in the ground. With the post held plumb, attach the top ends of both braces to the post with 3-in. deck screws.

6 Loosely set and brace the post at the opposite end of the fence line in the same manner as *Step 3,* keeping the overall above-ground height of the posts equal. Attach a leveled line between the posts. To do this, measure down a precise distance from both post tops (for example, 1 ft.) and mark reference lines. Tack or screw small spacer blocks of equal thickness to the same side of both posts, then attach mason's line to the blocks, aligning the line with the marks on the posts. (The spacer blocks will keep intermediate posts from throwing the string line out of alignment when you set the posts). Adjust the height of one of the end posts until the string line is level and remove or add gravel subbase as needed beneath this post to estab-

FIGURE B: Fill each post hole with 5 to 6 in. of compactible gravel subbase and tamp it down. The subbase will help water drain away from the post bottoms.

Post level

FIGURE C: Plumb end posts with a post level and brace them into position with 2 × 4 braces screwed to the posts and staked into the ground.

FIGURE D: Set intermediate posts with braces and stakes, using a scrap 2 × 4 spacer board between posts. Then fill the post holes with concrete.

2 × 4 spacer

FIGURE E: Snap a leveled chalk line along all the posts to mark cutting lines for trimming the posts to final height.

FIGURE F: Extend the chalk lines on the posts to all four faces with a pencil and trim the posts with a circular or reciprocating saw.

lish its new height. This top string line will serve as a reference for keeping intermediate post heights approximately the same as the two end or corner posts.

7 Attach a second leveled string line 8 to 10 in. up from ground level. Use spacers behind this string line as well (they should match the thickness of the spacers used for the top string line). These two string lines serve as reference lines to help keep the faces of intermediate posts lined up with one another. Plumb and brace intermediate posts and use a loose spacer to check the distance between each post and the string lines. We cut a piece of 2 × 4 to serve as a temporary spacer between posts to keep the distance between all posts uniform. Once the posts are in position, recheck to make sure the fence line is straight.

8 Fill each post hole with premixed concrete **(See FIGURE D).** Add just enough water to the concrete to form a stiff consistency. Overfill the holes 1 to 2 in. above ground level, then use a short wood block or masons trowel to slope the surface away from each post on all sides (called crowning) in order to direct water away from the posts. Before the concrete sets up, make sure the posts are still plumb and lined up. Readjust the braces, if necessary. Then remove the two string lines, but leave the post braces on until the concrete has fully cured (about two days).

9 Attach a level chalk line to the two end posts to mark post height **(See FIGURE E).** Snap a line onto all posts at once. Scribe pencil lines around all four sides of each post at the chalk line and trim the posts to height with a circular saw or reciprocating saw **(See FIGURE F).** *NOTE: 4 × 4 posts, like those shown here, are thicker than the maximum cutting depth of most circular saws, and must be cut in two passes from opposite sides of the post. Getting the cuts to line up can be tricky, so take your time.*

Adding stringers

10 Establish the locations of two stringer boards between the fence posts by measuring down from the post tops. On taller fences or fences with heavy siding, you'll need to add a center stringer to support the weight of the fence boards. In installations where stringers are made from dimensional 2× material, like 2 × 4s, and fit between each two posts, attach the stringers with galvanized 2-in. metal fence brackets **(See FIGURE G).** We centered our brackets on the inside faces of the posts and attached the brackets with 2-in. deck screws.

11 Measure and cut the stringers to length **(See FIGURE H).** *NOTE: It's a good idea to measure*

FIGURE G: Mark the stringer heights on the posts. Attach galvanized metal fence brackets at these locations, using 2-in. deck screws.

FIGURE H: Measure the distance between fence posts to determine the length of the stringers. Measure and cut the stringers to length.

all the spans between the posts first, even if you're confident that the distances are the same. This way, you won't gang-cut all the stringers only to find that some are too short. Cut stringers ¼ in. shorter than the span distance so they'll slip easily between the fence brackets.

12 Coat the cut ends of all the stringers with wood preservative to protect them from absorbing moisture and rotting **(See FIGURE I).**

13 Set the top and bottom stringers into the fence brackets and attach them with 1½-in. galvanized deck screws **(See FIGURE J).**

Modifying fence sections

14 The path of the fence shown here was interrupted by a large tree — a frequent problem encountered when installing fences. We decided to attach the fence to the tree rather than rerouting the fence. In these situations, build a modified fence section to fit the profile of the tree trunk from 2 × 2 dimension lumber. Attach it to the closest fence post with galvanized deck screws **(See FIGURE K).**

15 Drill a ⅞-in. hole through the bottom stringer of this fence section and drive a piece of galvanized pipe down through the stringer hole and into the ground **(See FIGURE L).** The pipe acts as a bottom brace for the fence section and is easier to install than digging another full-depth post hole this close to tree roots. It also is less damaging to the tree roots.

16 Anchor the top of the fence section to the tree by screwing an eyebolt into the tree trunk. Con-

FIGURE I: Coat the ends of the stringers with wood sealer to keep them from absorbing moisture and eventually rotting.

FIGURE J: Set the stringers onto the fence hangers and secure them with 1½-in. galvanized deck screws.

FIGURE K: Modify short lengths of fencing as needed to fit against obstructions like trees. Support these sections with temporary wood spacers and screw the framework to the closest fence post.

FIGURE L: In locations where full post depth is not possible, drive a length of ¾-in. galvanized pipe through the stringer and into the ground.

nect the fence section to the eyebolt with several lengths of heavy, braided wire cable threaded through the fence framing and a turnbuckle. Tighten the turnbuckle until the fence section doesn't wobble—but not so tight that it pulls the fence section away from the metal fence brackets **(See FIGURE M).** After the fence is built, check support cables periodically to make sure they're taut. Tighten the turnbuckle if there is too much play in the cables.

Attaching fence boards

17 Determine the length of your vertical fence boards and cut them to size. If you have a power miter saw, you can cut the boards quickly and easily by setting up a stop block on your work surface to index off each fence board at the correct cutoff length **(See FIGURE N).** Typically, the bottoms of the fence boards should be at least 2 in. above ground level to prevent contact with the ground, which can cause the boards to rot. The tops of the fence boards should not extend more than 6 in. above the top stringer, or they may warp.

18 Starting at one end post, plumb the first fence board and attach it to the stringers with 1½-in. galvanized nails or screws (use two fasteners per stringer). It's important that the first board be attached so that it is perfectly plumb—it becomes a reference board for all boards down the line. If it isn't plumb, the rest of the fence boards will be off, and the inaccuracy will get progressively worse as you go.

19 Attach the rest of the fence boards, checking frequently for proper alignment and plumb **(See FIGURE O).** A pneumatic nail gun makes quick work of attaching fence boards, but galvanized screws work equally well and make removing fence boards easy should some need replacement in the future. In the project shown here, we used one of the fence boards (painted white in the photo) as a spacer for establishing the *shadowbox* fence board pattern. If the boards in your design will butt against one another on the same side of the stringer, leave a ⅛-in. gap between them (8d nails serve as handy spacers).

20 Apply a finish to the fence (See page 81). We used oil-based, redwood-tinted stain, applied with an air-compressor-driven spray gun **(See FIGURE P).** Wear a respirator when spraying on a finish. Build and install a gate after the fence is complete (See pages 90 to 91).

FIGURE M: Attach fencing to trees by screwing a large eyebolt into the tree trunk. Secure the frame to the tree with cable and a turnbuckle.

FIGURE N: Cut fence boards to length. A power miter saw and a stop block allow you to gang-cut fence boards quickly and accurately.

FIGURE O: Set a mason's line as a reference to establish location for the tops of the fence boards, and attach the boards to the stringers with nails or screws, aligning the top of each board with the mason's line. Use a spacer board, where possible, to keep fence board spacing even.

FIGURE P: We used a compressor-driven spray gun to apply oil-based stain to this fence. Always wear a respirator when applying a sprayed finish.

FIGURE A: Measure the distance between the two gate posts and subtract 1½ in. for clearance to determine the actual width of the gate.

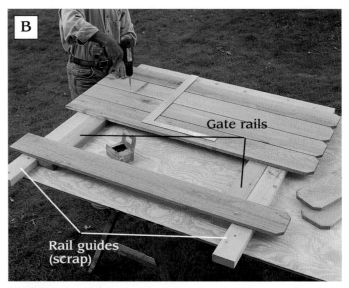

FIGURE B: Attach fence boards to the gate rails with screws. Scrap rail guides screwed in place keep the gate rails parallel during assembly.

FIGURE C: Measure and cut a diagonal cross brace to fit between the gate rails and screw the fence boards to it.

FIGURE D: Lay out and cut any decorative profiles in the top of the gate, being careful not to cut through the gate rail frame.

Gates

As with fences, there are many methods for building a gate. The one we constructed for our project fence is a typical residential gate, which consists of a simple 2 ¥ 4 frame with diagonal bracing covered with fence boards that match the fence.

1 Measure the distance between the inside faces of the gate posts on either side of the gateway **(See FIGURE A).** Subtract 1½ in. from this measurement to determine the actual width of the gate (which leaves ¾ in. of clear space on either side of the gate). The gate opening should be at least 36 in. wide to accommodate lawn and garden equipment or two people passing through at once. The width between the posts should not vary by more than ¼ in., top to bottom. Gate height will differ, depending upon the height of the fence, but

plan for the gate to hang at least 2 in. above ground.

2 Cut the gate frame rails and fence board siding to length and lay the gate framing members on a flat surface, fence board side facing up **(See FIGURE B).** Typically the top and bottom rails of the gate frame will align with the fence stringers. Screw the fence boards to the rails with 1½-in. galvanized deck screws, keeping each fence board perpendicular to the gate rails. Use two screws per joint. *TIP: To keep the gate rails parallel during this step, screw scrap-wood rail guides to your work surface, spaced so that the gate rails fit between them.*

3 Flip the gate over so the gate rails face up, and check the gate for square by measuring the diagonals. Select a length of stock for a gate cross brace that is longer than the diagonal distance between the gate

FIGURE E: Mark hinge positions on the gate and attach hinge leaves, screwing them through the fence boards and into the gate rails.

FIGURE F: Prop the gate into position, attach hinge hook hardware to the gate post and hang the gate.

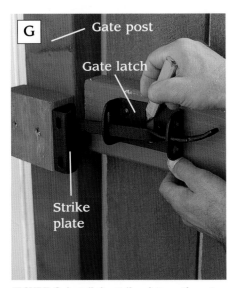

Gate post

Gate latch

Strike plate

FIGURE G: Install the strike plate on the gate post, align the latch and mark drilling locations.

FIGURE H: Bore holes through the gate rail for thumb latch hardware with a spade bit.

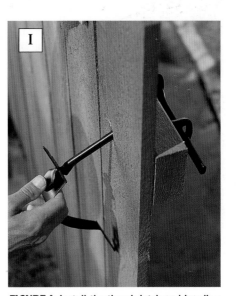

FIGURE I: Install the thumb latch and handle to the outside of the gate with screws.

rails. Lay it on top of the rails so it intersects the inside opposite corners of the rails. Mark the cutting angles so the cross brace will fit between the rails **(See FIGURE C).** Cut the cross brace to length and screw the fence board siding to it with 1½-in. deck screws.

4 Mark and cut any decorative profiles in the top of the gate with a jig saw **(See FIGURE D).** We chose a scallop that begins and ends one fence board in from either edge of the gate. Then stain or paint the gate to match the fence.

5 Measure and attach tee-hinge leaves to the gate, screwing them through the fence board siding and into the gate rails **(See FIGURE E).**

6 Prop the gate in the gateway with wood support blocks placed under the bottom rail. Provide at least

2 in. of clearance between the bottom of the gate and the ground. Measure and attach hinge hardware to the hinge-side gatepost and hang the gate **(See FIGURE F).** Test to make sure the gate swings freely and make any necessary adjustments before installing the latch.

7 Install the strike plate on the gatepost. Position the latch assembly on the upper gate rail, align it with the strike plate and mark pilot and latchbore hole locations on the gate rail **(See FIGURE G).**

8 Bore holes for thumb latch hardware with a spade bit, according to the manufacturer's instructions **(See FIGURE H).** Attach the latch to the gate.

9 Install the handle and thumb latch assembly to the outside of the gate **(See FIGURE I).** Test the operation of the latch mechanism and adjust as necessary.

Prefabricated fence panels

Prefabricated fencing comes in a variety of styles to suit many landscape designs (See page 79). The picket fence shown here is built with Gothic-style, 42-in.-high by 8-ft.-long fence panels.

1 Plot the fence line and set the posts as described on pages 84 to 86, locating the postholes so facing edges of adjoining posts will be 8 ft. apart (if using 8-ft. long panels). At this point, it's a good idea to take actual measurements of the panels—they can vary slightly from the stated length, and you'll want to space your posts to reflect any variation. Lay out your gate locations at this time as well. Plumb and brace the posts and set them in concrete.

2 Mark top and bottom stringer locations for each full-length fence section on the fence posts, and attach metal fence hangers to the posts with 2-in. galvanized deck screws. For this fence, we centered the fence brackets on the inside faces of each post. Set full-length fence sections onto the fence hangers and fasten them with 1½-in. deck screws **(See FIGURE A).**

3 Mark fence sections that will need to be cut to fit shorter spans between posts, measuring the distance between the inside faces of the posts **(See FIGURE B).** Plan these cuts where possible so that they fall on stringers rather than down the length of fence boards, and try to keep the spacing consistent between posts and the fence boards on either side. Attach fence hangers to these posts, and fasten the stringers of the cut panels to the hangers with deck screws.

4 We decided to modify a length of the prefab fencing for use as a gate in our project fence. The gatepost spacing on either side of the sidewalk required us to cut the gate to size by ripping the end fence boards. In cases like this, set the gate section into position and use the gate posts as references to mark cutting lines **(See FIGURE C).** Subtract an additional ¾ in. from each side to provide clear space between the gate and the posts. Lay out the gate so you'll cut the fence boards to even widths on both sides.

5 Cut a diagonal cross brace to fit between the two stringers and screw it to the stringers with 3-in. deck screws **(See FIGURE D).** Strengthen the gate frame by screwing the pickets to the cross brace with 1½-in. deck screws (use two screws per joint).

6 Sand the gate and fence members as needed with a palm sander using medium-grit sandpaper **(See FIGURE E).** Attach the gate to the fence posts with hinges, and install latch hardware (See pages 90 to 91 for more information on installing gates).

7 Seal the fence with several coats of oil-based primer and paint, stain, or water sealant **(See FIGURE F).** It's a good idea to cover sidewalks, grass and plants to protect them from drips or overspray, especially if you spray on the finish.

FIGURE A: Set posts, then attach full-length fence sections between the posts with metal fence hangers and galvanized deck screws.

FIGURE B: Mark cutting lines for fence sections that will need to be shortened using the fence post on each side as references.

FIGURE C: Set the gate section into place and mark the gatepost locations onto the panel. Subtract ¾ in. from each side to allow for clear swinging space and cut the gate to size.

FIGURE D: Measure and cut a cross brace to fit between the gate stringers and attach the cross brace to the stringers and fence boards with galvanized deck screws.

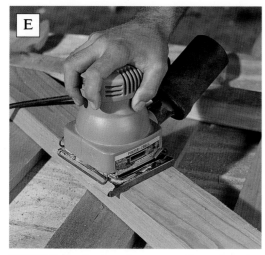

FIGURE E: Sand out rough spots or splinters from the gate and fence with a palm sander and medium-grit sandpaper. Hang the gate.

FIGURE F: Seal all wooden fence surfaces with primer and paint, stain or wood sealer. Be sure to wear safety glasses and a respirator if you decide to spray your fence.

Building Decks

A maze of stairs, platforms, planters and benches gives this richly finished deck an appealing, mysterious quality.

Building Decks

Only a generation or two ago, wood decks were a seldom-seen curiosity in the backyards of American homes. But today, in just about every type of neighborhood across the entire country, you're likely to find an abundance of decks sprawling out from patio doors or stepping gracefully down the hilly terrain. The reason for the explosion in popularity is twofold: as suburban housing developments have sprung up outside the crowded cities, the average yard size has increased dramatically; and, as leisure time has increased, we've come to focus our search for family relaxation first and foremost in our own backyards.

Building a simple wood deck is not difficult or expensive. In essence, it is only a raised wooden plat-

form supported by posts set in concrete. For many homeowners, a plain, square deck is more than adequate to meet their relaxation and entertainment needs. But if you aspire to creating an outdoor living area that is truly unique and has character, scale and function that go well beyond the ordinary, deckbuilding is an excellent vehicle for your pursuit.

On the following pages you'll find plenty of straightforward information on how to build a deck. But we've taken the information a step further. If you've ever seen a stunning, elaborate deck that's rich with attractive features and wondered to yourself "How did they build that?," then you'll enjoy examining the following chapters: in them you'll find the answers.

Airy screens, wooden planters and strategically placed foliage create a private retreat that doesn't feel like a fortress.

Own your own island in the sun by building a freestanding platform deck in your favorite corner of your yard.

An ordinary entry area is transformed into a shaded resort by adding an L-shaped, multi-level deck with a handsome arbor.

New outdoor living space is carved out from a hillside with retaining walls and an expansive wood deck.

A built-in bench provides a resting spot for travelers seeking to ascend the steep slope that is home to this multi-level deck.

Tiered planters form a transition between this deck and the thickly wooded yard that surrounds it.

An outdoor room, complete with an arbor-and-trellis ceiling and built-in furniture, can be created with a little bit of imagination and an impeccable sense of design.

A stunning view becomes a work of art when framed by the strong lines of this deck and overhead arbor.

Interesting angles and subtle step-downs are the stand-out features in this beautiful and highly functional deck.

Deck Basics

Whether you're building a deck as a simple addition to your yard or as part of a more ambitious landscaping project, begin by learning the basics of deck design and deck anatomy, and work toward drawing detailed plans of your deck and building site.

Basic deck anatomy

Before you make your final working drawings, you'll need to identify all the various structural components that will make up your deck. A simple deck platform typically consists of the following elements: footings, posts, beams, joists, and deck boards. If you'll be attaching the deck to your house, you'll also need to attach a ledger board to your home to support the deck framing. For a finished appearance, you can also install fascia boards around the deck perimeter.

Footings: Concrete footings must be sturdy enough to support the entire weight of the deck plus any loads applied to it. You can take one of several approaches to make the footings. The type you choose depends on the type of soil you're dealing with, as well as the height and size of the structure itself. If you're building a low, freestanding deck on firm, stable, well-drained soil, the footing can consist of a precast pier block placed directly on the ground, or set in a shallow hole filled with poured concrete. The pier blocks have inset wooden tops, and sometimes metal post anchors to which you attach the posts. In firm soil, you can also simply dig a hole (typically 12 to 14 in. in diameter) to the desired depth and insert a metal connector or post anchor into the wet concrete. The holes for these footings should be wider at the bottom than at the top to create a "bell shape" for greater stability. In very loose soil (such as sand or gravel), ready-made concrete tube forms are used to keep the sidewalls of the hole from collapsing into the space to be occupied by the poured concrete. In all cases, the bottom of the footing should extend below the frost line, and the top should be at least 3 in. above finished grade.

Posts: These usually are made from 4 × 4s or 6 × 6s, set on-end on top of the footings. They serve to transfer the weight of the deck to the footings beneath. If the deck will be 4 ft. or more above ground level, the posts may require cross-bracing.

Beams: These members provide the main horizontal support for the deck. One common type of beam consists of two 2 × 8s or 2 × 10s fastened to opposite sides of the posts with through-bolts or lag screws, or set into notches cut into the beams. Another common practice is to attach solid 4 × 6 or 4 × 8 beams to the tops of leveled posts with metal connectors. For low-level decks, you can attach the beams directly to leveled pier blocks or footings, eliminating the posts entirely.

Ledger boards: If the deck is attached to the side of the house, the wall of the house must support one end of the deck. In this case, you'll need to install a ledger board to which you attach the joists. The joists may either rest on top of the ledger or be hung flush against the face of the ledger. The method of attaching the ledger to the house depends on the type of house siding you're dealing with.

Joists: These typically consist of 2 × 6s or 2 × 8s attached to the beams to support the decking. Depending on your design requirements, the joists can either run across the tops of the beams, or be hung between them with joist hangers. On attached decks, the joists typically run perpendicular to the house wall, attached to the ledger at one end, with a 2 × 6 or larger header joist at the other end. Bridging or blocking installed between the joists may be required.

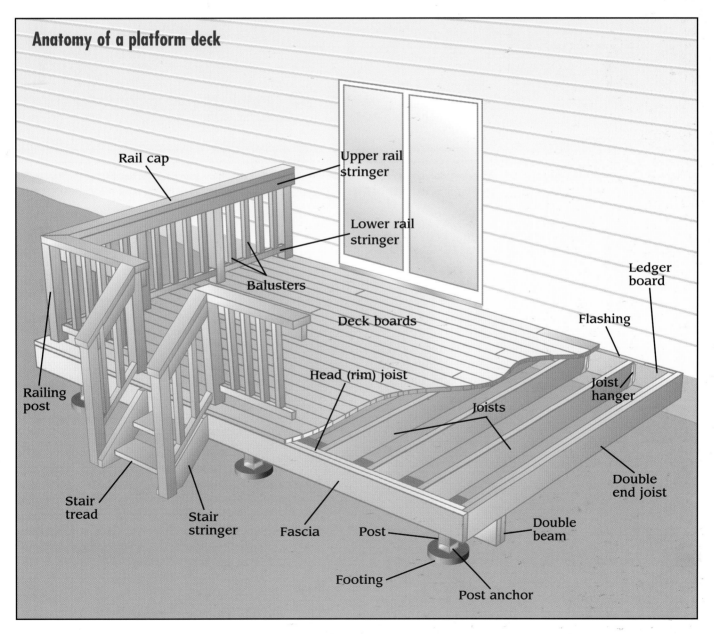

Anatomy of a platform deck

Rail cap

Upper rail stringer

Lower rail stringer

Balusters

Ledger board

Deck boards

Flashing

Head (rim) joist

Joists

Joist hanger

Railing post

Stair tread

Stair stringer

Fascia

Post

Double beam

Double end joist

Footing

Post anchor

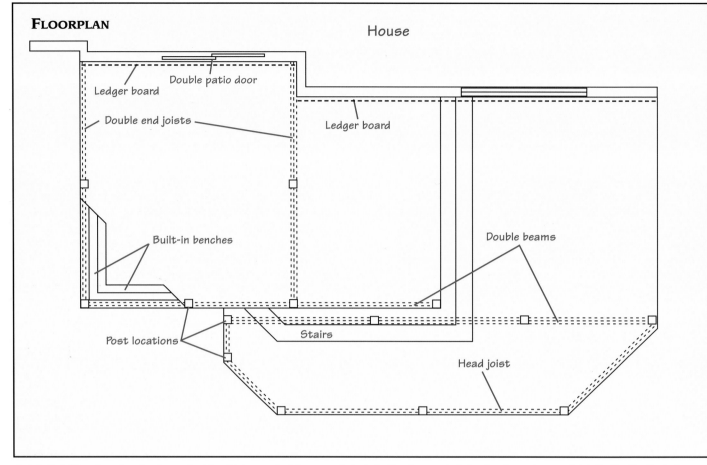

FLOORPLAN   House

Ledger board

Double patio door

Double end joists

Ledger board

Built-in benches

Double beams

Post locations

Stairs

Head joist

A detailed floorplan drawing is required to obtain your building permit. Include the above-noted structural members and details. For the final plan drawing, also indicate joists and joist spacing (24 in. on-center is suitable for most decks), overall dimensions and joinery plans.

Decking: The deck surface can be built with 2×4s or 2×6s (actual thickness is 1½ in.) laid flat across the joists and fastened to the joists with galvanized deck screws. Wider boards generally aren't used because they have a greater tendency to cup and split over a period of time. You can also use premilled deck boards, which are thinner (1¼ in. thick) but are usually cut from select lumber and feature rounded "bullnose" edges, rather than the sharp edges found on dimension lumber. Most deck boards are a nominal 6 in. wide (5¼ in. actual width). Because the decking is the most visible part of the structure, you'll want to choose the lumber carefully. For the sake of appearance, most professional designers and builders prefer to use natural redwood or cedar for decking, as well as for the other visible components, such as steps, railings, benches, and the like. Pressure-treated lumber is frequently used for the structural components (posts, beams, joists), but can be used for the decking as well if cost is the main concern. For more on choosing lumber, see page 102. To add visual interest, you can lay the decking in a variety of patterns (herringbone, diamond, or basketweave, for example—see pages 108 to 109). Because the decking pattern can influence the spacing

and location of joists, plan the substructure to provide support where deck boards meet.

Fascia Boards: Primarily a decorative element, fascia boards are often attached to the ends of the deck (and sometimes the sides) to cover the exposed ends of the deck boards. Made of the same material as the decking, fascia usually looks best if the bottom edge is flush with, or extends slightly below the bottoms of the end joists and headers. On low-level decks, make sure the bottom edges of fascia boards are at least 3 in. above ground level.

Drawing plans

Drawing deck plans is done in stages as your ideas and construction details are finalized. Your initial design plan should show the size and location of the deck in relationship to the house and other major features on the property. Use the drawing as a base for developing working drawings that detail the framework, joinery and decking pattern, then create final scaled "blueprints" that feature an overhead floorplan and an elevation drawing, along with materials lists and estimated costs (you'll need all of this information to obtain a building permit for your project).

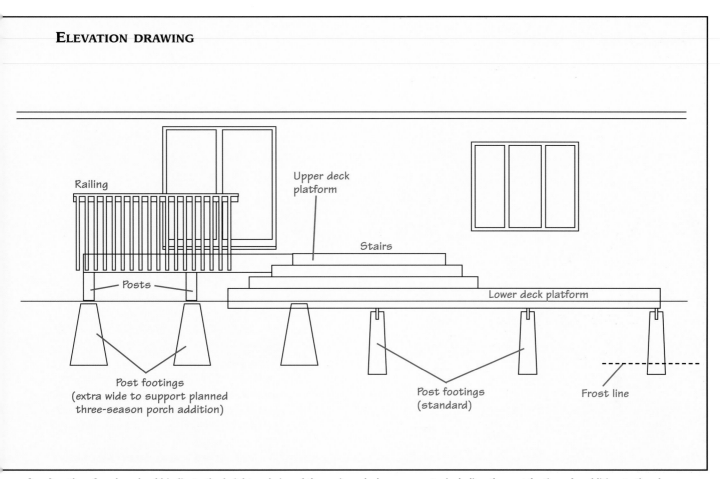

Railing

Upper deck platform

Stairs

Posts

Lower deck platform

Post footings
(extra wide to support planned
three-season porch addition)

Post footings
(standard)

Frost line

An elevation drawing should indicate the height and size of the various deck components, including the post footings. In addition to the above-noted elements, include dimensions, height above grade and indicate structural joinery methods.

For most deckbuilding projects, you should invest some time and money up front consulting with a professional designer or architect. Their input can actually save money in the long run, and will help ensure that you get results you're happy with from all your hard work. You should also contact your local building inspector early in the process. He or she will review your preliminary plans to suggest improvements and to identify any additional information you'll need to obtain your permit when your finished plans are ready for presentation.

Spans and Spacings

The spans and spacings between the various deck members—posts, beams, joists and decking—are determined by the size, lumber grade and wood species of these components, as well as the type of decking used, and the decking pattern. When planning spans and spacings, start from the top down by choosing the size and pattern of the decking first. Then, determine the joist spacing (for example, 16 or 24 in. on-center). Next, determine the span between beams, based on joist size and spacing. Then determine the post span based on the distance between joists. Finally,

Recommended spans & spacing

MAXIMUM DISTANCE BETWEEN JOIST SUPPORTS:

	Joist spacing (o.c.)		
Joist size	12"	16"	24"
2 × 6	11' 7"	9' 9"	7' 11"
2 × 8	15' 0"	12' 10"	10' 6"
2 × 10	19' 6"	16' 5"	13' 4"

MAXIMUM DISTANCE BETWEEN POSTS SUPPORTING BEAMS:

	Joist span			
Beam size	6'	8'	10'	12'
4 × 6	8'	7'	6'	5'
4 × 8	10'	9'	8'	7'
4 × 10	12'	11'	10'	9'
4 × 12	14'	13'	12'	11'

RECOMMENDED POST SIZE:

	Load area*				
Deck height	48	72	96	120	124
0' to 6'	4 × 4	4 × 4	6 × 6	6 × 6	6 × 6
6' and up	6 × 6	6 × 6	6 × 6	6 × 6	6 × 6

*To calculate "Load area" multiply the distance between the beams by the distance between the posts (in feet).

Designing for deck height

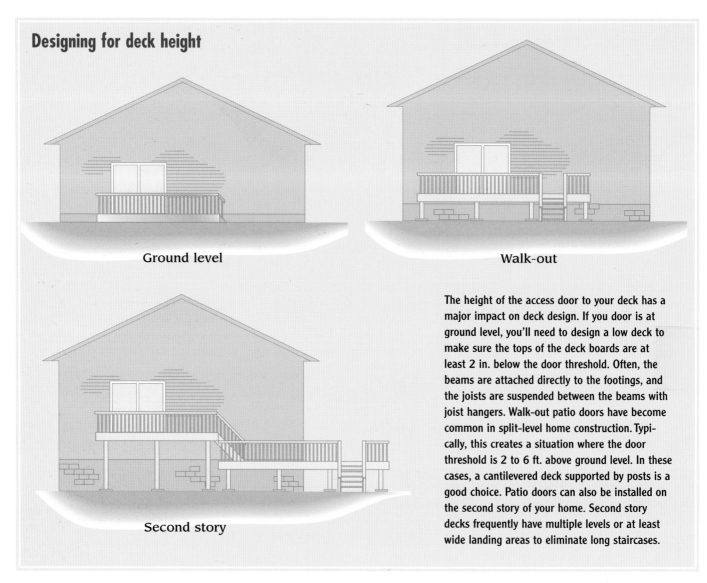

Ground level

Walk-out

Second story

The height of the access door to your deck has a major impact on deck design. If you door is at ground level, you'll need to design a low deck to make sure the tops of the deck boards are at least 2 in. below the door threshold. Often, the beams are attached directly to the footings, and the joists are suspended between the beams with joist hangers. Walk-out patio doors have become common in split-level home construction. Typically, this creates a situation where the door threshold is 2 to 6 ft. above ground level. In these cases, a cantilevered deck supported by posts is a good choice. Patio doors can also be installed on the second story of your home. Second story decks frequently have multiple levels or at least wide landing areas to eliminate long staircases.

choose the post size, which should be determined by the deck height and load area. Use the table on the previous page as a general design guide, but be sure to double-check your figures with local code requirements and have your plans approved before building the deck.

Bear in mind that designing the deck with larger-size components (2 × 8 joists and doubled 2 × 10 beams, for example) will enable you to increase spans and spacings, thus requiring fewer beams, posts, and footings, which can save you time and money. However, this will also raise the minimum height to which you can build the deck, which may or may not coincide with your plans.

The spans and spacings of these various components will determine the post and footing locations on the site, which must be indicated on your plan drawings. Many professionals prefer to cantilever the deck structure several feet beyond the supporting posts, to hide unsightly footings and piers. As a general rule, you can cantilever beams and joists a distance equal to ⅓ their allowable spans between supporting members.

For example, a beam with a 9-ft. span can be cantilevered up to 3 ft. beyond the perimeter post. A joist with a 6-ft. span can be cantilevered 2 ft. beyond the end beam. Check local codes. If you want to cantilever the deck, locate the footings accordingly.

Multi-level decks. Decks with multiple deck platforms are more complex to design and build than single-level decks, especially when it comes to framing and support. In some cases, it's possible to use the same structural network to support more than one deck platform. But frequently, the platforms are designed and built as independent structures, then connected via stairs, railings or single-step stepdowns.

Stairs, railings & other features

Be sure to include detailed drawings of stairs, railings and other deck features, like built-in benches or planters, in your drawings. If you're building a multi-level deck, include drawings for the transition between levels. See the chapters on these features for more design information.

Hand tools used in deck construction include: (A) speed square; (B) mason's line; (C) framing square; (D) hand saw; (E) aviator snips; (F) caulk gun; (G) 4 ft. carpenter's level; (H) combination square; (I) spirit level; (J) pencil; (K) line level; (L) 50 ft. roll tape; (M) rigid tape measure; (N) chalkline; (O) wood chisels; (P) utility knife; (Q) socket wrench; (R) hammer; (S) flat pry bar; (T) hand maul; (U) plumb bob.

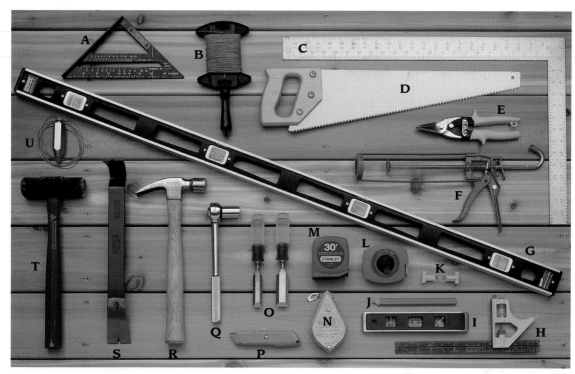

Power tools you'll need to tackle a deck-building project may include: (A) power miter saw; (B) portable table saw; (C) circular saw (preferably a worm-drive saw); (D) cordless drill/driver with replaceable battery pack; (E) ½ in. corded drill; (F) reciprocating saw.

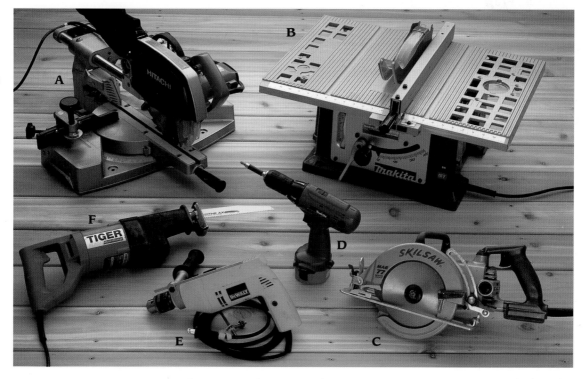

Tools & materials for building decks

Using quality materials and the right tool for the job will make your deckbuilding project run smoothly. In addition to obtaining the tools shown in the photos above, you may want to look into renting a gas-powered auger for drilling post holes. A compressor-driven nail gun is a big help when attaching decking.

The photos on the following pages show the various fastening devices and metal connectors used to join deck components. All fasteners and connectors should be galvanized to resist rust and be specified for exterior use. While metal connectors aren't absolutely necessary for assembling a deck, they provide a much stronger connection than nails or screws alone. Using the appropriate connectors to reinforce joints will extend deck life considerably, so it's well worth the relatively small amount of extra money you'll pay for these items.

Tips on buying lumber

When you go to buy lumber and other materials, make up an estimate sheet with columns for the sizes, lengths and quantity needed for the various structural components (posts, beams, joists, ledger, decking, etc.), as well as required hardware, concrete and other miscellaneous materials. For each item, add 5% to 10% extra to allow for waste, lumber defects, and building errors. If possible, hand-pick all lumber at the yard, even if you plan on having it delivered at a later time.

Take your list to several local outlets and do a bit of comparative shopping. Traditional lumberyards usually offer the widest variety of lumber sizes, lengths, and grades, and have knowledgeable personnel who can help you estimate the amount of materials you need. Large home centers and self-serve building emporiums generally sell lumber at cheaper prices, but have a limited selection of sizes and grades. However, these outlets often run sales, in which you can buy part of your lumber and other materials at a good discount.

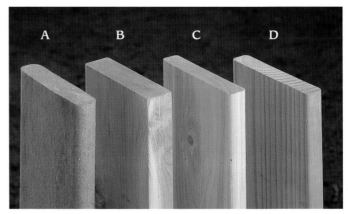

Decking options include: (A) composite deck boards; (B) 2 × 6 or 2 × 4 dimensional lumber; (C) 1¼ × 6 in. premilled cedar or redwood deck boards; (D) pressure-treated deck boards.

Masonry-related materials for footings include: (A) concrete tube forms (8 in. and 12 in. dia. shown); (B) pre-mixed concrete; (C) precast concrete piers (alternative to pouring footings).

Deck boards can be attached to the joists with 10d galvanized nails, but for more strength, use 3-in. deck screws. Some builders like to provide further reinforcement by laying a thick bead of construction adhesive along the tops of the joists before attaching the boards.

Fasteners:

• *J-bolts* (also called L-shaped anchor bolts) with nuts and washers are used to attach post anchors to concrete footings. These are installed while the concrete is still wet.

• *Lag screws and washers* are used to join larger deck components, such as 2× beams to the sides of posts, railing posts to the sides of the deck, as well as

certain types of hardware, such as metal stair cleats. They're often used in conjunction with lead lag screw shields to attach ledgers to masonry walls or concrete foundations.

• *Hex-head machine bolts, nuts and washers* have some of the same applications as lag screws (such as attaching double 2 × 10 beams to the sides of posts) but provide a stronger connection.

• *Galvanized nails* of various sizes provide the least expensive means of assembling deck components, but also make the weakest connection. Common nails have more holding power than box nails but are more likely to split the wood at board ends. Galvanized finish nails are used to attach decorative trims and moldings, where nail heads would be unsightly. These are usually countersunk with a nailset, and the holes filled with exterior spackle or wood putty.

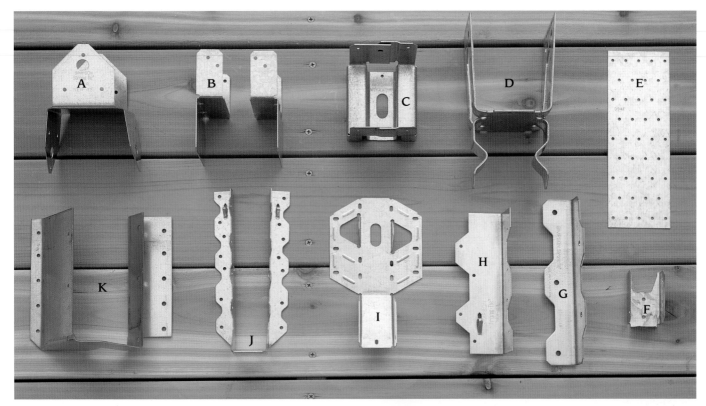

Galvanized metal connectors include: (A) one-piece post cap (4 × 4); two-piece adjustable post cap: (C) stand-off post anchor; (D) post anchor with concrete fins; (E) tie plate; (F) fence hanger; (G) staircase angle bracket; (H) right-angle connector; (I) skewable joist hanger; (J) joist hanger; (K) angled joist hanger.

• *Galvanized deck screws* (also called *all-purpose* or *bugle-head* screws) have perhaps the widest variety of applications in deck construction, and provide a stronger connection than nails. Coarse, aggressive threads and a bugle-head design enable you to power-drive the screws flush to the wood surface without the need of predrilling pilot holes, as you would for conventional wood screws. Don't confuse these with non-galvanized black drywall screws, which are meant for interior uses only.

Galvanized Metal Connectors:

• *Post anchors* are attached to concrete footings to hold the deck posts in place and to elevate the post base to help prevent moisture from wicking into the end grain.

• *Joist hangers* are used to attach joists to the ledger and head joist. On low-level decks, they're used between beams. Variations include angled joist hangers and double joist hangers. Similar hangers are available for 4× lumber. Special 1¼ in. joist nails are used to fasten the hangers.

• *Angle brackets* help reinforce inside corners, such as where a head joist meets an outside joist. Heavier angle irons may be used to reinforce post-to-beam connections.

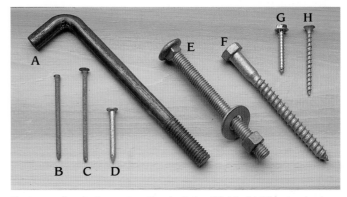

Fasteners for deck construction include: (A) J-bolt; (B) galvanized finish nail; (C) coated sinker; (D) joist-hanger nail; (E) carriage bolt with nut and washer; (F) lag screw; (G) hex-head screw; (H) deck screw.

• *T-straps and metal cleats* are used to reinforce post-to-beam attachments, as well as for butt splicing joists and beams.

Flashings: Galvanized sheet metal or aluminum flashing is used in conjunction with caulk to protect the ledger board, house siding, and the ends of deck boards from water damage. Preformed flashings of various sizes and shapes are available at hardware stores, lumberyards and home centers. If none of the preformed flashings fits your particular situation, you can make your own from flat stock, by bending it into the shape needed.

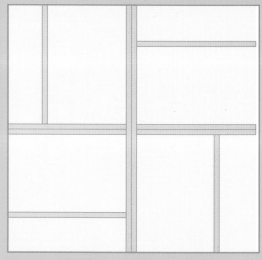

Basketweave pattern, sometimes called "parquet" pattern.

Herringbone pattern (sometimes called simply "diagonal pattern" if only one row of end joints is used).

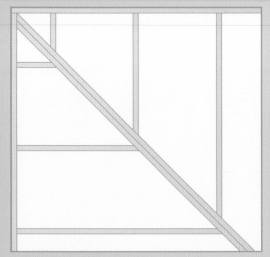

90° repeat pattern.

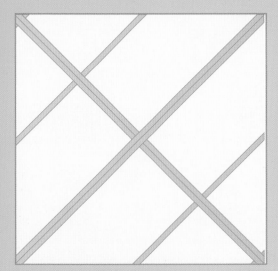

Concentric repeating mitered squares.

Deckbuilding: An overview

Deck layout

Careful layout work is the corner-stone of a successful deckbuild-ing project. If the corners are square and the footings are level and in the right spots, you'll enjoy the benefits throughout the entire construction process. But if the key structural members of the deck are mis-aligned, you'll spend the rest of the project trying to recover.

The conventional method for lay-ing out a deck is to use batter boards and mason's lines to outline the project area and to establish position for the footings that will support your deck posts.

Before you start laying out your deck, check to see that the site has adequate drainage. Make sure the ground slopes away from the house (at least 1 in. per 8 ft.), and that there are no low areas that will col-lect water. Also make sure any runoff from roof gutters is directed away from the deck site. To do this, you may need to connect the down-spout to a perforated drain pipe, placed in a gravel-filled trench that leads to a dry well on a lower part of the property. Also remove any sod, weeds, dead roots, wood scraps, or other organic matter from the site. Do not treat the soil with pesticides, weed killers, or other chemicals at this time. If desired, you can apply these later, after the substructure is built and you're ready to lay down the decking.

Provide a space convenient to the site for storing lumber and other materials. Stack the lumber neatly on scraps of wood to keep it off the ground. Do all the preparatory or organizational work you can do prior to setting your layout lines. Less activity around the lines once they're set decreases the probability that they'll be accidentally knocked out of alignment.

Creating the deck layout

The first phase of deck construction is to establish layout strings and batterboards to locate the footings for the deck posts. For decks attached to the house, first mark the ledger board location on the house wall and use this as a reference point to establish layout string lines for determining footing locations. Refer to your deck plan drawings for specific ledger details and post spacing.

1 Use a pencil, tape measure and level to mark a ledger board outline on the house wall **(See FIGURE A).** Mark the end of the ledger with a dotted line (normally, ledger boards are the same width as the deck joists). Mark another dotted line that represents the outside face of the end joist. If you'll be attaching a fascia board to the outside of the end joist (forming a double end joist), also mark its outside edge.

2 Measure in from the dotted line that indicates the end of the ledger and make a second reference mark to indicate the centerpoints of the posts that will be installed inside the end joist **(See FIGURE B).** Drive a nail at this post mark on the bottom edge of the ledger outline. It will serve as a tie-off point for the mason's line.

3 Erect a batterboard about 2 ft. beyond the corner post location, determined by your deck plan drawings. Use a tape measure squared to the house with a carpenter's square to find the approximate spot **(See FIGURE C).** *NOTE: Batterboards consist of pairs of scrap wood stakes connected to a wood crosspiece with deck screws. The batterboards should be tall enough so that they can be driven into the ground about 8 to 12 in. — their purpose is to hold layout strings taut.* Size the batterboards so that when they're driven into the ground, the top edge of the crosspiece will be roughly level with the bottom edge of the ledger board.

4 Run a mason's line from the nail you tacked on the house wall at the ledger site to the batterboard and pull it

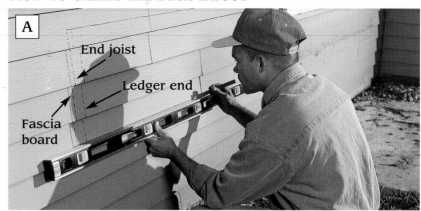

FIGURE A: Draw the outline of your ledger board on the side of the house, noting locations for end joists and fascia boards with dotted lines. Be sure the ledger outline is level.

FIGURE B: Mark the ledger outline as a reference for locating the corner posts. Drive a nail at this mark to serve as a layout line tie-off.

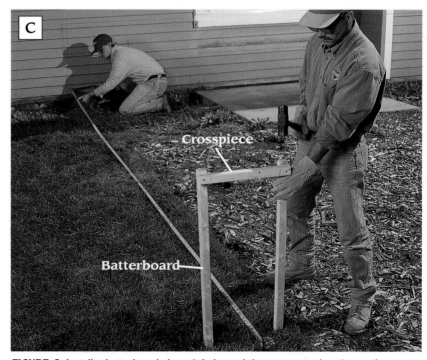

FIGURE C: Install a batterboard about 2 ft. beyond the corner post location so the crosspiece is roughly even with the nail you drove into the ledger outline.

FIGURE D: Tie off a mason's line to the nail in the ledger and run the line over the top of the batterboard crosspiece. Pull the line taut.

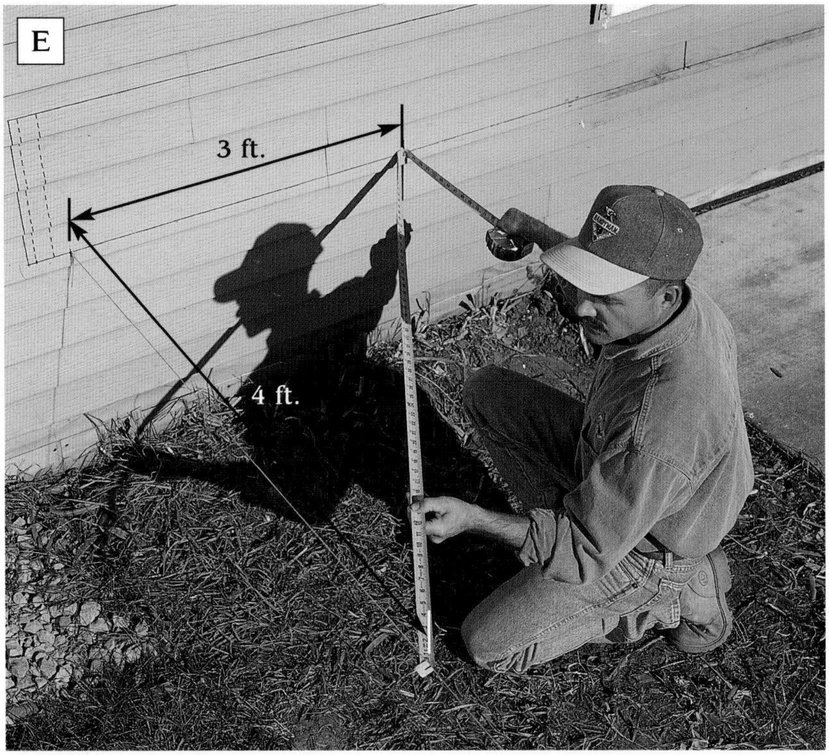

FIGURE E: Use the 3-4-5 triangulation method to square the layout line to the house. Adjust the line back and forth along the batterboard crosspiece until a 5-ft. section of the tape measure intersects both the 3- and 4-ft. index marks. This ensures that the line is square to the house. Drive a nail into the batterboard and tie off the string at this spot.

taut **(See FIGURE D).** With a helper, square the line to the house wall, using the "3-4-5" triangulation method. Establish the triangle as follows: Measure out 4 ft. along the string from the house wall and mark this spot with masking tape. Next, measure 3 ft. from the string at the ledger outline and make a second mark. Use a tape measure set at 5 ft. to measure diagonally between the two reference marks you've just made. Adjust the string back and forth on the batterboard until the distance between the other two reference marks is exactly 5 ft. **(See FIGURE E).** Drive a nail into the batterboard crosspiece to mark where the string crosses it, and tie off the string. The layout line is now square to the house.

5 Level the layout line established in *Step 4,* using a line level **(See FIGURE F).** Raise or lower the batterboard as necessary to make minor leveling adjustments.

Mark post locations

6 From the house wall, measure along the layout line and mark the line with masking tape at the middle of the corner post **(See FIGURE G).** To find the point, refer to the plan drawings for your deck and find the distance from the outside front face of the corner post to the house. Subtract half the thickness of the post from this distance (remember to use actual dimensions, not nominal), and mark your string line at that point. Repeat the batterboard squaring process to set a second layout line at the other end of the ledger, parallel with the first layout line. You've now established two of the three deck platform dimensions.

7 Position a second set of batterboards perpendicular to and approximately 2 ft. outside of the first two layout lines. The corner post marks on the first two strings should roughly align with the crosspieces of the new batterboards **(See FIGURE H).** Run a third layout line between these two batterboards so it intersects the corner post marks on the original two layout strings. Pull the line taut and tie it off to nails driven into the batterboard crosspieces. Level the third layout line by adjusting the batterboards.

FIGURE F: Suspend a line level from the layout line and adjust the batterboard up or down as needed until the layout line is level.

FIGURE G: Measure out from the house along the layout line to determine the center of the corner post. Mark the centerpoint with masking tape.

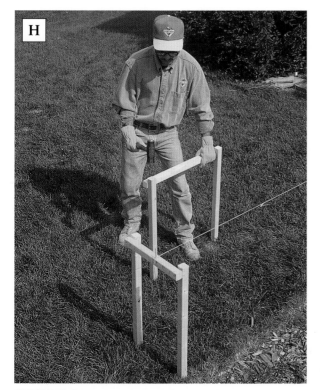

FIGURE H: Erect two more batterboards 2 ft. outside of and perpendicular to the first two layout lines. Run a third layout line between these batterboards so it crosses the corner post tape marks on the original layout lines.

FIGURE I: Check the layout for square by measuring diagonally from the ends of the ledger outline to both string intersection points. The layout is square when the diagonals are equal. Adjust the string lines if necessary.

Deck Layout **115**

FIGURE J: Mark the front layout line for additional post locations, using masking tape.

FIGURE K: Drop a plumb bob down from the post marks on the layout lines to mark the post locations on the ground. Drive a stake at each post location.

FIGURE L: Set up additional batterboards and layout lines to mark post locations for your entire deck. Once the batterboards and strings are removed, the stakes will serve as references for digging post holes.

The intersecting strings should just touch one another where they cross. Their intersection points mark the center of the corner posts.

8 Use a tape measure to check the length of both diagonals between the string intersection points and the ledger ends **(See FIGURE I).** Adjust the strings as necessary so both diagonal measurements are exactly the same, assuring a perfectly square deck layout.

9 Measure in from the layout string intersection points to locate the centerpoints of intermediate posts that will be positioned along the head joist of the deck. Use masking tape to mark post locations on the front layout line **(See FIGURE J).**

Stake the footing locations

10 Drop a plumb bob down from each masking-tape mark to establish the centerpoints of the posts on the ground. Drive a wood stake into the ground at each of these locations **(See FIGURE K).** These stakes serve as markers for digging and installing the tubular footings that will support the posts.

11 Since our multi-level project deck has two platforms, and each platform is larger than could be supported by a ledger and corner posts alone, we needed to install additional posts in the center areas of each deck platform. To pinpoint the centers of those posts, we tied off mason's line to layout strings already in place. We also erected more batterboard sets and ran string lines to establish our second, lower deck platform elevation **(See FIGURE L).** Regardless of the complexity of the deck you plan to build, keep all layout lines for each deck platform uniformly square and leveled at the appropriate height. This way, you'll ensure that footings for the posts will line up properly with deck framing members.

12 Make sure you've accounted for all post locations outlined in your deck plan. It's more difficult to determine post locations once you've taken down the layout strings. Remove the strings, but leave the batterboards in place.

Footings

After you've located and marked the footing positions on the deck site, the next step is to dig holes at the marks, and pour the concrete deck footings. Depending on your soil conditions, you may need to use a form to contain the concrete and keep the walls of the hole from collapsing. In the project featured here, we use tubular concrete forms to build the footings. The tubes come in various diameters and have a wax coating on the inside to keep the concrete from bonding to the form.

When your building department inspects your deck project, the footings are generally their primary area of interest. They'll check the depth to make sure the footings extend below the frost line (if applicable to your area of the country), and they'll check the diameter to make sure the footing is strong enough to support your deck. Contact your inspector to have him review your project after the footing holes are dug, but before you pour the concrete.

If you're only pouring a few shallow footings, it's easiest and cheapest to mix your own concrete on site. But if you'll need more than ½ cubic yard (about 14 cubic feet), look into having ready-mix concrete trucked in to your site (but don't schedule delivery until your footing holes and layout have been approved). Since each 60-pound bag of premixed concrete yields only ½ cubic foot of material, you'll need to mix upwards of 30 bags by hand just to create ½ yard. To put the numbers into perspective, if you're using a 12-in.-dia. tubular form, each 60-pound bag of premixed concrete will fill up about 9 in. of the form.

Before the concrete cures, you'll need to embed a device in the concrete for anchoring the deck posts. One option is to insert a metal J-bolt in the center of each footing, with the threaded end up. Or, you can install post anchors with preattached corrugated fins that are submerged into the concrete while it's still wet. In the project shown here, we use the J-bolt method, primarily because it's easier to control the height and position of the posts when using J-bolts.

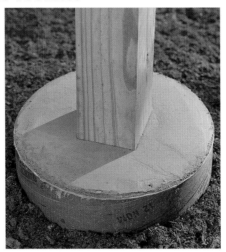

Set a J-bolt into the freshly poured concrete footing, centered with the threaded end sticking up. After the concrete cures, insert metal post anchor hardware over the J-bolt and thread a washer and nut to secure the anchor to the J-bolt.

Set posts directly into concrete. This is a little risky—if you manage to keep the post immobilized as the concrete sets up, you can end up with an almost-indestructible bond. But if the post slips, gaps are created and a loose fit (and water penetration) can result.

Post anchors with preattached corrugated fins can be inserted directly into the fresh concrete. Do your best to level the post anchors as you insert them. Do not disturb the anchors until the concrete has cured.

Footing options

In addition to the conventional method of pouring subterranean footings and embedding hardware into the fresh concrete, you may have other options for making deck footings.

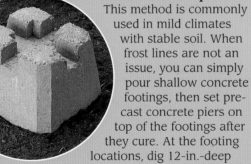

Precast concrete piers. This method is commonly used in mild climates with stable soil. When frost lines are not an issue, you can simply pour shallow concrete footings, then set pre-cast concrete piers on top of the footings after they cure. At the footing locations, dig 12-in.-deep holes (or as required by local codes) that are 3 in. wider in dimension than the base of the pier block (pier blocks are normally 12 × 12 in.). Tamp loose soil in the bottom of the hole, then shovel in a 2-in. layer of coarse gravel and tamp firmly. Pour concrete into the holes, filling them to within 3 to 4 in. of ground level. While the concrete is still plastic, but strong enough to support the pier, embed the pier about 1 in. deep into the concrete footing. Use a plumb bob to align the center of the pier block with the post centers marked on the guide strings. The top of the pier block should be level and at least 3 in. above ground. After the concrete cures, simply set 4 × 4 posts on-end into the recess at the top of each pier.

Above-ground tube footings. You can extend tubular forms one or more feet above grade to double as posts or columns to support the deck beams (common on hillside decks). If the tubes extend 2 ft. or more above the ground, you'll need to brace them with 1 × 4 or 2 × 4 braces as you would for a fence post. Insert a No. 5 reinforcing rod (rebar) into the footing after you've poured in the concrete, to prevent it from cracking. Because you'll be attaching the beams directly to the poured-concrete columns with metal connectors, you'll also need to make sure the tops of the form tubes are level to each other. Do this by attaching a string between the tops of the tubes, then leveling the string with a line level; or you can place a long, straight 2 × 4 on-edge across the tops of the tubes, and set a carpenter's level on top of the 2 × 4. Make any minor height adjustments when you install the tubes. Also run leveled strings out from the bottom of the ledger, centered over the post locations. Position the strings above the tubes to indicate the width of the beam, then measure down from the string to the tops of the tubular forms to indicate the beam width plus ½ in. Set the tubes to this height.

NOTICE: **Before you locate footings, make sure you know the exact locations of any underground electrical, gas, telephone, sewer and water lines within the deck area. Utility companies can provide you with this information; some offer a free locating service. Also check the original plot plans for your house, if you have them.**

Installing concrete tube footings

1 Dig post footings at each stake location to the appropriate depth (below frost line), as specified in building codes for your area. Dig each footing 3 to 4 in. deeper to allow for a drainage layer of compactible gravel subbase at the bottom. Depending upon the size and depth of your footings, as well as the number of holes you'll need to dig, it may be well worth the money to rent a one- or two-person gas-powered auger to excavate your footings **(See FIGURE A).** For holes shallower than 35 in., you could also use a post-hole digger.

2 Remove any loose soil from the bottom of each hole with a post-hole digger. Use a story pole to check the depth of the holes **(See FIGURE B)** and remove more soil, if necessary. The hole depth should be uniform for all footings. Add 3 to 4 in. of compactible gravel subbase, and tamp the bottom of each footing hole with a hand tamper or 4 × 4 scrap.

3 Measure the hole depth again, add 3 in., and cut the concrete tube forms to length with a hand saw or reciprocating saw. Make sure you cut the tubes evenly all around so the tube tops remain flat. Set the tubes into the footing holes **(See FIGURE C).** Each

FIGURE A: Dig post footings to the depth specified by building codes in your area. For large decks with many footings, rent a two-person gas-powered auger to excavate the holes.

Story pole depth marker

FIGURE B: Clear away any remaining loose soil from the bottom of each footing hole and check the depth with a story pole marked with a line at the proper depth. Add 3 in. of compactible gravel subbase and tamp this drainage layer down.

FIGURE C: Cut the concrete tube forms to length (depth plus 3 in.) and set them into the holes. Each tube should extend 3 in. above grade. Then backfill around the outside of each tube with soil and level the tops.

FIGURE D: Transport ready-mix concrete to posthole locations in a wheelbarrow. Lay a path of boards across your yard to make carting the cement easier and to protect your yard.

FIGURE E: Dump wheelbarrow loads of concrete into the tubular forms until they're nearly full to the top.

tube rim should extend 3 in. above ground level, which will keep the deck posts from absorbing ground moisture and rotting. Backfill around the tubes with soil, keeping each tube level. Then tamp the backfill.

4 For smaller decks with only a few footings, consider buying bags of premixed concrete for filling footings and prepare it in small batches yourself. On larger deck projects with multiple footings, have ready-mix concrete delivered to your site. If you must transport wet concrete a distance from the truck, use wide boards to make a path for the wheelbarrow **(See FIGURE D).** A path will spare your yard from wheel ruts and spillage and it also makes rolling the wheelbarrow easier.

5 Dump wet concrete from the wheelbarrow into each tube and fill it nearly full **(See FIGURE E).** If you have many footings to fill and a concrete truck waiting at the curb, time will be of the essence, so work carefully but quickly. Have a helper guide the concrete into the tube with a shovel as you pour. If some concrete does land outside the tube, don't shovel it back in, as it will be contaminated with dirt, which will weaken the footing as the concrete cures.

6 Top off each tube by shoveling in wet concrete until it overfills the tube **(See FIGURE F).**

7 Plunge a long length of scrap wood into the wet concrete, moving it up and down around the tube to settle the concrete and remove air pockets **(See FIGURE G).** If the concrete settles below the tube rim, refill it so it crowns the top of the tube.

8 Use a length of 2 × 4 to screed off the wet concrete level with the top of the tube **(See FIGURE H).**

9 Replace the layout lines between the batterboards and the house and re-level them, if necessary. Center a J-bolt over each tube, using a plumb bob dropped from the string lines. Insert the J-bolt into the wet concrete (hook end first), wiggling it slightly as you submerge it to remove any air bubbles **(See FIGURE I).** Leave about 1 in. of the bolt protruding above the concrete. Check the bolt with a try square to make sure it is perfectly vertical. Wipe any wet concrete off the J-bolt threads before it cures.

10 Allow the concrete to fully cure (about three days in dry weather). At this point in the deck construction process, you can remove the batterboards.

FIGURE F: Use a shovel to finish filling the tubular forms with concrete. Overfill the forms slightly.

FIGURE G: Plunge a length of scrap wood into the wet concrete and work it up and down to settle the concrete and remove air pockets.

Create a clean crown

Even if you don't use tubular forms for the body of your footings, you can create smooth, symmetrical appearance on the exposed portion of the footing by setting a 3 to 4 in. high section of tubular form on top of the loosely poured footing, then fill the form section and striking it off with a screed board.

FIGURE H: Run a short screed board (like a section of 2 × 4) over the top of the form to knock off excess concrete and create a flat, smooth surface.

FIGURE I: Reattach layout lines to the batterboards and drop a plumb bob down to locate the center of each tube. Insert a J-bolt into the wet concrete, leaving 1 in. of the threaded end above the surface.

Ledgers

Ledger boards are secured to the rim joist of a house to support attached decks. For small, low-level decks (100 square feet or less), the ledger can be the same size as the joists (typically a 2 × 6); on large decks, elevated (second-story) decks, or decks that will support heavy loads or additional structures, use a 2 × 8 or 2 × 10 ledger. In all cases, check local building codes to make sure your ledger board is in compliance.

In conventional wood frame construction, lag screws are used to attach the ledger to the rim joist of the house (typically a 2 × 10 or 2 × 12) behind the exterior siding and sheathing — the second story also contains a rim joist that's level with the second-floor floor joists. Do not attach the ledger to siding, wall studs, or stud wall sole plates.

Depending on the structural details of the house and the desired deck height, the joists can either rest on top of the ledger or be hung flush with it, using joist hangers. For free-standing decks, use an additional beam and header joist and back corner posts to take the place of the ledger.

Locating the ledger

In all cases, use your drawings as a guide to cut the ledger to length. Note that ledger will be 3 in. shorter than the overall width of the deck framing, to allow for attachment of the two end joists to the ends of the ledger. Locate the ledger so the finished deck surface will be 1 in. below the interior floor level or door sill. This will prevent water from entering the house through the door opening. Measure down 1 in. from the sill, then add the thickness of the deck boards to indicate the top edge of the ledger. Mark with a pencil. On wood frame houses, this should also place the ledger directly opposite the floor header joist on the other side of the exterior siding. If you're not sure of the header joist location, transfer the height of the interior floor level to the outside wall by measuring down from a nearby window or doorway. From this point, measure down 6 in., which should roughly indicate the center point of the header.

With a helper, align the top edge of the ledger to your mark, then brace or tack the ledger against the house wall. If the house has wood siding, tack the ledger to the wall with one duplex nail at the center; use a 2-ft. level to level the ledger, then tack nails at both ends. For solid masonry walls, stucco walls or masonry veneer walls, build temporary braces from 2 × 4s to hold the ledger in place.

ATTACHING LEDGERS TO LAP SIDING WALLS

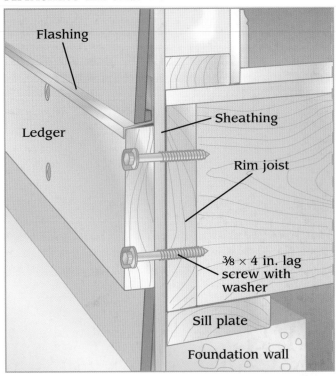

Attaching a ledger to an exterior wall with lap siding is a relatively uncomplicated task. See the projects description on pages 124 to 125.

ATTACHING LEDGERS TO STUCCO WALLS

Cut the ledger to length, then brace it in position against the stucco wall, aligned with the rim joist of the house. Outline the ledger onto the stucco, then add 1½ in. at each end of the outline for the end joists. Remove the ledger. Install a masonry cutting blade in your circular saw and set it to about ¾ in. cutting depth (the average thickness of stucco skins). Cut along the outline, stopping the cut short of the corners. Finish the cuts with a cold chisel and maul. Remove the stucco material, then cut through the wire mesh stucco underlay with aviator snips. Clear all the debris from the cutout area until you've exposed the wall sheathing in front of the rim joist. Finish installing the ledger as you would with lap siding (See pages 123 to 125).

ATTACHING LEDGERS TO CONCRETE

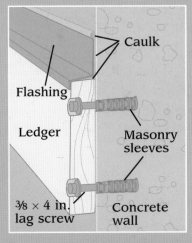

Cut the ledger to length, then drill pairs of counter-sunk guide holes, spaced about 2 ft. apart, to accept ⅜ × 4 in. lag screws. Brace the ledger against the wall, level it, then outline it, adding 1½ in. on each side for the end joists. Drill through the guide holes with a small masonry bit to mark drilling points for masonry sleeves. Remove the ledger. Drill ⅝ in. × 3 in. deep holes for masonry sleeves at the drilling points. Attach the ledger to the wall with lag screws driven through the guide holes and into the sleeves. Apply a heavy bead of polyurethane caulk between the top edge of the ledger and the wall, and another just above it. Cut flashing to fit (See page 124). Press the flashing firmly into the caulk bed. Run a bead of caulk across the top edge of the flashing. Cover the screw heads with caulk.

FIGURE A: Cut away the siding within the ledger layout area using a circular saw fitted with the proper blade. Set the blade depth to cut through the siding only.

FIGURE B: Cut the ledger board to size and mark each joist location on the ledger with a carpenter's square. Typical joist spacing is 16 in. on-center.

FIGURE C: Cut a strip of galvanized metal flashing to fit the length of the cutout area and slip the vertical flange up behind the flashing.

Attaching a ledger board

The following step-by-step photos show how to attach a ledger to a conventional wood frame house with wood, metal, vinyl or hardboard lap siding. Details for attaching ledgers to a masonry wall (such as a block foundation) or to stucco are discussed on page 123.

1 Mark a horizontal line ¼ in. above the top of the ledger outline you marked when laying out your deck footing locations (See pages 112 to 116). This additional space will leave room for installing a strip of galvanized flashing above the ledger. Remove the siding to accommodate the ledger board, flashing, end joist and fascia board, following your layout lines **(See FIGURE A).** *NOTE: For vinyl, wood or hardboard lapped siding, cut away the siding using a circular saw fitted with a carbide-toothed combination blade. If your siding is aluminum or steel, be sure to outfit the saw with a blade appropriate for cutting non-ferrous metals.* Regardless of the siding composition, set the blade depth to match the thickness of the siding only, so that you do not damage the wall sheathing beneath.

TIP: Flashing alternative

If you find it difficult or impractical to install galvanized flashing behind your home's siding, here's an easy alternative. When you install the lag screws or bolts through the ledger board, insert 6 galvanized washers over the lag screw shaft so that once the ledger is installed, the washers are sandwiched between the ledger and the siding. The washers will provide a gap that allows water to run freely behind the ledger and air to circulate, keeping the back face of the ledger dry. Be sure to keep the gap free from leaves and other debris that could trap water and defeat the purpose.

2 Use a hammer and wood chisel to finish the cuts at each corner of the cutout area that the saw blade can't reach. Square up the corners. Then install a strip of building paper to cover the sheathing behind the siding and staple it into place.

3 Measure and cut the ledger to size from 2× dimensional treated lumber. The width of your ledger board will vary, depending on the size of the joists you'll be installing — the ledger width should match or exceed the joist width. Test-fit the ledger in the cutout area. Mark joist locations on the ledger, using a carpenter's square **(See FIGURE B).** Typical joist spacing is 16 in. on-center.

4 Cut preformed galvanized drip flashing to fit the length of the cutout and slide the top edge behind the siding **(See FIGURE C).** Don't use fasteners to hold the flashing in place in place.

5 Set the ledger into the cutout so that the flashing wraps over the top. Level the ledger and temporarily tack it in place with several 3-in. framing nails or duplex nails. Mark the ledger for pairs of ⅜ × 4-in. galvanized lag screws, spaced every 2 ft. along the length of the ledger. Drill a ⅜-in. pilot hole for each lag screw, through the ledger board and sheathing and into the rim joist of the house **(See FIGURE D).**

6 Slip a washer over each lag screw and install the the screws with a socket wrench to secure the ledger to the house **(See FIGURE E).**

7 Run a thick bead of heavy-duty silicone or polyurethane caulk along the joint between the flashing and the siding to seal out moisture **(See FIGURE F).** It's a good idea to caulk the cracks along the sides and bottom of the ledger as well.

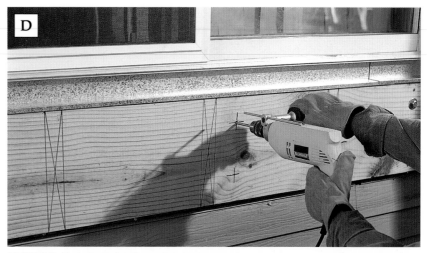

FIGURE D: Tack the ledger into place in the cutout area with framing nails or duplex nails. Mark the ledger for pairs of lag screws and drill a pilot hole for each screw.

FIGURE E: Use a socket wrench to drive the lag screws that secure the ledger to the house. Use washers with the lag screws.

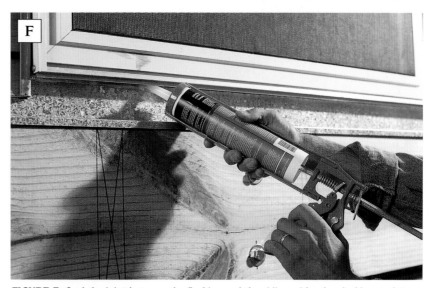

FIGURE F: Seal the joint between the flashing and the siding with a bead of heavy-duty silicone or polyurethane caulk.

Framing

Framing is the part of the deckbuilding process where your project actually begins to look like a deck. It's also labor-intensive and utterly critical to success. The framework of a deck, sometimes called the *undercarriage,* consists of a front joist called a header joist or rim joist, end or side joists, beams on some deck styles, and field joists that span between the header joist and the ledger, supporting the decking.

There's no single right way to frame a deck. Among the many variables are whether you're building a simple platform deck or a cantilevered deck; the size and height of the deck; the decking pattern you've selected; the number of levels in the deck project; whether the deck is free-standing or attached to a ledger on the house; and even whether or not you are bothered by the appearance of bulky galvanized deck hardware.

The order in which you install the frame members can also vary, depending on the project plan and the topographical features of the building site. The traditional method is to trim the post tops to level first, then attach beams or a header joist to the posts, parallel to the ledger. Then, the end joists and field joists are filled in between the beams or the header joist and the ledger. One drawback to this sequence is that it forces you to get the post heights exactly right, or the joists may not be square to the ledger and beams when you're finished. One way around this problem is to install the end joists first, supporting and leveling them in front with temporary braces. Once you know they're square and level, you can use them as a reference to mark cutting heights on the post tops, then finish the installation of the frame.

Using temporary braces to support the joists and even the header joists or beams is a particularly good idea when building on steep slopes or irregular terrain, where finding a reference point to measure from can be difficult. Weigh your framing options carefully before jumping in, from which type of fasteners to use to which assembly strategy you'd like to employ.

Anatomy of a deck frame

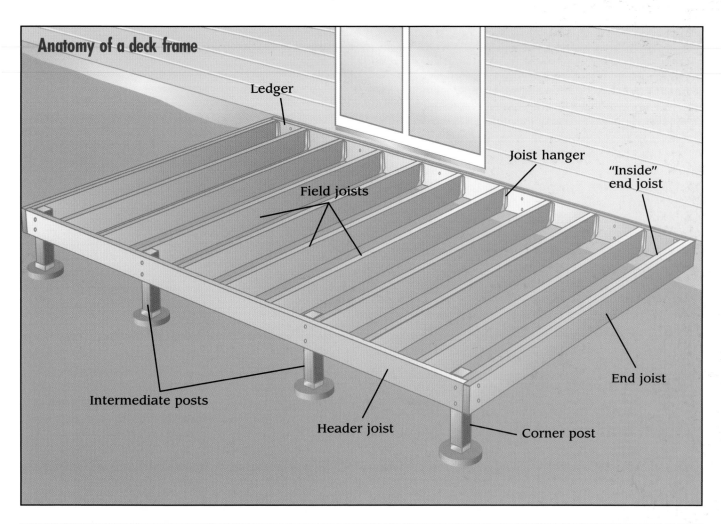

Ledger

Joist hanger

"Inside"
end joist

Field joists

End joist

Intermediate posts

Header joist

Corner post

Cantilevered decks

A cantilevered deck is one that is supported by posts and a main beam that runs parallel to the ledger board. The beam is positioned back from the front edge of the deck, which extends past the beam as much as one-third of its total length. Cantilevered decks are popular choices when building on slopes or building a deck with a high elevation. This is mostly because the undercarriage of a cantilevered deck consumes less real estate than a deck built with corner posts in front. The positioning of the main beam is the most crucial step when building a cantilevered deck. The top of the beam must be level with the bottom of the ledger board (if the ledger is the same thickness as the joists). This means that the posts supporting the beam must be level.

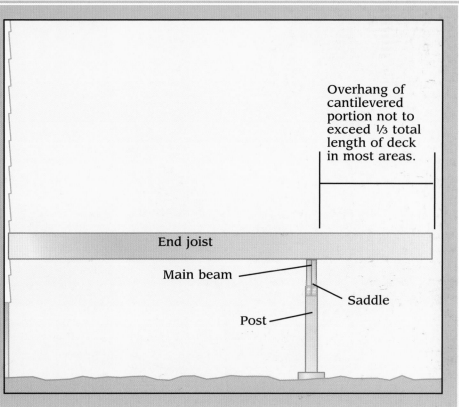

Overhang of cantilevered portion not to exceed ⅓ total length of deck in most areas.

End joist

Main beam

Saddle

Post

Options for joining frame members

There are nearly as many ways to fasten structural framing members as there are different styles of deck designs. Choosing the best method for your deck depends on the planned height of the deck (some methods will raise beams too high) and the type of fasteners used elsewhere on the deck — try to keep consistent. Whether you're installing a single or double beam also plays an important role in the decision. If you're using a double beam, try to select a fastening method where the beams are sandwiched together face-to-face, rather than attached to opposite sides of the post. In most cases, this means the doubled beam will rest atop the posts (the preferred arrangement). Where possible and practical, use metal fasteners. Make sure any end joints are supported from below.

SINGLE BEAM ATTACHED TO NARROW POST WITH LAG SCREWS

DOUBLE BEAM ATTACHED ON OPPOSITE SIDES OF POST WITH LAG BOLTS

SINGLE BEAM ATTACHED TO NARROW POST WITH T-STRAP

DOUBLE BEAM ATTACHED TO POST WITH BEAM SADDLE

SINGLE BEAM ATTACHED TO NARROW POST WITH SADDLE

SPLICED BEAM REINFORCED WITH T-STRAPS

SPLICED BEAM REINFORCED WITH PLYWOOD GUSSET

JOIST TOE-NAILED TO BEAM

JOIST HUNG WITH JOIST HANGER

JOISTS WITH SPLICE OVERLAPPING ON BEAM

JOISTS SPLICED WITH JOIST STRAP

FIGURE A: Cover the project area that will be beneath the deck with landscape fabric. Weight the fabric down with dirt to hold it in place (if your deck is elevated more than 3 or 4 ft., ignore this step).

FIGURE B: Cut end joists to length, then align one end of a joist against the end of the ledger. Tack the end joist to the ledger with a 3-in. deck screw.

Framing a deck

The construction techniques for this particular deck are a departure from the "norm" in that the doubled end and rim joists take the place of beams, with single joists of the same dimension hung between them. These perimeter members were installed and braced prior to cutting and setting the posts, so that we could cut and locate the posts with greater accuracy. The top end of each 6 × 6 post is notched to provide additional support for the beams.

The main platform consists of 2 × 12 beams and joists, attached to a 2 × 12 ledger. The lower platform consists of 2 × 10 beams and joists attached to the upper platform. For a lighter-duty deck, you can get away with 2 × 8 joists.

The following steps show how to construct the main platform only, although you'll notice that a second ledger is in place for the lower platform. Use the same procedures to build the lower platform. The beefed-up main platform was designed to carry the weight of an enclosed three-season porch, which will be added at a future date.

1 Roll sheets of landscape fabric over the deck project area to to inhibit weed growth beneath the deck **(See FIGURE A).** Cut the fabric around cement footings to keep the tops exposed and weight the fabric down along the seams and edges with dirt. In areas where termites are a problem, treat the project area with insecticide first.

2 Cut the end joists to length, according to your deck plan drawings. Construct temporary 2 × 4 braces attached to a plywood "foot" to support the joist near the end opposite the ledger. With your helper holding up one end of the joist, attach the other end flush to the end of the ledger near the top edge with a 3-in. deck screw **(See FIGURE B).**

3 Set a carpenter's level on top of the joist at the far end and level the joist by pivoting it up or down. Once it's level, fasten it to the 2 × 4 brace with several 3-in. deck screws **(See FIGURE C).** Repeat this process on the other end of the ledger to position a second end joist that is parallel to the first.

4 Screw the header joist flush to the ends of the end joists with 3-in. deck screws, spaced about 2 in. apart along the width of the header joist **(See FIGURE D).** Have a helper hold the opposite end of the joist while you drive the screws. *NOTE: You may need to shift the end joists one way or the other in order to align them with the header joist.* Once the header joist is secured to the end joists, drive additional deck screws through the end joists at the ledger every 2 in.

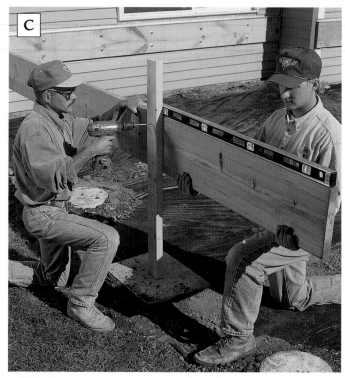

FIGURE C: Level the end joist near the far end with a carpenter's level and fasten the leveled joist to a temporary 2 x 4 support brace with several deck screws. Hang and level the other end joist to the ledger now.

FIGURE D: Cut the header joist to length, align it with the ends of the two end joists and fasten it in place with 3-in. galvanized deck screws, spaced at 2 in. intervals.

FIGURE E: Fasten diagonal supports to the 2 × 4 braces with a deck screw. Each diagonal support is outfitted with a stake at the opposite end, which is driven into the ground.

Overlap the "inside" joists at the corner post locations

FIGURE F: Reinforce the end and header joists by attaching a second joist to each on the inside face. Fasten the members together with deck screws in a staggered pattern. Overlap the ends of the "inside" joists at the corner post locations.

Pneumatic nail guns, powered by compressed air, are a suitable (and faster) alternative to deck building with screws. For heavy framing applications through 2× lumber, use 2¾-in. galvanized nails. Wear eye protection when using pneumatic nailers and follow all safety precautions.

5 Steady the deck assembly by screwing a diagonal brace to each 2 × 4 brace holding up the end joists. Attach a 12-in. stake to the opposite end of the diagonal brace with a deck screw and drive the stake into the ground. Then attach the diagonal brace to the vertical 2 × 4 brace with a deck screw **(See FIGURE E).**

6 For larger decks like this project deck, reinforce the perimeter joists by doubling them up. Attach a second joist inside the header and end joists with 3-in. deck screws, spaced every 2 ft. in a staggered pattern and screwed from inside the deck frame outward **(See FIGURE F).** (You can also laminate joists together and frame the deck with nails. See *TIP,* left). Overlap these "inside" joists in the corners where the header joist meets the end joists. Attach the "inside" joists to the ledger by driving 3-in. deck screws toe-nail style (diagonally) into the ledger.

7 Attach a mason's line along the length of the header joist, and set it off from the outside face of the joist with a spacer (such as a deck screw) at each end **(See FIGURE G).** Pull the string line taut and tie it off to a screw on either end of the header joist. Since most dimension lumber has a natural bow to it, the line will be used in the next step as a reference to straighten the double header joist.

FIGURE G: Attach a mason's line along the length of the header joist, and set it off from the outside face of the joist with a spacer. We used deck screws for spacers.

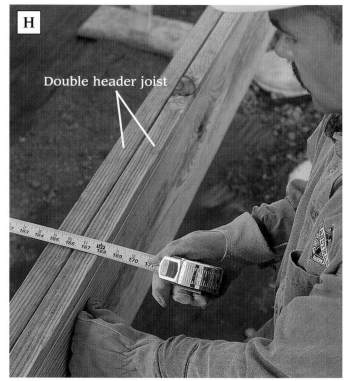

FIGURE H: Push or pull the header joist until it touches the string line, straightening the header joist. Measure the distance between the ledger and the inside face of the header to determine the length of the first "field" joist.

8 Push or pull the header joist near the middle of its span until it touches the reference line. Hold it in place. Measure the distance between the ledger (at the nearest joist or beam site marked on the ledger) and the inside face of the header joist and note this distance **(See FIGURE H).** Use this measurement to cut the first "field" joist or double beam to length.

9 Mark the location for the middle joist or beam (determined in *Step 8*) on the inside face of the header joist **(See FIGURE I).** Align and attach one side of a joist hanger to the header joist and ledger at the middle joist or beam layout marks, using 1¼-in. galvanized joist-hanger nails.

10 Set the center joist or beam into the joist hangers. Press the "loose" side of each hanger snug against the joist or beam to cradle it, align the hanger with the layout marks, then attach the hanger to the ledger and header joist with 1¼ in. joist-hanger nails. Fasten the hanger to the joist or beam with more nails **(See FIGURE J).** Drive a nail into each hole on the hangers. Check the entire deck frame for square by measuring the diagonals, and adjust the deck frame as needed by shifting the temporary braces and stakes until the diagonal measurements are equal. The deck platform is now square.

FIGURE I: Align and attach one side of a joist hanger to the header joist and ledger at the middle joist or beam layout marks, using 1¼-in. galvanized joist-hanger nails .

FIGURE J: Set the joist or beam into the hanger, align the loose side of the hanger with the joist layout mark, and fasten the hanger to the header, and then to the joist or beam, with 1¼-in. joist-hanger nails.

FIGURE K: Secure a metal post hanger to the J-bolt embedded in each concrete footing with a nut and washer. Tighten the nuts with a socket wrench.

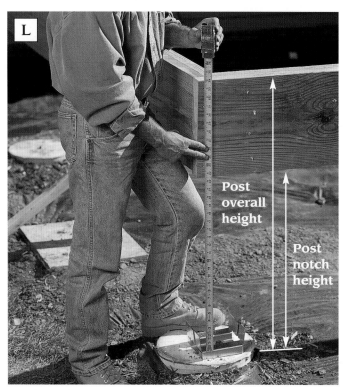

FIGURE L: Measure up from each post anchor to determine the overall height and notch height for each post.

FIGURE M: Trim each post to length by first cutting along all four faces at the post-end cutting line, using a circular saw set to maximum depth. If the thickness of your posts is less than that of our project deck posts, you may be able to complete these cuts with a circular saw alone.

Installing posts

11 Attach a galvanized post anchor to each concrete deck footing, securing it to the embedded J-bolt with a nut and washer **(See FIGURE K).**

12 Measure up from the bottom of each footing post anchor to the top edge of the deck frame in order to determine the overall height for each post. Take a second measurement from the bottom of the post anchor to the bottom edge of the deck frame. This measurement indicates where each post will be notched so the deck joists can rest on the posts **(See FIGURE L).**

13 Mark the post lengths and the notch locations on the faces of each post so you can cut all the posts at one time. *NOTE: For our project deck, we used 6 × 6 treated posts and cut notches in two faces for corner posts and one face for intermediate posts.* For large posts like these, set your circular saw to its maximum blade depth and cut along all four faces of each post to begin to trim them to length **(See FIGURE M).**

14 Because most circular saws cannot cut through a 6 × 6, even when cutting through all four faces, complete the cuts made in *Step 13* with a reciprocating saw or hand saw to cut the posts to length **(See FIGURE N).**

15 Start the notch cuts in each post with your circular saw set to maximum depth **(See FIGURE O),** then finish the notch cuts where the circular saw can't reach with a reciprocating saw or hand saw **(See FIGURE P).** Clean up the inside corners of each notch with a hand saw or wood chisel and hammer so the joists will rest cleanly on the posts. *NOTE: Photos O through R illustrate the procedure for notching and attaching a corner post.*

16 At each post location, fit the posts under the joists and into the post anchors on the concrete footings. Clamp a level to each post and adjust it to plumb, then nail the post to the post anchor with 6d galvanized common nails. Drill pilot holes through the posts and into the deck frame joists to accept two ⅜ × 4-in. lag screws with washers **(See FIGURE Q).** Fit each lag screw with a washer and drive the lag screws through the posts and into the joists to fasten them together **(See FIGURE R).** Once all the posts are attached to the deck, remove the 2 × 4 braces from the end joists.

17 Mark the remaining "field" joist locations along the inside of the header joist to match those you've marked on the ledger. Install a joist hanger on the ledger and header joist at each marked field joist

FIGURE N: Complete the cuts started in FIGURE M with a reciprocating saw or hand saw, if necessary, to finish trimming the posts to length.

FIGURE O: Start the notch cuts in each post by following the notch cutting lines with your circular saw set to maximum depth. In this photo, we're cutting the notches for a corner post.

FIGURE P: Finish the notch cuts where the circular saw can't reach with a reciprocating saw or hand saw. Clean up the notched areas with a wood chisel or hand saw so that the joists will sit squarely and evenly in the notches.

FIGURE Q: Set each post into place so the joists are resting in the post notches and the post bottoms are sitting in the post anchors. Plumb the posts with a level, nail them to the post anchors and drill ⅜-in. pilot holes through the posts and into the joists for lag screws.

FIGURE R: Fasten the posts to the joists with 4-in. lag screws fitted with washers. Install two lag screws per post, using a socket wrench.

FIGURE S: Attach galvanized joist hangers along the ledger and the header joists for hanging the field joists. Cut the joists to length, set them on the joist hangers and fasten them in place with joist-hanger nails.

FIGURE T: Prepare joists for angled installations by setting them into position over adjoining joists and marking the angles where the joists intersect on either end.

FIGURE U: Set your circular saw to match the angles you marked on the joist and make the end cuts.

location, then follow the procedure outlined in *Steps 9 and 10* to secure the field joists to the deck frame **(See FIGURE S).**

18 Some deck designs may incorporate angled corners into deck platforms to add visual appeal. We used angled header joists in the lower platform of our project deck. Prepare joists for angled installations by setting them into position over adjoining joists and marking the angles where the joists intersect on either end **(See FIGURE T).** Then set the angle on your circular saw to match the angle marks on the joist ends and make the end cuts **(See FIGURE U).** Joist hangers are available to match several regular angles used in deck construction. Attach the angled hangers to adjoining joists first with 1¼-in. galvanized joist nails, then set the angled joists into position on the joist hangers and fasten them in place **(See FIGURE V).**

V

FIGURE V: Attach angled joist hangers to adjoining joists with 1¼-in. galvanized joist-hanger nails. Then set the angled joist (or joists) into the hangers and fasten them in place.

The completed deck frame may be a little unconventional, but it's exceptionally sturdy and ready to take on the load of the three-season porch that is planned for the upper deck (someday).

Decking

Laying decking is probably the most satisfying part of the deckbuilding process. It goes quickly and provides a sense that the project is nearly complete. However, because the decking is the part that "shows," you'll want to take extra care when you install the boards. The deck will have a nicer, neater appearance if you strike a chalk line across the boards at nail or screw locations and use the lines as a guide to keep the fasteners in neat rows.

If you want to apply a wood preservative or another protective finish to the substructure or to the undersides of the deck boards, apply it before attaching the decking. Also, if you're incorporating benches or railings into the deck, attach the uprights or posts before laying the decking (See pages 150 to 161).

If possible, buy deck boards that are long enough to span the entire width of the deck. If you do need to butt boards in each run, stagger the joints, making sure they fall directly over a joist. Leave a ½-in. space between board ends to allow for wood expansion and contraction.

Deck boards can be laid in many interesting patterns (See pages 108 to 109). Note that most patterns other than simple straight rows require special joist layouts for support. You can use 2 × 6 lumber or 2 × 4 lumber (cedar, redwood, cypress and pressure-treated are the most common), or you can use 1¼ in. thick premilled deck boards (See page 106).

The subject of which deck board face should face up is currently under evaluation. Traditionally, deckbuilders have always installed boards with the bark side facing up, presuming that if the boards cup from exposure to moisture the cupping will be directed against the joist, preventing the surface of the deck from becoming uneven. But some industry experts assert that modern kiln-drying methods alter the character of the wood enough to reverse the direction of the cupping, so the boards actually cup toward the bark side. While everyone seems to have an opinion on the subject, the fact is that most professional deck builders pay little attention to which board face is facing upward.

Installing the decking

1 Start laying deck boards at the ledger side of the deck. Choose the straightest deck boards for the first row of decking and cut them to length so their ends overhang the outside edges of the end joists slightly—the best way to get a straight line at the sides of the deck is to trim the boards, using a straightedge guide, after they're all in place. Space the first row of decking about ⅛ in. away from the house siding. Screw the first row of decking to the joists and ledger with 2½-in. galvanized deck screws. Fasten additional rows of decking with pairs of deck screws at each joist location, centering the screws on the joists and setting the screws about 1 in. from the edges of each deck board. Use 16d common nails as spacers between the rows **(See FIGURE A).**

2 Arrange deck boards so that all splices (end joints) fall directly over a joist, and splices are not aligned on consecutive boards. Butt the board ends together so the seam falls midway across the joist. When driving screws close to board ends, drill pilot holes first **(See FIGURE B).**

3 Warped deck boards can be forced into alignment with the straight boards. Position the warped board so the concave edge faces away from the fastened

Drill driver tip options

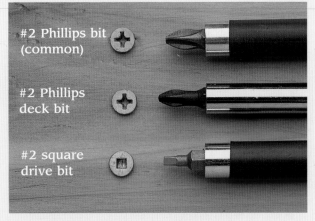

#2 Phillips bit (common)

#2 Phillips deck bit

#2 square drive bit

Three primary drill/driver bit styles are available for driving deck screws. A common #2 Phillips bit will easily drive deck screws through cedar or redwood decking without a pilot hole, but you may want to drill pilots if installing treated lumber. Specialty deck bits feature a hardened tip to withstand the torque that develops when you drive a screw through treated decking or 2× framing members. Square-drive screws are considerably more expensive than Phillips head screws, but they're less prone to stripping.

HOW TO LAY DECKING

A

FIGURE A: Fasten rows of decking, starting from the ledger side of the deck. Use 2½-in. galvanized deck screws, with 16d nails inserted as spacers between the rows.

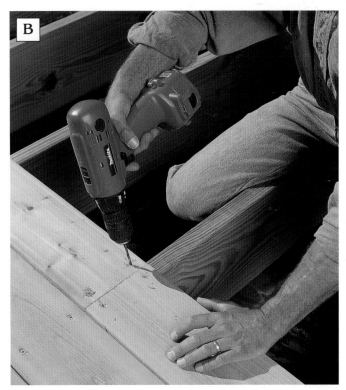

B

FIGURE B: Center board splices directly over a joist, with the seam between the boards located midway across the joist. Drill pilot holes for the screws to keep the board ends from splitting.

FIGURE C: Use a 2 × 4 lever to straighten warped boards. Tack the 2 × 4 to the joist, using a single screw. Pivot the board forward against the warped board to force it into alignment with the rest of the boards.

rows of decking. Fasten a piece of 2 × 4 to the end joist, butted up against the warped board by driving a single screw through the 2 × 4 into the inside face of the joist. Insert nail spacers between the warped board and the fastened row, then force the end of the warped board toward the fastened board by pressing the 2 × 4 against it, using the screw as a pivot **(See FIGURE C).** Drive deck screws to secure the board before it springs back. If the warp is severe, you may need to straighten the board at additional joist locations.

4 Proceed to lay rows of decking until you are within eight to ten rows from the end. Measure out to the end of the deck from the last row installed. Calculate the number of rows, including spaces, that it will take to reach the front of the deck, then mark the positions of each row on the joists **(See FIGURE D).** Adjust the spacing, if needed, so the outside edge of the last deck board row will end up flush with the end of the deck.

5 Snap a chalk line along the ends of the overhanging deck boards, about 1/16 in. beyond the outside edge of the end joists. Use a circular saw to trim off the overhanging boards, following the chalk line **(See FIGURE E).** Set the blade depth so the saw barely cuts through the decking to avoid marring the face of the end joists with the blade.

FIGURE D: About eight rows before the edge of the deck, measure the distance from the last row of installed boards to the edge. Calculate how many boards you'll need (include 1/8 in. for gaps between boards). Adjust the spacing if possible to avoid rip-cutting any deck boards.

FIGURE E: Snap a chalk line across the ends of the installed boards to mark a trimming line on each end of the deck. Trim the boards with a circular saw (use a straightedge for maximum accuracy). Take care to avoid cutting into the joist below the ends of the decking.

Installing decking around posts

STEP 1: Lay rows of decking until you are within one deck board's width from the post. Measure the distance from the edge of the closest fastened deck board to the face of the post.

STEP 2: Press a deck board up against the post. Draw a cutting line on the board face, parallel to the edge. The distance from the line to the edge of the board should be the same distance measured in STEP 1. Extend the lines created by the faces of the post onto the deck board until they meet the cutting line.

STEP 3: To cut out the notch, drill holes at the inside corners of the outline, then cut along the outline with a jig saw, connecting the holes. Square up the corners of the notch with a chisel or file.

STEP 4: Set the deck board into place and adjust the cutout area, if needed, until the board fits snugly around the post. Fasten it into place with deck screws.

Stairs

Decks higher than about 8 in. above grade will need at least one step to provide access between the deck and ground level. Steps also serve as a connection between two deck levels. If only one or two steps are needed, you can build a set of box steps which, as the name implies, are simple wooden boxes with deck boards on the top to create stair treads.

If three or more steps are required, you'll need to build a more conventional stairway in which the steps are attached to a set of stringers. The stringers are typically cut from 2 × 12s, which are secured to the deck joists or beams at the top end, and anchored to a footing at ground level. On outdoor stairs, the treads are made from 2 × 4s, 2 × 6s, or 2 × 8s attached to the stringers — wider boards, such as 2 × 10s or 2 × 12s tend to cup or warp when employed as single stair treads, thus are not recommended for exterior steps. Some stairways also incorporate risers to enclose the space between the treads as you typically see on interior stairs.

Building stairs, especially in longer runs, can get tricky. There are plenty of mathematic formulas to help you develop your design, but in the end it usually comes down to trial-and-error.

Basic design guidelines

Generally, outdoor stairs are not as steep as indoor stairs, having proportionally wider treads and lower rises. The staircase itself is also wider. For general access, the clear width between outer stingers should be at least 36 in. A stairway 5 ft. wide will accommodate two people side by side. All stairways wider than 4 ft. should include a third stringer placed midway between the two outside stringers, but installing a third stringer is also a good idea for prolonging the life of narrower staircase.

To build a comfortable set of stairs, you'll need to establish a suitable rise-to-run ratio: *Rise* refers to the height between the steps; *run* refers to the depth of the step, minus any overhang. As a general rule for outdoor stairs, the tread width (run) in inches plus twice the step height (rise) in inches should equal 24 to 26 inches. For exterior stairs, the rise (vertical distance between treads) should be between 4½ in. and 7 in. The tread depth should be a minimum of 11 in. Building codes often dictate acceptable run/rise relationships. In most deck situations, treads consist of two 2 × 6s, spaced ¼ in. apart, to create a tread run of 11¼ in. In this case, the formulas tell us that the riser height should be between 6½ and 7 in. This is the most common and useful outdoor step relationship.

The real trick to designing stairs comes when you try to actually incorporate the run and rise ratios into your design. By code, all stairs in a flight must have the same rise and run proportions (this is a safety issue: non-uniform sizing of stairs confuse our feet in a hurry and can easily cause injury from falls).

Measuring for stairs

To calculate the actual run and rise and the number of steps needed, first measure the vertical distance between the deck surface and the ground or between deck levels (total rise). Divide the total rise by the rough riser height (7 in. is a good starting point): the result is about the number of stairs you'll need in the staircase. More often than not, however, this formula usually results in a number of steps that is not a whole number. If this is the case, divide the whole number of steps into the total rise to get the exact riser height. Note that the number of stair treads required is always one less than the number of risers — the top "step" is the deck surface.

Next, multiply the exact riser height by two and subtract it from the overall ratio figure of 24 to 26 in. This will yield the ideal tread depth in the 10 to 12 in. range.

Finally, calculate the total run or *span* by multiplying the tread depth by the number of risers minus one. Knowing the span will enable you to identify and mark the bottom end of the staircase. If the stairs don't fit the space, adjust the tread/riser ratio by increasing one while decreasing the other. If this results in a tread/riser ratio that does not conform to acceptable limits you may need to redesign the stairway. For instance, on tall decks or steep hillside decks, you can use an "L" or "U"-shaped flight of stairs running parallel to the deck and incorporating one or more landings, rather than having a straight run of stairs running perpendicular to the deck.

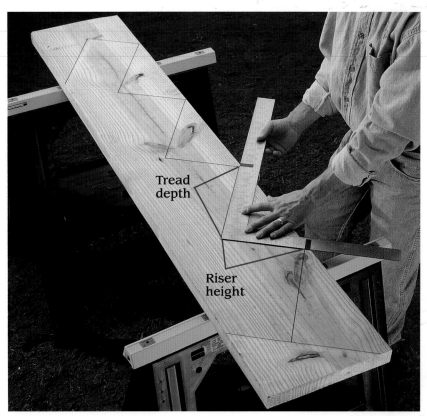

Note the riser and tread dimensions on a framing square and use the square as a layout tool for marking cutting lines or layout lines on the stair stringers.

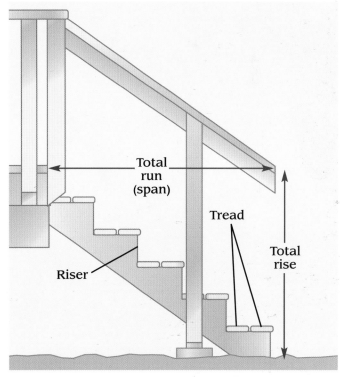

Designing stairs involves a little math and a little trial-and-error. The trick is to come up with a plan that has uniformly sized risers and treads that are in formation and terminate at a convenient location on the low end of the flight.

FIGURE A: Measure the overall height between deck platforms to determine the rise and run of the stairs. Be sure to take into account the thickness of the decking if you haven't already installed it.

FIGURE B: Use both legs of a framing square (one leg for rise and the other leg for run) to lay out a template stair stringer on a length of treated 2 × 12, according to your rise/run calculations. Mark waste areas with an "X".

Building deck stairs

Our project deck uses a system of "wraparound" stairs that provide easy access from all sides of both deck platforms. Every deck project will, of course, require its own unique stair system, depending upon the number of levels there are to the deck, its elevation from the ground and the deck's basic style. The following pages serve as an example for how to build wraparound-style steps for a low-standing, two-tiered deck. Modify your stair plans as necessary to accommodate the specific needs of your deck project.

1 Measure the overall rise between the two deck levels and use this distance to determine the rise/run ratio, following the formula discussed on page 143 **(See FIGURE A).** *Note: Be sure to allow for the thickness of the decking you plan to use if the decking on either deck platform isn't installed.*

2 Use both legs of a framing square (one leg for rise and the other leg for run) to lay out a template stair stringer on a length of treated 2 × 12, following your rise/run calculations **(See FIGURE B).** Be sure to account for the thickness of your treads and risers when laying out the stringer. Mark the waste side of the cuts with an "X" to keep your layout orientation clear. *Tip: For longer stringer layouts than shown here, mark the legs of your carpenter's square with pieces of tape to serve as quick layout references.*

3 Cut out the stringer with a hand saw, reciprocating saw or circular saw. If you use a circular saw, finish the inside corners with a hand saw where the circular blade won't reach **(See FIGURE C).** Set the template stringer into place on the deck and check it for accuracy. Then use it to mark the remaining stringers and cut them all to shape. Plan to install a stringer every 16 in. along the width of the stairway.

4 Set a stringer into place and level it. If the edge of the stringer that butts against the joist extends below the joist, measure down from the top of the joist to the top diagonal edge of the stringer **(See FIGURE D).** Use this measurement to determine the width of a plywood nailer that will support the top ends of the stringers where they rest against the perimeter joists.

5 Cut the nailers to size from ¾-in.-thick exterior treated plywood and attach them to the joist faces with rows of 2½-in. galvanized deck screws, spaced 10 to 12 in. apart, along the length of the joists **(See FIGURE E).** Use a tape measure and try square to mark each stringer location on the plywood nailers.

6 Place the two outermost stringers of the stairway against the nailer, level and square them to the

FIGURE C: Cut a stringer to shape following the layout lines. This first stringer will serve as a template for marking and cutting out the other stringers.

FIGURE D: Set the top of the stringer against the end joist of the upper deck platform so that it rests on the lower deck. Measure down from the upper deck to the bottom of the stringer to determine the width of the plywood nailer.

Plywood nailer

FIGURE E: Cut the nailer to size from treated plywood and attach it to the face of the header or end joist with 2½-in. galvanized deck screws, spaced 10 to 12 in. apart along the length of the joist.

FIGURE F: Level and square the outermost stringers for a staircase, aligning them with the layout locations on the nailer. Mark the bottom front edge of each stringer where it meets the decking. Then snap a chalk line to serve as a reference for installing the toe-kick.

FIGURE G: Mark and notch all the lower front edges of the stringers to make way for the toe-kick. Cut the toe-kick board to length, align it with the chalk line and attach it to the decking with screws.

2 × 4 toe-kick

FIGURE H: Fasten the bottom ends of the stringers to the toe-kick with two 2½-in. galvanized screws driven diagonally into the toe-kick from each side.

nailer, and mark the bottom edges of both stringers where they meet the lower deck **(See FIGURE F).** Snap a chalk line between these marks. The chalk line represents the front edge of a 2 × 4 toe-kick board that will be notched into the front lower edge of each stringer to anchor the stringers to the lower deck. Since the stairway wraps around the deck, follow the same procedure using stringers and chalk lines to establish toe-kick reference lines on adjacent sides of the deck.

7 Measure 1½ by 3½-in. notches in the front bottom corner of each stringer for the toe-kick board and cut the notches out with a saw. Measure and cut the toe-kicks to length from treated lumber.

8 Mark stringer locations on the toe-kicks using the nailer as a reference. Align the toe-kicks with the chalk lines, and set a stringer in place to check your layout. Fasten the toe-kicks to the decking with 3-in. deck screws, spaced 1 ft. apart **(See FIGURE G).** NOTE: *Since the stairs wrap around the deck, the toe-kicks in our project deck butt against one another at the outside corners of the deck where the adjacent stairways meet.*

9 Align the stringers with the nailer and toe-kick lay-out marks and attach the top end of each stringer to the nailer with pairs of 2½-in. deck screws driven diagonally into the nailer. Another alternative is to use galvanized stringer brackets (See *OPTION,* below).

OPTION: Stringer brackets

Stringer brackets, which work like joist hangers, cradle the bottom of the stringer and provide nailing flanges for attaching the stringers to the deck joists. Use 1¼-in. joist-hanger nails for fasteners.

I

Corner stringer dimensions
Top tread = C + D
Bottom tread = A + B

D

C

B

A

Toe-kicks

FIGURE I: Set an extra stringer into position in an outside corner, align deck boards to the lower tread, and use the formulas outlined above to determine the dimensions for the corner stringer.

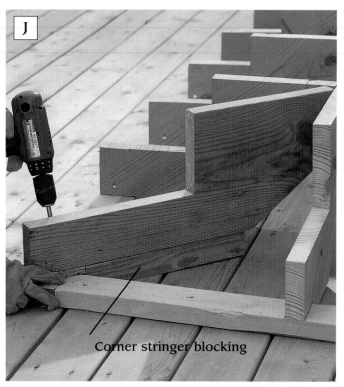

J

Corner stringer blocking

FIGURE J: Attach a length of extra blocking beneath corner stringers that are deeper than can be fabricated within the width of a 2 × 12. Fasten the corner stringers to the decking with screws.

10 Fasten the bottom end of the stringers to the toe-kick with two 2½-in. galvanized screws driven diagonally into the toe-kick from each side **(See FIGURE H).** Check each stringer with a carpenter's square before driving the screws to ensure that each stringer is perpendicular to the toe-kick.

11 Lay out and cut the corner stringer where adjacent stairways will meet. Establish the dimensions as follows: Set a spare stringer against the deck corner between the end stringers on the two adjacent staircases and line it up with the inside corner where the toe-kicks intersect. Lay two deck boards on the lower treads of adjacent stringers, tight against the riser edge of the stringer, and slide them until they intersect over the lower tread of the angled stringer **(See FIGURE I).** Then use the formulas in FIGURE I as references for determining tread depths. Distance A (starting 1 in. in from the outside toe-kick corner) plus distance B (front edge of the bottom tread to the corner where the deck boards intersect) equals the lower tread depth for the corner brace. Distance C (deck board intersection to stringer riser) plus distance D (top stringer tread) equals the top tread for the corner stringer. Add distances A through D to determine the overall length of the corner stringer. The riser heights remain the same.

K

FIGURE K: Construct treated-wood boxes for stairs that wrap around the end stringer of a stairway. Screw them to the stringer and to the decking with 2½-in. galvanized deck screws

FIGURE L: Measure and cut riser boards to fit each step leading up to the deck platform. Miter-cut riser-board ends at outside corners. Attach them to the stringers with 2½-in. galvanized deck screws.

FIGURE M: Cut and install the stair treads with pairs of 2½-in. deck screws, mitering the ends of the treads where they meet the corner stringers.

FIGURE N: Set 5 × 6 treated posts into 3-in.-deep trenches to serve as footings beneath box-frame steps. Be sure the tops of the posts are level in the trenches.

12 Cut the corner stringer to the proportions outlined in *Step 11*. The corner stringers for our project deck were so deep that they exceeded the width of a 2 × 12. We accounted for the extra width by fastening treated blocking beneath, extending the full width of the corner stringer base, less the corner width of the intersecting toe-kicks. Attach the corner stringers with 2½-in. deck screws driven toenail style into the deck **(See FIGURE J).**

13 Where stairs stop short of a deck corner or house wall, construct a treated wood box the same height as the bottom stringer tread, so that you can wrap the first step around the side of the end stringer and back to the end or header joist. Attach the box to the end stringer, upper deck, and lower deck with 2½-in. galvanized deck screws **(See FIGURE K).**

14 Measure and cut 1× or 2× riser boards (depending on your deck plan) to fit each step leading to the deck platform. Miter-cut the ends of the risers that meet at the corner stringers for a more finished appearance. Attach the risers to the stringers with 2½-in. deck screws, two screws per joint **(See FIGURE L).** If you plan to attach fascia boards to the deck, install them now in the same manner as the riser boards (See *OPTION*, next page).

15 Cut and install the stair treads with pairs of 2½-in. deck screws, mitering the ends of the

FIGURE O: Construct box frames that match the tread depth of the rest of the deck stairs. Set them on timber posts and screw the boxes to the deck joists.

FIGURE P: Attach stair treads to the tops of the box frames.

treads where they meet the corner stringers **(See FIGURE M).** Use two tread boards of equal width for wide treads and butt the inside tread board against the riser. As with decking, splices between tread boards should occur directly over a framing member to provide adequate support. Drill pilot holes before driving screws near the ends of tread boards.

16 For our project deck, we chose box-frame steps to transition from the lower deck platform to the ground. Box-frame steps are not supported by concrete footings but normally rest directly on the ground. We decided to use 5 × 6 treated posts as "footings" beneath our box-frame steps and dug 3-in. trenches to set the posts half their thickness below grade **(See FIGURE N).** Be sure the posts are level in the trenches.

17 Construct treated-wood boxes that match the tread depth of the rest of the deck stairs. Miter-cut the ends of boxes that join at the deck corners. Snap chalk lines where the top edges of the boxes will meet the deck joists. Set the boxes onto the timber footings, align them to the chalk lines and attach the boxes to the deck joists with 2½-in. deck screws driven every 12 in. Reinforce the box frames with perpendicular "webs" spaced every 16 in. **(See FIGURE O).**

18 Attach tread boards to the tops of the box frames with 2½-in. deck screws, screwing into the webs. Use two screws per joint **(See FIGURE P).**

Options for fascia installation

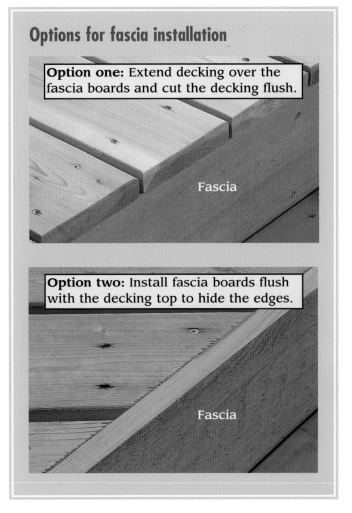

Option one: Extend decking over the fascia boards and cut the decking flush.

Fascia

Option two: Install fascia boards flush with the decking top to hide the edges.

Fascia

Railings & accessories

The numerous photos of successful deck projects sprinkled throughout this book have a common characteristic that sets them apart from ordinary decks that have gone unnoticed: the accessories. Uniquely designed railings that echo the setting of the deck, built-in benches and planters, overhead arbor-and-trellis structures . . . it's in these original touches that a deck can truly stand out from the crowd.

While some deck accessories are mainly decorative or fulfill a nonessential function, railings are indispensable features that are required by building codes on any deck that's more than 30 in. above the grade. To protect deck occupants from falling and becoming injured, the deck railing should be at least 36 in. high. And recently, a lot of news has been made in the building trades about the revised rules governing the spacing of the balusters. Previously, balusters could be as far apart as 6 in. But it was determined that gaps of that width pose a safety risk to small children, who in many cases managed to get their heads wedged in between the balusters. Under current code, railing balusters must be no more than 4 in. apart (See page 153).

But in addition to safety protection, railings contribute much to the overall appearance of a deck by giving it strong vertical lines and sometimes new textures. The classic railing design features 2 × 2 balusters attached to stringers that run between posts. The upper stringer is usually treated with a cap rail. But more ambitious designers have found that there are many creative ways to shake up the classic look and add even more interest to your deck project. Step-downs and curves are two popular ways to create a custom appearance, as are selecting unique building materials and incorporating other features (such as planters or benches) into the railing structure.

When choosing a railing style and any other permanent deck accessories, try to develop designs that share some common features with other parts of your deck, house or yard.

A simple planter box presents a perfect opportunity to make good use of any leftover deck supplies.

Built-in benches can be supported by posts attached to the undercarriage of the deck, or suspended from heavy vertical members, as in the above deck that's attached to timbers supporting an arbor.

Railings amplify angles. If you've gone to the effort of creating a deck with a complex footprint, show off your carpentry abilities by adding a railing that commands attention, like the one shown to the left.

Accessories abound in this well-equipped deck. Built-in seating, an overhead arbor, finely crafted railings and even an outdoor kitchen center make for a very unique and efficient outdoor living space.

Non-traditional materials, like the galvanized tubing used to make horizontal siding on this deck, add new textures and a sense of fun.

Steep slopes require that you take extra care to create a sturdy railing structure that does not interfere with the view.

Post caps and finials add flair to railing posts and to newel posts (the end posts on step railings). Wood caps and finials should be of the same material as the rest of the railing, but contrasting metal caps can be used effectively.

Balusters can be made from plain 2 × 2 stock, or you can dress up railings by using premilled balusters with decorative profiles.

Molded handrails may be required to provide a convenient hand grasp for people using the stairs. Most fit over 2 × 2 railing stringers

Railing requirements

Most building codes require decks that are more than 30 in. above the ground to have railings. Stairways with three or more steps also must have railings on one, or sometimes both sides of the stairs. Many codes require that stair railings have a grippable handrail (See photo above). Typically railings must extend a minimum of 34 in. to 36 in. above the deck surface. They need to be strong enough to provide support when people lean against them or even sit on them. Also, the railing should not have openings wider than 4 in., to prevent toddlers from squeezing through the railing. The code restricting baluster spacing contains a simple test for enforcing the code: a 4-in.-dia. sphere must not be able to pass between any two balusters in the railing. Nor should it be able to pass between the lower stringer and the deck surface. To be on the safe side, lay out balusters so they're no more than about 3¾ in. apart.

4-in.-dia. sphere

FIGURE A: Drill two 1-in.-dia., ½-in.-deep countersunk holes in the outside face of the notched area of each post, then drill a ⅜-in.-dia. pilot hole through each counterbore.

FIGURE B: Attach the top and bottom notched posts to the deck and the stair stringers with lag bolts. Check the posts with a carpenter's level to ensure that they're plumb.

Railings

The following pages show how to attach a railing to a short flight of steps. On stairways up to 8 ft. long, you'll need four posts — two at the top of the stairs (typically notched over the face of the end or header joist) and two at the bottom, fastened to the stringers near the first or second riser or anchored into the ground next to the stringers. On longer flights of stairs, you'll probably need to install a third post midway between the end posts. You can also adapt the stair railing design we show here to wrap railings around the perimeter of your deck, as we did for our project deck. Check building codes in your area for all railing requirements when you design your railings.

1 Measure the two railing posts for the top of the stairway and cut the posts to length — we used 4 × 4s for our posts. ***Note: be sure to account for the length of the post that will butt against the face of***

the end or header joist for fastening purposes plus the full post height above the deck platform. Use a reciprocating saw to cut a 1½-in.-deep notch along the face of one end of each post. The notch dimensions should match the length of the stair riser plus the thickness of the decking. Cut and notch the posts for the bottom of the staircase in the same fashion as the top two posts, but add an extra foot to the overall height of the bottom post or posts so they can be trimmed to the correct height once the layout is established. For the lag screws, drill two 1-in.-dia. × ½-in. deep counterbore holes with ⅜-in. pilot holes on the outside face of the notched areas **(See FIGURE A).**

2 Attach the top and bottom notched posts to the deck and stringers with ⅜ × 3-in. galvanized lag screws and washers, checking the posts with a carpenter's level to ensure that they're plumb **(See FIGURE B).** Be sure

FIGURE C: Tack the top rail into position on the inside faces of the stair posts and mark the cutoff height for trimming the bottom posts. The angle of the rail should be the same as the angle created by the noses of the stair treads.

FIGURE D: Use a reciprocating saw to trim the bottom posts to height, cutting along the line established by dry-fitting the top rail.

FIGURE E: Cut the ends of the top rails along the angled cutting lines so the rails will fit between the inside faces of the posts.

to keep the different post lengths in mind when attaching the four posts—longer posts get attached to the bottom of the staircase.

3 Position a top-rail board along the inside faces of the posts and angle it downward so that the top edge of the board marks the code-required height for the stair railing at both posts. Check this height at both post locations to make sure the distance to the treads is equal (be sure to measure from comparable points on the posts), then temporarily tack the board in place. Draw a trimming line along the top of the top rail where it intersects the bottom post **(See FIGURE C)**. Also mark the angles on the top rails where they cross the inside faces of the posts—the ends of the top rails will be trimmed so the rail can fit between the posts. Remove the top rails.

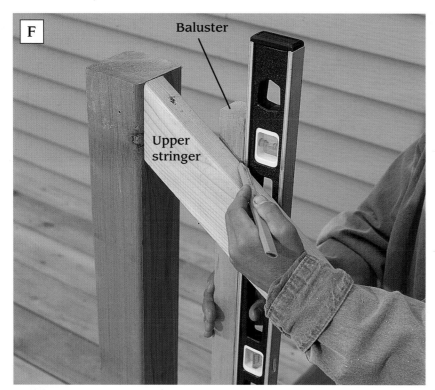

FIGURE F: Screw the top rails into place with 3-in. galvanized deck screws. Set a baluster into place against the outside face of the top rail and check it for plumb with a carpenter's level. Mark where it meets the top edge of the top rail.

4 Trim off the tops of the bottom posts with a reciprocating saw, following the angled trimming line you drew in *Step 3* **(See FIGURE D).**

5 Cut the 2 × 4 top rails to length along the angled cutting lines, using a power miter saw or circular saw **(See FIGURE E).**

6 Attach the top rails between the top and bottom posts with 3-in. galvanized deck screws. Next, determine the distance between 2 × 2 balusters, spaced evenly between the top and bottom posts along the length of the angled top rails. Set the first baluster into position on the top rail so that it is plumb with the nearest post and long enough to reach the bottom of the stair stringer (our balusters are fastened to the outsides of the top rails and down the full width of each stringer). Mark the cutting angle at the top of the baluster **(See FIGURE F).** Since the length and angle of each baluster on the stair rail will not change, use

FIGURE G: Use the first baluster as a template for marking the rest of the balusters, and cut them to size. Use a spacer block between balusters when you attach them to the top rails.

FIGURE H: Measure the distance between the railing posts to determine the spacing for the deck rail balusters (See page 153). The spacing should remain consistent around the entire deck, without exceeding the maximum spacing requirements set by the building codes in your area.

FIGURE I: Gang-cut the deck railing balusters to size on a power miter box. Tack a spacer block to your work table and index off of it to cut all of the balusters to the same size.

FIGURE J: Cut and attach handrails to the stair and deck railings, centering the handrails across the width of the posts. Fasten the railings from below by driving screws up through the top rails and into the bottom faces of the handrails, following a diagonal line.

this first baluster as a template for marking the rest of the balusters, and gang-cut them all to size. ***NOTE: To add visual appeal, we bevel-cut the bottoms of each baluster to align with the bottoms of the stringer.***

7 Attach the balusters to the top rails and stringers with 2½-in galvanized deck screws, using a spacer block between each baluster to maintain equal spacing **(See FIGURE G).** Drive two screws per joint.

8 Measure, cut and notch the posts for the perimeter deck railings and attach them to the deck using the technique outlined in *Step 1.* Install 2 × 4 leveled top rails between the deck railing posts, using 2½-in. deck screws. Measure and cut balusters to fit between the deck railing posts and measure the space between posts to determine baluster spacing. Adjust as necessary so the baluster spacing remains consistent around the deck perimeter **(See FIGURE H).**

9 Gang-cut the deck railing balusters on a power miter box. Use a stop block to ensure that the balusters are uniform in length **(See FIGURE I).** Install the deck railing balusters, attaching them to the deck and the top rails with 2½-in. deck screws.

10 Cut handrails for the stair and deck railings and center them over the width of the posts (we used 2 × 6s, but check the building codes in your area for allowable handrail size). Drive 2½-in. deck screws up though the top rails and into the bottom face of the handrail to fasten the handrail in place **(See FIGURE J).** Attaching them in this fashion hides the screw heads from view for a more finished look. You can also purchase molded handrail (See page 153) at most lumberyards and home centers.

Skirting options

Hide the unsightly crawlspace beneath a deck and discourage dogs, cats, raccoons or other pests from taking refuge under the deck by installing pre-fabricated lattice panels. If you don't care for the look of lattice panels, you can use just about any exterior wood to create your own skirt boards. For example, short cedar fence boards would have been highly suitable as a skirting material for the deck shown here.

Start the skirting project by attaching 2 × 2 or 2 × 4 nailers across the deck posts with deck screws **(See Top photo).** Install vertical nailers along the posts to support the ends of the lattice panels where they butt against one another.

Cut the lattice panels to size using a circular saw equipped with a fine-tooth plywood blade. When trimming the lattice panels to size, clamp them with cauls on both sides of the cutting line to keep the slats from separating and try to avoid cutting through the staples that hold the lattice strips together. Attach the panels to the nailers with deck screws **(See Bottom photo).** Drill pilot holes to avoid splitting the thin lath strips.

Attach nailing strips to the deck posts to create a surface for attaching the skirting.

Use deck screws to attach the skirting material (lattice panels are used above). Using screws allows you to remove the panels easily to access the area below the deck.

Benches

Built-in benches can provide both a practical and decorative touch to deck platforms. As you plan your your deck layout, take into account how you intend to use the deck and locate the benches accordingly. While there are many bench designs, most built-in benches rest on extended posts attached directly to the deck substructure for support. It's most practical to install the bench posts before you lay the decking.

1 Mark locations for the bench posts on the joists or beams. For our project deck, we used 4 × 4 posts. Cut the posts to height (usually around 18 in. above the deck) and attach the bench posts to the beams or joists with ⅜ × 4–in. lag screws, fitted with washers **(See FIGURE A).**

2 Build the seat frames for the benches, which usually consist of 2 × 4s joined to the bench posts with 2½-in. deck screws **(See FIGURE B).** Plan the seat depth to be 14 to 16 in. deep. We angled the ends of our benches to complement the corner angles of the deck platforms.

3 Attach the seat boards. Use the same type of lumber as you'll use for for the decking and fasten the seat boards with 2½-in. deck screws **(See FIGURE C).** Ease the edges and corners of the seat boards and sand them with medium-grit sandpaper.

FIGURE A: Cut the deck posts to length and attach them to the deck joists or beams with lag bolts and washers.

FIGURE B: Build the bench seat frames from 2 × 4s. The seat frames can either be rectangular for straight runs or L-shaped for corners. the above frames angle inward at the ends to echo the angles of the deck platform.

FIGURE C: Attach the seat boards to the seat frames with 2½-in. deck screws. Overhang the ends of the seat boards and trim them to length once they're installed. For benches that wrap around an outside corner, miter the seat boards in the corner for a more finished appearance.

Finishing

Decks are usually finished with either a clear, water-resistant top-coat or with exterior wood stain. In both cases, the primary objective is to protect the wood from rot and to preserve the color. Untreated deck woods, like cedar, usually turn gray as they're exposed to the weather (although in more natural settings the gray, weathered appearance can be quite appealing).

In some cases (particularly if you've used pressure-treated lumber to build your deck), painting may be a desirable finishing option. If you choose to go this route, use oil-based paint that contains abrasive silica particles. Standard porch enamel will become extremely slippery when wet. If your local building center doesn't stock silica-blended deck paint, you can usually get them to mix some in. Make sure to stir the paint well before applying it. A paint roller with an extension pole is the best tool for painting the main surface. Use a brush for details and to get paint down in between deck boards.

Tips for finishing your deck

• Do not apply deck finish in cold weather (below 50° for most products). You'll likely end up having to remove the finish and reapply it on a warmer day.

• Use a sprayer to apply clear sealant. If you don't own a compressor-driven sprayer, you can get by with a simple mechanical sprayer like the one shown on the following page.

• Dip smaller deck parts in a trough of finishing material before installing them for thorough penetration and coverage. To make a dipping trough, simply lay a piece of heavy sheet plastic over a frame (deck posts laid next to each other on-edge can be used to make the frame).

• Select a finish that can be refreshed without the need to remove the old finish. Many penetrating clear finishes can simply be reapplied year after year to keep your deck looking fresh and new.

Deck-finishing products include clear wood sealer-preservative (left) or an oil-based deck staining-sealer (right). Follow the manufacturer's instructions for the correct application method.

Smooth out rough areas on all exposed deck surfaces with medium-grit sandpaper. If your deck is built from cedar or treated lumber, wear a respirator to protect yourself from inhaling irritants.

Vacuum the deck before finishing. Use a wet/dry shop vacuum to remove sawdust and sandpaper grit.

Use a low-pressure sprayer to apply clear wood sealer-preservative to deck surfaces. For stain-sealers, brush or roll on the finish or use a compressor-driven paint sprayer.

Part 2
Yard & Garden Structures

Introduction

For most of us, yards and gardens are extensions of our homes into the outdoors. They expand available living space, providing refreshing places to putter, relax and entertain. But to function well as parts of the home, your yard and garden may need some structural improvement. Maybe what's lacking is more shade or a private place to put a comfy chair. It could be that your garden is missing a crowning touch, like an arched gateway or a landscape bridge to showcase your flowers and other ornamental plants. Or it could be that your needs are entirely practical — a way to extend the growing season of your spinach or a place to store all your gardening and landscaping tools, including that lawn tractor and garden tiller.

Whatever the case, you'll find a wide range of solutions featured in the pages of *Part 2 — Yard & Garden Structures*. The heart of this part of *Outdoor Living* is a collection of nine yard and garden projects you can build, covering a range of uses and levels of construction complexity. You'll find everything from a screened-in gazebo that will challenge your building skills to a simple compost bin you can assemble in just a few hours. Other projects include an arbor/trellis that creates an airy room in the out-of-doors, a handsome gateway to frame the entryway to a garden, and an attractive footbridge to span a waterway, pond or planting bed. We've also included no-nonsense plans for a stick-built tool shed and cold frame.

Two projects — a tractor shed and greenhouse — are built from kits. Kits can be a sensible alternative to building from scratch for many reasons. Time is a precious commodity these days. A kit saves you time at the lumberyard or home center, because you don't need to create elaborate shopping lists first, pick through stacks of lumber or drive back and forth to buy more supplies when you unexpectedly run low. Kits come with nearly everything required for installation, and it doesn't take a shop-full of tools to get good results. You may be surprised by how easy it is to build a structure that seemed just a little beyond your skills, your available time and even your project budget.

Though some of the projects here may seem ambitious at first glance, don't be daunted. Each yard and garden structure is presented in methodical detail, complete with dimensioned drawings, scores of full-color photos and illustrations, or both, as well as thorough step-by-step instructions. Most projects also include an exhaustive cutting list to make your calculations easy. From layout to setting posts and from framing to installing ornamental trim, every major construction phase is clearly explained.

In the end, regardless of whether you erect an arbor from scratch or a shed from a prefabricated kit, you'll have the satisfaction of building it yourself, with sensible information guiding you every step of the way. But more importantly, you'll finish the "remodeling" your outdoor "living room" has needed all along.

A few tools, a stack of lumber and some hard work are the basic ingredients for making any outdoor structure. But along with these critical elements, you'll need a solid recipe — a well-conceived plan that combines the ingredients, safely and efficiently.

OUTDOOR BUILDING BASICS

Once you've selected that perfect shed, footbridge or gazebo project for your yard, it's important to organize your efforts systematically so the process of building your project will go smoothly and successfully. The pages that follow cover the kinds of issues you'll need to address as you proceed. In brief, here is an overview of some key points to keep in mind.

Select a site

Regardless of which type of yard or garden structure you're planning, do not underestimate the importance of selecting the best site for the project. Likely as not, the structure you'll erect will become a long-term fixture on your property. Choose a spot that will maximize the utility of your project and beautify your surroundings. For instance, if you plan to build an unscreened gazebo, steer clear of shady, damp areas that attract pests like mosquitoes. If you are building an arbor/trellis, track the sunlight at different times and anticipate how your new arbor will eventually shade the area around it. Be sure that nearby plants can tolerate partial or full shade, and plan accordingly. Even though a tool shed may be most convenient if it is positioned near the edge of your property, your next-door neighbor will probably have a view of that shed on a daily basis, too. It's always a good idea to share your plans with the neighbors before you build, so there will be no surprises or ill feelings afterward.

Apply for a permit

Assume that any permanent structure you build will be subject to local building codes and will require a building permit. It always pays to check with your local building department and apply for the proper permit or permits whenever you build. The permit cost generally is affordable, and you'll benefit from your local building inspector's expertise when it comes to constructing a project that meets standards for public safety and solid construction. If you decide to forego the permit and the inspector pays you a visit, you may be subject to fines and even have to remove or disassemble all or part of your project so the inspector can review your work in stages. Consider a permit to be as much a part of the building process as choosing a design, buying materials or driving that first nail.

Gather your tools

You won't need a workshop full of tools to build most of the projects in this book, but a selection of the right tools will make your work easier and probably help you produce better results. See pages 168 to 169 for a review of the essential tools to consider renting, borrowing or buying, so you'll have them on hand right from the start.

Shop for building materials wisely

It's important to set a project budget up front and to stick to it as your project develops. But don't let the initial sticker shock kill your inspiration. Almost every building material you'll need to buy will be sold in a number of options and ranges of cost. Shop wisely. If your trellis project budget is tight, estimate what you might save by building with pressure-treated lumber instead of cedar or redwood. The cost savings might surprise you.

Siting a project: Move from rough ideas to specific layout

In many cases, you will have a number of possibilities for siting your new structure in your yard. To determine which spot will work best, start by asking some general questions, such as how its location will impact your other yard features, like flower beds and walkways, as well as sunny and shady areas and your general sight lines. Use extension cords, rope or a garden hose to "rough out" the shape of your project and to help get a sense for how its overall proportions will integrate with the rest of the yard. Once you've selected a site, develop an accurate layout. Using stakes or batterboards, outline the site and identify key points where digging needs to occur. Keep in mind that you still may need to move your building site if you discover too many surprises, like rocks and roots, when digging.

Before you start digging, **contact your local utility companies to flag buried power lines or gas and plumbing pipes. These companies usually will stake out rights-of-way for you at no charge to avoid the possibility of having you cut a cable or pipe. And don't forget about your own utilities. Make sure you won't be interfering with your own well, septic tank or underground sprinkler system.**

OUTDOOR BUILDING GUIDELINES

❑ **Watch out for buried lines.** Contact your local public utilities to identify the location of buried power lines and gas lines before you dig. Utilities will usually provide line location identification as a free service.

❑ **Research building codes.** Most municipalities enforce outdoor building restrictions. Footing and framing requirements on outdoor structures as well as minimum distance from city land and other property lines are common areas subject to regulation.

❑ **Discuss plans with your neighbors.** Your outdoor building project will likely be within the field of vision of your neighbors. As a courtesy, share plans with neighbors and give them the chance to raise objections or concerns before you start working.

❑ **Be aware of your physical limits.** Working outdoors can be highly strenuous, especially on hot, humid days. Drink plenty of water and take breaks when you can. Work with a partner, if possible.

Key information for permit applications:

• Plot location and complete address where the project will be built

• A site drawing that identifies the location of your project in relation to other permanent structures and property lines

• Detailed elevation and plan drawings that indicate overall size, materials and types of fasteners to be used

• Your estimated building cost

• Anticipated completion date

PERMITS

Whether or not you need a building permit to erect permanent outdoor structures depends on the type and size of the project and your local codes. In some places, the exterior structures presented in this book may be well outside the purview of the local building inspector. But in others, you will need to apply for a permit and have the inspector pay a visit or two to the worksite.

How do you know if you need a permit? Ask! Even before finalizing your design, consult the municipal building and zoning department where you apply for permits. These folks will lead you through the application procedure. In most cases, you'll need to complete a form that describes your project, including overall dimensions, construction details and approximate cost. You might have to submit a sketch showing where the new construction will be located in relation to your house and property lines. The permit fee is usually based on a percentage of the project's cost.

Regulations for houses are far more complex than those that govern garden outbuildings. Your inspector's primary concerns probably will be setback requirements and sound construction practices. Setback requirements refer to the minimum distance a structure must be from your property lines.

As far as sound construction practices are concerned, your building inspector can let you know of particular code requirements that apply in your area.

Work safely

Safety is no less of an issue when you are building outdoors than it is when you are working within the confines of your basement or garage workshop. You'll need protective goggles to shield your eyes when using striking tools, driving fasteners, cutting lumber or operating power equipment. Ear protection is advisable if you'll be using a circular saw, router or gas-powered equipment for long periods of time.

When cutting, routing or sanding pressure-treated lumber, wear a dust or particle mask, and do not incinerate wood scraps when you are finished. If you finish your project with a spray-on wood preservative, paint or stain, wear a cartridge-style respirator to protect your lungs from airborne particles.

Building taller outdoor structures will likely require a ladder and possibly even scaffolding. Follow the safety ratings for load and height as specified on this equipment, and exercise extra precaution when carrying supplies or operating power tools on a ladder.

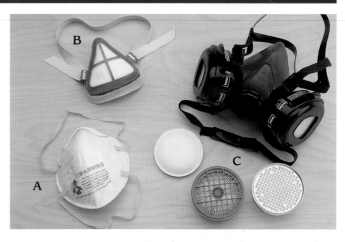

Protect against dust and fumes. A particle mask (A) or dust mask (B) are designed to keep out finer particles, like sawdust, but neither will protect you from fumes or particles from spray-on finishes. In these instances, choose a respirator (C) with the appropriate filter or cartridge instead.

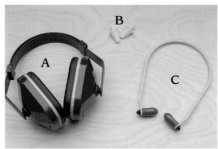

Protect your hearing when operating gas-powered machinery or most power tools. Earmuffs (A), expanding ear plugs (B) or corded ear inserts (C) all are good choices, but be sure they have a noise reduction rating (NRR) of at least 25 decibels for best hearing protection.

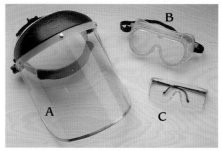

Shield your eyes from dust, wood chips and other flying debris by wearing a face shield (A), safety goggles (B) or safety glasses (C). Do not assume that your prescription glasses offer enough protection — most do not — and they won't shield your eyes from the sides.

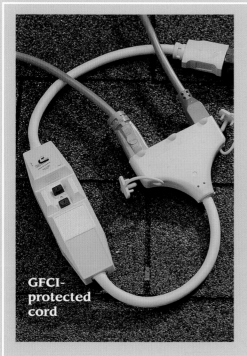

GFCI-protected cord

WORKING WITH POWER

When using power tools outdoors, avoid working in damp conditions. Also, make sure tools are plugged into a GFCI-protected outlet. GFCIs (ground-fault circuit interrupters) instantaneously cut off power if the tool or power cord short-circuits. Plug-in types are available for unprotected outlets. Or, you can buy a GFCI-protected extension cord like the one shown to the left. Also, make sure the electrical circuit has enough ampacity to handle the power tools and equipment you'll be using. A 20-amp, 110-volt circuit will handle most portable and stationary power tools. Don't overload circuits by running too many tools at once.

Ladder ratings are printed on labels that are required by law on any new ladder you purchase. Make sure your ladder is designed to support enough load and to be used in exterior conditions. Choose a Type I or Type II class extension ladder. These ratings indicate the safe weight a ladder will bear: 250 lb. for a Type I ladder; 225 lb. for Type II; and 200 lb. for a Type III. The same strength ratings are applied to stepladders.

Tools for Exterior Construction

Part of what makes building an outdoor structure enjoyable is that you don't need a shop full of high-precision woodworking tools to tackle the job. However, adding a few more tools to your arsenal and renting a few others will speed your building process, improve your accuracy and almost invariably save you time and labor in the long run. And these days, more and more power tools are cordless, which really helps when you are building outdoors and at a distance from the nearest power source. Here is an overview of the tools you may want to buy, borrow or rent when building your project.

Power tools for outdoor building will dramatically speed the process of cutting and fastening parts, and the assortment shown here is easy to transport to your jobsite. A few you'll want to consider using are: (A) power miter saw; (B) portable table saw; (C) circular saw (preferably a worm-drive saw); (D) cordless drill/driver with replaceable battery pack; (E) ½-in. corded drill; (F) reciprocating saw.

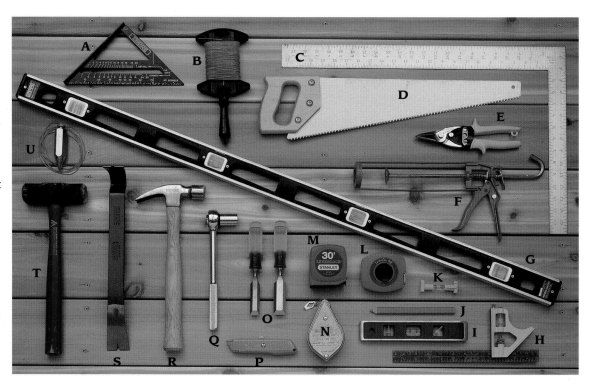

A basic set of hand tools for building outdoor structures includes: (A) speed square; (B) mason's string; (C) framing square; (D) hand saw; (E) aviator snips; (F) caulk gun; (G) carpenter's level (4 ft.); (H) combination square; (I) spirit level; (J) pencil; (K) line level; (L) 50 ft. roll tape; (M) rigid tape measure; (N) chalkline; (O) wood chisels; (P) utility knife; (Q) socket wrench; (R) hammer; (S) flat pry bar; (T) hand maul; (U) plumb bob.

A sod kicker is a hand-operated blade attached to a roller that enables you to remove sod in usable strips that can be replanted elsewhere. It shears away an even top layer of turf. Unless you are planning to remove sod often, rent this tool rather than buy it.

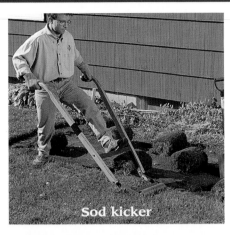

Sod kicker

A plate vibrator compacts subbase material more quickly and easily than a hand tamper, and it's relatively inexpensive to rent. When pouring a concrete slab, you'll want to use a plate vibrator first to ensure that the subbase beneath the concrete is compacted uniformly.

Plate vibrator (power tamper)

PNEUMATIC NAIL GUNS

Pneumatic nail guns, powered by compressed air, offer several advantages over driving screws or hammering nails. A squeeze of the trigger both drives and countersinks the nail, and you usually can keep one hand free to hold your work. A variety of nail options are available for these tools so you can drive everything from brads to heavy framing nails. You'll need an air compressor to power most guns, but cartridge-style nailers are also available and require no compressor. Pneumatic nailers and compressors are expensive to buy but widely available to rent.

TOOL OPTIONS FOR DIGGING POST HOLES & FOOTINGS

"Clamshell"-type posthole digger

Two-man gas-powered auger

One-man gas-powered auger

If you have only a few shallow footings or post holes to dig, use a clamshell-type posthole digger (left). For deeper or larger holes, or if you have a lot of holes to dig, rent a gas-powered auger (right and inset) from a tool rental shop. Gas-powered augers come in one- and two-person models and will save you considerable time and labor over hand digging. Depending on the model, the weight of the motor either helps to drive the auger into the ground or makes withdrawing the auger easier.

Lumber for outdoor building projects

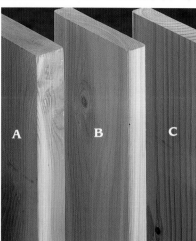

Parts of your outdoor structure that are sheltered from the elements or painted can be made of ordinary dimensional softwood (A). Use cedar (B) or pressure-treated lumber (C) for parts like posts and railings that come in contact with the ground or must remain exposed. Cypress and redwood are other options, depending on your region.

Options for creating footings

Masonry-related materials for footings include: (A) concrete tube forms (8- and 12-in.-dia. shown); (B) premixed concrete; (C) precast concrete piers (an alternative to pouring footings).

BUYING LUMBER & FASTENERS

Lumber, fasteners and miscellenous metal hardware will make up the bulk of your project expense. Study your lumber and fastener options so you can maximize your project budget dollars.

Lumber: When you go to buy lumber, make up a shopping list with columns that identify the sizes, lengths and quantity you need. For each lumber item, add 5% to 10% extra to allow for waste, lumber defects and building errors. If possible, hand-pick your lumber at the yard, even if you plan to have it delivered, to get the best boards in the stack.

Creating a shopping list for your project can be time-consuming, but it will save countless trips to the lumberyard. Making a shopping list is not simply a matter of adding up the total length of all your project parts and dividing by common board lengths to determine the amount you'll need. Instead, you must consider how your project parts will fit on the board lengths you buy and how you can make most efficent use of the lumber. It helps to draw various board sizes to smaller scale and sketch your parts right on the boards. Use these sketches as cutting diagrams later.

Fasteners & hardware: Outdoor structures should be built with corrosion-resistant fasteners. The most common and least expensive option is to buy galvanized steel fasteners. However, galvanized coatings will react with the tannins in some woods, like cedar, creating small black spots. The stains are harmless, but they can be unsightly. Other fastener options that won't stain your wood include teflon-coated, aluminum, stainless-steel and brass, but these will be more expensive and are not made in all styles.

A host of galvanized metal brackets is available for connecting posts, beams and joists. While this hardware is sturdy and convenient, it isn't particularly attractive for connections that show. For aesthetic reasons, we opted to use other fastening methods, like toe-nailing, for most of the projects in this book.

Shopping for building supplies to construct an outdoor structure can be a bit daunting, especially if you've never built a sizable project before. You'll likely need framing lumber, plywood sheathing, a variety of screws, nails, bolts and nuts and an assortment of galvanized metal hanger hardware. If your structure has a roof, you'll need shingles and building paper, roofing nails, roofing cement and metal drip edge. Depending on the condition of the construction site, you may need to buy a load of sub-base material (usually compactible gravel) along with suitable posts and piers or tube forms and concrete.

To make the shopping task less intimidating and a little more affordable, here are a few tips to keep in mind:

• Think of your project as a series of smaller projects that start from the ground up. Make a separate shopping list for your project's base, framing and sheathing, windows or doors, decking and railings and roof. Shorter lists will give each trip to the home center or lumberyard more focus and will help you avoid estimation errors.

• If possible, buy your supplies over an extended period of time, so you can do some materials comparison shopping and take advantage of sales as they occur.

The following pages cover a variety of building materials you may need for your project.

Coarse sand is used as a base material for setting landscape pavers and natural stones as well as beneath concrete. It offers fair drainage and adequate compaction around posts and piers and beneath slabs.

Pea gravel is used mostly as a drainage material, but it can also double as a border treatment around plantings. It is not recommended for use as a base material beneath pavers or concrete slabs.

Compactible gravel is an inexpensive subbase material used widely for landscape construction projects. Known in some regions as "Class V" or "Class II" (lower numbers denote smaller aggregate), it improves drainage and can be tamped to create a stable base.

River rock is used mostly as a drainage material when backfilling or providing drainage in a post hole. It can also be used for decorative or loose-fill purposes. River rock is sold according to the diameter of the stones (3/8 in., 3/4 in., and 1 1/2 in. are typical). As a general rule, use smaller diameter stones for drainage fill. 1 1/2-in.-dia. river rock is shown here.

Loose-fill choices

If you want to create ground cover around plant bedding areas or simple walkways through your yard and to garden projects, a number of natural loose-fill options are available. Smaller aggregates, mulch and bark are the most common. These materials are commonly sold by the bag or by the yard, depending upon where you shop and how much you need. Examples shown here are: (A) crushed limestone; (B) 3/8- to 3/4-in.-dia. river rock; (C) cypress mulch and; (D) cedar bark chips.

Concrete footings (See pages 185 to 188) extend down into the ground and create a stable base for posts and joists. A footing can be formed by either pouring concrete directly into a hole in the ground or by filling a tubular form (as shown here). Tubular forms keep the sides of the hole from collapsing and they also slow down the curing speed of the concrete, which strengthens it.

Concrete slabs (See pages 285 to 290) provide a broad, stable base and a hard, flat surface for larger structures, like sheds and gazebos. Generally, several inches of earth are removed from the slab area first and replaced with a compacted layer of gravel or sand to drain water away from the slab and keep it from shifting later. A wood form is constructed to give the slab its shape, then wet concrete is poured directly into the form.

ESTIMATING CONCRETE

Concrete is calculated and sold in volume units of cubic feet and cubic yards. You'll need to determine the total volume of concrete required for your footings or slab in order to purchase an accurate amount. If you buy ready-mix concrete that comes delivered in a truck, your supplier will want your estimate in terms of cubic yards. Should you decide to buy premixed dry concrete instead from your local home center, it comes packaged in 60-pound bags that yield ½ cubic ft. Doing the math can be a bit befuddling, especially when it comes to calculating the volume of tubular footings. Fortunately, a handy chart is printed right on the pre-mix bags to help you estimate the number of bags you need for various-sized slabs and footings. Your ready-mix supplier can help you determine yardage if you explain the dimensions of your slab or the diameter, height and number of footings you need to pour. Or, use the chart below to help you figure what you need, based on some common concrete yields. If you calculate your own quantities, round up 10% to be safe.

Concrete quantity	Yields		
	4-IN.-THICK SLAB	8-IN.-DIA. FOOTING	12-IN.-DIA. FOOTING
¼ yard (14 bags*)	20 square ft.	14 @ 16 in. deep 5 @ 42 in. deep	6 @ 16 in. deep 2 @ 42 in. deep
½ yard (27 bags)	40 square ft.	28 @ 16 in. deep 10 @ 42 in. deep	12 @ 16 in. deep 4 @ 42 in. deep
1 yard (54 bags)	80 square ft.	57 @ 16 in. deep 21 @ 42 in. deep	25 @ 16 in. deep 9 @ 42 in. deep

*Bag quantities are 60-pound dry-mixed concrete

Ready-mix. When you purchase concrete and have it delivered, the concrete comes already mixed and ready to pour. Buying ready-mix is economical when you need several yards of concrete. You'll pay a delivery charge regardless of the size of the order, which makes batches of 1 yard or less more expensive. Have helpers with wheelbarrows on hand when the concrete arrives and create a path with boards to protect your lawn and make smooth wheelbarrow runs. You'll need to move quickly.

Rent a mixing trailer when you need more concrete than can feasibly be mixed in a wheelbarrow. You can haul this mixer behind your truck or car. They come powered by either a gas or electric motor. Some trailers can be filled with ready-mix at your concrete supplier so you are ready to pour when you get home.

MIXING CONCRETE YOURSELF

Mixing concrete is hard work, and the logistics can be daunting. You have two options: If your project requires only small amounts — setting posts, for example — consider buying premixed concrete in a bag. It comes already packaged in the proper ratio of portland cement, sand and gravel. All you need to do is add water and blend the mixture in a wheelbarrow with a hoe.

A second alternative is to purchase the ingredients in bulk and mix them yourself — a cheaper but more labor-intensive process. Portland cement is sold in 1-cubic-ft. bags weighing 94 pounds. The gravel and sand are sold in bulk, by weight. If you have a pickup or a trailer, you can buy the ingredients, haul them home and shovel them into piles. Otherwise, you can have sand and gravel delivered by the truckload.

When mixing from scratch in a wheelbarrow, mix the cement and sand first. They must be blended to a uniform color, showing neither light nor dark streaks. Add water little by little, until the entire mixture is evenly moist. Mix in the gravel last. If you add gravel before the water it probably will be too difficult to mix by hand. If you get carried away with the water and the mix seems too soupy, add small amounts of cement, sand and gravel in the same proportions you used in the original mix.

For those instances where you use a power mixer, you'll blend the mixture in a different order. With the mixer stopped, load in the gravel and some water. Start the mixer, and while it is running, add the sand, cement and (as long as the mix seems to need it) more water. Keep the mixer running for at least three minutes, or until the contents are a uniform color. Add water a little at a time until you get a mix of the right consistency. Pour the concrete as soon as possible.

If you are mixing concrete yourself, here are some recommended proportions for slabs and footings.

Slabs (light traffic):
1 part cement, 2 parts sand, four parts gravel

Slabs (heavy traffic):
1 part cement, 1½ parts sand, three parts gravel

Footings:
1 part cement, 2 parts sand, four parts gravel

Treat end grain with sealer. Even if you apply no finish at all to your outdoor project, coat the ends of project parts with waterproofing wood sealer to keep them from absorbing moisture and eventually rotting. This is especially important with posts or joists that come in contact with the ground.

FINISHING PRESSURE-TREATED WOOD

Despite the infusion of chemicals into pressure-treated wood, it still will take finishes such as stains and paints with pleasing results. One thing to keep in mind when finishing treated lumber is that you should let it dry thoroughly first, before topcoating with a finish. The labels on cans of exterior finishes will usually specify a recommended drying time for treated lumber (often several months). Be sure to follow the instructions on the can carefully, just as you would for applying a finish to other exterior woods.

At some point in the building process, you'll find yourself standing in the paint department of the local home center, staring at the wide assortment of finishes available to you. The world of exterior wood finishes used to be simple. Once, there were only three basic categories: paint, stain or varnish. No more. While those broad categories are still useful, they aren't as clear-cut anymore. What, for example, distinguishes paint from solid-color stain?

To choose a finish, first ask yourself what you want the finish to accomplish. The ideal finish would never need maintenance, would keep moisture out of the wood to prevent cracking and cupping, would prevent degradation from the sun's ultraviolet (UV) rays and inhibit fungal growth. There is no such finish, of course. All finishes do provide some protection from moisture, the sun and fungi, but each type of finish is better at some of these jobs than others. And the amount and kind of maintenance required varies with the finish.

In choosing an exterior wood finish, ask yourself a few questions:

• Do I want the wood grain to show through? Or do I need to conceal it?

• How much time and effort am I willing to expend for surface preparation, like priming, before applying the finish?

• Am I willing to spend the time recoating periodically, or do I want the finish to last indefinitely?

• Do I really need to apply a finish at all, or am I willing to allow the wood to age naturally and turn gray?

See the next page for an overview of the basic finish categories available for protecting outdoor structures.

Exterior wood finish options

A. Leave it bare: With rot-resistant woods, like pressure-treated pine, cedar, redwood or white oak, you can forego a finish entirely. The wood will turn to gray slowly, thanks to the UV effects of the sun, but it shouldn't rot and requires no routine maintenance.

B. Paint: Paint does the best overall job of protecting wood outdoors. It provides a tough, protective coating over all kinds of wood, and its pigments block out the sun's UV rays. Be sure to prepare your project for paint with a coat of exterior-grade primer first. If you paint flat walking surfaces, add anti-skid particles to the paint first (most paint suppliers stock them) to keep the final finish from becoming slippery when wet.

C. Solid-color stains: Solid-color stains look and behave like thinned paint, forming a protective, scuff-resistant film over wood surfaces. You can have them mixed in a host of different colors. They're a good choice for projects made of pressure-treated wood or a mix of different woods, because the stain will hide differences in wood tone and grain pattern.

D. Semi-transparent penetrating stains: Semi-transparent stains penetrate the wood surface, are porous and do not form a surface film like paint. As a result, they will not blister or peel even if moisture moves through the wood. Use a penetrating stain when you want to preserve the texture and grain pattern of wood but enhance or change its color. A good choice for all vertical and horizontal wood surfaces, including walkways.

E. Water-repellent preservatives: Water-repellent preservatives are popular treatments, advertised as a way to retain the natural appearance of wood while protecting it from cracking and warping. They contain no pigment and darken the wood only slightly. However, the effectiveness of some preservatives is debatable, since they have been known to peel or allow wood to turn gray unless fortified with plenty of UV inhibitors. Plan to recoat annually.

F. Varnishes: Exterior-grade varnish, often called marine or spar varnish, provides a beautiful glossy finish, but it can fail if the wood is not protected from direct exposure to sunlight. Moisture and damaging UV rays can cause the varnish to peel. Professional-grade marine varnishes, intended for finishing boats, are good performers. However, you'll need to apply multiple coats for best protection, and the varnish can be quite expensive. Varnished wood generally requires recoating every year or two when the surface begins to dull.

No finish

Paint

Solid-color stains

Semi-transparent
penetrating stains

Water-repellent
preservatives

Varnishes

ENTERTAINMENT STRUCTURES

Few pleasures in life rival the time spent
outdoors on a beautiful afternoon or evening.
Whether you're relaxing with a good book,
hosting a garden party or barbecue, or simply
soaking up some sun, that time will be even more
enjoyable if your surroundings are pleasant,
attractive and well appointed.
Plantings, groundcovers and the general condition
of your yard go a long way toward letting your
surroundings shine to their fullest potential.
But a perfectly placed, well-crafted structure or two can
be the key ingredient in transforming
a nice yard into a showplace you're proud
to call your outdoor home.

GAZEBO

A luxurious retreat that graces any setting, this gazebo offers the ultimate in sophistication. Follow along as we show you how to build one in your own yard or garden.

All sorts of gazebo designs are possible. We tend to think of them as being hexagonal or octagonal, but a gazebo can be square or rectangular, even oblong. It can stand alone or be incorporated into a deck. Style is a big part of design. We chose a style with a Victorian flavor for our gazebo. The shape of the railing balusters and the corner brackets are the primary contributors to that Victorian flavor.

The construction of this gazebo owes a lot to the prefab units that are so commonplace these days. Many of the parts can be cut in the shop, if you have one, and elements like the railing and the screen frames can be preassembled in a workshop, then hauled to the site for installation.

This gazebo project is not especially complex or time-consuming to make, as far as gazebos go. But neither is it designed with the beginning carpenter in mind. It involves some of the trickier construction techniques, including cutting compound miters, as well as production style manufacturing of some parts (especially the balusters) that would be very unwieldy without good power tools. If you are just beginning to develop your carpentry skills, consider a gazebo kit. And read this chapter closely. It is a thorough treatment of how these charming structures are made.

Gazebo Project:
A 7-step overview

1. Lay out the site & pour the footings (185 to 188)
2. Build the undercarriage (188 to 192)
3. Install the decking (192 to 195)
4. Install the roof supports (195 to 200)
5. Build the roof (200 to 203)
6. Install railings & trim (204 to 207)
7. Finishing touches (208 to 212)

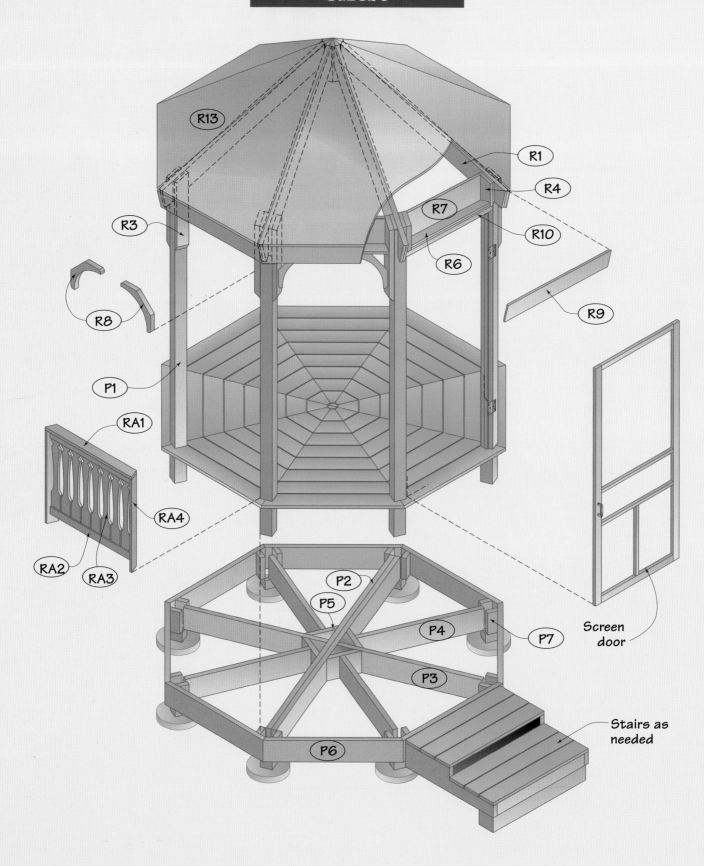

R13

R1

R4

R7

R10

R3

R6

R8

R9

P1

RA1

RA4

RA2

RA3

P2

P5

P4

P7

P3

P6

Screen
door

Stairs as
needed

Cutting List

OVERALL DIMENSIONS ($97\frac{1}{4} \times 97\frac{1}{4} \times 134\frac{5}{8}$")

KEY	PART NAME	QTY.	SIZE	MATERIAL
PLATFORM				
P1	POSTS	8	$3\frac{1}{2} \times 3\frac{1}{2} \times 96\frac{5}{8}$"	CEDAR
P2	DOUBLED JOIST	2	$1\frac{1}{2} \times 7\frac{1}{4} \times 89$"	PRESSURE TREATED
P3	LONG JOIST	2	$1\frac{1}{2} \times 7\frac{1}{4} \times 43$"	PRESSURE TREATED
P4	SHORT JOIST	4	$1\frac{1}{2} \times 7\frac{1}{4} \times 37\frac{11}{16}$"	PRESSURE TREATED
P5	JOIST HUB BLOCKING	4	$1\frac{1}{2} \times 7\frac{1}{4} \times 10\frac{7}{16}$"	PRESSURE TREATED
P6	RIM JOIST	8	$1\frac{1}{2} \times 7\frac{1}{4} \times 38\frac{9}{16}$"	CEDAR
P7	RIM JOIST BLOCKING	16	$1\frac{1}{2} \times 3\frac{1}{2} \times 7\frac{1}{4}$"	CEDAR
P8	DECKING - RING 1	8	$1 \times 5\frac{1}{2} \times 39\frac{3}{16}$"	CEDAR
P9	DECKING - RING 2	8	$1 \times 5\frac{1}{2} \times 34\frac{3}{8}$"	CEDAR
P10	DECKING - RING 3	8	$1 \times 5\frac{1}{2} \times 29\frac{5}{8}$"	CEDAR
P11	DECKING - RING 4	8	$1 \times 5\frac{1}{2} \times 24\frac{7}{8}$"	CEDAR
P12	DECKING - RING 5	8	$1 \times 5\frac{1}{2} \times 20\frac{1}{8}$"	CEDAR
P13	DECKING - RING 6	8	$1 \times 5\frac{1}{2} \times 15\frac{5}{16}$"	CEDAR
P14	DECKING - RING 7	8	$1 \times 5\frac{1}{2} \times 10\frac{9}{16}$"	CEDAR
P15	DECKING - RING 8	8	$1 \times 5\frac{1}{2} \times 5\frac{13}{16}$"	CEDAR
P16	DECKING CENTER	1	$1 \times 2\frac{9}{16} \times 2\frac{9}{16}$"	CEDAR
ROOF				
R1	RAFTERS	8	$1\frac{1}{2} \times 5\frac{1}{2} \times 63\frac{1}{2}$"	CEDAR
R2	FILLER BLOCK	6	$1 \times 3\frac{1}{2} \times 9\frac{1}{2}$"	CEDAR
R3	VERTICAL BATTEN	14	$1\frac{1}{2} \times 3\frac{1}{2} \times 24$"	CEDAR
R4	BATTEN AT DOOR	2	$1\frac{1}{2} \times 3\frac{1}{2} \times 5\frac{1}{8}$"	CEDAR
R5	HUB	1	$5\frac{1}{2} \times 5\frac{1}{2} \times 12$"	CEDAR
R6	HORIZONTAL FRIEZE	8	$\frac{3}{4} \times 3\frac{1}{8} \times 30\frac{3}{4}$"	CEDAR
R7	VERTICAL FRIEZE	8	$\frac{3}{4} \times 8\frac{7}{8} \times 28\frac{11}{16}$"	CEDAR
R8	BRACKET	14	$1\frac{1}{2} \times 5\frac{1}{2} \times 15\frac{5}{8}$"	CEDAR
R9	FASCIA	8	$\frac{3}{4} \times 5\frac{3}{4} \times 40$"	CEDAR
R10	DOOR HEADER	1	$1\frac{1}{2} \times 3\frac{1}{2} \times 33\frac{1}{2}$"	CEDAR
R11	FILLER AT HEADER	2	$\frac{3}{4} \times 1\frac{1}{4} \times 33\frac{1}{2}$"	CEDAR
R12	DOOR STOP	3	$\frac{1}{2} \times 1 \times 80$"	CEDAR
R13	SHEATHING	8	$\frac{3}{4} \times 40 \times 58$"	AC PLYWOOD
RAILING				
RA1	CAP RAIL	7	$1 \times \frac{1}{4} \times 33\frac{1}{2}$"	CEDAR
RA2	TOP/BOTTOM RAIL	14	$1\frac{1}{2} \times 2\frac{1}{2} \times 31\frac{3}{8}$"	CEDAR
RA3	BALUSTER	56	$\frac{3}{4} \times 3\frac{1}{2} \times 24$"	CEDAR
RA4	BATTEN	14	$\frac{3}{4} \times 3\frac{1}{2} \times 31$"	CEDAR
SCREEN (QUANTITY TO MAKE 7 SCREENS)				
S1	STILE	14	$\frac{3}{4} \times 1\frac{1}{2} \times 82\frac{3}{4}$"	CEDAR
S2	TOP RAIL	7	$\frac{3}{4} \times 1\frac{1}{2} \times 29$"	CEDAR
S3	BOTTOM RAIL	7	$\frac{3}{4} \times 3\frac{1}{2} \times 29$"	CEDAR
S4	HORIZONTAL MULLION	7	$\frac{3}{4} \times 1\frac{1}{2} \times 29$"	CEDAR
S5	FILLER	7	$\frac{3}{4} \times \frac{3}{4} \times 29$"	CEDAR
S6	MOUNTING BATTEN	8	$\frac{3}{4} \times 1\frac{1}{4} \times 82\frac{3}{4}$"	CEDAR
HARDWARE REQUIRED				
SCREENING		50 linear ft.	32-36" wide roll	
SCREEN DOOR		1	32×80"	
HINGES		2	2×3"	
HANDLE		1		
POST ANCHORS/J BOLTS		8		
BUILDING PAPER			100 sq.ft	
SHINGLES			100 sq.ft	YOUR CHOICE
SCREW EYES & HOOKS		28 PAIR		
CARRIAGE BOLTS		32	$\frac{3}{8} \times 6\frac{1}{2}$"	W/NUTS & WASHERS
DECKING SCREWS		2"		
NAILS				
LAG SCREWS		8	$\frac{5}{16} \times 4$"	W/WASHERS

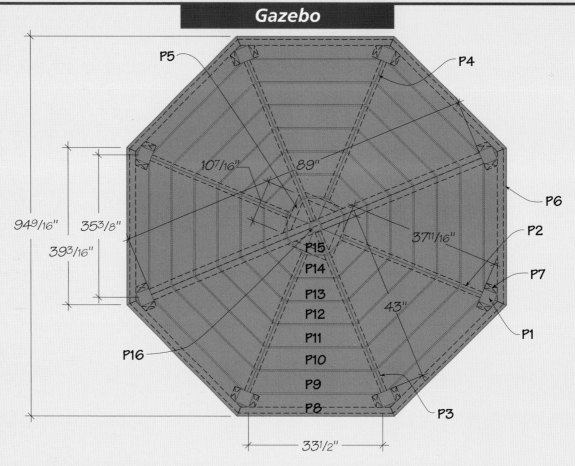

PLAN VIEW - FLOOR PLATFORM (FRAMING/DECKING)

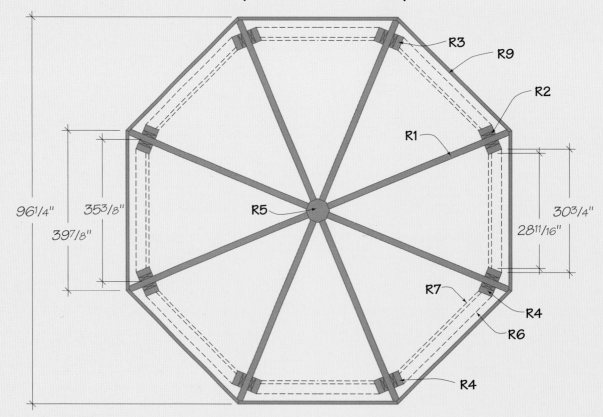

PLAN VIEW - ROOF FRAMING

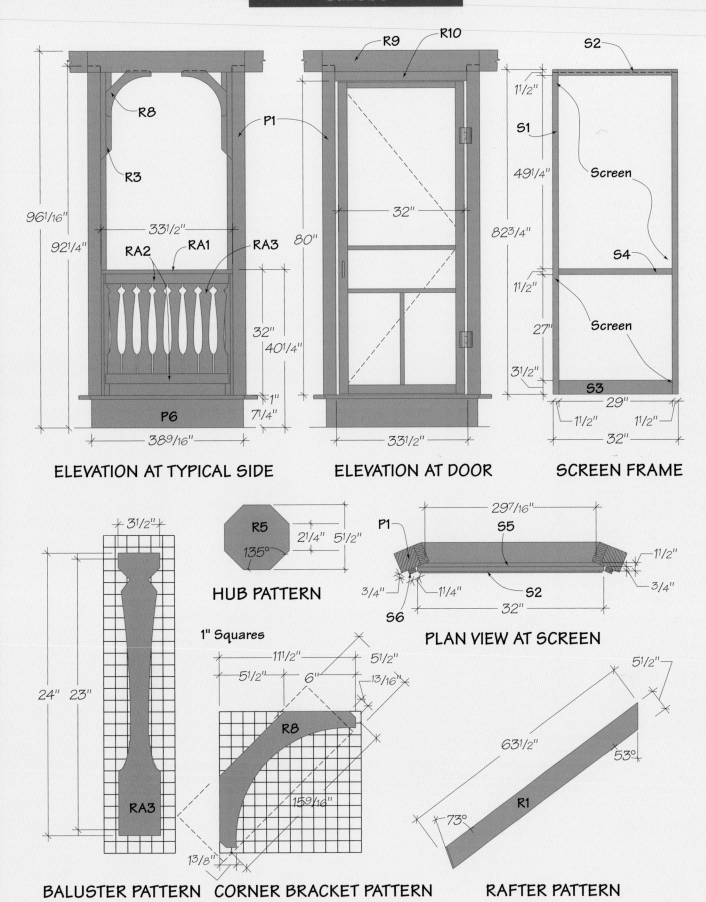

ELEVATION AT TYPICAL SIDE

ELEVATION AT DOOR

SCREEN FRAME

HUB PATTERN

PLAN VIEW AT SCREEN

BALUSTER PATTERN

CORNER BRACKET PATTERN

RAFTER PATTERN

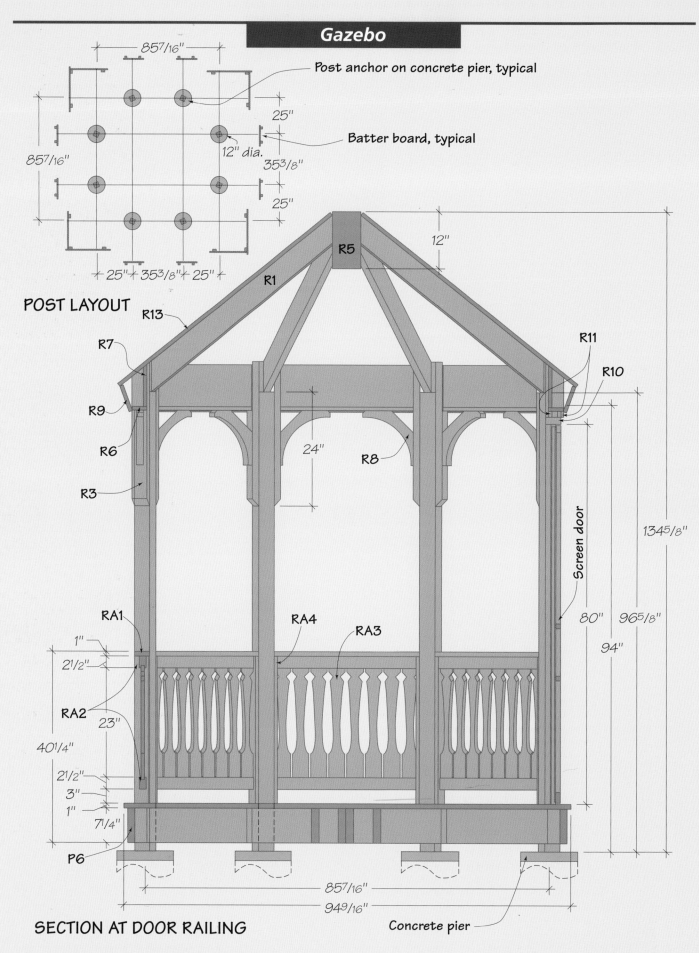

85⁷/₁₆"

Post anchor on concrete pier, typical

25"

Batter board, typical

85⁷/₁₆"

12" dia.

35³/₈"

25"

POST LAYOUT

25" 35³/₈" 25"

R5

12"

R1

R13

R7

R11

R10

R9

R6

24"

R8

R3

134⁵/₈"

Screen door

96⁵/₈"

RA1

RA4

RA3

1"

2¹/₂"

80"

94"

RA2

23"

40¹/₄"

2¹/₂"

3"

1"

7¹/₄"

P6

85⁷/₁₆"

94⁹/₁₆"

SECTION AT DOOR RAILING

Concrete pier

Building a gazebo is a major undertaking for even the most experienced home carpenter. It requires some familiarity with all the basic construction skills, from working with concrete to framing to finish carpentry. It also requires a good deal of organization and project coordination. You'll need to draw up detailed plans, get a permit and arrange to have the structure inspected at key points. But don't be discouraged. After all the hard work and attention to detail, you'll emerge with a classically beautiful outdoor structure that will dramatically improve your ability to enjoy your yard and garden. And if you can manage to build a gazebo, you'll know you can tackle just about any outdoor building project.

ONE: Lay out the the site & pour the footings

Laying out the gazebo building site is best accomplished by driving stakes into the ground and running strings from stake to stake, outlining the perimeter of the project. The strings will help you determine where to remove sod and exactly where to dig holes for post footings. The strings also help you determine when the site is level.

You need some pointed wooden stakes, a small sledge hammer (maul), mason's string, a 4 ft. carpenter's level, a line level, a framing square, and a long tape measure. It's also good to have a helper.

We used batterboards and mason's string to establish the layout for the gazebo posts. Start by setting up stakes and batterboards (the crosspieces on the assemblies) so the batterboard is positioned one or two feet behind a rough corner location. Drive another stake so it forms a perpendicular corner with the first stakes (See Photo 1:1). Then, connect the new stake to the original batterboard with another batterboard (perpendicular

Crosspieces

Photo 1:1 Drive pairs of wood stakes a couple of feet directly behind the corners of the planned project site. Attach horizontal crosspieces to the stakes to form batterboards. By tying mason's strings to the crosspieces of the batterboards and adjusting the height and position of the strings and crosspieces you can pinpoint the post locations for your layout. Here, a third stake and second crosspiece are being installed to form a corner.

Photo 1:2 Even though the gazebo has 8 corners, you'll need to start with a square layout area (See Post Layout illustration, previous page). In the photo, the mason's strings are checked for square using the 3-4-5 triangle method: measure out from the corner 3 ft. in one direction and 4 ft. in the other; mark the points with tape; adjust the positions of the strings until the distance between the points is exactly 5 ft.

to the first) at the same height. Tie a mason's string to each batterboard and stretch them out along what you intend to be the edges of the project's footprint. When you are a foot or two beyond the adjacent corners of the project, set up another batterboard at each corner. Stretch the string tight and tie it to this new stake. Check the string with a line level and adjust the height of one of the new batterboards to bring the string to a level position (See Tip, next page). Use this string as a reference for leveling other strings. Position the bat-

terboards at the opposite corner from the corner at which you started. Tie mason's strings to the batterboards to establish the four corners of the square. As shown, the square should have 85½-in.-long sides.

Check the strings to make sure they are square to one another and the correct distance apart. This will require you to slide each string back and forth along the batterboard it is attached to until the layout is correct. Use a squaring method (such as the 3-4-5 method shown in Photo 1:2) to make sure

1:3

Photo 1:3 Once you have tied and adjusted all the strings to identify the post locations, use a plumb bob to transfer the locations (the points where the strings intersect) to the ground. Drive a stake to mark the position of each post.

1:4

Photo 1:4 The completed layout of the project area identifies exactly where to dig post holes and allows you to gauge the depth of the holes. Mark the positions of the strings on the batter boards, then remove the strings before you start digging. Re-tie the strings so you can check your work when you finish digging.

the strings are square. Mark the position of each string on the batterboards in case they slip out of position or need to be removed temporarily.

Once the corners of the string layout are squared up, set up more batterboards (two per side, spaced evenly, as shown in the *Post Layout* diagram on page 184). Tie mason's strings between opposing, intermediate batterboards, level them and adjust them until the distances between strings match those shown on the diagram. Mark their positions on the batterboards.

Drop a plumb line from each point (eight points in total) where a cross-string is attached to one of the original squared strings *(See Photo 1:3)*. Drive a stake at each spot to mark centerpoints for digging post holes.

Double-check the layout to

LEVELING LINES ON BATTERBOARDS

Line level

Batterboard

To level the mason's strings when using batterboards, suspend a line level from one layout line and adjust the batter board up or down as needed until the layout line is level. Secure the batter board to the stakes at this height. This will set the height "permanently," allowing you to adjust the line from side to side as you square up the layout. Use the height of the first line as the baseline for setting additional lines to the same height.

make sure the corners are square, the strings are the correct distance apart and all the strings are level. Make sure the marks on the batterboards reflect the correct string positions. When you are done leveling the strings and marking the batterboards *(See Photo 1:4)*, you can remove all the strings tem-

DEALING WITH ROOTS & ROCKS WHEN DIGGING

Gas-powered augers will not cut through large roots or magically wind their way past rocks. If you strike a large rock while digging a post hole, you have two options: either grab a shovel and pry bar and see if you can extract or move the offending rock; or relocate the structure.

A large root can be more of a problem. It is very tempting to try to cut through roots with a power auger—it is even reasonable to expect your auger to chew through smaller to medium sized roots. But if you feel the blade begin to bog down, stop the machine immediately. In trying to work through tough obstacles, the blade can become embedded. Since many power augers don't have reverse gearing, a stuck blade presents quite a problem. It will leave you few solutions other than disengaging the motor and trying to turn the drive shaft in a reverse direction with a pipe wrench to free the blade. This is exactly as difficult and laborious as it sounds.

Before you begin digging, arm yourself with a few tools to deal with those unavoidable obstructions: a "clamshell" post hole digger for removing dirt around the obstruction; a heavy pry bar for dislodging stones; and a "spud bar" (a weighted bar with a flat cutting blade) for cutting roots.

And as always, check with your utility companies before digging (See page 164).

Photo 1:5 Dig the post holes. We used a gas-powered auger since our post holes needed to be about 4 ft. deep and there were eight of them. The holes should be at least 18 in. deep and extend a few inches past the frost line for your area. Make sure you have your yard flagged for buried lines before you start digging (See page 8).

Photo 1:6 Set tubular forms (if needed) in the holes and level and plumb the forms. Pack gravel or dirt around the forms to hold them in place.

Photo 1:7 Overfill the forms slightly with concrete, then shape the concrete surface with a masonry trowel to create a slight crown that sheds water.

Photo 1:8 Before the concrete sets, transfer the locations of the post center-points to the footing. Set a J-bolt (for attaching post anchors) into the concrete at each centerpoint. The threaded end should stick up about 1 in.

porarily to create access for digging post holes.

Dig the post holes *(See Photo 1:5)*. A power auger is the quickest tool for creating the post holes, but in rocky or rooty soil, such a machine can be tough for even the burliest of handymen to control. The alternative is a clam-shell post hole digger. By whichever means you choose, dig the post holes, making sure each one extends down below the frost line in your area.

If the soil is firm and your post holes have straight walls, you can pour the concrete directly into the holes. In loose soil conditions, however, tubular forms may be necessary. Cut the forms to length (a reciprocating saw or hand saw works well) and place a form in each post hole (the top should be a couple of inches above grade). Pack gravel around the outside of the form to hold it plumb and centered *(See Photo 1:6)*.

NOTE: Arrange for inspection of the footing holes before pouring concrete.

Calculate the amount of concrete needed to fill the holes/forms to grade and choose a delivery method (See pages 14 to 15). Overfill the forms or post holes slightly with concrete. As you pour the concrete, work the material lightly with a stick to eliminate air bubbles. Trowel the surface to smooth it and to crown it slightly so it sheds water *(See Photo 1:7)*.

Working quickly, re-tie the mason's strings in their marked positions on the batterboards. Use the lines as references for positioning a J-bolt at the centerpoint of each post location (don't just center the bolt on the footing.) Set a J-bolt into the wet concrete at each centerpoint *(See Photo 1:8)*. Allow the concrete to set up overnight before proceeding.

Photo 2:1 Attach a metal post anchor to the J-bolt in each footing. Position the post anchors so one of the nailing flanges is square to the center of the layout. To secure the post anchors, thread a washer over the threaded top of the J-bolt, then tighten a nut onto the bolt with a socket wrench.

Nailing flanges

Photo 2:2 Screw 2 × 4 braces to two adjacent sides of each post, about halfway up. Fit a post level onto each post and use it as a guide for leveling and plumbing the post. When the post is in the correct position, drive a stake into the ground next to the free end of each brace and attach the stake to the brace.

Post level

Photo 2:3 Rip a 22½° bevel on one edge of a 2 × 4 to prepare the stock for cutting the blocking that's attached to the posts. A portable table saw is a perfect tool for performing this operation on-site.

TWO: Build the undercarriage

The undercarriage of the gazebo is composed of the posts and the joists that support the floor platform. The posts must be installed so all the inside faces would be perpendicular to straight lines if they were extended out from the center of the gazebo. The 4 × 4 posts are mounted to the footings with metal post anchors that are attached to the J-bolts set in the footings. The lengths of the posts will vary according to the above-grade height you want for the floor platform. The best bet is to let the posts run overlong; you can trim the tops after the deck is constructed.

To begin setting up the posts, mount all the metal post anchors. Line up the anchors and fasten them to the J-bolts with washers and nuts *(See Photo 2:1)*. Erect the first two posts on directly opposite sides of the gazebo. Attach them to the post anchors by driving joist hanger nails through the predrilled holes in the anchor tabs. Attach a pair of 2 × 4 braces to each post with deck screws, then drive stakes and loosely attach the free ends of the braces to the stakes. Using a post level as a guide, level and plumb each post then tighten the brace screws at the stakes to hold the post in position *(See Photo 2:2)*. You can go ahead and erect all eight posts at this point, but you might be better off putting them up in pairs as you hang the joists— they can create a bit of a traffic jam in the working area.

Before attaching the joist hangers to the posts, you'll need to cut and install 2 × 4 blocking to each post at joist height. The blocking creates a surface for attaching the joist hangers and also creates nailing surfaces for attaching the rim joist boards. To make the blocking pieces, bevel-rip 2 × 4s so one edge is 22½° *(See Photo 2:3)*. We used a

2:4

Square edge of blocking faces inward

Beveled edge of blocking faces outward

Photo 2:4 Cut 7¼-in.-long pieces of the beveled blocking stock and attach one to each side of one post. The tops should be flush with the layout marks for the top of the joist. Use 3 in. deck screws to fasten the blocking.

2:5

Photo 2:5 Use a water level to transfer a joist layout mark to the post opposite the post you attached the blocking to. Water levels are very accurate tools for setting layout lines with consistent heights. Unlike strings and line levels, there is no risk that a water level will sag and cause errant readings.

Photo 2:6 Nail double joist hangers to the inside faces of the two opposite posts. Position each hanger so the top of the doubled joist that will rest in it will be flush with the joist layout lines. Use joist hanger nails to attach the joist hangers: they have much greater shear strength than deck screws. TIP: *Slip two cutoff joist pieces into the hanger as a guide for positioning it.*

portable table saw to make this cut. Before installing the blocking, draw layout lines for the tops of the joists (and blocking) on each post. If the building site is not level, find the post at the highest point and begin there. Measure up 9¼ in. from the top of the footing and scribe a reference mark for the top of the joist. Attach a piece of blocking on each side of the post so the tops are flush with the reference line. The beveled edges should face outward and follow the octagonal outline of the gazebo *(See Photo 2:4)*.

Use a line level and mason's strings (or better yet, a water level) to transfer the joist height mark to the other post *(See Photo 2:5)*. Attach blocking to the sides of each post at the joist height marks.

Attach a double joist hanger to the two opposing posts. The hangers should be positioned so the joist will be flush with the joist lines when installed (set pieces of scrap joist material into each hanger for reference). Attach the hangers with joist hanger nails *(See Photo 2:6)*.

The joist structure is built by hanging a doubled, full-width joist between two opposite posts: all other joist members depend on the doubled joist for interior support. Cut two full-length joists (See Cutting List) and screw them together face to face (you may want to use construction adhesive as well). Hang the first joist *(See Photo 2:7)*.

Cut and hang the single joists that fit at right angles against the doubled joist *(See Photo 2:8)*. Attach joist hangers to the posts and on the doubled joist for support.

The four remaining joists are attached to blocking that's inserted between perpendicular joists at the center of the gazebo undercarriage. Cut blocking pieces to length (See Cutting List), with 45° miters at each end. Attach the blocking

Photo 2:7 Set the full-diameter-length doubled joist into the two opposing double joist hangers (you'll want a helper for this). Check to make sure the doubled joist is level (shim the low end if it is not), then secure it with joist hanger nails driven through the flanges of the joist hangers.

pieces between the installed joists
(See Photo 2:9). When all four
pieces are installed, measure out
from each blocking piece to the rim
joist, at a right angle, to find the
required length of the remaining
joists. Subtract about ¼ in. from
each joist length measurement to
allow for movement.

Cut the remaining joists to
length and hang them with joist
hangers (See Photo 2:10).

Cut and install the rim joists. The
rim joists extend from post to post,
forming the outer perimeter of the
floor platform. The ends of each
rim joist are cut at a bevel. Two
beveled rim joist boards butt
together to form a 45° angle at
each post.

In an ideal world, all the rim
joists would be the same length
and would have the same bevel
angle, so you could cut them all at
once without changing the set-up
on your saw. But in real life, the
joists probably will vary in length
and bevel angle. To mark the 2 × 8
rim joists for cutting, tack a 2 × 8 to
two adjacent posts. Make sure the
beveled post blocking is flush
against the back face of the rim

Photo 2:8 Install
posts, then hang
the longer half-
joists that are
attached directly to
the doubled joist,
using single joist
hangers. By accu-
rately transferring
the joist layout line
from one of the
doubled joist posts,
you'll ensure that
the tops of the rest
of the joists all are
level with one
another.

Photo 2:9 Miter-
cut pieces of 2 × 8
to fit between
joists at the hub
area of the under-
carriage. The block-
ing creates flat,
square surfaces for
hanging the rest of
the joists. Attach
the blocking by
tacking it in place
with deck screws,
then toe-nailing
with 16d common
nails.

Photo 2:10 Hang
the four shorter
half-joists between
the posts and the
joist hub blocking
with single joist
hangers. Once all of
the joists are
installed, you can
go ahead and
remove the braces
supporting the
posts.

2:11

Photo 2:11 Mark the rim joist stock for cutting by tacking boards in place, then extending a line from the midpoint of each post to the board. Use a square (a speed square is shown here) to extend the cutting line.

Photo 2:12
Nail the rim joist in place with 16d casing nails. Angle the nails toward the miter joint between the rim joists to help draw the joint together.

2:12

joist, and that the ends of the rim joist extend past the blocking by a couple of inches on each end. Use a speed square or framing square to extend a cutting line at each end of the rim joist *(See Photo 2:11).* The cutting line should start at the midpoint of the post face and extend out at a right angle. Mark each end of the rim joist, remove it and cut it (set your circular saw or table saw blade angle to match the angle of the cutting line on each joist board).

Cut and attach two rim joists, using 16d casing nails. *(See Photo 2:12).* Install the rest of the rim joist boards one at a time.

NOTE: Arrange for inspection of the framing before installing decking.

THREE: Install the decking

Because the decking is the part of the floor that "shows," you'll want to take extra care when you install the boards. The deck will have a nicer, neater appearance if you strike a chalkline across the boards where they fall across joists

BARK SIDE UP OR BARK SIDE DOWN?

The subject of which deck board face should face up is currently under evaluation. Traditionally, deckbuilders have always installed boards with the bark side facing up, presuming that if the boards cup from exposure to moisture the cupping will be directed against the joist, preventing the surface of the deck from becoming uneven. But some industry experts assert that modern kiln-drying methods alter the character of the wood enough to reverse the direction of the cupping, so the boards actually cup toward the bark side. The best advice is to ask your lumber distributor which method they recommend.

and use the lines as guides to keep the fasteners in neat rows.

If you want to apply a wood preservative or another protective finish to the substructure or to the undersides of the deck boards, it's not a bad idea to apply it before attaching the decking (See pages 174 to 175).

The floor platform for our gazebo is decked with ⁵⁄₄ × 6 in. (nominal) cedar deck boards. Because of the configuration of the platform framing, the decking is installed in a concentric, octagonal pattern. Study the drawing *Plan View-Floor Platform* on page 182. Note that the ends of the deck boards are mitered at 22½°. Each board extends from the centerline of one joist to the centerline of the adjacent joist. Also note that the outermost decking boards need to be notched to fit around the posts.

Snap chalklines along the centerlines of all the joist tops for reference when measuring for and installing the deck boards.

Begin installing deck boards at

Photo 3:1 Measure the distance from the outer post face to the edge of the rim joist joint, then add ¼ in. (for overhang) to that distance. Use this measurement to lay out the front cut of the notch you'll need to make in the deckboard to fit around the post.

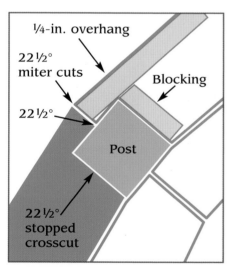

Deck board notching detail: The outer-ring deck boards must be notched to fit around the posts. Each deck board is mitered at 22½° to form 45° joints. A 22½° stopped crosscut that parallels the end miter cut is made to form one edge of each notch. The other sides are cut into the mitered ends, also at a 22½° angle, to follow the front post edges.

Photo 3:2 Use a sliding T-bevel as a guide for drawing a line parallel to the end of the deck board. The parallel line, scribed 1¾ in. from the end of the board, defines the edge of the cutout area for notching the deck board to fit around the post.

the perimeter of the floor platform and work your way around the gazebo, toward the center, mitering the ends of the adjoining boards so they are flush and the edges are aligned. First, cut a 22½° miter at one end of an outer ring deck board. A power miter saw is the best tool for this job (many have positive stops at 22½°), but make a test cut first, then butt the cut ends together and check to make sure they form a 45° angle.

Mark the cutout lines for the notch that will fit around one end post (See *Illustration,* previous page). Start by measuring straight out from the midpoint of the post at the rim joist height *(See Photo 3:1).* The edge of the measuring tool should follow the rim joist joint. Add ¼ in. to establish the recess of the cutout edge from the outer edge of the deck board (the deck board edges should overhang the outer rim joist by ¼ in. all around). With a protractor

DRILL DRIVER TIP OPTIONS

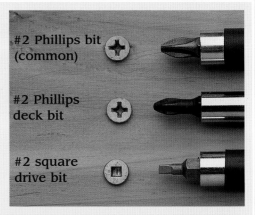

Three primary drill/driver bit styles are available for driving deck screws. A common #2 Phillips bit will easily drive deck screws through cedar or redwood decking without a pilot hole, but you may want to drill pilots if installing treated lumber. Specialty deck bits feature a hardened tip to withstand the torque that develops when you drive a screw through treated decking or 2× framing members. Square-drive screws are considerably more expensive than Phillips head screws, but they're less prone to stripping.

Photo 3:3 Cut out the notches in the outer ring of deck boards so they'll fit around the posts.

Photo 3:4 Cut the deck boards one at a time to fit between the joists, then attach them with 2½ in. deck screws driven through the deck boards and into the joists. Try to keep the screw heads aligned over the joist. Drill pilot holes when driving screws near the edge of a board.

or T-bevel, extend a cutting line into the end of the deck board at a 22½° angle.

From the outer corner of the mitered deck board end, measure in 1¾ in. (half the post width). Extend a cutting line from this mark to intersect with the first cutout line *(See Photo 3:2)*. Cut out the notch with a jig saw *(See Photo 3:3)*.

Cut and notch the other end of the deck board to fit around the post at the opposite end of the opening. Attach the board to the rim joists with 2½ in. deck screws. TIP: *When driving screws close to board ends, drill pilot holes first.* Fill in the remaining outer-ring (notched) deck boards, striving for tight miter joints between deck boards. Then, cut and install boards for the inner rings — you may need to make small relief cuts in the second-ring boards to accommodate the inside edges of the post. To cut the inner-ring boards, begin by mitering one end of a board at 22½°, then lay the board in position and mark the point where each board falls over the midpoint of the joist. Use your T-bevel to extend cutting lines from the end mark. NOTE: *While the mitered ends should fit together tightly, leave a ⅛ in. gap between parallel deck board edges: use 16d common nails as spacers.*

Install the rest of the deck boards *(See Photo 3:4)*. When you reach the "hub" of the platform, cut and install an octagonal fill piece to complete the deck board installation.

FOUR: Install the roof supports

Rafters resting atop the posts support the gazebo roof. The rafters are secured to the posts with battens that extend up along the sides of the post and overlap the rafters. Blocking is needed to fill the gaps between the battens

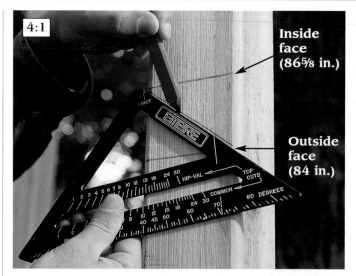

4:1

Inside face (86⅝ in.)

Outside face (84 in.)

Photo 4:1 Scribe cutoff lines on the posts. Since you've made a painstaking effort to ensure that the joists are level, you can simply measure up from the decking 84 in. on the outside face of each post and 86⅝ in. on the inside face, then connect the points with a straightedge on each side.

4:2

Photo 4:2 Working from a ladder, trim off each post at the cutoff line. Because of the thickness of the 4 × 4 stock, you'll need to make a cut from each side to clear the cut. Trim off most of the excess first to prevent the cutoff piece from breaking off and splintering.

4:3

Photo 4:3 Set up a table saw (we used a portable model on the job site) to chamfer the edges of a 6 × 6 block at each corner, creating the octagonal hub. With the blade set at 45°, measure out toward the fence 3⅝ in. from the point where the blade will contact the workpiece. Lock the fence in position.

and the rafter, since the posts are much thicker than the rafters. The rafters are cut from 2 × 6 stock, the filler blocks from ⅝ decking, and the battens from 2 × 4s. Depending on the actual dimensions of the lumber you use, you may need to install shims between the the fillers and the rafters (if the ⅝ decking is too thick for the opening, use 1× stock and shims).

The first task in creating the roof support system is to trim the posts to length, at an angle matching the roof pitch. Since the gazebo floor is level, you can measure the same distance up each post to mark it for cutting (no need to use a line level or a water level). The roof pitch is 9-in-12. Rather than get-ting caught up in trying to use a protractor, try this simple approach: Measure 84 in. up from the floor and scribe a line across the outside face of the post. Mea-sure 86⅝ inches up the inside face of the post, and scribe a line across that face. Now, scribe angled lines across the post sides that connect the two points. Set the sliding T-bevel to the angled line scribed on the first post, and use the bevel to mark the mitered cutting lines on the remaining seven posts *(See Photo 4:1)*. Trim the posts along the cutting lines *(See Photo 4:2)*. A circular saw will yield the straight-est cut for most people, but you could use a reciprocating saw or a hand saw instead.

The center of the roof frame is an octagonal wood hub with faces wide enough to support the rafters. Since the hub needs to have a diameter of 3⅝ in., it must be formed from a 6 × 6 post. Chamfer off the corners of a post section so it is octagonal. A table saw is the best tool for this task. Position the rip fence so the blade tilts away from it. Adjust the fence so it is 3⅝ in. from the blade. Now, tilt the saw blade away from the fence at a 45° angle. Double-check to make sure the cut will start the correct distance from the fence *(See Photo 4:3)*. Guide the block along the fence to trim off all four corners *(See Photo 4:4)*. Because you'll need to remove the saw blade

Photo 4:4 With your table saw blade set at 45°, trim off all four corners of a piece of 6 × 6 stock to make the hub for the roof structure. Lay out the cuts so the uncut faces of the octago-nal hub will be 2¼ in. wide. Cut the hub to length.

22½° bevel

17° miter

Photo 4:5 Make compound miter cuts at the lower rafter ends. Set the saw to cut a 22½° miter, then tilt the blade to cut a 17° bevel. Align each workpiece on the saw bed so the blade will exit halfway through the thickness of the board. Cut all eight rafter ends before changing the saw setup.

guard to make these cuts, use extra care as you work. Cut the post section to length to make the hub.

Lay out and cut the rafters, referring to the drawing *Rafter Pattern* on page 183. Note that the top end of each rafter is miter-cut to join the hub but has a square face to seat against the hub. The bottom end of the rafter is mitered at a different angle than the top. It is also beveled from both sides, forming a point (these cuts are *compound miter cuts*). The bevels create flat surfaces for the fascia boards to seat against. Because the bottom rafter ends are much trickier to cut than the tops, cut them first, then cut the rafters to length by making a simple miter cut at the top of each board.

Set up your miter saw to make the first compound miter cut at the bottom end of each rafter. The miter angle should be 17°, and the bevel angle is 22½°. Cut one side of all eight rafter bottoms *(See Photo 4:5).* To make the second bevel cut on the other side of each rafter bottom, keep the saw set up for a 22½° bevel the same direction, but swing it 17° to the opposite side of the zero point. With the cut side of the board facing down, position a rafter so the saw blade will exit the board midway through its thickness, resulting in a point that extends the full width of the rafter end and has symmetrical sides *(See Photo 4:6).* Make the bottom-end double bevels on each rafter.

The filler blocks are mitered at the top and bottom to follow the lines of the rafters. We used cutoff pieces of deck boards, ripped to 3½ in. wide, to make the fillers. The 5/4 (nominal) deck boards were actually exactly 1 in. thick, so attaching one on each side of the rafter extended the rafter width from 1½ in. to 3½ in. — the exact width of a 4 × 4 post. Because all the strips are cut to the same size and

Photo 4:6 Remove the rafter, swing the saw to 17° on the other side of the zero point, turn the workpiece over, align it with the blade and make the other side of the cut (keep the bevel at the same 22½° angle as the first cut. The peak of the resulting two-sided cut should fall at the midpoint of the rafter. Cut all eight rafters, then cut each to length with a simple 17° miter at the high end.

37° miter

6½ in.

Stopblock

Photo 4:7 Cut filler blocks to fill the gaps between the rafters and the sides of the posts that occur when the rafters are set and centered on the posts. Rip 1-in.-thick stock to 3½ in. (we used a 5/4 deck board), then cut off pieces with the saw set for a 37° miter cut. The edges of the filler blocks should be 6½ in. long (a stop-block will help you cut more accurately and quickly).

4:8

at the same angle, the fastest way to produce them is to attach a stopblock to the table of your miter saw *(See Photo 4:7).* Set the saw for a 37° cut and set the stopblock so the edges of the blocks will be 6½ in. long. You'll need 16 filler blocks.

The 2 × 4 battens lap the rafter/post joints on each side. The 14 regular battens are 24 in. long. To allow clearance for the door framing, the battens in the door opening area are square-cut to 5⅛ in. long. Bevel-cut the 14 regular battens at 45° on the bottoms for appearance. Then miter-cut the tops of all 16 battens at 37° to follow the roof slope line *(See Photo 4:8).*

To assemble the roof frame, lag-screw the rafters to the hub and sandwich the rafters between the filler blocks and battens atop the posts: the filler blocks are attached to the rafters, then lag bolts are driven through the battens and filler blocks and the rafters. The tricky part is getting the first three rafters mounted on their posts and attached to the hub. Once this is done, the framework will be self-supporting, and you can work in a straightforward manner.

One reasonable approach at the beginning is to attach two rafters to the hub before lifting them up onto the posttops. Working on the ground, toe-nail two opposing rafters to the hub. The tops of the rafters should be flush with the top of the hub. To reinforce the joints, drill a counterbored pilot hole for a ⁵⁄₁₆ × 4-

Photo 4:8 Cut the 2 × 4 battens that are attached over the joints between the posts and rafter/fillers to secure the connection. All 16 battens are mitered at the top at 37°. The battens that fit over the screen openings are 24 in. long and beveled at 45° at the bottoms. The two that get attached at the top of the door opening are square-cut to 5⅛ in. at the bottom.

4:9

Photo 4:9 Attach two opposing rafters to the hub while the parts are still on the ground. Toe-nail the rafters to the hub to hold them in place. Make sure they're centered on the hub face, flush with the top and plumb. Reinforce each joint by driving a ⁵⁄₁₆ × 4 in. lag screw through the rafter and into the hub.

4:10

Photo 4:10 Raise the rafter/hub assembly and balance it on two opposite posts. Toe-nail each rafter end to the post tops with two 16d nails per side to hold the assembly in place. Don't install the battens and fillers yet: wait until all rafters are positioned so you can make adjustments if needed.

Photo 4:11 Install the rest of the rafters, toe-nailing or screwing them toe-nail style to the hub and the post. Inspect to make sure all the bottom end overhangs are equal and the rafters are evenly spaced, plumb and flush against the hub faces and the post tops. Secure all rafters at the top with one lag screw apiece.

Photo 4:12 After nailing or screwing a filler strip to each rafter (the bottoms of the fillers should rest on the posts and the sides should be flush), install the battens. Tack them in place with nails, then drill two counterbored guide holes for bolts through each batten and into the rafter. Drive another pair of guide holes into the post.

in. lag screw (with washer) and drive one lag through each rafter, about 2 in. down from the top, and into the the hub (See Photo 4:9).

Set up sturdy stepladders (See page 167) next to two opposite posts. With a helper, lift the two-rafters-and-hub assembly onto the posts and adjust it so the overhang is equal on both posts (See Photo 4:10). The rafters should be centered on the posts. Toe-nail each side of each rafter to the post below with 16d common nails or 3- to 4-in. deck screws, making sure the fastener head is countersunk. These alone should hold the assembly in place and allow you to move one of the stepladders under the hub and the other to a new post. Toe-nail or screw the rest of the rafters in position (See Photo 4:11). Check to make sure all the rafters overhang the posts equally and are plumb. Drive a lag screw through each rafter top and into the hub.

Attach the filler blocks and battens. So they don't interfere with the roof sheathing, the tops of these parts should be 1 in. below the tops of the rafters. Nail the filler block to the rafters first, then tack the battens in position. Drill counterbored pilot holes for ⅜ × 6½-

in. carriage bolts (See Photo 4:12). Insert a pair of bolts through each batten and into the rafter. Attach washers and nuts and tighten (See Photo 4:13). Make sure the bottoms of the short battens in the door opening are at the same height (See Photo 4:14).

Cut and attach the fascia boards. Use ⁵⁄₄ deck boards for the fascia. These extend from rafter-end to rafter-end, enclosing the perimeter of the roof and giving it a finished appearance. The ends of each fascia board must be cut with a compound angle so they seat tightly to the rafters and to the adjacent boards. The miter angle for the end cuts is 22½°. For this gazebo, a 10° bevel accounted for the inward cant of the rafter ends: but you should measure the amount your rafter ends cant in from vertical to make sure the compound cut is correct for your project. Cut the fascia boards (you'll need to change your saw setup for each board end. Attach the fascia boards with 10d finish (casing) nails (See Photo 4:15). If you're concerned about the small black marks that can be created by galvanized metal on cedar (See page 170), use aluminum nails for this relatively visible joint.

Photo 4:13 Attach washers and nuts to the 3/8 × 6½-in. carriage bolts to complete the rafter/post connections.

Photo 4:14 Attach the shorter, square-bottom battens to the posts that frame the door opening.

Photo 4:15 Cut fascia boards to cover the rafter ends and nail them in place with 10d nails. Measure the inward angle of the rafter ends — ours canted in at 10° — and combine that bevel angle with a 22½° miter angle to make the compound miters cut on each end of each board.

FIVE: Build the roof

We installed fiberglass 3-tab shingles over ¾ in. exterior sheathing on this gazebo. The size and configuration of the roof allows you to cut two pie-wedge-shaped segments from each 4 × 8 sheathing sheet. Choose sheathing that has at least one presentable face: it will be visible from inside the gazebo.

Check the dimensions of your roof frame to confirm the sheathing dimensions shown in the Cutting List on page 181. The roof should be constructed of eight wedge-shaped pieces of plywood sheathing, each of which covers one section of the roof. The wedges should meet in a point at the top of the roof, but leave a ¼ in. gap between sheathing boards. Lay out the sheathing pieces on full sheets of plywood. To make sure the angles of the triangular shape are correct, start measuring in a corner and mark the base (low) end measurement. Measure and mark the midpoint of the base on the edge of the plywood. Use a framing square to mark a perpendicular line at the midpoint, then extend that line up toward the peak of the triangle. Mark the length of the sheathing piece on the line, then draw cutting lines to the corner and to the endpoint of the base line. Cut out the shape with a circular saw. Test the fit of the sheathing piece to make sure the edges fall over rafter and fascia locations. If it fits correctly, use the first piece as a template for laying out the other seven pieces. Cut all eight sheathing pieces *(See Photo 5:1)*.

Attach the sheathing. We used a pneumatic nailer *(See Photo 5:2)*, but you could use deck screws or 10d galvanized common nails instead. Cut and install the drip-edge molding next, using roofing nails (if your drip edge is aluminum, be sure to use aluminum nails). The proper approach here is to cut wedges out of the flange that overlays the sheathing so you can bend the material to follow the roof-edge contour. The end of one strip should overlap the end of its neighbor by about 1 in., and joints between pieces should fall over a straight run, not at the seam.

Staple building paper onto the sheathing (local codes in the area this gazebo was installed in required 30# building paper). Begin attaching the building paper at the eaves and work your way toward the peak of the roof *(See Photo 5:3)*. Use the reference lines printed on the building paper as a guide for aligning pieces. Higher courses should overlap lower courses by 2 in., and each piece should overlap the adjoining ridges by 6 in. Trim off any paper that extends past the front edge of the drip edge.

Lay a shingle starter course all the way around the eave edge of the roof. The shingles in the starter course should be turned upside-down so the tabs are on the high side. The exposed edges of the shingles should overhang the drip edge by 3/8 in. all around. Also make sure adjoining shingles are square. The end shingles should overlap the seams between roof sections *(See Photo 5:4)*. Drive one roofing nail near the top of each tab. Make sure all nail heads are in areas that will

Photo 5:1 Lay out and cut the wedge-shaped roof sheathing from plywood sheets. You should be able to cut two sheathing pieces from each 4 × 8 plywood sheet. Test the first piece to make sure it fits before you cut the rest of the pieces. Note that there should be a gap of around 1/8 in. between sheets when installed, to allow for expansion.

Photo 5:2 Attach the roof sheathing to the rafters. We used a pneumatic nail gun, but 2 in. deck screws or #10d ring-shank nails will also do the job.

Photo 5:3 Attach drip-edge molding to the bottom edge of the roof deck. Make release cuts in the molding flange so it can be bent around corners without buckling. Then, staple building paper to the roof deck, starting at the bottom.

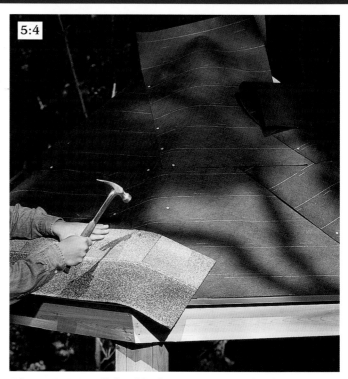

Photo 5:4 Install the shingle starter course. The shingles in this row are installed upside down. Overlap the sheathing seams and make sure adjacent shingles are aligned and flush to one another.

Photo 5:5 Install the first course of right-side-up shingles. Position the shingles so the slots point down. Drive one roofing nail above each slot, and stagger the seams so they don't align with the starter course seams.

Photo 5:6 Work your way up the section, making sure to stagger shingle tabs and slots. Overlap the seams between roof sections, then trim off the ends after finishing each course. Shingle all the sections.

be covered by the next course of shingles. Don't forget to peel the cellophane strip off the back of each shingle before you apply it. Tɪᴘ: *Run a bead of asphalt roof cement near the eave to bond the starter course to the building paper.*

Install a course of shingles directly over the starter course *(See Photo 5:5)*, but with this course, position the shingles so the tabs are lower (standard installation). Also, shift the shingles over by one-half tab so the slots and seams are not aligned. Drive one roofing nail about an inch above each slot.

After each course, trim the shingles at the seams between roof sections. This will prevent conspicuous bulging when the ridge caps are applied. Shingle all the way up to the peak *(See Photo 5:6)*. The roof sections on most gazebos are small enough that trying to use the traditional shingling method of staggering slots by half-tab thicknesses may not work out well. In such a case, simply adjust the shingles as you start each course so the seams are not aligned. Try to preserve some uniformity in the stagger pattern.

When the roof is shingled all the way up to the peak, go back to the ridges and install "ridge caps" to cover the seams between roof sections. To make a ridge cap, cut a shingle into thirds. Starting at the bottom of the roof slope, fold a ridge cap across the ridge and nail it in place. Work up the ridge, installing the ridge caps — make sure to cover the nail heads in the lower shingles — *(See Photo 5:7)*. When all the ridge caps are installed, trim the bottom edges to follow the line of the regular shingles.

Trim the non-mineralized backing off of a ridge cap shingle and fit it over the peak. You'll need to cut a small slot in each side of the peak cap shingle so it can be folded to fit *(See Photo 5:8)*. Nail the peak shingle down securely and cover the exposed nailheads with roof cement.

Photo 5:7 Cut ridge cap shingles and install them over the ridges between roof sections, starting at the bottom and working your way up.

Photo 5:8 Slit a ridge cap shingle so it can be folded without tearing, then tack it over the peak of the roof. Depending on how much of the peak is exposed on your roof, this may take more than one shingle. Trial and error is the best method for solving the issue. Nail the shingle down and cover the nailheads with roof cement.

Photo 6:1 Cut out the balusters on your band saw or with a jig saw after laying out the pattern. We ganged two together at a time to speed up this time-consuming task.

Photo 6:2 Cut slots in the top and bottom rails to house the ends of the balusters. A dado-blade set mounted in your table saw is the perfect tool for this task.

Photo 6:3 Measure to determine how long to make the rails for each opening. Clamp the 1 × 4 battens to the posts first and measure from the inside faces of the battens.

SIX: Install railings & trim

The railings and trim are two focal points that give this gazebo its elegant appearance, so we decided to invest a bit of time and energy in creating them. If this seems like too much work, you can buy ready-made deck-railing balusters. In fact, you can also purchase railing stringers and cap rails in premilled form, eliminating the need to rip and slot the top and bottom rails on a table saw, as we do here.

Using a power miter saw with a stopblock, cut 1 × 4s to make the balusters. Make a cardboard template using the *Baluster Pattern* on page 183 as a guide. Stack two or three boards face-to-face and bind them with masking tape. Trace the pattern, then cut out the shape on the entire stack *(See Photo 6:1).*

Make the top and bottom rails. The rails that form the top and bottom of the railing structures are made from 2 × 4s ripped to 2½ in. wide on a table saw (some lumber yards carry 2 × 3s). All rails are machined with ¾ in. wide by ½ in. deep slots, cut lengthwise, to accept the ends of the balusters. Use a dado-blade set mounted in your table saw *(See Photo 6:2).*

The rails are mitered at 22½° on the ends to match the angles of the post sides. Then they are attached to 1 × 4 battens which are fastened to the posts. After the slots are cut, cut and clamp 1 × 4 battens to the posts in each railing opening. Measure between the battens to determine the required lengths of the top and bottom rails *(See Photo 6:3).* Miter-cut the rails to fit.

To assemble the rail frames, lay a rail slot-side-up on your worksurface. Mark the midpoint of the railing, then mark a point ³⁄₁₆ in. from the midpoint. Lay a bead of construction adhesive in the slot and insert a baluster so the edge is aligned with the second mark *(See Photo 6:4).* Using a ⅜ in. dowel as a spacer, insert the rest of the balusters. It is important to maintain even spacing between balusters, so let "leftover" space in the slot fall between the end balusters and the posts. Drive a pair of finish nails through the rail to hold each baluster in position (we used a pneumatic pin nailer). Lay a bead of construction adhesive in the other rail and fit it over the free ends of the balusters *(See Photo 6:5).* Check the assembly with a framing square and adjust as needed, then nail the second rail to the baluster ends. Attach the battens to the railing assembly so the tops are flush with the top railing *(See Photo 6:6).* Construct all seven railing assemblies, custom-measuring for each.

Set the railing assemblies into the correct openings and attach them by nailing or screwing the battens to the posts. Cut cap rail from ⁵⁄₄ deck boards. Each cap rail should fit between two posts, and the ends should be mitered to match the post angles (22½°). Attach the cap rail to the top rails of the railing assemblies with con-

Photo 6:4 Apply construction adhesive into the bottom rail slot (assemble one section at a time). Arrange the balusters in the slot using a 3/8-in. dowel as a spacer. Start in the middle and work toward the ends.

Photo 6:5 Apply construction adhesive in the top rail slot and fit the top rail over the free ends of the balusters. Use the midpoint mark on the rail to set the layout (a baluster should start 3/16 in. on each side of the midpoint). Use a 3/8 in. dowel spacer to set the rest of the gaps (any overage can be picked up outside the end balusters). Drive a nail through each rail and into each baluster end.

Photo 6:6 With the railing section upside down, attach the 1 × 4 battens to each end of the section. The battens should be flush with the top of the top rail.

Photo 6:7 Insert the railing section into the opening and attach it by nailing through the battens and into the posts. Cut the cap rails to fit and attach with construction adhesive and 10d finish nails. Make and install all the railing sections.

Photo 6:8 Install the horizontal frieze boards at the top of each frame opening. Set the nailheads with a nailset. The board ends are mitered at 22½°.

Photo 6:9 Bevel the tops of the vertical frieze boards to follow the roof slope, then miter-cut the ends. Nail the vertical boards into the top of each opening.

Photo 6:10 Drive finish nails through the horizontal frieze boards and into the bottom edges of the vertical boards to draw the joint together.

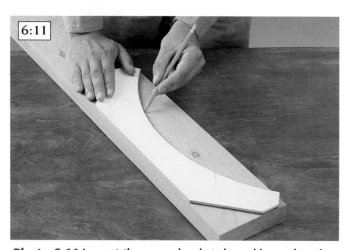

Photo 6:11 Lay out the corner brackets by making and tracing a hardboard template, according to the *Corner Bracket Pattern* shown on page 181.

Photo 6:12 Nail the corner brackets in place at the top corners of the screen frame openings, centered on the post battens. Don't install them in the door opening.

struction adhesive, then toe-nail the ends to the posts with 10d casing nails *(See Photo 6:7)*.

The primary trim parts on the gazebo are the corner brackets at the tops of the openings between posts, and frieze boards that are installed between the fascia and the underside of the roof on the interior of the gazebo. You'll need both horizontal and vertical frieze boards to box in the frieze area. Cut the horizontal boards first, mitering the ends to follow the post angles. The bottoms of these boards should be flush with the bottom edges of the fascia boards. Install the horizontal boards by toe-nailing them into the posts with finish nails *(See Photo 6:8)*. Set the nailheads with a nailset throughout the frieze. The vertical boards are beveled on the ends and on the top edge to fit snugly between the horizontal frieze boards and the roof. Measure the opening and the bevel angles (they should be 22½° on the sides and 37° on the top), then cut the boards to fit with a jig saw or on your table saw. We needed to use 1 × 8 stock to fit the openings. Insert the vertical boards into the openings *(See Photo 6:9)* and secure them by nailing up through the horizontal boards with finish nails *(See Photo 6:10)*.

Make a template for the corner brackets from cardboard or hardboard, using the pattern on page 183 as a guide. Lay the template onto a 2 × 6 and trace the pattern onto the board *(See Photo 6:11)*. Cut out the shape with a jig saw or band saw. Make all 14 corner brackets.

Attach a corner bracket at each post opening (except the door opening), using casing or finish nails driven into pilot holes *(See Photo 6:12)*. The brackets should be centered on the rafter-support battens.

Building Stairs

Generally, outdoor stairs are not as steep as indoor stairs, having proportionally wider treads and lower risers. The clear width between outer stringers should be at least 36 in.

To build a comfortable set of stairs, you'll need to establish a suitable rise-to-run ratio: *Rise* refers to the height between the steps; *run* refers to the depth of the step, minus any overhang. As a general rule for outdoor stairs, the tread width (run) in inches

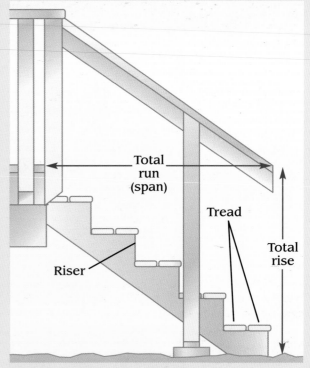

Designing stairs involves a little math and a little trial-and-error. The trick is to come up with a plan that has uniformly sized risers and treads that are in formation and terminate at a convenient location on the low end of the flight.

plus twice the step height (rise) in inches should equal 24 to 26 inches. For exterior stairs, the rise (vertical distance between treads) should be between 4½ in. and 7 in. The tread depth should be a minimum of 11 in. Building codes often dictate acceptable run/rise relationships. For most structures with decking, treads consist of two 2 × 6s, spaced ¼ in. apart, to create a tread run of 11¼ in. In this case, the formulas tell us that the riser height should be between 6½ and 7 in. This is the most common and useful outdoor step relationship.

The real trick to designing stairs comes when you try to actually incorporate the run and rise ratios into your design. By code, all stairs in a flight must have the same rise and run proportions (this is a safety issue: non-uniform sizing of stairs confuse our feet in a hurry and can easily cause injury from falls).

STRINGER BRACKETS

Stringer brackets, which work like joist hangers, cradle the bottom of the stringer and provide nailing flanges for attaching the stringers to the deck joists. They are a quick and convenient substitute for building stringers from scratch. Use 1¼-in. joist-hanger nails for fasteners.

Photo 7:1 Measure the total rise of the gazebo deck at the door opening to begin planning your stairs. Measure from the lowest point of ground outside the door opening.

Photo 7:2 Design and build your stairs (See previous page). Here, we buried a landscape timber at the foot of the stairs for support and rested the inside edge of the construction on the footings. A ledger attached to the rim joist keeps the staircase from pinching in, but is not attached to the staircase due to ground swell issues.

Photo 7:3 Use the same decking and amount of overhang to make the stair treads as were used on the gazebo deck.

SEVEN: Finishing touches

By now, your gazebo project is nearing completion and only a few optional finishing touches remain. Because the floor of the gazebo is raised by more than a foot, you'll need to provide a step at the doorway. You have several options, depending on how much distance there is between the floor and ground and a few other factors. The simplest solution is to attach a simple stair stringer bracket to the rim joist (See previous page). But we opted for a slightly more elegant approach.

Measure the distance from the ground to the top of the gazebo floor (called the stair *rise*) at the doorway opening *(See Photo 7:1).* Design your stairs (See previous page). We chose to build a two-step box frame that is attached to the rim joist *(See Photo 7:2).* We used deck boards to make the stair treads *(See Photo 7:3).*

After the steps are installed is a good time to apply the finish to the gazebo, unless you're using a wood like cedar that is naturally moisture resistant and can be left untreated (See pages 174 to 175). We applied redwood stain with UV protection to the project.

Prepare the gazebo for the finish. Preparation steps include setting nailheads with a nailset (it's usually not that important to fill nail holes or screw holes with putty, but if you do, be sure to use a moisture-resistant exterior wood filler), sanding down any rough edges, and sanding out any footprints, stains or blemishes that would show up through the finish *(See Photo 7:4).* We also hosed down the gazebo and let it dry before applying the redwood stain *(See Photo 7:5).*

Just about every region of the country is plagued by some type of flying pest, be they gnats, mosquitoes, yellow jackets, blackflies or anything else. Consequently,

Photo 7:4 Sand all the exposed wood surfaces to prepare them for finishing (and to clean them after all the construction traffic).

Photo 7:5 Apply your finish of choice before installing the screen frames. We used semi-transparent redwood stain.

screens and a screen door may be in order for your gazebo. You can make a set that can be removed for winter storage, and it isn't hard for someone who's just constructed a gazebo.

Rip eight post battens to 1½ in. wide from 1× stock. Cut them to length to extend from floor to rafter. Apply finish. Snap a plumb chalkline on the inside face of each post, right down the center. Nail a batten to each post, centered on the chalkline (See Photo 7:6).

Each screen frame consists of two stiles and three rails. The object here is to make a simple frame upon which to stretch window screening. You don't want fat frame members impinging on the openness of the gazebo. Since the frame will be clipped to the posts and won't move, it doesn't have to be particularly stiff or rigid or wrack-resistant. The stiles and two of the rails therefore are cut from 1 × 2 stock. The third rail, the bottom one, is subject to inadvertent kicks and bumps from chair legs, so it is wider with enough strength to resist these indignities. Cut the

bottom rail from 1 × 4 stock.

To determine the required dimensions of each screen frame, measure straight across the opening from batten to batten (See Photo 7:7). It's a good idea to cut a stick to that length and test-fit it between all the battens, top and bottom. Subtract 3 in. from that measurement, and cut all the rails to that length. The stiles should be the same length as the battens.

In keeping with the simplicity objective, the frames are assembled with reinforced butt joints. Two 3-in. galvanized screws secure each joint. Lay out the stiles and set the rails between them. Obviously, the bottom rail (the wide one) is flush with the bottom end of the stiles, and the top rail flush with the stile tops. The middle rail should be at railing height. Pull the stiles tight against the rail ends and square up the assembly by measuring the diagonals (See Photo 7:8). Drill and countersink two pilot holes at each joint. Drive the screws. Remove the clamps. The process is the same for each of the seven frames needed.

Cut, but don't attach, molding to

Photo 7:6 Nail a mounting batten to the inside face of each post in each screen frame opening. Apply finish to the battens first and center them on a centerline on the post.

Photo 7:7 Measure between the post battens to determine the width of each screen frame. Subtract 3 in. to find the rail length. The stiles should be the same length as the post battens.

Photo 7:8 Cut the rails and stiles for each screen frame. Dry-fit the parts and check for square. Join the frames with butt joints reinforced with glue and 3-in. screws.

Photo 7:9 Roll out the window screening, set a frame on top of it, and trim it to rough length. Measure the length and cut the screening to that length for the rest of the frames.

Photo 7:10 Slip a 2 × 4 under each end of the frame and clamp the middle of the frame to your worksurface, creating a bow. Staple the screening to the top and bottom rails, then release the clamps to stretch the screening taut.

Photo 7:11 Staple the screening to the stiles and the middle rail. Try to keep the staples within the area that will be covered with the molding.

Photo 7:12 Miter-cut window stop molding to frame the screen opening and tack it to the frame, concealing the staples. Also tack molding over the middle rail.

surround the openings in the frame. These are to cover the edges of the screening and the staples that secure it. Use strips of astragal or bead molding, or simply thin flat strips — we used window stop molding. Assuming you will apply a finish to the frames, now is the time to do it.

When the finish is dry, attach the screening. To begin, cut the screening to length plus a few inches, using a utility knife. Spread out the screening and lay the frame on top of it. Keep the screen mesh as straight as possible and parallel to the frame edges. Trim the screening along the frame edges *(See Photo 7:9)*.

Turn the frame over and lay the screening on top. Staple the screening to the bottom rail. Start in the center and work toward the bottom corners of the frame, driving staples about 6 in. apart. Smooth the screening as you work to eliminate wrinkles. Keep the staples in a tidy line, so it will be easy to cover them with the molding in the next step. Place a 2 × 4 under each end of the frame and apply C-clamps at the center, forcing the frame into a concave bow. Stretch the screen to the top of the frame, pulling it taut. Drive a staple at the center of the top rail *(See Photo 7:10)*, and work out to the corner, stapling every 6 in. The screening will now be stapled at the top and bottom, but not the sides.

Release the clamps, and the frame will spring back flat, stretching the screening nice and tight. Now drive staples along the two sides and across the middle rail *(See Photo 7:11)*.

Nail the molding to the frames with brads or small finishing nails *(See Photo 7:12)*. Trim off the excess screening *(See Photo 7:13)*.

Attach a mitered wood strip to the molding side of each screen frame, flush with the top edge *(See Photo 7:14)*. The mitered strips fill

Photo 7:13 Trim off the excess screening next to the molding material with a utility knife.

Photo 7:14 Nail miter-cut filler strips to the top of each screen to fill the gaps next to the frieze boards.

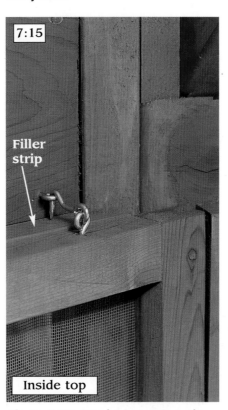

Filler strip

Inside top

Photo 7:15 Attach screw eyes to the frieze boards and attach eyebolts to each top corner of each window frame. Fit each screen frame into its opening and fasten it in place with the eyebolts.

Outside bottom

Photo 7:16 Use the same method to fasten the bottoms of the screen frames. The screw eyes are driven into the post battens.

7:17

Photo 7:17 Purchase a wood-frame screen door and hang it in the door opening, following the manufacturer's installation instructions. Set the door on wood shims when marking hinge locations.

7:18

Photo 7:18 Attach the hinges, making sure there is a slight gap between each side of the door and posts. Once the door is hung, install a door closer and handle/latch assembly.

the gap between the screens and the frieze inside the gazebo. To size the strips, set the screen in place and measure.

Attach screw eyes to the top and bottom edges of each screen, near the corners. Attach eyebolts to the frieze boards (See Photo 7:15) and to the post battens (See Photo 7:16) so they align with the screw eyes. Install the screens by hooking the screw eyes through the eyebolts.

Buy a wooden screen door, hinges, door closing hardware and a latch. You can make either of two choices when it comes to the door width. If the stiles of the door are wide enough, you can cut or plane a bevel on both of them so a 32-in.-wide door will fit between the posts. Or you can make some thin beveled strips to nail to the posts, squaring the opening, and use a 30-inch door. Whichever approach you take, the door should be hung so it opens out.

In a nutshell, the procedure is to stand the door in the opening. To get the proper clearance at the bottom, slip a couple of wood shims between the floor and the door. Allow a slight gap on the sides of the door as well. When the door is centered and shimmed, mount the hinges. This is a matter of holding the hinge in place and marking the mounting screw locations (See Photo 7:17). Drill pilot holes. Screw the hinges to the screen door, then to the posts (See Photo 7:18). Attach the door closing hardware and latch.

GATEWAY

A delightful hybrid between the pergola and the trellis,
this stunning gateway project transforms
a simple back yard into a magical garden.

Gateway Project: *A 3-step overview*

1

Build the gateway arches (218 to 222)

2

Build the trellises (223 to 228)

3

Assembly and installation (229 to 232)

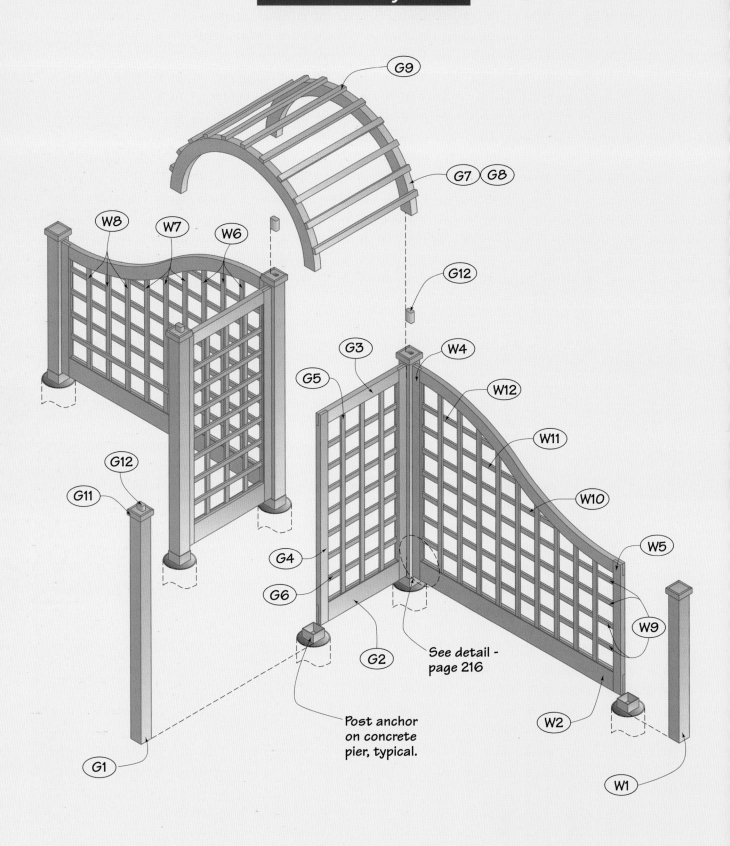

G9

G7 G8

W8 W7 W6

G12

G3 W4

G5 W12

W11

G12

G11 W10

W5

G4

G6 W9

G2

See detail -
page 216

Post anchor
on concrete
pier, typical.

W2

G1

W1

OVERALL DIMENSIONS (37" × 196½ × 91½")

KEY	PART NAME	QTY.	SIZE	MATERIAL
ARCHWAY				
G1	POST	4	3½ × 3½ × 66"	CEDAR (4 × 4)
G2	BOTTOM RAIL	2	1½ × 5½ × 29"	CEDAR (2 × 6)
G3	TOP RAIL	2	1½ × 3½ × 29"	CEDAR (2 × 4)
G4	STILE	4	1½ × 2½ × 61¼"	CEDAR (2 × 4)
G5	VERTICAL SLAT	6	½ × 1¼ × 54¼"	CEDAR (1 × 6)
G6	HORIZONTAL SLAT	14	½ × 1¼ × 26"	CEDAR (1 × 6)
G7	ARCH SEGMENT	18	1 × 5 × 16"	CEDAR (5/4)
G8	ARCH SEGMENT	4	1 × 5 × 8"	CEDAR (5/4)
G9	ARCH RUNG	11	1 × 1½ × 34½"	CEDAR (2 × 4)
G10	POST CAP	8	¾ × 3½ × 3½"	CEDAR
G11	MOLDING	16	½ × 1½ × 4½"	CEDAR (2 × scrap)
G12	LOOSE TENONS	4	1¼ × 2 × 3"	CEDAR
WING TRELLISES				
W1	END POST	2	3½ × 3½ × 42¾"	CEDAR (4 × 4)
W2	BOTTOM RAIL	2	1½ × 5½ × 69¾"	CEDAR (2 × 6)
W3	CREST RAIL	2	1½ × 8 × 74¾"	CEDAR (2 × 10)
W4	TALL STILE	2	1½ × 2½ × 61¼"	CEDAR (2 × 4)
W5	SHORT STILE	2	1½ × 2½ × 38"	CEDAR (2 × 4)
W6	VERTICAL SLAT	6	½ × 1¼ × 54"**	CEDAR (1 × 6)
W7	VERTICAL SLAT	6	½ × 1¼ × 46¼"**	CEDAR (1 × 6)
W8	VERTICAL SLAT	6	½ × 1¼ × 34¾"**	CEDAR (1 × 6)
W9	HORIZONTAL SLAT	8	½ × 1¼ × 66¾"	CEDAR (1 × 6)
W10	HORIZONTAL SLAT	2	½ × 1¼ × 51¼"	CEDAR (1 × 6)
W11	HORIZONTAL SLAT	2	½ × 1¼ × 40¼"	CEDAR (1 × 6)
W12	HORIZONTAL SLAT	2	½ × 1¼ × 28⅜"	CEDAR (1 × 6)
W13	POST CAP	2	¾ × 3½ × 3½"	CEDAR
W14	MOLDING	8	½ × 1½ × 4½"	CEDAR (2 × scrap)
HARDWARE REQUIRED				
NAILS			¾", 1¼"	STAINLESS STEEL
DECK SCREWS			#8 × 2½"	
CONSTRUCTION ADHESIVE				
WATERPROOF GLUE				
POST ANCHOR/STAKES		6	3½ × 3½ × 24"	STEEL

NOTICE: Part dimensions are based on ideal installation conditions. For best results, confirm measurements on actual project before cutting parts.

Gateway

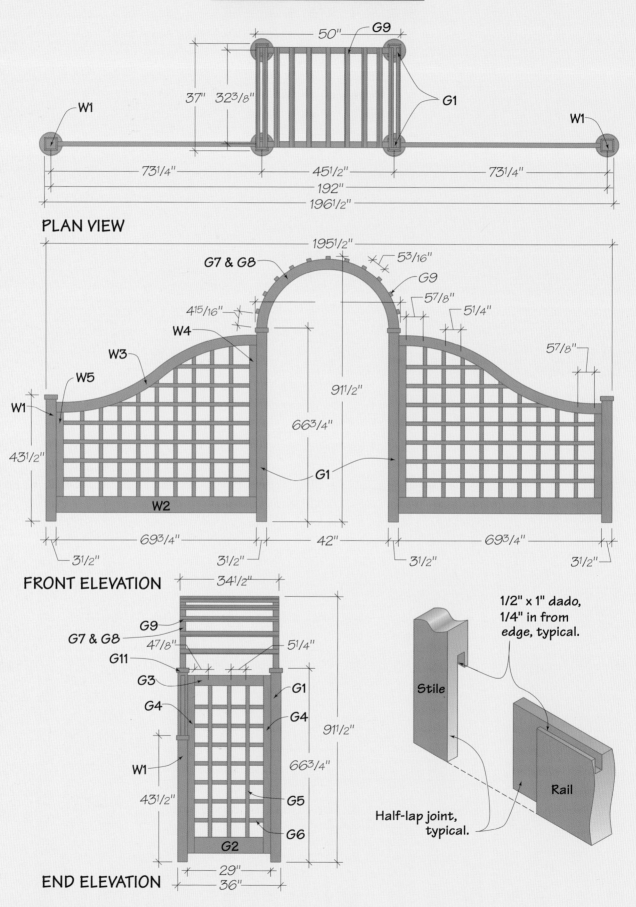

PLAN VIEW

50" G9

37" 32³/₈"

G1

W1   W1

73¹/₄"   45¹/₂"   73¹/₄"

192"

196¹/₂"

FRONT ELEVATION

195¹/₂"

G7 & G8   5³/₁₆"

G9

4¹⁵/₁₆"   5⁷/₈"

W4   5¹/₄"

W3

W5   91¹/₂"   5⁷/₈"

W1

66³/₄"

G1

43¹/₂"

W2

69³/₄"   42"   69³/₄"

3¹/₂"   3¹/₂"   3¹/₂"   3¹/₂"

END ELEVATION

34¹/₂"

G9

G7 & G8

4⁷/₈"   5¹/₄"

G11

G3   G1

G4   G4

W1

G5

43¹/₂"

66³/₄"

91¹/₂"

G6

G2

29"

36"

1/2" x 1" dado, 1/4" in from edge, typical.

Stile

Rail

Half-lap joint, typical.

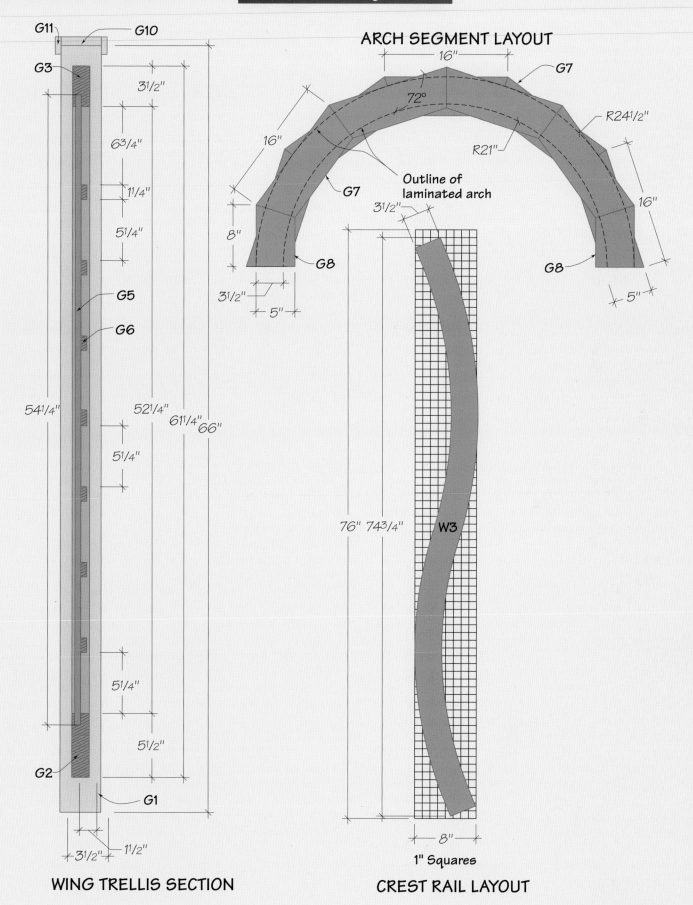

ARCH SEGMENT LAYOUT

G7

16"

72°

16"

16"

R24 1/2"

R21"

G7

Outline of
laminated arch

3 1/2"

8"

G8

3 1/2"

5"

16"

G8

5"

G11
G10
G3

3 1/2"

6 3/4"

1 1/4"

5 1/4"

G5

G6

54 1/4"
52 1/4"
61 1/4"
66"

5 1/4"

3 1/2"

76" 74 3/4"

W3

8"

1" Squares

5 1/4"

5 1/4"

5 1/2"

G2

G1

3 1/2"
1 1/2"

WING TRELLIS SECTION

CREST RAIL LAYOUT

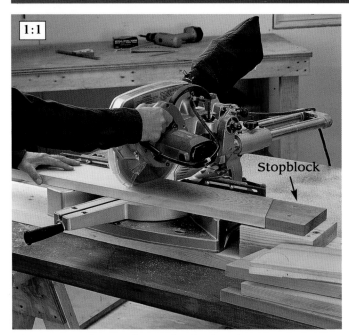

Photo 1:1 Miter-cut the overlapping board segments at a 72° angle to make the "bricklaid" blank that will be cut into the arch shape. A stopblock speeds up the process.

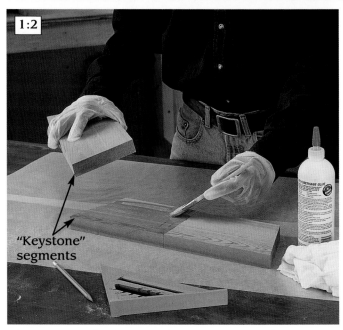

Photo 1:2 Apply glue up to the centerline on the face of one of the three "keystone" segments. Also apply glue to the mating face of another keystone segment, stopping at the centerline.

For a romantic entrance into your yard or garden, you can't beat this elegant arched gateway with side trellises. It is a project you can tackle and handle easily with common woodworking tools. Get started in midwinter, about the time the spring seed and bulb catalogs appear in the mailbox. By the time the frost is out of the ground, you'll have your trellis subassemblies constructed and ready for assembly out in the yard.

Build the gateway arches

Building the arches is the most difficult and time-consuming part of this project. You *can* rip thin strips of wood, smear them with glue, and bend them around a form. Known as *glue-lamination bending,* this technique produces a good strong product. But ripping all the strips needed is a lot of work and fairly wasteful of material. We chose to save time and material by *bricklaying* segments to create a blank for each arch, as shown in the drawing on page 217. Two layers of blocks cut from 5⁄4 × 6 cedar are glued up in an overlapping sequence, resulting in excellent strength. Cut the arches out from the "bricklaid" blanks once they are glued and dried.

Prepare the blocks for the arch blanks. You'll need stock that's a full inch thick and at least 5 in. wide to make the mitered blocks that are fastened together to form the blanks for the two arches. Because 5⁄4-in.-thick cedar is not readily available in the area where this gateway was built, we used cedar deck boards to make the stock. The nominal 5⁄4 boards are actually exactly 1 in. thick, so all we needed to do to prepare the stock was to rip-cut the bullnose off each deck board, resulting in 5-in.-wide stock. The majority of the blocks used to make the glue-up blanks are miter-cut at a 72° angle and measure 16 in. along the longer edge. These parts are easy to cut with a power miter saw or radial-arm saw. Simply set the saw to 18° (18° from 90° yields a 72° angle) and cut all 18 of these blocks. We made a stopblock to speed up the process and guarantee uniform parts *(See Photo 1:1).* For the ends of the arches you also need four blocks that are mitered on only one end and measure 8 in. along the longer edge.

Assemble the blanks. In a masonry arch, the *keystone* is the wedge-shaped stone at the crest of the arch that keeps all the other stones in place. In our bricklaid blank, the counterpart to a masonry keystone is the three-part block oriented horizontally at the arch's crest. Begin assembly of this element by drawing setup lines on three blocks for each arch (six blocks total). With a pencil and square, draw a centerline across the width and top edge of each of the blocks. These lines are used to align the blocks during glue-up. The complete glue-up will require around 20 clamps and nearly a pint of water-resistant glue (we used polyurethane glue). Collect your clamps and glue, and pile up the blocks close at hand before you start. Select one of the pieces with the layout marks and spread a nice even coat of glue over the face on one side of the centerline *(See Photo 1:2).* Then, spread glue on a sec-

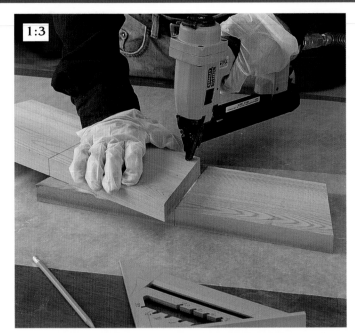

Photo 1:3 Arrange the two blocks so the centerlines and ends align, then nail the blocks together to hold them in place while you assemble the glue-up. Keep the nails away from the edges so they don't interfere with the saw when cutting out the arches — the nail being driven above did not get in the way, but was a little too close for comfort.

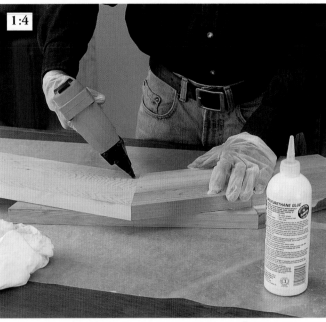

Photo 1:4 Add the third "keystone" block to the assembly and nail it in place. The remaining blocks all "key" off these three, so be sure to get them oriented correctly. Continue adding blocks until the glue-up is completed with the square-cut end blocks. Work quickly so you can get the assembly clamped up before the glue sets.

ond keystone block. Set this second block glued-face to glued-face on the first block, aligning its end with the centerline on the face. Then, align the centerline on the edge of the overlying block with the end of the first keystone block. When everything lines up, nail the blocks together — we used a pneumatic pin nailer *(See Photo 1:3)*, but you can use 6d finishing nails. Position the nails near the center of the overlap so they won't get in the way when cutting the arch contour. Glue the other overlying keystone block to the first block in exactly the same way, butting the ends of the two overlapping blocks together *(See Photo 1:4).*

Finish gluing up the blanks. You'll need to clamp the glued-up arch blanks together, but wait until the entire unit is glued and nailed together because clamps will keep the assembly from lying flat. When all the blocks are in place, you can go back and apply clamps. So con-

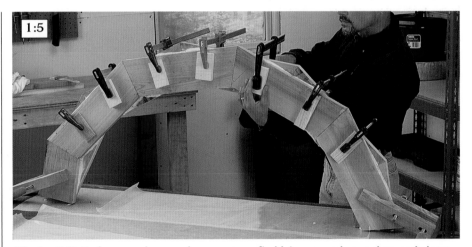

Photo 1:5 Grab any and every clamp you can find lying around your shop and clamp the blocks together. Try to get at least one clamp situated over every block.

tinue along, gluing and driving nails to hold the blocks in place. One layer of the arch is made up of five full blocks (those with two angled ends); the other layer is made up of four full blocks and two of the short blocks with only one angled end. When the first arch is finished, apply clamps around the perimeter of the glue-up *(See*

Photo 1:5). Clamps that can apply pressure a couple of inches in from the edges of the glue-up are best. But as you can see in the photo, we used fast-action bar clamps, some Quick-Grip clamps, and C-clamps, which are ideal for this, along with some handscrews and even some pipe clamps, which are not the best. You need about 20

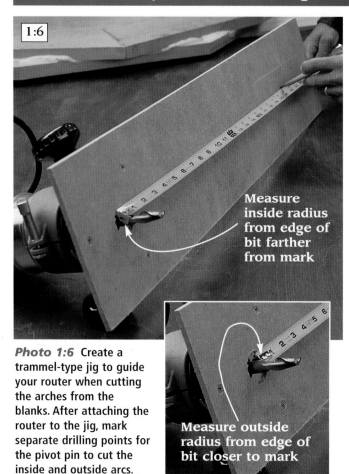

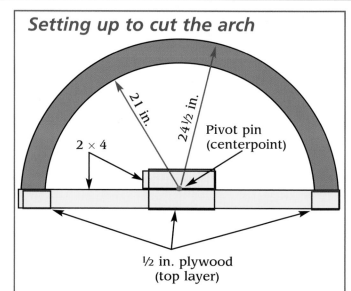

Setting up to cut the arch

21 in.

24½ in.

2 × 4

Pivot pin (centerpoint)

½ in. plywood (top layer)

The pivot pin for the router trammel (a 6d finish nail works well) must be even with the ends of the arch blank and centered between the legs of the arch. On a flat surface, lay a 2 × 4 so it spans both legs of the arch and is flush with the end of each leg. Slip a ½ in. plywood spacer over each end of the 2 × 4 and clamp the assembly to your worksurface. Lay a smaller 2 × 4 scrap against the top edge of the larger 2 × 4 as a spacer, then attach a piece of ½ in. plywood to the assembly so it covers the seam between 2 × 4s. Drive the pivot pin (nail) into the plywood at the trammel pin centerpoint, then slip each pin hole in the trammel over the nail to cut your arcs.

Measure inside radius from edge of bit farther from mark

Measure outside radius from edge of bit closer to mark

Photo 1:6 Create a trammel-type jig to guide your router when cutting the arches from the blanks. After attaching the router to the jig, mark separate drilling points for the pivot pin to cut the inside and outside arcs.

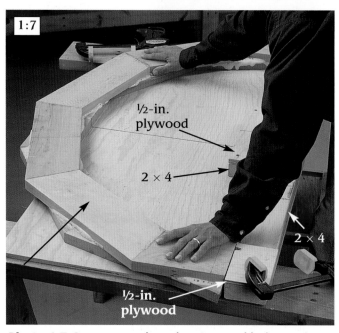

½-in. plywood

2 × 4

2 × 4

½-in. plywood

Photo 1:7 Set up to cut the arches. Secure a blank to a piece of scrap plywood, then secure a 2 × 4 to the worksurface so it spans the feet of the arch. Add ½ in. plywood spacers at the ends of the 2 × 4 and over the midpoint of the 2 × 4, where the pivot pin will be driven (See Illustration, above).

Photo 1:8 With a spiral up-cutting bit in your router, set the trammel jig over the pivot pin in the outside radius location and cut the outside arc. Take several passes, deepening the cut each time. Then, set the inside radius pin hole over the pivot pin and cut the inside arc.

clamps for each assembly. Set the assembly aside and let the glue dry overnight. With all your clamps thus freed, you can glue up the second arch in the same way.

Rout the arches. While the arches could be cut out with a jigsaw or a band saw, your best chance for creating two smooth, even (and identical) arches is to cut them with a router. We used a custom-made hardboard trammel (a pivoting jig used to swing an arc) and a router with a ½-in.-dia. × 2 in. spiral up-cutting bit to cut out the arches. The finished arches are 3½ in. wide. The radius of the outside edges is 24½ in., and the inside edge has a radius of 21 in.

Cut a piece of ¼ in. hardboard to about 12 × 36 in. to make the trammel. Install a spiral up-cutting bit in your router. Measure the distance from the router bit to the edge of the router foot, add a couple of inches, then drill a guide hole slightly larger in diameter than the bit in to the trammel, centered side to side. Remove the base from your router and set it on the trammel so the guide hole is centered on the bit clearance hole in the base. Use the base as a guide for marking the holes for the screws used to attach the base to the router. Drill guide holes at the marks and attach the trammel to the base. Then, measure and mark locations for the guide holes for the trammel pivot pin that will hold the trammel in position while cutting the arc (we used a 6d finish nail for the pivot pin). When measuring back, make sure to mark the drilling points so they align with the guide hole for the bit. The pin hole for cutting the outer radius of the arch should be 24½ in. back from the point of the bit closest to the pin hole, and the pin hole for cutting the inside radius should be 21 in. back from the point of the bit farthest from the pin hole *(See Photo 1:6 and inset photo)*. Drill the pin holes with a ⅛-in.-dia. bit.

Secure one of the arch blanks to a flat work surface and set up with 2 × 4 and ½ in. plywood spacers to make the router trim cuts *(See Photo 1:7 and Setting up to cut the arch, previous page)*. Adjust the cutting height of the router bit to about ¼ in. Slip the trammel over the pivot pin in the set-up assembly, then make your first cutting pass *(See Photo 1:8)*. It doesn't matter if you start with the inside or outside radius, but before cutting, make sure there are no nails in the cutting path of the router bit. Cut all the way through the blank in several passes, lowering the bit about ¼ in. after each pass. Trim both arches in this manner.

Cut mortises in the arches & posts. The arches are joined to the posts with mortise-and-loose-tenon joints. To make these joints, cut mortises in the bottoms of the arches and the tops of the posts, then make a loose tenon to be housed spline-style in opposing mortises. NOTE: *Wait until it's time to install the gate-*

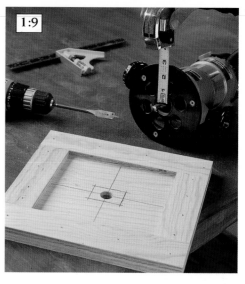

Photo 1:9
Make a router jig for cutting 1¼ × 2 × 1½-in.-deep mortises into the ends of the posts and the arches. Make a plywood frame to capture the router base and attach it to a small piece of plywood. Base the size of the jig on the distance from the edge of the router bit you'll be using to the edge of your router base (called the setback). In this case, the width of the framed opening should be the setback plus 1¼ in. The length should be the setback plus 2 in. Drill a starter hole for the bit in the middle of the plywood base and rout out the mortise in the base by following the edge guides created by the frame.

Photo 1:10 Screw the jig, in turn, to the top of each post to cut mortises for the loose tenons. Each mortise must be centered on the post end. Drill a starter hole into the workpiece then hog out the mortise in multiple passes. We used a 2 in. spiral up-cutting bit to remove the waste.

way to cut the posts to finished length: uneven ground may require you to vary their height somewhat. To make the mortises, use a router guided by a tenoning jig *(See Photo 1:9)*. Attach the jig to a post top with screws and rout out a mortise with the same spiral up-cutting bit used to shape the arches *(See Photo 1:10)*. Make the mortises as deep as your bit will allow (preferably, at least 1½ in.). You'll need to make multiple passes to get to full depth: don't try to remove all the waste in one shot. Remove the jig, then use it to

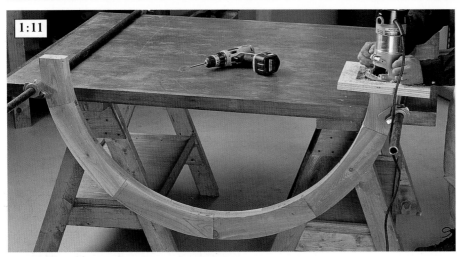

Photo 1:11 Use pipe clamps or bar clamps to pin the arches against your workbench, steadying them so you can cut mortises for the loose tenons, as you did with the posts.

Photo 1:13 Lay out the positions for the "rungs" on the arches by measuring out in straight lines, beginning at the peak of the arc. The reference marks for the rungs should be 6⅜ in. apart. Mark each rung by measuring from the previous mark.

Photo 1:14 Attach the rungs to the arches at the marked reference points to create the top of the archway.

Photo 1:12 Cut a piece of stock to 1¼ × 2 in., then round over the edges with a file to match the radius of your router bit. Slice the stock into 3-in. lengths to make the loose tenons.

rout mortises in the other post and in the ends of the arches (See Photo 1:11). We used pipe clamps to hold the arches and a quick-clamp to hold the post.

Cut some stock to 1¼ × 2 in. to make the tenons that fit into the mortises in the posts and arches. You'll need at least 12 in. of stock. After the stock is cut to size, round over the edges to match the round corners of the mortises, which should equal the radius of your router bit (See Photo 1:12). Then measure the depth of the mortises, multiply by two and subtract ⅛ in. to determine the required length of the tenons. Cut the tenons to length, test the fit to make sure they're snug, then set them aside until you install the gateway in your yard.

Join the arches together. The arches are connected with 11 evenly spaced 1 × 2 "rungs" that follow the curved arch tops. To plot out their positions on the arches, start by making a mark at the very top of one arch, exactly in the center. Using a steel rule, make another mark on the arch where the 6⅜ in. mark on the rule cuts across the arch, measuring from the center mark (See Photo 1:13). Mark the positions for all five rungs on each side of the centerpoint, measuring out 6⅜ in. in straight lines from the previous mark. Transfer the marks onto the other arch, then screw the rungs to the arches, centered on the marks and flush at the ends *(See Photo 1:14).* Use 2½ in. screws (we used stainless steel) to attach the rungs.

Build the trellises

With their elegantly sloping top rails, the trellis wings that flow out on either side of the arch are the most distinctive feature of this gateway project. When combined with the custom trellis frames installed between the archway posts, they also lend the structure a feeling of substance and even romance. Although building the trellis features is somewhat time consuming and requires a table saw, simply compare your final results to the standard lattice sheets you can buy at building centers, and you'll be happy you put forth the effort.

Make the archway trellises. Because they're square, the trellis frames that fit into the sides of the archway are easier to make than the trellis wings, so it's a good idea to build them first and learn the techniques as you go. Each trellis frame holds a gridwork of ½-in.-thick × 1¼-in.-wide lattice strips. The top rails and the stiles for the archway trellises are 2 × 4s, and the bottom rails are 2 × 6. To make the lattice strips, we planed clear cedar 1 × 6 (actual size is ¾ × 5½ in.) down to ½ in. thick, then ripped 1¼-in.-wide strips on the table saw. This yielded four 8 ft. strips per board, so we were able to cut lattice for the entire project from nine 8-ft.-long 1 × 6s.

Choose some nice, clear 2 × 4s and cut them to length (See Cutting List). The ½-in.-wide × 1-in.-deep slots that are cut along the length of the boards capture the ends of the lattice strips. It would be possible to cut these slots using a router and the same jig used to cut the slots in the curbed top rails of the wings trellises, but it's faster and safer to cut them on a table saw. If you have a dado-blade set, you can make the slots in a single pass. Otherwise, set up your saw for a 1-in.-deep cut and run the frame pieces through it in several passes until you've cut ½-in.-wide grooves *(See Photo 2:1).* The inside shoulders of the grooves should start at the centerlines of each board, with the outside shoulders ending up ¼ in. from the faces of the workpieces. The offset grooves allow for the overlap between vertical and horizontal slots (you'll need to pay close attention to the orientation of the offset grooves when cutting the lap joints and assembling the frames).

The joints at the corners of the frames are simple lap joints. Since we used a dado-blade set to cut the slots, we also used it to make the lap cuts. Cut a lap in each end of each frame member *(See Photo 2:2),* removing wood on the faces of the boards containing the slots (this will result in ¾-in.-deep × 3½-in.-wide lap cuts.

While not difficult, assembling the trellis units does

Photo 2:1 Cut ½-in.-wide × 1-in.-deep slots in the edge of each square trellis frame rail and stile. We used a table saw and dado-blade set to make these cuts. The slots are offset ¼ in. from the center.

Photo 2:2 Use the dado-blade set to remove waste wood in a hurry, cutting the half-laps at the end of each rail and stile. Pay attention to the orientation of the offset slots.

demand a pretty spacious assembly table. A sheet of plywood laid across a pair of sawhorses is good. The lattice strips don't need to be glued into the framework. A spot of waterproof construction adhesive at each intersection between horizontal and vertical slats may be used to prevent twisting.

Join each bottom rail to two stiles to make a U-shaped frame (don't attach the top rail yet: it should be left off to create access to the slots for installing the lattice strips). Apply glue to the laps and join them together. Check to make sure the joints are square, then reinforce them by nailing or screwing *(See Photo 2:3).*

Install the vertical slats in the frame first. We made a 5¼-in.-wide spacer from plywood to help position the

Photo 2:3
Assemble the bottom rail and stiles of each square trellis frame, using glue and nails. Leave the top rail off so you can insert lattice strips.

Photo 2:4 Fit the vertical lattice strips into the bottom rail, using a 5¼ in. wide spacer as a guide. Secure the strips by driving two or three nails through the bottom rail and into each strip.

Photo 2:5
Install the horizontal lattice strips, starting at the bottom rail. Use the 5¼ in. spacer to set the distance between strips. Pin the strips in place with nails.

slats accurately *(See Photo 2:4)*. Once the slats are positioned, secure them into the bottom rail slot with two or three nails.

When all the vertical strips are locked in place, slide the horizontal strips into the slots in the stiles and distribute them evenly. Use the same spacer to set the positions, beginning at the bottom. Secure both ends of each horizontal lattice strip with nails *(See Photo 2:5)*.

When the latticework is assembled, install the top rail. Apply glue to the lap joints, then slip the top rail in place. Be sure the strips fit into the slot in the rail. Check for square and use the spacer to help hold the positions of the vertical slats at the top of the frame. Nail through the lap joints and into the tops of the slats *(See Photo 2:6)*.

Make the wing trellises. The wing trellises are built in much the same fashion as the square archway trellis units. The difference lies in the gracefully curved top rails on the wings. Because of their contours, making them is a bit more involved than making straight rails. And as a consequence of the rail shape, the lattice slats are not all exactly the same lengths. And you'll need to use a router to cut the slots for the lattice strips, since the table saw can't follow a curve.

Make the stiles and the bottom rails the same way you made them for the archway trellis frames. The only difference is in the lengths of the pieces. The slots and laps are cut the same way.

The top rails for the wing trellis frames are made by creating a template and using it as guide to rough-cut the shapes from a 2 × 8, then refining the cut by trimming along the template with a router and pattern-following bit.

Draw the rail pattern to scale on a piece of ¼-in.-thick hardboard, using the grid drawing on page 217 as a guide. Cut out the hardboard template with a band saw or a jig saw. With a belt sander or a drum sander chucked in a drill press, sand the edges of the template to smooth out the curves. The ends should form flat, square lines to join neatly to the frame stiles.

Lay the template onto an 8-ft.-long 2 × 8 and trace the pattern of the rail. Trim the extra length from the board, then rough-cut the shape with a jig saw. Cut to within about ⅛ in. of the line (See Photo 2:7). Cut out the rough shapes for both top rails. Next, use double-faced carpet tape to tack the template securely to each rough-cut rail (See Photo 2:8). Install a pattern-following bit in your router (pattern-following bits are flush-cutting bits with a collar at the top of the shank to ride along a template without cutting into it). The workpiece secured, rout around the template with the pattern-following bit set to full cutting depth (See Photo 2:9). The goal here is to create edges on the rail that are as smooth as the template edges. Because the cutting depth of the bit will be less than the thickness of the stock, you'll need to flip the workpiece over, reattach the template to the other side, then shape the rest of the edge.

We used a router with a straight bit and a special jig to cut the slots into the bottom edges of the top rails. Before undertaking this step, note that unlike the slots in the other frame members, the slot in each top rail is a full 1 in. thick because it must accommodate both vertical and horizontal lattice strips. The router "jig" we used is really only two guide blocks that are clamped to the base of the router (See Photo 2:10). A pair of spacers the same width as the workpiece are positioned between the fences before they're clamped in place. Set the fences so they are parallel and one is ¼ in. away from the bit (the bit will be offset slightly). Before cutting the slot, drill 1-in.-dia. × 1-in.-deep holes near the ends of rails. Locate the holes so they're centered side to side and the centerpoint is 3½ in. away from the ends of the rails. The holes are starter holes for the router bit you'll use to cut the slots.

Once the starter holes are drilled, the next challenge is to secure the curved rails so they can be routed accurately and safety. We clamped wood screw clamps to each end then clamped the wood screws to sturdy sawhorses. Set a straight router bit to 1 in. cutting depth (if you're using a soft wood like cedar — with harder woods, set a shallower cutting depth and cut the slots in progressively deeper cuts). Set the guide-fence jig so the fence that is ¼ in. away from the bit is on the left side (you'll be pulling the router backwards as you work). Engage the router and cut one side of the slot (See Photo 2:11). When you reach the end of the rail, stop the router and reposition yourself to cut back toward the direction you started from. The fence that's ¼ in. away from the bit should be on the other

Photo 2:6 Install the top rail after all the strips are in place. Glue and nail the lap joints at the corners, and nail through the rail and into the tops of the lattice strips. Use the spacer to make sure strips don't slip out of alignment during nailing.

Photo 2:7 Use the full-size hardboard template to lay out the shape of the top rail for the trellis wings. Using a jig saw, rough-cut the shape to within about ¹⁄₁₆ in. of the cutting line. Take care not to cut into or past the cutting lines.

Photo 2:8 Use double-faced carpet tape to secure the hardboard template over the rough-cut curved rail.

Photo 2:9 Install a pattern-following bit in your router and rout around the rough-cut top rail, smoothing out the shape as you follow the template. After routing all the way around, remove the template and tape it to the other face of the workpiece. Rout the edge form this side to finish the smoothing cut.

Photo 2:10 Clamp wood blocks to your router base to set up the router for slot-cutting the curved rail. Use cut-off pieces of the rail material to set the distance between blocks. Secure the blocks so the bit is offset (the edge should be ¼ in. away from one block).

side of the workpiece. Start the router and cut the other side of the slot (See Photo 2:12). The router base should contact as much of the workpiece as possible as you rout. If the router begins to bog down, stop the cut and raise the bit so you're removing less stock, then cut the slot in multiple passes. Cut slots in both top rails.

Cut half-laps in the ends of the wing trellis top rails to mate with the half-laps in the tops of the stiles. Once again, the curves of the rails make it difficult to perform this operation on a table saw. We simply laid out the half-laps, then used a circular saw to remove strips of wood to the correct depth in the waste area (See Photo 2:13). Then we removed the strips of left-over wood and smoothed the joint with a chisel (See Photo 2:14).

Join the bottoms rails and stiles (but not the top rails) with glue and nails, making sure the lap joints are square. Dry-fit the top rail into position. Cut the vertical lattice strips so they're each a couple of inches longer than their finished length. Dry-fit the strips in the bottom rail slots of one wing, using the 5¼ in. spacer as a guide. The lattice strips should overlay the top rail. The top ends will need to be trimmed to follow the curve of the top rail. At the high point of each intersection between the top rail and the strips, measure up 1 in. and mark each strip. (See Photo 2:15). Then, use a straightedge to extend the mark toward the lower point of intersection, following the line of the top rail (See Photo 2:16). Remove the lattice strips and trim them to length on the cutting lines.

Replace the strips in the bottom rail and dry-fit the top rail over the free ends and check to make sure none of the strips are too long. Nail the bottom ends in place. Four of the horizontal lattice strips on each trellis are square cut to fit between

Photo 2:11 Drill a starter hole for your router bit, then fit the router with guide blocks over the curved edge of the rail. Rout out one side of the slot area.

Photo 2:12 Rout back along the opposite face of the work-piece, this time with the positions of the guide blocks reversed. The resulting slot should be ¼ in. from each edge of the work-piece. Cut the slot to full depth in several passes.

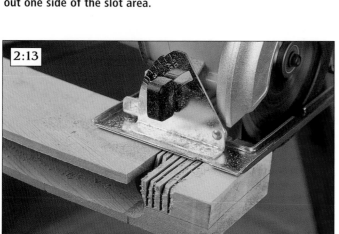

Photo 2:13 Use a circular saw to cut out the waste wood to make the half-laps at the ends of the curved top rail. Cut ¾-in.-deep saw kerfs from the end of the board to the lap shoulder.

Photo 2:14 Clean up and smooth the half-lap joints with a sharp wood chisel.

the stiles. Position them in the stile slots, using the spacer for reference. The top three horizontal strips on each trellis need to be contoured on the end that inter-sects the top rail (the contoured end is fitted into the slot in the top rail). Dry-lay them in position and mark the contours as you did for the vertical rails. Cut them to fit, then nail the horizontal strips in place, starting at the bottom *(See Photo 2:17).* Install the lattice strips on both trellises.

Join the top rails to the stiles with glue and nails. You'll notice that there are ½ in. gaps between some

of the lattice strips and the shoulders of the slots. These gaps need to be filled with filler blocks. Use cut-off pieces of lattice strip to make the blocks, trimming them so they'll be flush with the bottom edge of the top rail. Set the blocks into the gaps, then secure them with glue and nails *(See Photo 2:18).* If you're using a hammer and finish nails, not a pneumatic nailer, drill pilot holes first. Now, cut filler blocks to fit between the ends of all the slats in all bottom rails and attach them with glue and nails *(See Photo 2:19).*

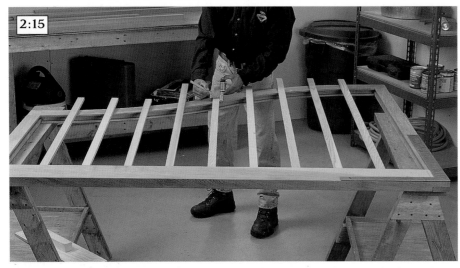

Photo 2:15 Join the bottom rail and the stiles for each wing frame with glue and nails. Dry-fit vertical lattice strips in the bottom slot. To mark the strips for trimming, start by measuring up 1 in. from the high side where each strip crosses the top rail.

Photo 2:16 Extend cutting lines across the top of each vertical lattice strip by following a straightedge that's roughly parallel to the curve of the frame.

Photo 2:17 After the vertical strips are cut to fit, pin them into the bottom rails. Then begin installing the horizontal strips, starting at the bottom. Use the spacer and fasten the strips at the stiles as you work.

Photo 2:18 When all the vertical and horizontal strips are fitted into the top rails, glue and nail the lap joints, then cut spacers to fill the gaps between strips and the top rail slots (there will be a ½-in. gap on one side of each strip). Use cutoff pieces of lattice to make the spacers. Secure them with glue and nails.

Photo 2:19 Fill the gaps between lattice strip ends in all bottom rails of each trellis frame, and secure the fillers with glue and nails. NOTE: If you're using a hammer and nails, not a nail gun, it's a good idea to drill pilot hole for the nails first. You can do this easily by chucking one of the finish nails you're using into your drill and using it as a drill bit.

Photo 3:1 Lay out the location for the gateway using batterboards and mason's strings.

Photo 3:2 We used one-piece stake-and-post-anchor hardware to secure the posts, rather than messing with pouring footings. Drive the stakes at the post locations, doing your best to get them level and aligned correctly. A chunk of 4 × 4 placed in the saddle portion absorbs the blows from the maul.

Photo 3:3 Drive stakes and use a mason's string so you can check to make sure the post anchors are all aligned with one another. Measure from the bottom of the post-anchor saddle to determine the required height of each post.

Photo 3:4 Trim the posts to the correct height with a circular saw. It's likely the heights will all be a little different to account for uneven terrain.

Assemble & install the gateway

The gateway is not designed to be freestanding. One way to anchor it to the ground is to pour concrete footings and attach the posts to the footings with metal post anchors (See page 188). But if you'd rather not go to all that effort, use stake-and-post-anchor hardware. These anchors are equipped with an integral, two-sided metal stake that you simply drive into the ground at the post locations. Then you fit the post into the saddle portion of the device and tighten the nuts and bolts to cinch the saddle around the post.

Lay out the site & install the archway. Use batterboards and mason's string to lay out the post locations for the gateway (See pages 185 to 186 Gazebo).You should have strings intersecting at each post location. Make sure to level the strings *(See Photo 3:1)*. Drive the stake-and-post anchors at each post location. Before driving them, cut a scrap of 4 × 4 about 6 in. long and place it in the saddle to absorb the shock of the sledge or maul. Drive the stake about halfway in, then stop and check to make sure it is going in straight, using a level *(See Photo 3:2).* Adjust as needed, then finish driv-

3:5

Photo 3:5 Attach the archway (square) trellises to the archway posts by driving 3-in. deck screws through the trellis frame stiles and into the posts.

3:6

Photo 3:6 Set the archway post-and-trellis assemblies into the saddle of the post anchors and tighten the bolts to hold them in place (inset photo).

ing the hardware home. Drive all the stake/anchors so the bottoms of the saddles are at grade. Any compensation for uneven ground will be made by adjusting the heights of the posts when they're trimmed.

Drive stakes at the ends of the main run of four posts and connect them with a line level. Set the line at the highest anchor and measure the distance from the bottom of each post saddle to the line *(See Photo 3:3)*. Also check the height of the two archway post anchors. The highest anchor (the one closest to the level line) should be fitted with a 66¾-in.-long post. For the other posts (if different) add the amount away from the line they are than the high post to 66¾ in., and cut to that length with a circular saw *(See Photo 3:4)*. Be sure you don't trim off the an end with a mortise cut for a loose tenon.

Attach the square archway trellises to the posts that form the four corners of the archway. The tops of the trellis frames should be the same distance (2 in.) down from the post tops. To attach the frames, lay the posts on their sides on a worksurface, making sure the mortised post ends are at the same end (the top). Position a few ⅞-in. spacers next to each post to support the the frame and raise it to the correct position. Drill pilot holes, then drive 3½ in. screws through the slots in the frame stiles and into the posts *(See Photo 3:5)*. Drive a screw every foot or so. Join the frames and posts into two assemblies that form the "walls" of the archway.

Set one of the assemblies

into the post anchors and press it down to make sure it's well seated. Tighten the bolts on the post anchors so the saddles fit snugly around the bottoms of the posts. The assembly should be freestanding at this point. Install the assembly on the other side of the archway and tighten the saddle bolts *(See Photo 3:6 and inset)*.

Set a loose tenon in each post-top mortise in the archway. You may need to rap the tenons lightly to seat them — if you find you need a hammer or mallet to drive them in, they're too big and should be sanded down a bit. Once again with a helper, raise the top of the archway so it rests on top of the posts. Carefully position the top so the mortises in the bottoms of the arches line up over the free ends of the loose tenons *(See Photo 3:7)*. Pull down carefully on the top, if necessary, until the posts and the arches butt together flush. To pin the top in place, drive a pair of 6d finish nails into each tenon: one nail through the post and the other through the arch.

Attach the end posts to the short ends of the wing trellises the same way you attached the taller posts to the archway frames *(See Photo 3:8)*. Set the short posts into their anchors and tighten the bolts until snug. Loosely clamp the free end of each wing to the shared archway post. Adjust the wing trellis frame until it is centered on the shared post and perpendicular to the archway frame. The bottom rails should all align. Tighten the clamps so the wings don't slip out of position, then attach them to the shared posts with 3½ in. screws driven through pilot holes in the frame stiles *(See Photo 3:9)*. This essentially completes the installation of the primary gateway parts. Check to make sure everything is square, then cinch up the post anchor bolts so they're good and tight (but do not overtighten them).

Photo 3:7 Fit a loose tenon into each post-top mortise. With a helper, lower the archway top into position. Press down on the archway, if needed, until the tenons are fully seated in the archway mortises. Don't glue the tenons; but it's a good idea to drive a 6d nail through both the post and archway to pin the tenons in place at each joint.

Photo 3:8 Attach the wing trellis frames to the outer posts with 3-in. deck screws.

Photo 3:9
Set the wing trellises into the appropriate post saddles and adjust their positions until they're level, plumb and at a right angle to the archway trellis frames. Join the wings to the shared post with 3½-in. deck screws.

Photo 3:10
Cut filler strips to fill the gaps between the arches and the posts, then miter-cut 1 × 2 trim to conceal the joint. Attach the trim pieces with stainless steel finish nails.

Photo 3:11 Cut and attach a flat post cap to th each post, then conical the cap

Photo 3:12 Apply your finish of choice. We used clear wood sealer.

Finishing touches. The transition molding overlaps the top edges of the post. It punctuates the jump from the 4 × 4 post to the smaller-sectioned arch, and it offers a vehicle for sealing the top of the post.

The legs of the arches will be recessed about ¾ to ⅞ in. per side from the parallel faces of the posts in the archway. Measure the exact size of these gaps and cut ¾-in.-high filler strips to fit. The outer faces and ends of the strips should be flush with the posts. Attach the filler strips to the post arches with construction adhesive.

Rip-cut ½- × 1½-in. strips of molding to apply over the joints between the posts and arches. Miter-cut the ends to wrap around the posts. Attach the mitered molding with 6d finish nails (See Photo 3:10). The tops of the molding strips should be flush with the tops of the filler strips. When the molding is installed, apply clear caulk to the seams between the pieces on the post top. This will retard water penetration.

Cut 3½-in.-square pieces of ¾-in. cedar to cap the short posts on the ends of the gateway wings. The post caps help prevent water from wicking into the exposed end grain at the post tops. Attach them with construction adhesive and 6d finish nails. Knock the cap edges back with a file or sander if they project out past the faces of the posts.

Cut ½- × 1½-in. strips of wood to frame the tops of the short posts, concealing the seams between the post caps and the posts. Miter the ends and install as with the frames around the arch/post joints (See Photo 3:11).

Set any exposed nailheads with a nailset and sand down any rough areas on the gateway. Wipe clean, then apply your finish of choice. We applied clear wood sealer to protect the wood.

LANDSCAPE BRIDGE

Graceful and engaging, a landscape bridge can brighten backyards or gardens even in the flattest and driest surroundings. Add a little romance to your living spaces (and have some fun in the shop) by building this "portable" bridge yourself.

3/8" x 4" Carriage bolt, typ.

OVERALL DIMENSIONS ($51 \times 122\frac{1}{2} \times 47\frac{3}{4}''$)

KEY	PART NAME	QTY.	SIZE	MATERIAL
MAIN STRUCTURE				
A	JOIST	4	$1\frac{1}{2} \times 11\frac{1}{4} \times 120''$	PRESSURE TREATED
B	BLOCKING	6	$1\frac{1}{2} \times 10\frac{3}{8} \times 13\frac{1}{2}''$	PRESSURE TREATED
C	FASCIA	2	$\frac{3}{4} \times 3\frac{3}{4} \times 46\frac{1}{2}''$	CEDAR
D	RAIL POST	4	$3\frac{1}{2} \times 3\frac{1}{2} \times 45\frac{1}{4}''$	CEDAR
E	RAIL POST	4	$3\frac{1}{2} \times 3\frac{1}{2} \times 39''$	CEDAR
F	HANDRAIL	2	$1\frac{1}{2} \times 3\frac{1}{2} \times 48\frac{1}{2}''$	CEDAR
G	BALUSTER RAIL	4	$1\frac{1}{2} \times 2\frac{1}{2} \times 48\frac{1}{2}''$	CEDAR
H	BALUSTER	22	$1\frac{1}{2} \times 1\frac{1}{2} \times 23\frac{1}{4}''$	CEDAR
I	RAMPED HANDRAIL	4	$1\frac{1}{2} \times 3\frac{1}{2} \times 31''$**	CEDAR
J	RAMPED BALUSTER RAIL	8	$1\frac{1}{2} \times 2\frac{1}{2} \times 31''$**	CEDAR
K	RAMPED BALUSTER	28	$1\frac{1}{2} \times 1\frac{1}{2} \times 24\frac{3}{8}''$	CEDAR
L	POST BRIM	8	$1 \times 4\frac{1}{2} \times 4\frac{1}{2}''$	CEDAR
M	POST CAP	8	$1 \times 3\frac{1}{2} \times 3\frac{1}{2}''$	CEDAR
N	DECKING	22	$1 \times 5\frac{1}{2} \times 47\frac{1}{2}''$	CEDAR
O	RAIL CLADDING	4	$\frac{3}{4} \times 1\frac{1}{2} \times 48\frac{1}{2}''$	CEDAR
P	RAMPED RAIL CLADDING	8	$\frac{3}{4} \times 1\frac{1}{2} \times 31''$	CEDAR

** INDICATES CUT TO FIT

HARDWARE REQUIRED

DECK SCREWS		$\#8 \times 3'', 2\frac{1}{2}''$	
CARRIAGE BOLTS	20	$\frac{3}{8} \times 4''$	W/NUTS & WASHERS

NOTICE: Part dimensions are based on ideal installation conditions. For best results, confirm measurements on actual project before cutting parts.

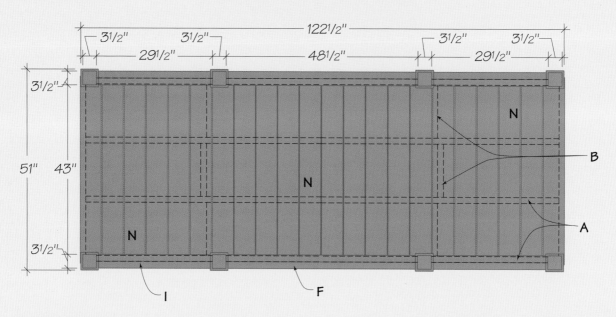

PLAN VIEW

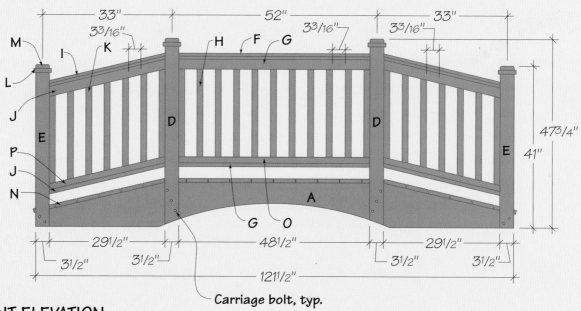

FRONT ELEVATION

Carriage bolt, typ.

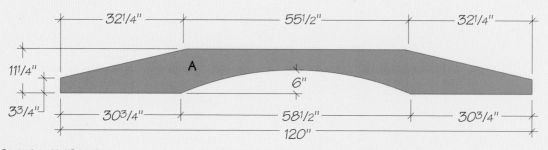

JOIST LAYOUT

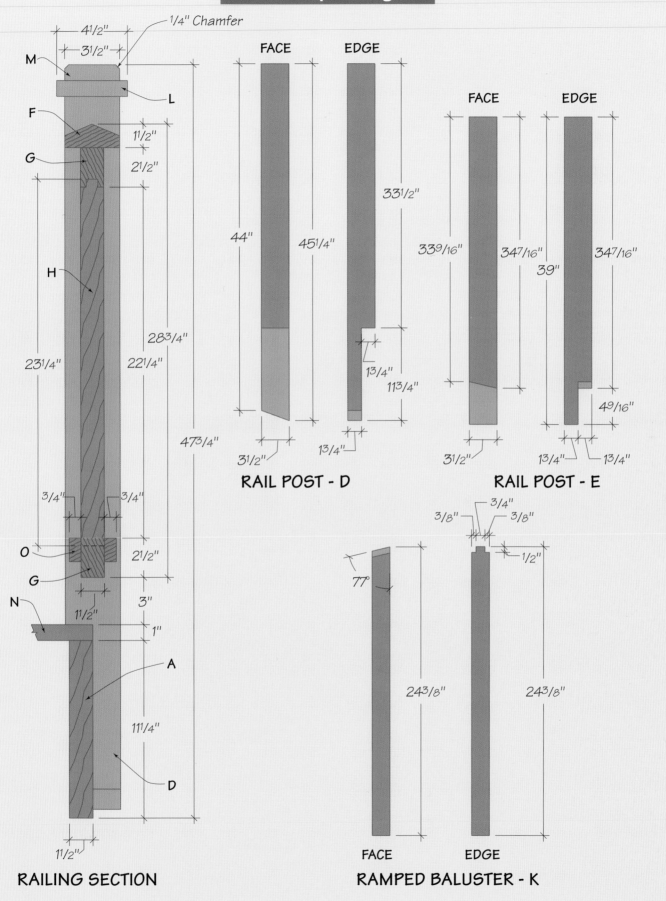

1/4" Chamfer

4 1/2"
3 1/2"

M

L

F

1 1/2"

G

2 1/2"

H

28 3/4"

23 1/4"

22 1/4"

47 3/4"

3/4"   3/4"

O

2 1/2"

G

N

3"

1 1/2"

1"

A

11 1/4"

D

1 1/2"

RAILING SECTION

FACE   EDGE

44"

45 1/4"

1 3/4"

11 3/4"

1 3/4"

3 1/2"

RAIL POST - D

FACE   EDGE

33 1/2"

33 9/16"   34 7/16"   34 7/16"

39"

4 9/16"

3 1/2"   1 3/4"   1 3/4"

RAIL POST - E

3/8"   3/4"   3/8"

1/2"

77°

24 3/8"   24 3/8"

FACE   EDGE

RAMPED BALUSTER - K

Photos by Apple River Studios

Photo 1 Use a 1-in.-wide strip of ¼-in.-thick hardboard to flex an arc for laying out the arches at the bottoms of the joists.

Photo 2 Cut the tapers at the ends of the joists with a circular saw and straightedge. The tapers create the "rise" in the bridge.

Photo 3 Stagger the blocking that fits between joists to create access for attaching the blocking boards to the joists. The tops of the blocking must be beveled to match the slope of the tapered joists.

Photo 4 Attach fascia boards to the ends of the joists at each end of the bridge. The fascia also must be beveled to follow the slope line of the joists.

Function and beauty combine in this appealing landscape bridge. In addition to providing a lovely landscape feature to look at, it's wide enough and sturdy enough to allow you to push a lawn mower or small wheelbarrow across. The obvious use of a bridge like this is to span a small stream: It's especially useful if the stream divides your property, making access to the far side difficult. But even without a body of water to cross, a bridge can enhance and beautify your yard. Use it to span a hollow, swale or rocky outcropping. Or create the illusion of a stream by spreading landscaping stones in a meandering path beneath the bridge.

Reduced to its essentials, the bridge consists of four joists joined with blocking, posts, deck boards and a railing on each side. As shown, the bridge is about 12 feet long and four feet wide, but you can scale it to suit your needs and the appearance you want for your yard

(but try to maintain a walkway that's at least 32 in. wide). This landscape bridge is a carpentry project that's best built in your shop, then moved to the site for assembly, installation and finishing.

Build the joist framework

The landscape bridge is supported by four arched and tapered joists connected with 2 × 12 blocking. A beveled fascia board is attached to each set of joist ends to cap the ends of the bridge. The four joists are cut from 10-ft.-long 2 × 12s. Lay out and cut one joist then use it as a template for making the other three.

The arcs at the bottom edges of the joists can be laid out by flexing a 1-in.-wide strip of ¼ in. hardboard between the end points of the arc. Mark the end points along the bottom edge, 30¾ in. from each end. Then, find the midpoint of the 2 × 12 (60 in.), measure up 6 in. and drive a small nail. Clamp the hardboard strip to the work-piece so the ends fall across the endpoint marks and the peak of the strip is pressed against the nail. Trace the arc onto the board *(See Photo 1)*. Remove the strip and cut out the arc with a jig saw. Sand the edge of the cut smooth.

Taper the ends of the joist: First, measure up 3¾ in. from the bottom edge on each end of the joist and make a reference mark. Then, measure 31⅜ in. along the top edge from the top corner above each reference mark. Connect the marks at each end to make cutting lines. Make the taper cuts with a jig saw or circular saw and a straight-edge *(See Photo 2)*. Lay out and cut the rest of the joists.

The joists are connected with pieces of blocking cut to 13½ in. long and 10⅜ in. wide from 2 × 12 stock. Fascia boards beveled on the top edges are nailed to the ends of the joists. Because of the angle of the tapers cut on the joists, the blocking will need to be trimmed a bit. You can plane the blocking flush with the top edges of the joists after it is installed with a hand plane or hand-held power plane. Otherwise, hold them in place between the joists and mark the amount of stock that needs to be trimmed away. Bevel-cut to the lines with a circular saw, jigsaw or table saw.

The blocking should be aligned with the "break" on the top edges of the joists (where the taper levels off). But to allow you to screw through the joists and into the ends of each piece of blocking, stagger the blocking.

Working on a flat surface, line the pieces of blocking up so the tops are flush with the tops of the joists and install them by end-screwing through the joists and into the blocking. Drive three #8 × 3 in. deck screws per joint *(See Photo 3)*.

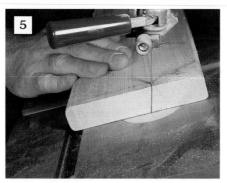

Photo 5 Notch the ends of the deck boards to fit around the posts. The notches in the deck boards need to be cut at an angle to fit against the posts.

Photo 7 Clamp each post to the joist framework and adjust it so it's level and plumb before you attach it. The deck board shown is dry-fit as a spacer.

The top edges of the fascia boards are beveled at a 13° angle. Cross-cut the boards to length, then rip the bevel on a table saw or with your circular saw. Attach the fascia boards to the ends of the joists *(See Photo 4)*.

Install the posts

The posts are cut with half-laps to make lap joints where they fit against the joist framework. The deck boards that intersect with the posts are notched to fit. The surest way to lay out the half-laps for the end posts is to notch and dry-install the end deck boards, then cut the posts to fit over them. To mark the end deck boards for notching, first mark the inside edge of each post on the outer joists. The posts should be flush with the ends of the joist framework, so

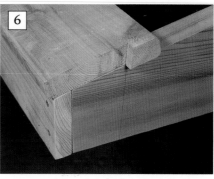

Photo 6 The deck boards at the ends of the bridge are flush with the outer joists in the notched area and overhang the joists and fascia by ½ in. elsewhere.

Photo 8 Drill counterbored guide holes for the carriage bolts that secure the posts. Drive bolts into the guide holes and secure with washers and nuts.

measure in 3½ in. from each end. Then, lay the deck board across the joists so it overhangs the fascia by ½ in. Extend the line for the post edges up onto each end of the deck board. Measure in ½ in. at the top of the cutting line and draw a cutting line parallel to the end of the board. With a band saw, jig saw or hand saw, make the ½-in.-deep cut at the edge of the notch, following the cutting angle *(See Photo 5)*. Remove the wood from the notched area by making the long cut parallel to the board end. Notch both ends. Test the fit of the deck board *(See Photo 6)* then screw it temporarily in place (you'll want to remove it before installing the posts so you can get better access to the fasteners). Notch and install both end boards.

Cut the end posts to length, then

Photo 9 Trace the joist arch profile onto the bottom of each post.

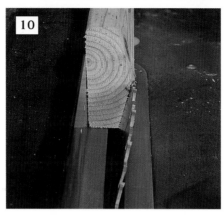

Photo 10 Chamfer the top of the hand rail stock at 15° from both directions.

cut half-lap joints in the posts so they fit over the end deck boards and are flush with the bottoms of the joists. The easiest way to cut the half-laps is to use a dado-blade set installed in your table saw (See *Cutting half-laps*, right). Keep in mind that the shoulders of the half-laps in the end posts must slope to follow the tapers at the ends of the joists. To cut them, you'll need to set the table saw miter gauge to a 13° angle when making the initial pass or two at the top of the half-lap notch. Cut the first half-lap, then position the post and clamp it in place *(See Photo 7).* Check with a level and framing square to make sure the post is vertical

and plumb. Cut all four end posts, checking to make sure they fit correctly, then attach them to the joists with two ⅜ × 4 in. carriage

Cutting half-laps

Notching a post to create a half-lap for a lap joint is easy to do with a table saw and dado-blade set. When notching large stock, like the 4 × 4 post at right, you'll need to make at least two passes of increasing depth to keep the blades from bogging down. Using a miter gauge as a guide, feed the workpiece through the blades in the outlined area (Photo 1), leaving a narrow nub of uncut material for the workpiece to ride on. Make another pass to full depth, then knock off the nub with a hammer (Photo 2). Flatten the shoulder and cheek of the notch with a chisel (Photo 3).

bolts at each end post, driven into counterbored guide holes. Drill the counterbore and guide holes, then drive the carriage bolts through the guide holes with a hammer *(See Photo 8).* Secure the carriage bolts with washers and ⅜-in. nuts.

Install the higher midposts. Unlike the end posts, these posts have square half-laps, which makes them easier to cut. Simply cut the posts slightly overlong, then cut a half-lap at the bottom of each post. Set a deck board on the joists as a spacer. Clamp each post in place, then trace the arc of the outer joist onto the bottom end of the post *(See Photo 9).* Cut the arc shape with a jig saw then attach the posts with carriage bolts, as with the end posts. Remove the deck board spacers.

Build & install the railings

The deck railings are formed by capturing 2 × 2 balusters between top and bottom rails, then capping the top rail with a wide handrail. Each rail is made in three sections to fit between the posts. The balusters have tenon-style tongues on top to fit into grooves that run the length of each top rail. At the bottom, the balusters are left full size and fit into dadoes cut across the bottom rail. To hide the bottom rail/baluster joints, 1 × 2 cladding is attached to the outer faces of the bottom rails. Double-check all Cutting List measurements against the actual distances between your posts before cutting the parts for the railings — it's reasonable to expect to find some variation.

The baluster rails are cut from 2 × 3 stock (you'll probably need to rip-cut 2 × 4s to width), and the handrails are fashioned from 2 × 4s. The handrails are chamfered on top to shed water and make them more comfortable to hold. Although you won't be cutting the handrails to fit until the railing is installed, go ahead and cut the chamfers now. When the chamfers are cut, the handrails will slope from 1½ in. thick at the middles to ¾ in. thick at the edges. To produce these chamfers, you need to make two bevel-rip cuts. While the chamfers can be cut with a circular saw, the best tool for this job is the table saw. Raise the blade and tilt it to 15°. Set the fence so it's ¾ in. away from the point where the blade will meet the stock, then cut the first chamfer. Turn the workpiece over and make the second bevel cut to complete the chamfer *(See Photo 10)*.

Miter-cut the ends of the short handrail sections at 13° angles. Be sure the cuts on the ends of each handrail section are parallel. Sand the handrails thoroughly and set them aside.

The balusters are joined to the top rails with tongue-and-groove joints. Cut the groove (¾ in. wide × ½ in. deep) in the bottom edge of the rail. This can be done with a router and ¾-in. straight bit, using edge guides. But we used the table saw and dado-blade set. Cut grooves in all top rails *(See Photo 11)*.

Before making the bottom baluster rails, make the balusters so you can use them to guide your work. Begin the process by ripping and cross-cutting stock to the dimensions specified by the Cutting List. The balusters for the level section of railing are square-cut, but those for the angled railing sections are mitered at 13° on the top ends to follow the slope of the handrail (which follows the slope of the joist tapers). Cut the tongues at the ends of each baluster by setting up your dado-blade set to make a ⅜-in.-deep × ½-in.-wide rabbet cut, then run all four faces of each baluster end through the blade (this will create tongues that are ¾ in. thick and ½ in. deep). Attach an auxiliary fence to your miter gauge to guide the workpieces. Also attach a reference block to your rip fence to align your workpieces — the reference block should be ½ in. outside the point where the blades contact the workpiece *(See Photo 12)*. To cut the tongues on the mitered balusters, simply adjust the miter gauge so the end of each baluster butts flat against the reference block.

The bottom rails are cut with a series of dadoes to accommodate the bottom ends of the balusters. Start by laying out the dadoes on the straight rails that fit on the flat portion of the bridge. Tip: *Cut the rails for each side of the bridge to length then lay them next to one another edge-to-edge so you can lay out baluster locations on both rails at the same time.* Outline baluster locations at each end, then mark the midpoint of the rail and center a baluster at that point. Lay out field balusters from the middle to the ends on each side. There are 11 balusters in total, so the spacing should be about 3³⁄₁₆ in. between balusters. Depending on the actual size of your stock, you may need to play with the spacing a bit, though. This is why it helps to have

Photo 11 Cut a ¾-in.-wide × ½-in.-deep groove in the bottom of each top rail to hold the baluster tongues.

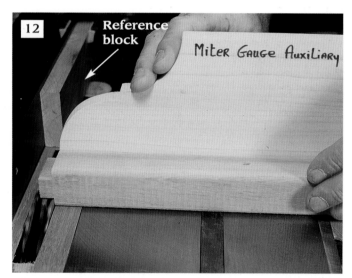

Photo 12 Cut the tenon-style tongues in the top ends of the baluster by running each face through the dado-blade set.

all the balusters cut so you physically lay them on the rails for reference. To avoid confusion as you are cutting, shade the waste areas with a pencil. Set up the dado cutter at its maximum cutting width and adjust the depth of cut to ½ in. Move the rip fence out of the way; you'll use the miter gauge to guide the rails across the cutter. Run the rails over the dado head to remove the wood in the dado locations. Again, you can save some time by ganging the rails together.

The setup is slightly different for cutting the dadoes in the angled rails that fit into the ramped sections of the bridge. For these, the dado set must be tilted at a 13° angle. Plus, you'll need to make two passes for each dado, with the blades set at different heights to create a smooth-bottomed dado with the correct pitch. The first, shallower, cut should be ¼ in. deep at the lower side. The shallower bite of the second cut should be the same depth as the higher side of the first cut.

Photo 13 Set the cutting angle of the dado-blade set to 13° and cut dadoes in the bottom rail to hold the balusters in the ramped railing sections. The low end of the second pass should be the same height as the high end of the first pass.

Photo 14 Secure the balusters in the bottom-rail dadoes with glue (we used polyurethane glue) and one 3-in. deck screw driven into each baluster. When using polyurethane glue, moisten the wood slightly before applying the glue.

This gets a little tricky, so it's a good idea to practice a few cuts on some 2 × 2 scrap first. And be sure to lay out the baluster positions carefully, as you did for the rails for the flat portion. Cut all the dadoes for these four rails *(See Photo 13)*.

Assemble the railing sections using glue and 3-in.-long deck screws. Lay out all the parts for a section on a flat surface. To begin, apply glue to the baluster dadoes in the bottom rail. Use a disposable brush to spread the glue evenly. Apply glue to the tongues on the baluster tops, too. Fit the top railing groove over the baluster tongues and fit the bottoms of the balusters into the corresponding dadoes in the bottom rail. Drill a pilot hole and drive one deck screw through the bottom of the bottom rail and into each baluster end *(See Photo 14)*. Check with a framing square or by measuring the diagonals to make sure the section is square, and adjust as needed. Then, drive screws through the top rail and into the baluster tops. It's not a bad idea to clamp the section in two directions while the glue sets to keep it from falling out of square. Assemble all railing sections in this manner.

Install the decking & apply the finish

The decking adds greatly to the weight of the bridge structure. Because it is not time consuming to install, consider cutting the boards to fit in your shop, then moving them to the installation site.

Install the deck boards you've already cut and notched to fit around the posts by sliding them under the posts, then driving a pair of 3 in. deck screws through the boards and into each joist. The end boards should overhang the fascia by ½ in. All deck boards that do not butt up against a post should overhang the outer joists by ½ in. Lay the deck boards across the joists, using 16d common nails as spacers between boards. If the deck board layout doesn't come out

exactly right, make adjustments of less than 1 in. total by ripping one board (the last board before the flat area of the walkway is a good choice). If you need to remove more than 1 in., spread it out over two or more deck boards to preserve some uniformity. When building the bridge, we did not need to make any adjustments to the deck board widths. The screw heads should be countersunk.

Once the decking is installed, go ahead and install the railing sections. Set 3 in. spacers at each end of the opening, set the railing section onto the spacers and attach it to the posts at each end with deck screws. Then, measure the distances between posts and cut the pieces of the chamfered handrail to fit (you'll need to miter-cut the ends of the shorter sections). Attach the handrail with construction adhesive and a few screws driven up through the top rail and into the hand rail in each section. To conceal the dadoes and baluster bottoms, rip-cut some 1× stock to 1½ in. wide, then cut pieces to clad both sides of the bottom rails. Round over the edges then attach the cladding with 6d stainless steel finishing nails.

Cap the posts. The caps have two parts, a square cap made of 5⁄4 deck boards, which overhang the post by ½ in. all around, and a smaller, chamfered cap that is centered on top of the square cap. Cut the parts to the dimensions specified by the Cutting List. The chamfers on the smaller cap are formed by trimming with a chamfering bit in a router table, or by hand-filing. Once the pieces are cut, installation is a matter of aligning them on the post and fastening them. The lower cap piece can be attached with two or three screws driven at slight angles into the post top. The "cap" is nailed to the brim with finish nails.

Finally, apply a coat of stain or water sealer to the bridge, if desired.

Arbor/Trellis

An arbor is an open, overhead structure supported by posts and
typically used to train plants and to provide shade.
A trellis is a vertical matrix of slats or lathe that can also be used to train plants,
while creating an exterior "room divider."
When combined, these structures form an Arbor/Trellis that adds
tranquility and privacy to your yard.

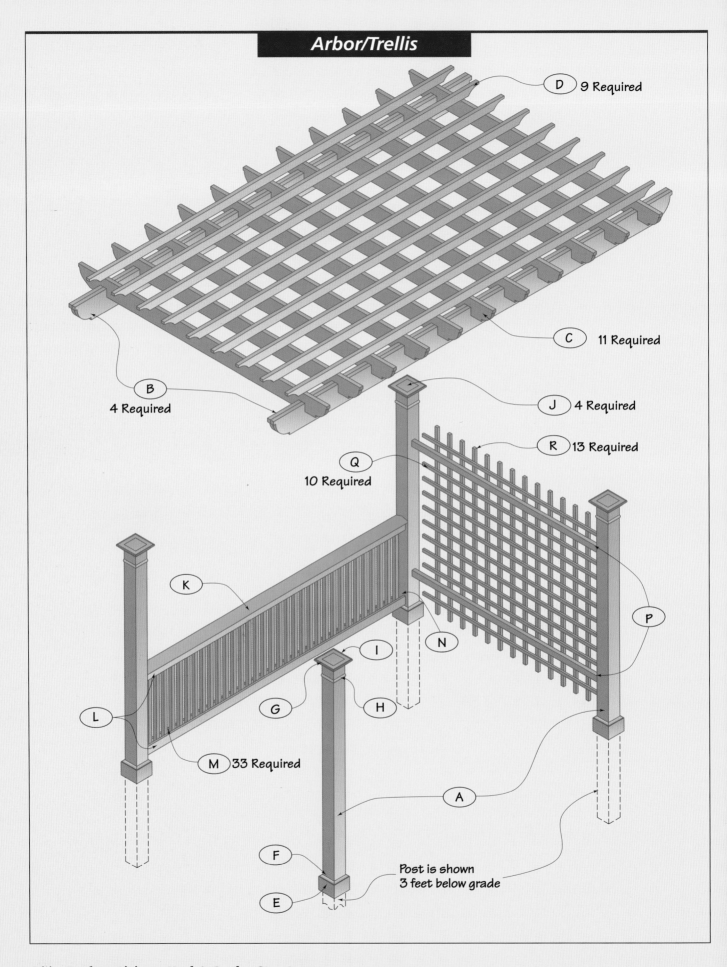

D 9 Required

C 11 Required

B
4 Required

J 4 Required

R 13 Required

Q
10 Required

K

N

I

P

G

H

L

M 33 Required

A

F

E

Post is shown
3 feet below grade

Cutting List

OVERALL DIMENSIONS (120 × 192 × 112$\frac{1}{2}$")

KEY	PART NAME	QTY.	SIZE	MATERIAL
MAIN STRUCTURE				
A	POST	4	5$\frac{1}{2}$ × 5$\frac{1}{2}$ × 131"	EXTERIOR LUMBER
B	BEAM	4	1$\frac{1}{2}$ × 9$\frac{1}{4}$ × 192"	EXTERIOR LUMBER
C	RAFTER	11	1$\frac{1}{2}$ × 7$\frac{1}{4}$ × 120"	EXTERIOR LUMBER
D	PURLIN	9	1$\frac{1}{2}$ × 3$\frac{1}{2}$ × 176$\frac{1}{2}$"	EXTERIOR LUMBER
E	BASEBOARD	16	1 × 5$\frac{1}{2}$ × 7$\frac{1}{2}$"	EXTERIOR LUMBER
F	QUARTER-ROUND MOLDING	16	$\frac{3}{4}$ × 3/4 × 7"	PINE
G	COVE MOLDING	16	$\frac{5}{8}$ × 2$\frac{3}{4}$ × 9$\frac{1}{4}$"	PINE
H	HALF-ROUND MOLDING	16	$\frac{1}{2}$ × 1 × 6$\frac{1}{2}$"	PINE
I	COVE FILLER BLOCKS	16	1$\frac{1}{2}$ × 1$\frac{5}{8}$ × 5"	PINE
J	POST CAP	4	1 × 5$\frac{1}{2}$ × 5$\frac{1}{2}$"	EXTERIOR LUMBER
RAILING				
K	HANDRAIL	1	1$\frac{1}{2}$ × 5$\frac{1}{2}$ × 126$\frac{1}{2}$"	EXTERIOR LUMBER
L	STRETCHER RAILS	4	$\frac{3}{4}$ × 3$\frac{1}{2}$ × 126$\frac{1}{2}$"	EXTERIOR LUMBER
M	BALUSTERS	33	1$\frac{1}{2}$ × 1$\frac{1}{2}$ × 34$\frac{1}{2}$"	EXTERIOR LUMBER
N	MOUNTING BLOCK	4	1$\frac{1}{2}$ × 1$\frac{1}{2}$ × 3$\frac{1}{2}$"	EXTERIOR LUMBER
O	HANDRAIL MOUNTING BLOCK	4	1$\frac{1}{2}$ × 1$\frac{1}{2}$ × 2$\frac{1}{4}$"	EXTERIOR LUMBER
TRELLIS				
P	MOUNTING STRETCHERS	2	1$\frac{1}{2}$ × 2$\frac{1}{2}$ × 90$\frac{1}{2}$"	CEDAR
Q	HORIZONTAL SLATS	10	$\frac{3}{4}$ × 1$\frac{1}{4}$ × 84"	CEDAR
R	VERTICAL SLATS	13	1 × 1$\frac{1}{4}$ × 78"	CEDAR
HARDWARE REQUIRED				
	FINISH NAILS		6d, 8d, 12d, 16d	ALUMINUM
	DECK SCREWS		#8 × 2", #8 × 3"	GALVANIZED

> **NOTICE: Part dimensions are based on ideal installation conditions. For best results, confirm measurements on actual project before cutting parts.**

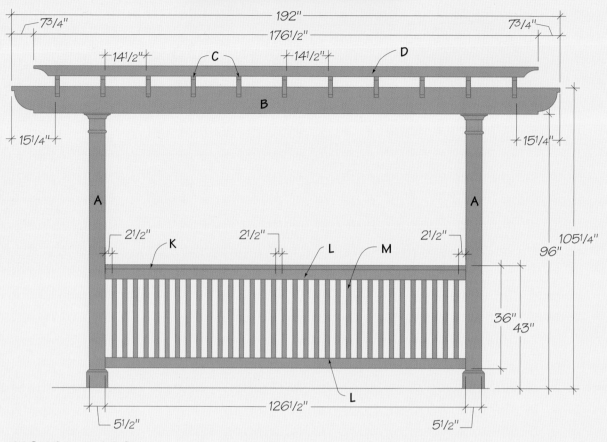

FRONT ELEVATION

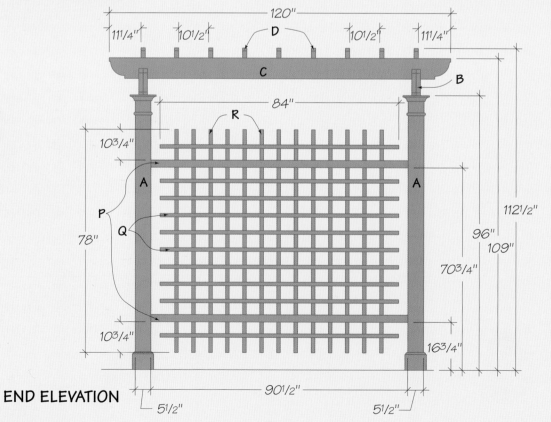

END ELEVATION

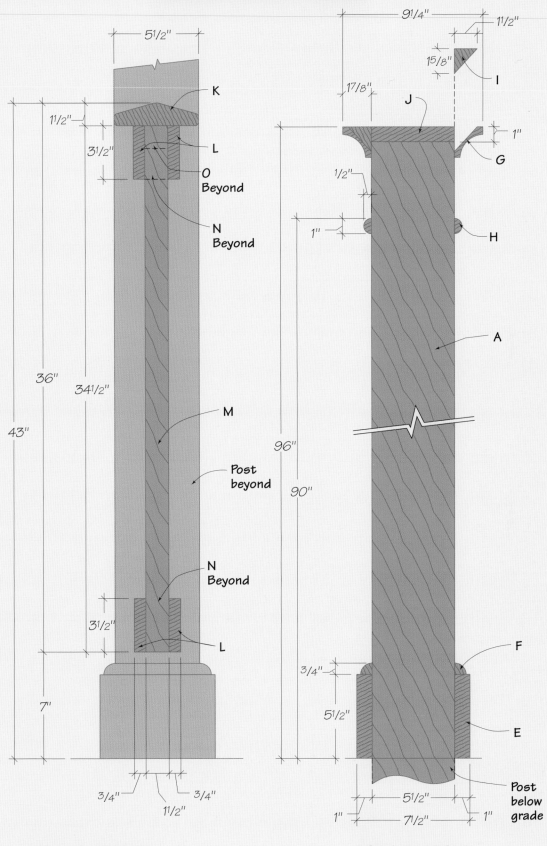

RAILING SECTION

POST SECTION

A pleasant refuge from the harsh sun is under the spreading, leafy branches of a tree. Unfortunately, it takes a tree years to mature enough to provide this kind of haven. An arbor structure, like this arbor/trellis, can provide a comparable escape after only a couple of weekends' work.

The arbor consists of four 6 × 6 posts supporting an open roof of beams and rafters. The open roof itself can screen and moderate the sun's rays, but it is really intended as a support for those spreading vines. The posts have been decorated with moldings, and the ends of the overhead beams and poles have been sculpted with cove and ovolo shapes. To make the arbor more of an "outdoor room," you can add a railing or two and a trellis wall. These are the basic elements of an arbor/trellis structure. You can recombine them in any form to meet your own needs.

Lay out the project area: A complete description of how to accomplish this using batter boards and masons' strings as guides can be found on pages 185 to 187. Once the layout is established, the strings will mark the

DETAIL 1: Cut the posts so they're a little longer than the finished height once they're set in concrete. Then, measure to the proper height on one of the posts and transfer the line to the other three posts using a line level and masons' string. Trim all posts to the same height with a circular saw.

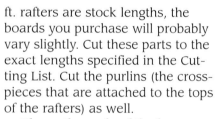

Line level

Masons' string

outer edges of the posts. Mark each post hole with a spike or stake.

Dig the post holes. Your best bet probably is to use a clamshell-type post-hole digger (See page 169) to make the holes. For posts set in concrete, make the holes at least three times the width of the posts. In cold areas, the hole must extend below the frost line. If you're unsure of the frost line depth in your area, contact your local building inspector. Dig the holes deeper than required and backfill with 2 to 4 in. of gravel.

Cut each post longer than its finished height, including the depth of the hole. Set, brace and level the posts. After all posts are in place and the concrete has set, run a line level from post to post as a guide, then trim them to equal height with a circular saw *(See page 189 and Detail 1, above)*. To prevent the tops of the posts from wicking moisture and rotting prematurely, cut post caps from ¾-in.-thick stock and attach them to the post tops with construction adhesive and deck screws. The edges of the caps should be flush with the edges of the posts.

Cut the parts. While the 10 ft. beams and 16

ft. rafters are stock lengths, the boards you purchase will probably vary slightly. Cut these parts to the exact lengths specified in the Cutting List. Cut the purlins (the crosspieces that are attached to the tops of the rafters) as well.

Shape the ends of the beams, rafters and purlins. To give the pergola a handsome, traditional appearance, the ends of the beams, rafters and purlins are trimmed to classic shapes — the ovolo (or quarter-round) on the beams and rafters, and a cove shape on the purlins. While it is possible to lay out the cuts from a pattern, then cut to the lines with a jigsaw, you'll get better, more consistent results if you use a router guided by a template to trim the ends. If you take this approach, you need to begin by making three templates from ¼-in.-thick hardboard. Use the grid drawing as a guide for the ovolo shapes *(See Detail 2)* and cut a simple cove in the ends of the purlins. Make rough cuts to within about ⅛ in. of the cutting lines using a jig saw, then smooth out the cuts (here is where the "production work" comes in to play) using a router with a 3-in. piloted pattern bit to

DETAIL 2: Use this profile drawing as a guide for laying out the hardboard ovolo template used to make the end profiles on the rafters and beams. For the rafters (made from 2 × 8s) enlarge the drawing 243% on a photocopier. For the beam ends (2 × 10s), enlarge the drawing 310%.

follow the hardboard template. Adjust the cutting depth so the bearing rides along the edge of the template. Guiding the router along the template edge trims the work to match the template. After making the cuts, smooth the edges with a file and coarse sandpaper.

Erect the beams. Two beams support the overhead framing. Each beam is formed by two 2 × 10s, nailed together face to face. Each beam spans two posts. The first task in erecting the beams is, of course, nailing the 2 × 10s together with 8d galvanized common nails. While the beams are still on the ground, lay out the locations of the rafters on the tops. Use a framing square to mark both beams at the same time *(See Detail 3).* With a helper and a pair of sturdy stepladders, lift the beams onto the posts and secure them by toe-nailing through the edges of the beams and into the post caps. If you prefer, you can use metal saddle fittings that fit onto the post tops. Tabs on the saddles are fastened to the beams with joist hanger nails. Once the beam is set onto the post, adjust it so the ends overhang the posts an equal amount.

Notch the rafters to fit over the beams. The notch depth is not criti-

DETAIL 3: Use a framing square as a guide for gang-marking the rafter locations on top of the arbor/trellis beams. Follow the spacing shown in the drawing on page 246.

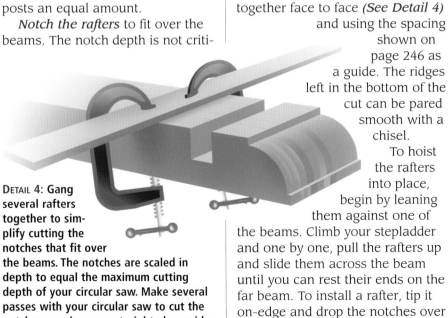

DETAIL 4: Gang several rafters together to simplify cutting the notches that fit over the beams. The notches are scaled in depth to equal the maximum cutting depth of your circular saw. Make several passes with your circular saw to cut the notches, moving your straightedge guide about ¼ in. after each cut. Clean up the bottoms of the notches with a chisel.

cal, as long as they are deep enough to securely lap the beams and not cut more than halfway the rafters. We simply set the circular saw we used to cut the notches to its maximum cutting depth (2½ in.) then cut out the notches with multiple passes of the saw. Lay out the cuts first by ganging the rafters together face to face *(See Detail 4)* and using the spacing shown on page 246 as a guide. The ridges left in the bottom of the cut can be pared smooth with a chisel.

To hoist the rafters into place, begin by leaning them against one of the beams. Climb your stepladder and one by one, pull the rafters up and slide them across the beam until you can rest their ends on the far beam. To install a rafter, tip it on-edge and drop the notches over the beams. Toe-nail through the rafter into the beam *(See Detail 5).*

Install all 11 rafters.

Install the purlins. The 2 × 4 purlins are installed much the same way as the rafters, except they aren't notched. Hoist the purlins up onto the rafters. Lay out position marks on the end rafters. One by one, roll the purlins on-edge, align them at the position marks and toe-nail them to rafters.

While the posts can be left plain if you prefer, we added some decorative trim to enhance the traditional appearance of the arbor/trellis. The "post trim package" consists of a plain board, capped with a quarter-round molding, installed as a baseboard. Around the top of the post, we installed mitered 2-in. cove molding. Several inches below that is a half-round molding *(See Detail 6).* Trimming out each post is a straightforward matter of cutting four pieces of each element, with mitered ends, and nailing them to the post. Use stock moldings and

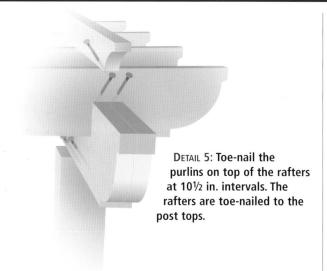

DETAIL 5: Toe-nail the purlins on top of the rafters at 10½ in. intervals. The rafters are toe-nailed to the post tops.

cut all the pieces to fit, one at a time (as opposed to cutting everything to a uniform measurement). Fasten the pieces with galvanized finish nails.

The railing shown with this project is completely optional. What it does is establish a boundary that can transform the arbor/trellis into an outdoor room or a gallery. The railing is quite simple to make and mount. Although we use square balusters, you could buy profiled deck balusters and use them instead. You can also alter the spacing of the balusters, but do not place them more than 4 in. apart. Cut the railing balusters to length from 2 × 2 stock. Set up a stopblock for your power miter saw or radial arm saw and cut all the pieces to the same size quickly and efficiently. Cut a few extra balusters. Also, save the short cutoff scraps.

INSTALLING COVE MOLDING

The only real complication encountered when trimming the posts involves the cove molding that attaches like crown molding at the top of each post. The primary hitch is the need to make and install "blocking" to support the molding. The size cove molding specified typically does not have a right-angle back. It is intended to be installed between a wall and a ceiling, so it has narrow flats to seat against wall and ceiling and a relieved back to bridge out-of-square seams. Since the molding won't seat against a ceiling, it needs back support. Measure and cut triangular blocking to provide the support. Also use the blocking as a jig when miter-cutting the cove molding to fit: with blocking behind it, orient the cove molding as if the fence of your saw were a "wall," the bottom of the molding resting on the saw table. This will create compound angle cuts that create perfect miter joints when the molding is installed.

You'll need at least four 2¼ in. pieces to help you space the balusters during assembly. These pieces later are used to mount the handrail. You also will need four 3½ in. pieces to use when mounting the railing assembly to the posts.

Cut the rails (both the stretcher rails and the handrail) to fit between the posts on the side or sides where the railing is installed. The handrail should be chamfered twice, so its top surface is peaked to shed water. It is easiest to do this cut with a stationary saw, such as a table saw or radial arm saw. It can, however, be done with a circular saw.

Assemble the stretchers and balusters. Begin by laying out three balusters and two of the stretcher rails. Position a baluster roughly at each end of the assembly, and one at dead center. Lay the stretcher rails on the balusters, one at the top, one at the bottom. Nail the rails to the center baluster. With the first baluster in place, slide two more balusters into position beneath the rails, one on either side. Use the 2¼-in.-long pieces of the baluster stock to space and align the balusters. Nail the new balusters in place. Keep adding balusters, using the spacer blocks to position the new ones, checking periodically to ensure that they are square to the rails. When all 33 balusters are nailed in place, turn the assembly over and set the second two stretcher rails in place. Align these rails and nail them to the balusters.

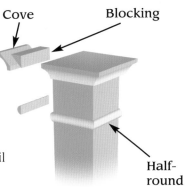

Cove   Blocking

Half-round

Mount the railing assembly. With some assistance from a helper, carry the railing assembly to the installation area. Clamp temporary supports to the posts and set the railing assembly in place. Slip a mounting block (a 3½-in.-long piece of 2 × 2) between the stretcher rails, align it so it is flush with the stretcher rails top and bottom and mark its location on the post. Do this at the top and bottom on both posts. Move the railing

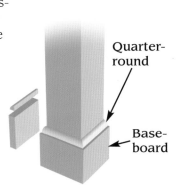

Quarter-round

Base-board

DETAIL 6: Trim out the posts with decorative molding for a more elegant appearance. The cove molding, half-round molding and baseboard with quarter-round all are mitered at each corner.

assembly out of the way. Screw a mounting block to the posts at each marked location. Lift the assembly back into position. Drive nails through the stretcher rails into the mounting blocks. *(See Detail 7).*

Mount the handrail. The spacer blocks you used to help assemble the railing are now used to mount the handrail. Set the handrail in place atop the upper stretcher rails. Select four spots for the mounting blocks and mark the handrail. Remove the handrail and screw the mounting blocks to the underside. Put the handrail back, settling the mounting blocks down between the stretcher rails. Drive nails through these rails into the mounting blocks.

We added a trellis to this project design to function as a screen, creating a bit of privacy without completely blocking the passage of light and breezes. It can, of course, support vines and other climbing plants. There are many options you could choose for trellising: you could create a three-walled room using trellising, railings or a combination of the two; you could trellis all four walls and create doorways in one or two of the trellis walls; or, you could make a walk-through by "walling" parallel sides. Cut the trellis parts. The trellis consists of two mounting rails, 10 horizontal slats and 13 vertical slats. Cut the parts to the dimensions specified in the Cutting List.

Fasten the vertical slats to the mounting rails. The slats, both vertical and horizontal, are located 6 in. apart, on center. Mark out the locations of the vertical slats on the mounting rails. On the vertical slats, mark the bottom edges of the two mounting rails. Pick a slat to get started. Apply a dot of construction adhesive and press the slat into place. Use a try square to ensure that the slat is perpendicular to the mounting rail, and check the alignment marks. Nail or screw the parts

Hand rail

Mounting blocks

DETAIL 7: 2 × 2 mounting blocks are attached to the posts to mount the stretcher rails and to the stretcher rails to mount the hand rail

together (if you own a pneumatic stapler, this is a perfect opportunity to use it. One by one, align the rest of the slats on the bottom mounting rail, making sure each is at right angles to the rail. Using a spacer made from scraps expedites this setup work. After all the slats are fastened to one rail, line up the second rail and fasten the slats to it.

Turn the trellis assembly over and attach the horizontal slats to the vertical slats and the rails. Use spacers to align the horizontal slats *(See Detail 8)*. The gap between the mounting rails and the adjacent horizontal slats is 4⅛ in. Cut a couple of scraps to that width. Lay them on the vertical slats, tight against one of the rails. Slide a horizontal slat against them and adjust its position end-to-end. Fasten this slat to each of the vertical slats. Use these same spacers to position and attach a slat on either side of both rails. Now cut a couple of spacers that are 4¾ in. wide. Use these in the same way to position the other horizontal slats.

Mount the trellis to the posts. Clamp scraps of wood to the posts where the mounting rails are to be attached. With a helper, lift the trellis into position and rest it on the clamped-in-place supports. Drill angled pilot holes through the rails into the posts. Drive a screw into each hole, securing the trellis to the posts. Unclamp the temporary supports.

DETAIL 8: Use spacers as guides for installing the horizontal trellis slats. The gap between the outer slats and the rails is narrower than the gaps between inner slats.

4¾ in.   4⅛ in.

GARDEN STRUCTURES

The appeal of the garden is hard to capture in words.
To the casual observer, it is far from glamorous:
toiling in the dirt and weeds under the hot sun or in the
cold and rain. But for those in the know,
the appeal and the rewards are as obvious as they are
hard to describe. Like any other pursuit,
how well we enjoy the pleasures of gardening is greatly
impacted by the tools we have at our disposal.
And even though the basic "tools" for the gardener are
quite simple — sun, dirt, seeds, a shovel
and a watering can chief among them — adding a new
garden structure, like a greenhouse or even
a basic cold frame, opens up a whole new world
of garden possibilities.

COMPOSTING PEN

This clever design makes a potentially unsightly structure a pleasant addition
to your garden area — and it provides a great way to recycle
organic wastes as fertilizer for your plants.

Cutting List

OVERALL DIMENSIONS (43 × 82½ × 37")

KEY	PART NAME	QTY.	SIZE	MATERIAL
SCREEN PANELS (PER UNIT, 7 UNITS REQUIRED)				
A	TOP/BOTTOM	2	1 × 3 × 36"	PRESSURE TREATED PINE
B	SIDE	2	1 × 3 × 34"	PRESSURE TREATED PINE
C	CORNER BLOCKS	4	1½ × 3½ × 3½"	PRESSURE TREATED PINE
BIN COMPONENTS				
D	POST ELEMENT	6	3½ × 3½ × 36⅞"	PRESSURE TREATED PINE
E	BRACES	2	1 × 2⅜ × 32⅝"	PRESSURE TREATED PINE
F	BRACES	2	1 × 2⅜ × 29⅞"	PRESSURE TREATED PINE
HARDWARE REQUIRED				
DECK SCREWS			#8 × 2½"	GALVANIZED
HOOKS & EYES		8	¼ × 2½"	
FENCING (OR POULTRY) STAPLES			¾"	
WIRE MESH FENCING			36" × 25'-roll	

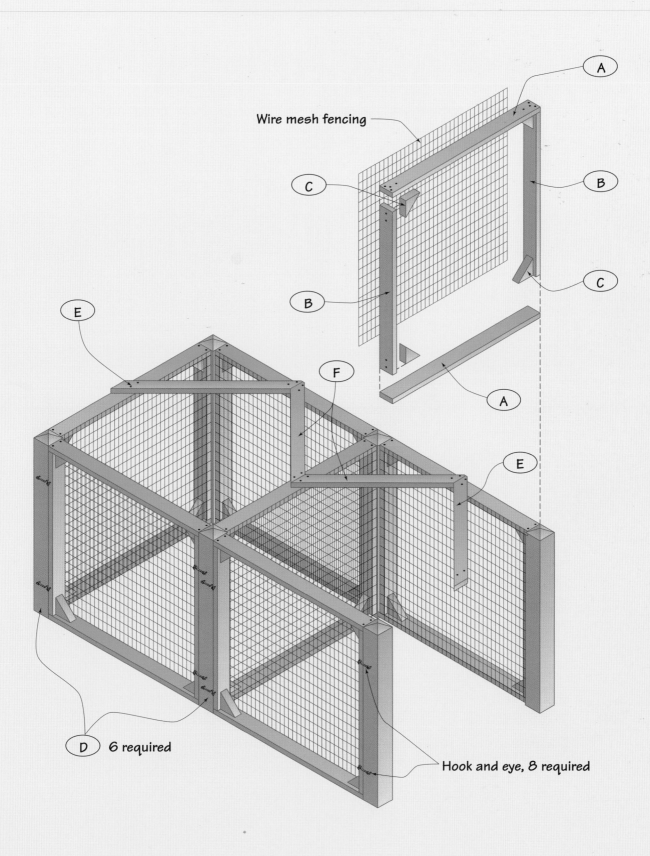

Wire mesh fencing

A

C

B

C

B

F

A

E

E

D 6 required

Hook and eye, 8 required

Composting Pen

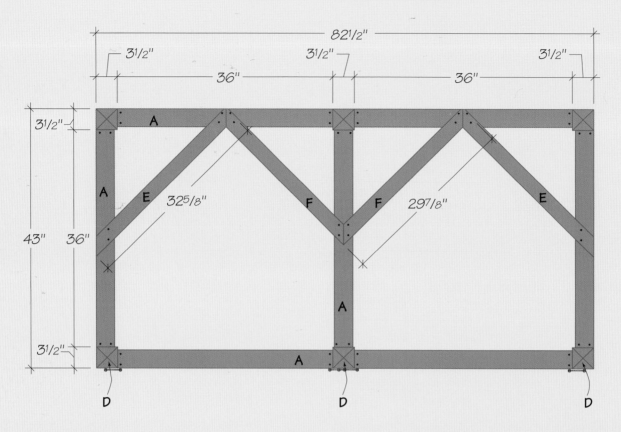

82¹/₂"
3¹/₂"   3¹/₂"   3¹/₂"
36"   36"
3¹/₂"
43"   36"
A   A   A
A   E   32⁵/₈"   F   F   29⁷/₈"   E
3¹/₂"
A
A
D   D   D

PLAN VIEW

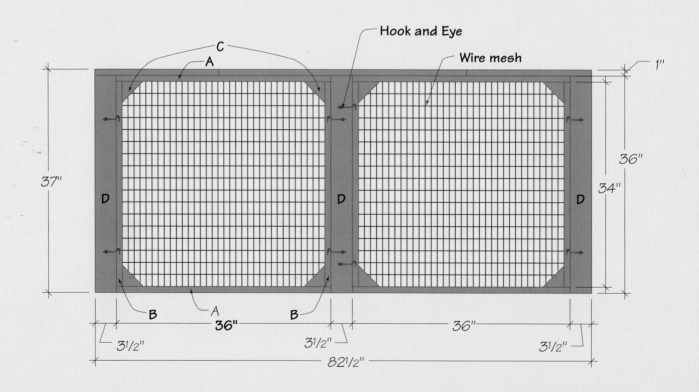

Hook and Eye
Wire mesh
C
A
1"
36"
37"   34"
D   D   D
B   A   B
36"   36"
3¹/₂"   3¹/₂"   3¹/₂"
82¹/₂"

Maintaining an attractive, tidy yard with healthy shrubs and trees, beautiful flowers and a lush lawn can produce a mountain — well, at least more than a molehill — of garden trash like grass clippings, pruning cutoffs and leaves. The costs of landfilling all this good organic material are driving many homeowners to turn back to an old-time solution: composting. Given some time and a little encouragement (in the form of shredding and periodic turning), those garden and yard wastes can be transformed into a nutrient-rich soil amendment. It doesn't take a lot of work on your part to produce compost, but it does require some forbearance. If you value tidiness and attractiveness, the vision of a loose, unsightly heap of decomposing organic matter is off-putting.

But here's a solution: This composting pen allows you to tidy up that pile, and in the bargain, organize and structure this practical garden process. The structure shown has two cubicles. But the modular nature of the construction makes it easy to expand into a three- or four-cubicle unit.

Once assembled, the composting pen can be carried by two people, so it doesn't have to be permanently sited. But if you think it appropriate, you can anchor it to the ground with foot-long pieces of rebar driven through the frames into the ground.

Make the posts & screen frames

Cut the 4 × 4 posts that support the screens. To improve the appearance of the composting pen and to prevent pooling on the post tops, we beveled the post tops on all four sides. There are several ways this can be accomplished: we used a power miter saw *(See Photo 1)*. After cutting the frame pieces to size, save the cutoff pieces to make the 28 corner blocks needed for the screens.

Photo 1 Bevel all four sides of each post top at a 45° angle. A power miter saw is an excellent tool for this task. Set up the saw and position the workpiece so the blade exits at the midpoint of the post end.

Photo 2 Attach the frame tops and bottom to the sides using construction adhesive and galvanized deck screws to fortify the joint. Be sure to drill pilot holes before driving the screws.

Photo 3 Corner blocks cut from the cutoff pieces of the frame strengthen each frame and help keep it from falling out of square. Attach the corner blocks with construction adhesive and deck screws driven through the frame and into the blocks.

The 3-in.-wide stock for the tops, bottoms and sides is ripped to width from 5⁄4 × 6-in. stock (actual size is approximately 1 × 5¼ in.), which is usually made for use as deck boards. Some of the narrow strips left over from ripping can be used to make the diagonal braces installed later. After ripping the stock, cross-cut the screen frame parts to length.

The four strips making up each frame are joined together with construction adhesive and galvanized deck screws. Apply a modest bead of adhesive to the end of a side, and butt the overlapping top or bottom against it. Drill pilot holes and drive two screws into the joint (See Photo 2).

When the basic frames are assembled and squared, cut the

Photo 4 Apply a finish to the posts and frames before attaching the mesh. The finish improves the appearance of the project and also helps extend its life by protecting the wood.

NOTICE: We used pressure-treated pine to build this project. It is an inexpensive building material that withstands ongoing exposure to moisture and insect infestation. And when painted or treated (we used a redwood-colored, UV-resistant wood stain) it can be as attractive as any other exterior wood. But because the chemicals used to treat the lumber are potentially health threatening, you should take plenty of precautions when handling pressure-treated stock. The greatest hazard is created by sawdust generated when the wood is cut, so always wear a particle mask when sawing or drilling treated lumber. Also wear gloves when handling it and clean up sawdust and cutoff scraps immediately. Do not burn any wood or sawdust that has been pressure-treated.

Photo 5 Use masking tape to mark cutting lines on the metal mesh. The mesh used here is a galvanized product with ½ in. grids sold in 36-in.-wide rolls.

Photo 6 Attach the mesh to the fronts of the frames with fencing staples. These galvanized fasteners are sometimes called U-nails. Drive a staple every 6 in. along each side of the frame. Make sure no cut wires extend past the edges of the frame.

corner blocks. Apply adhesive to one of the corner blocks and press it firmly into an inside corner. Drill pilot holes and drive screws through the frame members and into the angled edges of the block, drawing the blocks tight *(See Photo 3).* Assemble all seven frames.

If you are going to paint or stain the compost bin, the time to do it is before the mesh is attached. You'll be able to get finishing materials onto all the surfaces and edges. We applied redwood-colored UV-protected wood stain to the parts *(See Photo 4).*

Cut seven 3-ft.-square pieces of the wire mesh. We used 36-in.-wide rolls of galvanized wire mesh with ½ in. grids. To mark the mesh for cutting, lay a frame on top of it and apply masking tape at the cutting point *(See Photo 5).* Cut the mesh to length with aviator snips. Use aviator snips. Make the cuts as close as possible to a crosswire in the mesh, so you don't have sharp ends jutting out. Using fencing staples (galvanized U-shaped nails), attach a piece of mesh to each of the wooden frames *(See Photo 6).* The middle divider has mesh on both sides of the frame.

Assemble the composting pen

Select a frame and clamp a post to each side. The bottoms of the posts should be flush with the bottom of the frame. Drill pilot holes and drive screws through the frame sides into the posts *(See Photo 7).* Make up two more subassemblies like this one—a frame with a post attached to each side. Use one of the remaining frames to connect two of the subassemblies. Clamp the frame to a post in each subassembly, align these parts, then screw them together. Clamp another frame to the assembly and screw it in place at the third post-and-frame subassembly *(See Photo 8).* When you are through, you will have two bins that are connected and open in the front.

Mount the removable frames. These provide access to the bins so you can turn the composting materials easily, or reach in to shovel the compost out once it has decomposed sufficiently. Each of these frames is held in place with four ordinary hook-and-eye latches. Stand the removable frames in the openings in the assembly and clamp them to the posts. Drill pilot holes, then screw the hooks into the posts near each corner.

Photo 7 Attach the frame between posts with galvanized deck screws. Make sure the bottoms of the frames align with the bottoms of the posts.

Photo 8 Complete the post-and-frame assembly by driving screws into the last frame and into a shared corner post. You can do this step in your construction area or move the assembly parts on site and join them together there.

Mark the spots where the screw eyes fall onto the frames, then drill holes and attach the screw eyes *(See Photo 9 and Photo 10)*.

Mount the diagonal braces at the top corners of the cubicles. The braces simply stiffen the unit and keep the sides from flexing in and out. Miter one end of each of the four cutoff strips of 5⁄4 deck board left over from ripping the frame stock. Lay the braces in place on the tops of the bins and mark the cuts to be made to the other ends *(See Photo 11)*. Trim the braces to the cutting lines, then screw them to the bins.

Install the composting pen in your yard. Choose an inconspicuous site that is convenient to your gardening areas. Avoid installing the pen near any permanent structures (the one built here is fairly attractive compared or other designs, but little can be done about the odors that can be created). To help keep the pen stationary, drill holes in the bottom frames on each end and drive a 12-in.-long section of rebar through each hole and into the ground *(See Photo 12)*.

Using the composting pen

Raw materials for the compost can be accumulated in one cubicle. After you mow your grass, empty the clippings into one of the units. After weeding the garden, thinning plants, pruning shrubs and bushes, add the accumulated organic waste to the clippings. Even compostable kitchen scraps can be added to the compost recipe. Periodically, open up the front of the bin and shred the decomposing material. The newly shredded material is then transferred into the second cubicle. Before long, it is broken down by microbial activity and is ready to be spread in the garden.

Photo 9 Attach the screw eye hooks to the posts first, then mark the spots where they fall across the posts with a pencil. Attach the eyebolts for the screw eyes at these spots. The screw eyes hold the removable frames in place but allow you to remove them easily for turning or removing compost.

Photo 10 Make sure the screw eyes at the center post are far enough apart that they do not interfere with one another.

Photo 11 Lay the mitered frame braces across the tops of the bins and scribe cutting lines at the free ends using a combination square. The braces greatly increase the sturdiness and wrack-resistance of the composting pen. Apply a finish to the frame braces before attaching them with screws.

Photo 12 Stake the composting pen in place by driving 12-in.-long pieces of rebar through holes drilled in the bottom frame pieces near each end of the unit.

COLD FRAME

A cold frame lets you get a jump on the growing season come spring or even prolong your fall harvest. In just an afternoon, you can use this plan to turn an old window sash and a sheet of plywood into a versatile, portable cold frame.

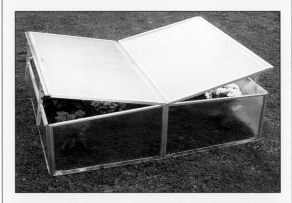

OPTION: BUY A COLD FRAME KIT

If you'd rather not build your cold frame from scratch, you can build one using a pre-fabricated kit instead. The one shown here is composed entirely of precut parts that come ready to assemble. The light panels are made of polycarbonate plastic, and the framework is aluminum. Kit-built cold frames come in a number of shapes and styles, but the primary difference between them is the number of light panels that open up for plant access.

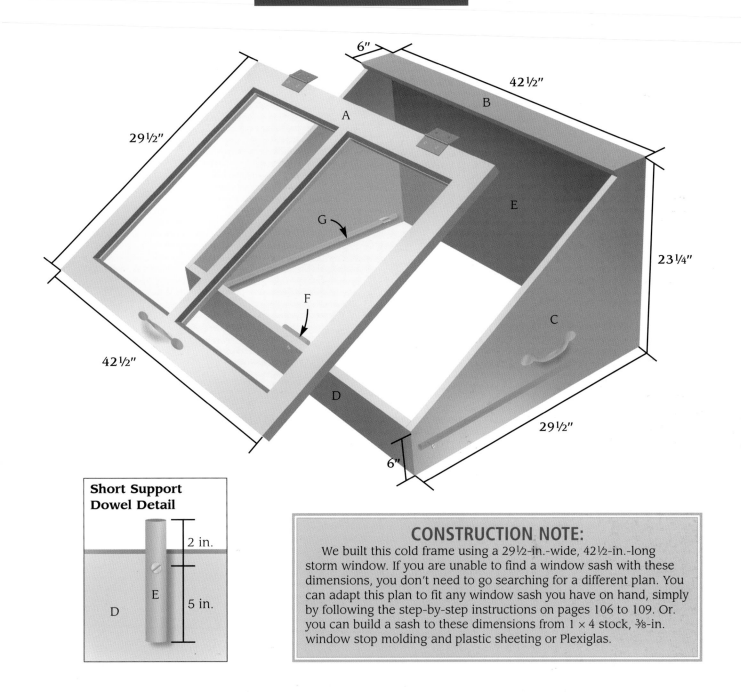

Short Support Dowel Detail

2 in.

5 in.

E

D

CONSTRUCTION NOTE:

We built this cold frame using a 29½-in.-wide, 42½-in.-long storm window. If you are unable to find a window sash with these dimensions, you don't need to go searching for a different plan. You can adapt this plan to fit any window sash you have on hand, simply by following the step-by-step instructions on pages 106 to 109. Or. you can build a sash to these dimensions from 1 × 4 stock, ⅜-in. window stop molding and plastic sheeting or Plexiglas.

Cutting List

OVERALL DIMENSIONS (42½ × 29½ × 23¼")

KEY	PART NAME	QTY.	SIZE	MATERIAL
A	WINDOW SASH	1	1⅛ × 29½ × 42½"	N/A
B	TOP	1	¾ × 6 × 41"	EXTERIOR PLYWOOD
C	SIDES	2	¾ × 29½ × 23¼"	"
D	FRONT	1	¾ × 6 × 41"	"
E	BACK	1	¾ × 41 × 22½"	"
F	SHORT SUPPORT	1	¾-DIA. × 7"	HARDWOOD DOWEL
G	LONG SUPPORTS	2	¾-DIA. × 26½"	HARDWOOD DOWEL

In the project shown here we use an old storm window sash of a specific size to build a cold frame. However, these step-by-step instructions are designed so that you can build your cold frame with a sash of any size.

1 Measure the length, width and thickness of your window sash. Record these dimensions.

2 Determine how wide to make the side panels for the cold frame. Starting from one corner of a sheet of ¾-in. exterior plywood, measure off the width of the sash along the bottom edge of the plywood and make a mark. Draw a 2-ft.-long perpendicular line from this mark using a carpenter's square as a guide. This line represents the back edge of the side panel.

Back-of-side-panel line
(about 2 ft. long)

3 Draw a reference line 6 in. to the left of the back-of-side-panel line. Both lines should be parallel and the same length.

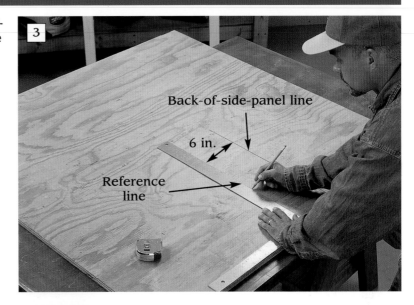

Back-of-side-panel line

6 in.

Reference line

4 Lay out the sloping edge of the side panel. Start by measuring 6 in. up from the lower left corner of the plywood to mark where the bottom of the slope begins. The top of this sloped line intersects the reference line you drew in Step 3. To find this point of intersection, subtract 1 in. from the width of your sash. Using a metal rule, measure out that amount (sash width minus 1 in.) and pivot the rule at the bottom-of-the-slope point until it intersects with the reference line. Connect the top and bottom slope points with a straight line.

Lay out the top of the side panel: Draw a line from the top of the sloped line over to the back-of-side-panel line to mark the top of the panel. This line should be parallel to the bottom edge of the side panel.

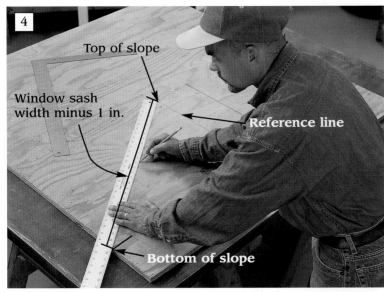

Top of slope

Window sash width minus 1 in.

Reference line

Bottom of slope

5 Lay out cutting lines for the sash on the side panel. Notice in the drawing on page 105 that the sash fits into a notch at the top of the side panels. To mark for this notch, draw a short line in from the top of the sloped line. Use a square to make this short line perpendicular to your sloped line and as long as your sash is thick. At the bottom of this sash notch line, draw a second line parallel to the sloped top line back to the left edge of the plywood. When you cut out the side panel, you'll cut along the sash notch line and the inside sloped line.

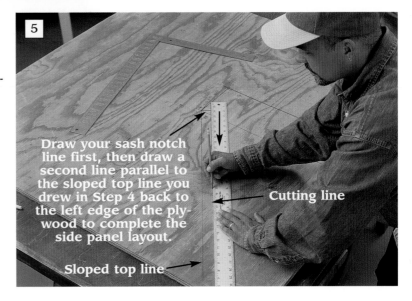

Draw your sash notch line first, then draw a second line parallel to the sloped top line you drew in Step 4 back to the left edge of the plywood to complete the side panel layout.

Cutting line

Sloped top line

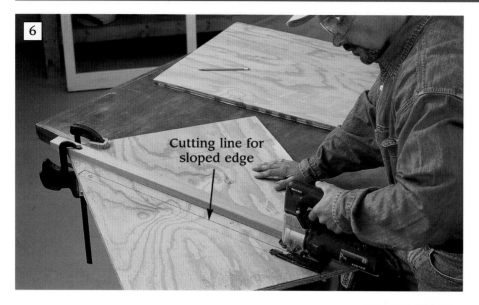

6 Cut out the side panel using a jig saw and a straightedge guide. Be sure to cut the sloped edge along the cutting line you drew in Step 5, not the original top slope reference line.

Use this first side panel as a pattern to trace the other side onto a piece of plywood, then cut out the second side.

Cutting line for sloped edge

7 Measure and cut the front, top and back pieces. The length of the these parts should be equal to the length of your sash, less 1½ in. Both the front and top are 6 in. wide. One long edge of the front must be beveled to correspond with the sloped edges of the sides. The top must also be beveled along one edge to match the sash notch angle. The other long edges of the front and top are square. Use the side panels as a reference for determining the bevels you'll need to cut on the top and front. Then rip the front and top pieces to width with a circular saw set at the appropriate bevel angles. Cross-cut the parts to length.

Rip and cross-cut the back panel to size. Its length should be 1½ in. shorter than your sash length. The width of the back is ¾ in. shorter than the height of the sides.

Layout line for bevel cut

8 Glue and screw the cold frame together. Assemble the back and side panels first. Run a bead of moisture-resistant wood glue along the ends of the back, set it in between the side panels and fasten the parts with countersunk 1½-in. galvanized deck screws. A couple of wood screws clamped to the bottom edges of the sides make it easy to stand the sides upright while you fasten the parts together.

To complete the box assembly, attach the top and front panels between the sides with glue and screws, making sure the beveled edges are correctly oriented on the side panels.

Prime all inside and outside surfaces of the cold frame box, then topcoat with two coats of exterior-grade latex paint.

9 Attach the long lid supports: Cut the long dowel supports so they're about 3 in. shorter than the width of the cold frame. Hold each dowel 1 in. up from the inside, bottom edges of the side panels. Drill a pilot hole 1 in. from the ends of the dowels closest to the cold frame front and through the side panels. Slip a bolt through each pilot hole and fasten with a washer and locknut to hold the dowels in place while allowing them to pivot. Install broom clips to the side panels near the opposite ends of the dowels to hold them in place when not in use.

Install the short lid support. This support, mounted to the front of the cold frame, holds the sash open at two settings for ventilation. Cut a 7-in. length of ¾-in.-dia. dowel, and mark it 2 in. from one end. Position the dowel so the 2-in. mark is about 1 in. below the top edge of the front panel, centered from side to side. Drill a pilot hole through the dowel where you've marked it and through the front panel. Install the dowel with a bolt and nut. When you pivot the dowel one way or the other, it will hold the sash open either 1 in. or 4 in.

Pivot bolt
Broom clip
Short lid support

10 Fasten 3-in. lift handles to the side panels of the box and to the lower rail of the sash. Refer to the drawing on page 105 for general placement of the handles, and be sure to use galvanized or brass handles and screws. Place them so the cold frame balances comfortably when you lift it up.

Install the sash. Attach two hinges to the top of the sash, about 6 in. from each end. We used 3-in. galvanized butt hinges, but brass hinges would work, too. Set the sash in place on the cold frame, and fasten the hinges to the top of the cold frame.

11 Drill lid support holes in the sash. The long lid supports fit into 1-in.-dia. holes drilled ¼ in. deep into the bottom of the sash. The holes hold the lid supports securely to prop the sash open. To mark the sash frame for the holes, simply prop the sash open and trace around the ends of the supports. Drill the holes with a Forstner bit in a drill/driver.

GREENHOUSE

The crown jewel in any gardener's crown, a personal greenhouse opens up countless new possibilities for the true gardening enthusiast. And when built from a kit, like the one above, they're a snap to build.

Greenhouse Project: *A 3-step overview*

1 Assemble the frame (271 to 274)

2 Install panels & roof vents (276 to 278)

3 Hang the door (278 to 279)

Greenhouse styles

In addition to the freestanding greenhouse featured in this chapter, you can also find kits for greenhouses that are attached to your house (left) or are designed to cover a deck or patio (above).

GREENHOUSE ACCESSORIES

Part of the fun of building a greenhouse is customizing it by adding a few unique bells and whistles. Kit manufacturers can get you started down this trail with a few optional devices.

A hydraulic lifter activated by changes in temperature can keep your greenhouse from turning into a steamroom if it gets warm outside and you're not around to manually open the vents. As the temperature rises, the hydraulic oil expands and lifts the vent.

This photo shows a louvered exhaust fan that can be wired to a "smart" thermometer. If the temperature in the greenhouse rises above a predetermined level, the thermometer signals the exhaust fan to kick in and vent the hot air. Another type of thermometer (seen at the far right of the photo) records the minimum and maximum temperature in the greenhouse on a day-to-day basis.

Kit manufacturers and many nurseries also sell shelves, racks and tables designed for use in a greenhouse.

Floor options for greenhouses

Loose fill such as bark or landscaping rock is a suitable floor material for most light-use greenhouses. You'll still need to provide a frame or curb to contain the material and anchor the structure.

The paver-and-landscape-timber foundation used in our featured project is made by bolting four landscaping timbers together, then setting pavers into a bed of sand, as you would for any paver patio project. In addition to its attractive appearance and durability, the hard surface make it practical and easy for the homeowners to run power service to their greenhouse.

GREENHOUSE KITS

Of the many yard and garden structures for which kits are available, greenhouses may make the most sense. The typical built-from-scratch greenhouse (with its inevitable broken glass panels or cloudy, unappealing plastic) can't compete with the durability and appearance of the high-strength polycarbonate panels featured in most quality greenhouse kits. And after all, a greenhouse is really nothing more than a skeleton that supports a see-through skin.

The greenhouse parts are delivered packaged in just a couple of elongated cardboard boxes. Don't tear open all the packaging! The parts for each subassembly—the gable-end walls, the side walls and so forth—are bundled together. You can avoid confusion by leaving each bundle intact and unopened until you are actually ready to assemble the parts.

Every gardener worth his or her mulch has wished for a greenhouse at one time or another. For the handyman, a small greenhouse project seems eminently do-able. Seems do-able, that is, until you get deep into designing the framing and sorting through the glazing options. Then it looks awfully complicated.

At that point, a greenhouse kit looks better and better. All the vexing decisions involving materials choices have been made. The design will have been tested and proven. All you have to do is spend a weekend assembling the parts, then the gardener in you can cut loose.

The greenhouse kit we selected is the Danish-made *Juliana* model, distributed in this country by *GardenStyles* of Bloomington, Minnesota. The greenhouse has virtually unbreakable polycarbonate glazing panels that mount in a framework of extruded aluminum members. Everything is cut to precise (metric) measurements. With a little help, you can easily assemble and glaze the unit in a weekend.

In a nutshell, the process is to assemble each of the walls before setting any of them up. The structure is light enough that any wall

Photo 1:1 To avoid confusion, wait until you're ready to assemble each wall section before opening the bundle containing the parts to make the section. Check the parts against the inventory as you lay them out in roughly the sequence they're installed.

can be lifted and carried by one person. You set up the walls, then add the roof framing and the roof-vent frames. Then the entire unit is glazed, the door is hung and the structure is anchored to its foundation.

Site preparation is minimal. You'll probably want to remove sod from the site, and it should be level and reasonably well compacted. But this is an easy job, because you don't need to set up batterboards and run lines outlining the perimeter. The foundation almost sites itself. For the project shown here, the homeowner chose to install a loose-paver floor framed with landscape timbers *(See page 270).*

SECURING YOUR GREENHOUSE TO THE FOUNDATION

When preparing your construction site, take into account that the greenhouse will need to be fastened somehow to the earth. If you're laying a paver or loose-fill foundation, install landscape timbers around the perimeter of the construction area (See Photo, previous page) so you can simply screw the greenhouse sill plates to the timbers (See Photo, left). Normally, this is done after the kit is completely assembled. Drill holes through the sill and drive 3-in. screws through the holes into the wood. If you're pouring a concrete slab to support the greenhouse, insert threaded J-bolts (See page 187) into the fresh concrete. Position the J-bolts so the greenhouse sill plates will be centered on top of them.

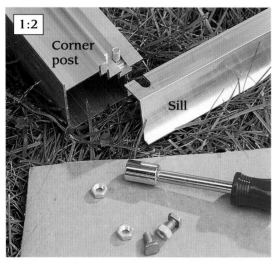

Photo 1:2 Mechanical fasteners are used to join the frame members. Here, square-headed bolts fit into T-slots in the corner post. An open slot on the sill is fitted over the threaded end of the bolt.

Photo 1:3 Diagonal braces are fastened across the struts that function as studs in the front wall frames surrounding the door opening. The braces make the walls more rigid, which is especially useful on the front wall due to stress from opening and closing the door to the greenhouse.

Photo 1:4 Connecting plates are used to join the rafters together at the peak.

Photo 1:5 "L"-angled connector plates join the rafters and the corner posts at the eave area of the greenhouse. The ends of the braces are attached to the same "L" connector on the post.

Photo 1:6 Install the door header between the tallest struts in the front wall.

Photo 1:7 Once the front wall is completed, assemble the side walls, back wall and back wall gable one at a time.

ONE: Assemble the framing

Start assembly of the frame walls with the front wall, then build the side and back walls. After all walls are complete, erect them and join them together.

Front wall: Unpack the parts for the front wall and practice arranging them according to the diagram in the assembly instructions *(See Photo 1:1)*. By laying out the parts in the proper arrangement, you'll see what needs to be done. Each part in the drawing is numbered, and that number is printed on the actual part in the bundle. The instructions include small drawings of each connection that must be made to assemble this wall, so consult them wherever a detail isn't immediately obvious.

As you study the instructions for assembling the front wall, you will see there's a sequence suggested. This general sequence can be followed when building the side walls and back wall as well.

• Begin assembly at the bottom left corner of each wall frame, connecting the sill to the corner post *(See Photo 1:2)*.

• Move across the sill, installing diagonal metal braces that connect the struts ("struts" correspond to wall studs). *(See Photo 1:3)*

• Next, the two rafters are joined together at the peak, using a special plate — it will be marked. Slide this unit into position so it can be joined with angle plates to the two corner posts *(See Photo 1:4)*.

• Connect the corner posts to the sill by bolting an angle plate and horizontal and diagonal braces to the post *(See Photo 1:5)*.

• Connect horizontal braces to the doorway studs, then add the door header *(See Photo 1:6)*.

With a sense of direction established, break out the bolts and nuts and begin connecting the parts. You'll see immediately that each strut has a continuous slot formed into it to accommodate a bolt head.

Photo 1:8 Begin erecting the wall frames. Start with the back wall and one of the side walls. The frames are lightweight, but you'll need two people to connect them.

Photo 1:9 The side walls and gable walls are joined at shared corner posts. The side walls are connected to the corner posts with screws.

1:10

Photo 1:10
After all four walls are erected, raise the ridge pole and fit the ends into the open "V's" formed at the tops of the front and back gable peaks. With the green-house model shown here, the pole has flanges that fit into slots in the rafters. You'll need to flex each wall outward momen-tarily to slip the pole into place. Make sure your ladders are set up on firm ground.

Mating parts have either holes or notch-like slots for the bolts. Thus the connection points are pretty obvi-ous. Alignment adjustments are made by moving the bolt in the slot. As you join the parts, thread nuts onto the bolts and tighten them with a nut driver.

You should note that the sills and corner posts don't meet in a closed corner; instead there's a gap or notch, which is for the side wall's sill. The same is true at the joint between the corner post and the rafters. An angled plate is bolted first to the corner post. A cross brace and a diagonal brace go on the bolts that secure the plate to the post. After the door and wall posts and the braces are all secure, you bolt the rafters to the corner post via the angled plate. A gap is to be left between post and rafter, so the side wall's top plate, which doubles as a rain gutter, can link into place.

Don't worry too much about getting all the parts perfectly aligned and squared up at this point. The wall will take shape and assume a reasonable rough align-ment as you bolt the parts together, and that's all you need to focus on at this point. Later, as the walls are set up and joined together, the alignment will become more refined. And installing the glazing will force everything into perfect alignment.

For now, bear in mind that you may need to loosen a few nuts to allow parts to shift so one wall can be connected to its neighbor. In other words, you don't need to tighten the nuts "for the ages," you just may need to loosen them to make slight adjustments after they are installed.

The other walls are assembled one by one. Just do one at a time, and don't open a bundle of parts until you are going to assemble them. Lay out the parts according to the diagram in the manufacturer's assem-bly instructions. It is reasonable to follow the same general sequence you'll follow when assembling the front wall. Start at the lower left corner of the layout and work your way up and across the unit, roughly aligning them and bolting the parts together.

The rear gable wall closely approximates the front wall—it simply lacks the doorway. The side walls are composed of only seven pieces, and they lack corner posts *(See Photo 1:7)*. This is because the gable walls contain the structure's corner posts.

Erect the wall frames. Lift the rear gable wall and stand it on the foundation. While your helper holds

Photo 1:11
Fasten the rafters to the ridgepole and the side wall sills. The holes and slots are predrilled so you don't need to worry about spacing the parts.

1:11

that wall, lift a side wall and bring it into position *(See Photo 1:8).* The sill and plate of the side wall fit into the spaces left for them in the gable wall. While you should get a good fit at the sills, you may need to loosen some of the bolts in the gable walls to adjust the space for the plate/gutter. Attach the side wall to the back wall post *(See Photo 1:9).* After the first side wall is locked in place, connect the second side wall to the gable wall.

Erect the front gable wall last. The other three walls should be pretty much self-supporting, so you and your helper can each take a side of the rear wall and get it tied into the structure quickly.

Install the roof frame. The primary roof member is the ridge. The heads of the mounting bolts catch in slots in the undersides of the rafters, and the bolt shanks pass through short slots cut in the flange on the bottom of the ridge.

Thread a nut on a bolt, catch the head in the rafter's slot and slip the bolt a couple of inches down the slot. Turn the nut finger tight, just to hold the bolt in place. Do this with one bolt at each rafter. Set up stepladders inside the greenhouse, one at each gable wall. You

hold one end of the ridge, and a helper holds the other end. You both go up the ladders, lift the ridge up and clear of the structure, then lower it into place *(See Photo 1:10).* One of you probably will need to push the rafters out a bit so the ridge can drop into place, with the flange beneath the rafters. Pull the rafters tight against the ridge, and the bolts can be slid up the slot and right into the niches cut for them in the ridge's flange. Tighten the nuts with a nut driver, and the ridge is secure.

Struts, which correspond to rafters in a stick-framed roof, are installed next *(See Photo 1:11).* The locations for the struts are clearly indicated by holes bored in the ridge's flange. You slip a bolt into the continuous slot in the strut, lay the strut's end on top of the ridge flange and the bolt shank will drop through the hole in the flange. Thread on the nut and tighten it. At the lower end, the struts bolt to the side wall top plate in the same way.

Photo 2:1 Slip the rubber gasket that holds the top edge of the roof panel over the ridgepole flange at the top of each roof panel opening. Also snap a gasket into the bottom edge of each roof panel.

Photo 2:2 After securing the top edge of the roof panel in the gasket at the top of the opening, flex the panel and snap the bottom edge in position. The sides should rest on the rafter ledges.

TWO: Install the panels & roof vents

The greenhouse is glazed with special polycarbonate panels. Polycarbonate is the plastic used in safety goggles; it is virtually unbreakable. The panels have a corrugated core, which provides insulation value. The outside of the panel has a UV coating to retard the degradation of the material from the sun's ultraviolet radiation.

When you unpack the glazing, you'll see that each panel is cut to a precise size to fit specific openings in the framework. No cutting is necessary. A protective film masks the panels to protect them from scratching during shipping and installation.

There are two methods for securing the panels into the building frame (and other kit manufacturers have their own altogether different approaches). One way is to bond the panels into the frames with silicone caulk, then secure them with spring-wire clips that are fitted into the frame channel, locking the panel into place. In effect, the clips "clamp" the panel in place until the caulk sets, bonding the panel.

The greenhouse kit we installed featured a somewhat newer technology for installing the polycarbonate panels. Instead of caulk and spring clips, semi-rigid plastic gaskets are snapped in place over the panel frames to immobilize the panels within the frames.

The assembly instructions should provide a diagram so you can easily determine which panels are used where. Snap a rubber gasket onto the ridgepole flange at the top of the outer panel openings *(See Photo 2:1)*. Also attach a rubber gasket to the bottom edge of each panel. Then, fit the top edge of each panel into the rubber gasket at the top of the correct panel opening *(See Photo 2:2)*. Fit the bottom edge into the top side wall sill (you'll probably need to flex the panel slightly to do this). The sides of the panel should rest on the rafter ledges at the sides of the panel openings. Fit the plastic outer gaskets over the top ridges on the rafters and snap them down to pin the sides of the panels in place *(See Photo 2:3)*.

As you work, you may discover that here and there you need to loosen an assembly bolt or two to adjust the align-

Photo 2:3 Snap the plastic gaskets over the rafters to press the panels snugly against the rafter ledges.

Photo 2:4 After installing the shorter fixed panels in the interior roof openings, frame out each opening to accept a roof vent.

Photo 2:5 Assemble the roof vents. The vent frames are wide enough to span two panel openings. To assemble them, install the polycarbonate panels and attach the support rods that are used to prop the vents in an open position.

Photo 2:6 Slip the top rail of each roof vent assembly into the channel near the top of the ridgepole (See inset photo), then slide the vents into position. The lips at the side edges of the vent panels should fit over the tops of the rafters.

ment of the frame so a panel will fit its opening.

The upper third or so of each inner roof panel opening is covered with an operating vent window. Before assembling the windows, install the shorter fixed panels in the lower two-thirds of each opening, then install the top frame that separates the fixed and vented panels in the openings (See Photo 2:4).

To assemble and install the vented windows, first unbundle the parts and lay them out. As with other components, the assembly is pretty clearcut. Slip bolts through the predrilled holes, joining the parts together, and tighten the nuts. After the vent frames are assembled, bolt a prop to each one (See Photo 2:5). Install the panels into the openings.

The vents are hinged by means of interlocking grooves formed in both the ridgepole and the vent-frame hinge rail. The vent is slid into place from one end of the ridge (See Photo 2:6).

Photo 3:1 Assemble the door that came with your kit, in this case by screwing the corners together (all holes are predrilled and all hardware provided). Attach the hinges and door latch.

THREE: Hang the door

Open up the door bundle and lay out the parts. It will looks like an aluminum storm-and-screen door, complete with a lever-type latch with a lock. Holes for the assembly screws are already drilled. All you have to do is drive the screws to assemble the door.

Four hinges are provided. The leaves with the pins are attached to the doorpost, while the leaves with the sockets are installed on the door (See Photo 3:1).

The latch mechanism fits into the door stile, and the lever is screwed to the stile surface.

The polycarbonate panels in the door shown here were installed using a different method from the one described in the previous sec-

Photo 3:2 The door panels in this kit were installed using a slightly different system than was used to install the roof panels. The first step is simply to line the frame opening with silicone caulk.

Photo 3:3 Press each panel into the bed of silicone in the frame opening. Then, insert spring clips between the panels and the frame ledges to secure the door panels.

tion. They required the silicone-and-spring-clamp method discussed on page 276.

For the best bond, the panels and the aluminum frame need to be dry. For this reason, the distributor recommends that you keep the glazing panels on the cardboard packing rather than laying them on the grass. Wipe the adjoining surfaces with acetone to remove any grease or solvents. You don't need to scrub the surfaces; a quick pass with a soft rag dampened with acetone will do the trick. But to clean the edges of the panels, you need to peel the masking from the inside surface. The blue-colored masking identifies the surface with the UV coating.

Run a bead of caulk around each frame opening (See Photo 3:2). Then, set the panels into the appropriate frame openings. Snap spring clips between the panels and the tops of the frame flanges to hold them in place (See Photo 3:3). After the panels are installed, hang the door onto the pins to mount it to the greenhouse.

Install any trim pieces or additional accessories, like plastic end caps for the ridge and sill or a door catch to hold the door open (See Photo 3:4).

Front wall frame

Door

Photo 3:4 Hang the door with the hinges provided and test the operation. Then, mount the door catch to the door frame and the front wall frame so the door can be held in an open position (inset photo)

SHEDS

If your house has a yard, you can use a shed.
It is that simple. Garages are for cars,
basements are for household storage and laundries.
But a shed is for tools that you need to keep
your yard in good repair.
Lawn mowers and tractors, rakes and shovels,
bags of fertilizer or peat moss, tillers, chainsaws. . .
The beauty of the shed is that you can fill it
with just about anything, and it will be there
waiting for you when you need it.
Built from a kit or from scratch, a shed keeps
your tools right where the action is.

KIT-BUILT SHED

For ease of installation and economy, the kit-built shed is a popular solution to backyard storage problems. The wood-paneled, 10 × 12-ft. shed shown here goes together in much the same way as any other kit-built shed.

A shed kit typically includes the wall framing members and sheathing, door, roof frame, roof sheathing, trim and hardware, including fasteners. You can usually order a prefab plywood floor platform. You'll need to provide paint and the roof covering materials.

Kit-built Shed: A Six-step overview

1 Prepare the site (284 to 287)
2 Pour the slab (287 to 290)
3 Build the walls (291 to 295)
4 Frame & deck the roof (296 to 299)
5 Shingle the roof (299 to 301)
6 Finishing touches (301 to 302)

Photo 1:1 Mark the rough layout area (indicated by the small flags above) then use batterboards and mason's string to pinpoint the exact positions of the corners. Check to make sure the layout is exactly square. The 3-4-5 method is being used here: measure out 3 ft. and 4 ft. on the strings that form one corner and mark the points with tape. Measure the distance between the points. If the distance is 5 ft., then the corner is square. Check at all four corners.

Photo 1:2 After the layout is squared and you've checked to make sure the dimensions are correct, level the layout lines. Attach a line level to one of the strings and adjust the batterboards it is tied to until the string is level (you can do this by raising or lowering the crosspieces on the batter boards or by simply adjusting the height of the stakes that support the crosspieces).

If you've ever compared the price of building outdoor structures from scratch to buying a kit, you may have been surprised. While it seems logical that the kits would cost more (after all, much of the work has already been done), that often is not the case. Whether you're pricing playsets or fences or sheds, kits frequently are less costly. So you may ask yourself, "How do they do that?" Well, does it matter how? The real point is that if time and money are issues for you, it's hard to go wrong by buying a shed kit. And because you do have to construct a foundation, assemble all the parts and shingle the roof, you'll still get to experience the satisfaction of doing it yourself.

The 10 × 12-ft. shed kit we bought and assembled is made by *Handy Home Products* of Warren, Michigan. It features a gambrel roof and is clad in *T1-11* plywood. Plywood floor platform kits are available, but because the primary use for this shed is to house a lawn tractor, a more durable concrete floor was a better choice.

Regardless of how excited you might be about setting up your new shed kit, you need to do some planning and site preparation work before you bust open the kit. Your first stop should be the local building department. In fact, you might want to check into building requirements even before you buy the kit. Though it is unlikely, you don't want to get stuck with a kit that local building regulations prevent you from assembling. Explain your plans and find out if any rules govern or restrict your work. Will you need a building permit (most sheds will). Are there setback requirements? Are on-site inspections required? These are the kinds of questions to ask before you begin.

Before you being preparing the construction site, make a call to your local public utility companies to have them check the property for buried lines or pipes (See Page 167).

Building regulations and utilities both can impact your site selection. Access is another key element. It may well be that the number of possible locations for the shed are very limited in your small yard. But for someone with a spacious yard (or with limited street access), the location of the shed can create a lot of extra hauling work. Ask yourself: "Will I need to cart gravel and concrete a considerable distance? Will I be able to have the shed package dropped right beside the slab? Will I have to carry every stick and nail from one end of your property to the other?" If you answer "Yes," you may want to investigate other site options.

ONE: Prepare the site

For small structures like this shed, a plain 4-in.-thick concrete slab makes an excellent foundation. In most cases, you can simply strip away the vegetation and topsoil, and cast the slab in forms set up directly on the undisturbed subsoil. Where drainage is sub-par, you'll need to excavate deeper, add drainage rocks/gravel, compact the fill, then cast the slab on top of that.

Lay out the slab. A formed concrete slab is laid out much like any other square work area: by driving stakes and batterboards and connecting them with masons' strings. Once the strings are in position and leveled, you adjust them up and down and side to side as needed to assess the grade of the site and mark out the exact corners of the forms.

Lay out the perimeter of the slab with batterboards and masons' string, remembering to include the thickness of your form boards (add 3 in. to both dimensions —a 10 × 12 slab like the one shown here will have a layout area of 123 × 147 in.). For this slab, you can begin with either the length or the width. Just make sure the strings delineating the sides are parallel and the stakes that support the batterboards are planted at least 2 ft. outside the project area. Then, lay out the perpendicular sides, again with the stakes planted a couple of feet beyond the edge of the slab. The points at which strings cross will show the actual corners of the slab plus forms. Check to confirm that the corners form right angles. We used the *3-4-5 method (See Photo 1:1)* to check our layout for square.

Once you've established a square layout, level the strings so you can use them as a guide for excavating for the pour *(See Photo 1:2)*. Slip a line level onto one of the strings and adjust the height of the batterboard to bring the string to level (you can do this either by raising or lowering the stakes, or by detaching the batterboard crosspiece and reattaching it at a higher or lower position). Adjust the other strings, using the line level, so they are at the same height as the leveled string. Once the strings are squared and leveled, mark the positions of the strings on the batter boards so you can remove and re-tie them without having to go through the whole procedure again.

Excavate and prepare the base for the slab. A firm, well drained subbase is critical to a long-lasting slab. Serious cracks and settling usually can be traced to a poor subbase. In most cases, undisturbed soil supports a concrete slab best. If you must use fill—to provide enhanced drainage under the slab, for example—be sure to compact it well. Small areas can be compacted with a hand tamper or a heavy lawn roller. If you need to use gravel fill over the entire site, rent a compactor.

To begin the excavation, remove sod, weeds, roots and any other organic matter from the site so you're down to bare dirt *(See Photo 1:3)*. If the turf is in good shape and you need fresh sod, use a sod stripper (See page 11). To create access for the forms, excavate to 1 ft. beyond the perimeter of the area to be formed (this

Photo 1:3 Remove all sod and loose debris from the work area so you can accurately assess the grade and the soil condition. Clear the ground at least 1 ft. outside each layout line.

Photo 1:4 Make a story pole marked to indicate the distance of the highest point of the site from the level lines. Then mark off the excavation depth above this line and use the story pole as a guide for excavating to an even depth.

Photo 1:5 Compact the soil in the worksite with a plate vibrator or hand tamper, especially if you have filled in with any new subbase material.

Photo 1:6 Drive stakes around the perimeter of the construction area to support the form boards. When laying out the area, add 3 in. to each direction to allow for the thickness of the form boards.

is the main reason the batterboards are installed well outside the work area). To determine the required depth of the excavation, add the thickness of the slab (4 in., in this case) to the thickness of the subbase, if needed (also 4 in.). Subtract 1 in. (the approximate amount the slab should project above grade). Make a story pole to quickly measure this distance at the layout strings (you'll need to figure in the distance of the strings above the highest grade point, of course). Excavate to the required depth, checking periodically with the story pole *(See Photo 1:4)*.

Photo 1:7 Attach the form boards (2 × 4s are used most often) to the stakes with deck screws. Screws can be backed out easily when it's time to break the forms.

When the excavation is finished, check for soft or mucky spots. If you find any, they should be dug out and filled with sand or gravel. Then, add subbase fill if needed. The best subbase is compactible gravel (sometimes called Class V or Class II). Dump a load of fill into the work area and compact it until it's 4 in. thick. We didn't add subbase, but we compacted the soil with a plate vibrator anyway *(See Photo 1:5)*.

Construct the forms. To build concrete slab forms, most people use 2 × 4 (they're only 3½ in. wide, but enough of the concrete will settle into the subbase that the slab will be close enough to 4 in. thick after the pour). The form boards need to be braced with wooden stakes—usually 1 × 2 or 2 × 2. Begin setting up your forms by driving stakes into the ground, spacing them about 2 or 3 ft. apart. Line up each stake so its inside face touches the layout string *(See Photo 1:6)*. You may need to use a level to extend the plane of the stake up to reach the layout string. Pound in the stakes so the tops are slightly less than 3½ in. above ground (if they're higher than the form boards you won't be able to tool the concrete). All stakes must be driven straight and true if forms are to be plumb.

Cut the form boards to length (if you use more than one board to make any of the runs, make sure the seam between boards is reinforced with a stake directly behind it). Position the form boards inside the stakes and attach them by driving screws through the stakes and into the forms — avoid driving all the way through the forms. Also screw through the ends of the form boards and into the mating form boards to reinforce the corners. Check to make sure all the form boards are plumb and aligned with the layout strings. Now you can remove the layout strings.

TWO: Pour the slab

Preparing. Make sure to order enough concrete — coming up short can be disastrous. For the 10 × 12-ft. slab shown here, we only needed 1½ yards, but we ordered two full yards to allow for waste and just to be safe. Before the truck arrives with your concrete, a few pieces of information should be marked on the form boards. One is locations for the J-bolts that are installed in the fresh concrete to secure the shed sills to the slab. Typically, the J-bolts are positioned about 4 ft. apart. We planned to embed three ½-in.-dia. × 5-in.-long J-bolts about 3 in. deep into the edge of the slab, spacing three along each side and the back, and two near the corners along the front. The resulting 2-in. projection of threaded bolt is about right for securing 2 × 4 sills.

The second marking is for con-

Ramp for wheelbarrow

Photo 2:1 Begin placing the concrete at the corner of the work site furthest from the access point. Try to get the concrete as close to the correct thickness when you unload it to minimize the need to move the material around. Begin striking off with a screed as soon as you can. Make sure to have plenty of help on hand for the pour.

trol joints, if you choose to cut them in the slab (See *Controlling Cracks,* page 289). On this project, it just happened that the control joints would fall on the centerlines of the sides, which also were locations of J-bolts.

The day the concrete is to be delivered, be sure you have the tools you need at the job site. Basic items needed for a typical job include at least one wheelbarrow (preferably two or three, with eager pushers), a shovel, a long straightedge (usually a 2 × 4) for screeding the concrete, a bull float or darby, an edger, a groover for cutting the control joints, a float, a trowel, and a ready water supply.

There is no getting around one basic fact of pouring a concrete slab: you will need help when the truck arrives. The deliveryman will discharge the concrete directly into the forms if he can get the truck close to the job site. He will not push a wheelbarrow for you. If concrete can be discharged directly

from the truck into the forms, usually with a chute, you still will need one or two helpers to strike and finish it before it cures.

Just before the concrete is scheduled to arrive, dampen the subbase — this is especially important in hot weather, to keep the dry subbase from sucking water out of the concrete and causing weakening during the cure. Likewise, wooden forms should be hosed down. To make breaking the forms easier, coat the insides with vegetable oil. Set the reinforcing steel (re-bar or re-wire) in place if you are going to use one of these products instead of cutting control joints — in a slab of this size you can go either way (See page 289).

Placing. When the truck arrives, have a clear path laid out between the delivery area and the site. Also, construct a ramp so you can get your wheelbarrows up and over the form boards. Begin loading your wheelbarrows then dumping them in the formed area *(See Photo 2:1)*.

Photo 2:2 Use a straight 2 × 4 (a 12-footer is shown here) to strike off the concrete so it is level with the tops of the form. Make sure there are no ridges or dips. Move the screed board in a back-and-forth sawing motion.

Photo 2:3 Smooth the concrete surface with a bull float (a rental item). When pushing the bull float, tip the leading edge up slightly so it doesn't dig in.

Photo 2:4 On the pull stroke, raise the back edge of the bull float slightly. Float the concrete until the surface is smooth and even, but avoid overworking it.

Concrete should not be dumped in piles, then dragged out with a rake or hoe. Doing this will tend to separate the ingredients, because mortar (the sand and cement) tends to flow ahead of coarse aggregate. Too much water and fine material rise to the surface, and this can cause scaling and dusting of the cured surface. Instead, start in the far corner from the entry ramp and place the concrete in even rows that are roughly the thickness of the planned slab. This entails backing up with the wheelbarrow as you unload it, so it's important not to overfill the wheelbarrow to the point that you can't control it. With a shovel, fill in with concrete at the edges of the forms and move it around as needed for even coverage. Work the nose of the shovel between the form and the concrete to settle out voids. But do take care not to overwork the material.

Tooling. You should begin screeding (also called "striking off") the concrete before all the concrete is placed. Use a straight 2 × 4 (we used a 12-footer) as a screed. Rest the 2 × 4 on top of the forms. The object is to skim off the excess concrete in a sawing motion so the surface is flush to or just slightly higher than the top of the form *(See Photo 2:2)*.

When all the concrete is placed and screeded, smooth it with a bullfloat or a darby (both tools can be rented). A bullfloat has a long handle and is used to smooth areas too large to reach with a darby. Work the bullfloat as you would a sponge mop. As you push the tool away from yourself, tip the front up so it will compact the concrete without digging in *(See Photo 2:3)*. As you pull the bullfloat back toward yourself, run it flat on the concrete to cut off bumps and fill holes *(See Photo 2:4)*. The darby is short and low-handled, giving you more control in the easy to reach areas. It is moved across the concrete in a sawing motion. After smoothing, cut the top inch or so of the concrete away from the forms using a pointed trowel.

As soon as the floating is completed, push the J-bolts into the concrete. The bolts should be positioned at the spots you marked on the forms, set about 1¼ in. from the inside edge of the form board. As the concrete sets up, slice it away from the forms with a mason's (bricklayer's) trowel *(See Photo 2:5)*.

Monitor the concrete as it cures. When water rises to the surface of the concrete, then evaporates, it is time to edge the concrete and cut control joints. Run the edging tool along an edge (choose a less visible spot). If the concrete holds the rounded shape of the metal edging tool, finish the first edging operation, applying with firm, steady

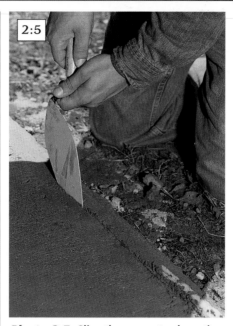

Photo 2:5 Slice the concrete along the edges of the form as it begins to set up, using a trowel. This creates a smoother edge and makes the form boards easier to release.

Photo 2:6 Once the bleed water has disappeared from the concrete surface, tool the edges of the slab with an edging tool. You should probably wear gloves when performing this job.

CONTROLLING CRACKS

Concrete is constantly expanding and contracting, which causes stress and, inevitably, cracks. You can't prevent the cracking, but you can control it. Two techniques are used to control cracking. One is the use of steel reinforcement (rebar and rewire), which serves purposes beyond crack control. For smaller slabs like the one shown here, reinforcement is not required. So we chose the other option: cutting "control joints."

Control joints encourage the concrete to crack in straight lines and at planned locations. We cut one control joint along the centerline of the slab. A control joint should cut about one-quarter of the way through the slab. Slabs wider than about 10 to 12 ft. should have more than one control joint, including a longitudinal control joint down the center. If possible, the panels formed by

Option 1: Cut control joints with a groover after the concrete has stiffened, but before it has hardened.

Option 2: Cut control joints with a circular saw and masonry blade after the concrete has set up.

control joints should be approximately square. All control joints should be placed as continuous (not staggered or offset) lines. Cut

them with a groover while the concrete is fresh, or with a circular saw and masonry blade after the concrete has set.

pressure *(See Photo 2:6).* Tip the tool up slightly as you work, so it doesn't dig into the concrete. And don't press down too hard. Gouges and depressions created by the various finishing tools are difficult to remove at this stage. (edging the slab for the shed is not as critical as it is when you're pouring a sidewalk or patio with exposed edges.)

Control joints (See Controlling Cracks, previous page). The next step is adding the control joints. Use a board at least 6 in. wide as a straightedge to guide the jointing tool and to kneel on as you work. It's a lot easier to do the job if you use a 2 × 12, which will give you a lot more space for kneeling. Before cutting the control joints, snap a chalk line across the slab to mark the line of the joint. Lay the 2 × 12 across the forms, parallel to the chalk line. Press the groover firmly into the concrete and guide it along the 2 × 12 as you cut the joint. Keep the nose of the tool slightly elevated. After you've moved all the way across the slab and roughed out the joint, turn around and slide the tool back through the groove, smoothing and finishing it.

Floating usually is the last step in finishing outdoor concrete. Use a wooden or metal hand float to further smooth the surface. Work the float flat on the con-crete, in wide, arc motions. But don't press too hard. It is hard to erase gouges made at this point.

NOTE: Sometimes concrete is troweled to make it even smoother and more dense on the surface. But this extra smoothness isn't desirable inside the shed, because it can be slippery when wet. An alternative is to trowel the concrete, then scarify the surface with a stiff-bristled brush after the last troweling. The first troweling is done immediately after floating. If you need to kneel on a board to reach areas, you can float an area and then trowel it before moving the board. Hold the trowel flat against the concrete. The second troweling should be done later, when your hand leaves only a slight impression in the concrete.

Curing. Keep the concrete damp while it cures. It takes about a month for typical concrete to cure to its full strength. The first 5 to 7 days, depending on the weather, are the most crucial. During this time, you must make sure the concrete has a chance to cure slowly by keeping it moist. Cover it with plastic sheeting, damp burlap or straw and sprinkle it periodically. The forms can be removed after several days. For best results, allow a few extra days of curing time before using the surface.

Photo 2:7 Proper curing is critical to the durability of your new concrete slab. If the concrete dries too quickly it will be subject to a number of possible defects, including spalling (flaking off of the surface) and cracking. For a full week after the pour, keep the slab covered with a plastic tarp. Once or twice a day you should dampen the surface with water, then recover it. Dampen it even more frequently in hot weather.

Photo 3:1 Set the sill boards in position lengthwise on the slab and use a square to mark a refence line aligned with the center of each J-bolt onto the tops of the sills.

Photo 3:2 Measure the distance from the center of each J-bolt to the edge of the slab, then measure along the sill reference line that same distance and mark a drilling centerpoint.

THREE: Build the walls

After the slab has been cast and has cured for a good week, you can erect the shed, starting with the walls. Even if you don't build a *Handy Homes* model similar to the one shown here, you can be confident that yours will go together in much the same way. Study the directions supplied with the shed, and follow them to the letter.

Drill guide holes for the J-bolts. Cut the sills to length from pressure-treated 2 × 4 stock (some shed kits will not include sill plates because the kits are meant to work on a variety of foundations, including plywood platforms, where sill plates may not be required). The side sills are just under 12 ft. long. The end sill is 10 ft. long. The two front sills, located on either side of the doorway, are 28 in. long. Lay each sill on the slab and set it against the J-bolts. Transfer the J-bolt locations to the sills using a square — we used a combination square *(See Photo 3:1).* Measure the distance of the middle of each J-bolt from the edge of the slab, then use this measurement to mark a drilling point for the guide hole in the sill, at the reference line *(See Photo 3:2).* Drill holes and check the fit, but don't bolt the sills in place yet.

Inventory the parts. The paperwork packed with the shed skit should include a list of all the parts. Now's the time to make sure you have everything you need. Spread the parts out and collect each subassembly's components in one spot. This will help you get a sense of what's involved in the work ahead, it will organize the parts so you can work efficiently, and it will reveal

Photo 3:3 Using the slab as a worksurface, begin constructing the walls of the shed. Start by screwing the back wall components together with 3-in. deck screws.

3:4

Photo 3:4 Attach the precut wall sheathing panels to the wall frames with 2-in. siding nails. Follow the manufacturer's directions carefully when assembling the walls, paying special attention to the overhang and setback amounts for the sheathing panels.

3:5

Photo 3:5 Erect the walls one at a time, beginning with the back wall. Set the guide holes you drilled in the sill over the J-bolts, level and plumb the wall, then attach a staked brace or two to hold the wall in position temporarily.

anything that's missing (See Photo, page 124). If something is missing, you can, of course, call and have a part sent. But you may find it more convenient to make the part.

Construct the back wall. Move the frame members for the back wall — the sill, the extension wall braces, and the center wall supports — onto the slab. Join the two center wall supports with the precut cross-lap joint. Butt the extension wall braces against the ends of the horizontal element of the center-wall support unit next. Drive 3 in. deck screws through the braces into the ends of the support *(See Photo 3:3).*

Butt the sill against the ends of the braces and the vertical support. The middle of the sill (60 in. from each end) should line up on the centerline of the vertical support. Marke sure all the vertical elements are perpendicular to the sill (measure diagonally from brace to brace to check this; the diagonal measurements should be equal). Screw through the bottom face of the sill into the ends of the three vertical frame members.

Set the two large wall panels in place on the framework. They should butt edge-to-edge over the center of the center support, and their bottom edges should overhang the top of the sill by ½ in. Nail them to the frame members with 2-in. siding nails, spacing the nails about 8 in. apart *(See Photo 3:4).* Place and nail the wing panels next. You'll need to slip 2 × 3s under the outside edges of these wings to support them. Nail the wings to the wall frame members.

Erect the back wall. Erecting the back wall is a simple matter of lifting it onto the J-bolts, making sure it is level and plumb, then temporarily attaching a 2 × 4 brace to the outside of the wall. Stake the brace to the ground to hold the wall in place until the other walls are installed to support it *(See*

Photo 3:5). If it is necessary to plumb the back wall, slip cedar shims between the wing panels and the end studs. Then, tighten washers and nuts onto the threaded J-bolts sticking up through the sill *(See Photo 3:6).*

Construct the side walls. The side walls are conventional stud walls, and they can be constructed and erected just like conventional stud walls. The sills on the side-walls should be shorted by 3½ in. each to provide clearance for the front and back wall sills. For the same reason, the end studs should be cut 1½ in. short at the bottoms. Lay out the sill and the top plate, and arrange the studs between them. The studs are located 24 in. on-center (except for one of the end studs, which is 20⅝ in. from the adjacent stud). When the layout is set, drive 3-in. screws through the sill and the top plate and into the ends of the studs.

Make sure the frame is square (measure the diagonals), then lay the side wall panels over it. Align the top edges of the panels flush with the top plate. The ends of the panel should be flush with the end studs. The bottom edges should overhang the top of the sill by ½ in. Drive 2-in. siding nails through the panels into the plate, studs and sill *(See Photo 3:7).* Build both side walls, but do not erect them yet.

Construct the front wall. Because it contains the door opening, the front wall is the trickiest to construct. Position the right front wall panel on a flat surface (the week-old concrete slab is an excellent work area). The door should be facing up. Lift the panel enough to slide the center front wall support under the panel above the door, edge up. The panel should, of course, be lined up on the center-line of the support. Lift the other edge of the panel and slide the extension-wall brace under the panel, aligning its centerline with

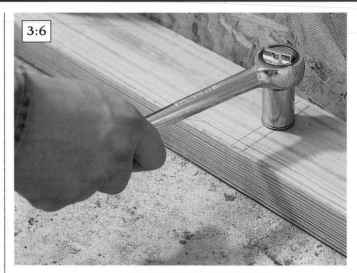

Photo 3:6 After level and plumb are established, secure the walls by threading washers and nuts over the J-bolts and tightening the nuts with a socket wrench. Get them good and snug, but take care not to overtighten the nuts.

Photo 3:7 Construct the short sidewall frame by driving 3-in. deck screws through the sill and top plate and into the ends of the studs. The ends of the sill are cut short to allow for the width of the front and back wall sills.

Photo 3:8 Attach the sheathing panels to the sidewalls with 2-in. siding nails spaced at 8-in. intervals. Set the completed sidewalls out of the way until after both the back wall and front wall are set up.

3:9

Photo 3:9 Construct the front wall with the framing members slipped in beneath the sheathing panels. Because of the door and framed door opening, the front wall is usually the trickiest of the four to put together, so take your time.

3:10

Temporary battens

Photo 3:10 Cut some temporary battens (we used the waferboard packing material from the shed kit) and screw them across the door seams to keep the door shut securely when the wall is erected. Finish up the construction of the front wall by screwing up through the sill and into the bottom ends of the wall studs.

the panel's edge. The bottom end of the extension-wall brace should be aligned 2½ in. from the bottom edge of the wall panel. Additional support for the wall panel can be provided temporarily by sliding a piece of 2 × 3 stock under the door.

With the panel well supported, drive 2-in. siding nails through the edge of the wall panel into the front wall support and the wall-extension brace. Space the nails approximately 8 in. apart. (Don't drive any nails into the temporary support, of course.)

Place the wing-panel on the extension-wall brace. Use a length of 2 × 3, set on edge, under the wing panel as a temporary support while you align and nail the wing to the brace.

Bring the left front wall panel into position next. The door will be supported by the temporary support you still have under the right-hand door. The section above the door must rest on the front wall support, and the outer edge should rest on an extension-wall brace. Position this brace 2½ in. from the bottom edge of the wall panel, as you did on the right side. Place the two ⅜-in.-thick door spacers between the latch-edges of the two doors, and make sure the two wall sections are aligned properly.

Nail through the left wall panel into the front wall support and the extension-wall brace *(See Photo 3:9).* Use 2-in. nails and space them approximately 8 in. apart. At the gable peak, toe-nail through the trim on the right panel into the trim on the left panel. Position the left wing panel, in the same fashion that you did the right wing panel, and nail it to the assembly.

Screw the trim to the wall panels above the door next. After the wall is erected, you will permanently attach this trim by driving fasteners from inside the shed. But this trim will help hold the wall components together while you set it up, so for now, drive four screws through the trim into the wall panels.

Secure the doors with temporary battens by scabbing two pieces of the waferboard packing material across the joint between the doors *(See Photo 3:10)*. Align one at the bottom, and drive three screws through each batten and into each door. Position the piece at the top so it laps over the top trim you just installed. Screw this piece to the doors and the trim.

Finally, screw the sills to the bottom ends of the extension-wall braces, then nail the wall panels to the sills. Each sill should extend ⅛ in. past the edge of the front wall assembly. (The assembly should measure 119¾ in. across the bottom, while the outside ends of the sills should be 120 in. apart.)

Erect the front wall. Before erecting the front wall, cut a brace like the one you used for the rear wall and have it ready.

Stand the wall upright, slide it into alignment with the J-bolts, then lift it and drop it over the bolts. Get the wall roughly plumbed, and screw the brace to the wall. Drive a stake into the ground beside the far end of the brace. Square up the wall again so it's perfectly plumb then screw the brace to the stake. The last job is to slip a washer over each J-bolt, then thread the nut onto it. Tighten the nut.

Before erecting the sidewalls, open the doors in the front wall. Back out the screws in the battens that are keeping the doors closed. When the doors are open, permanently attach the trim above them by driving screws through the interior side of the wall panels into the trim boards.

Erect the sidewalls. Set one of the sidewalls onto the J-bolts *(See Photo 3:11)*. The end studs of the sidewall should rest on the ends of the front and back sills. Be careful

Photo 3:11 Position the sidewalls over their J-bolts, making sure they're flush with the sides of the front and back walls. Attach washers and nuts to the J-bolts. Note: Unless you're a world-class hurdler, it's wise to remove the temporary battens from the door before installing the sidewalls so you don't get trapped inside the shed.

not to disturb the front and back walls. Plumb the side wall at the front, and drive nails through the front wall into the adjacent sidewall studs, tying the two together *(See Photo 3:12)*. Install the washers and nuts on the J-bolts, and tighten the side wall against the concrete slab.

Construct and erect the second side wall in the same way.

Install the trim. Attach the "weatherstrip" to the inside of the door on the right side (viewed from inside the shed), so the strip covers the gap between the two doors. Use the 1¼-in. screws provided, locating them about 8 in. apart.

Step outside the shed, close both doors, and mount the hasp and staple. The staple is mounted on the left door, the hasp on the right. You want to install them so that the hasp, when closed onto the staple, covers the mounting screws for both pieces.

Install the rest of the trim. This includes the soffit end caps, the front and back wall trim, and the corner trim *(See Photo 3:13)*.

Photo 3:12 Drive siding nails through the sides of the front and back wall panels and into the end studs of the sidewalls to complete the basic wall structure of the shed.

Photo 3:13 Attach the trim boards before proceeding with the roof installation. The trim kit includes the top trim pieces for the front wall, corner trim, and the soffit end caps being installed in this photo.

TRACTOR SHED Step Four: Build the roof

FOUR: Frame & deck the roof

Assemble the trusses. The trusses are delivered in halves. You must join two halves with a pair of gussets to form a complete truss unit.

First, measure across the side wall plates. Hook your tape over the outside of one side wall and measure across to the outside of the other wall. Subtract 1 in. for the thickness of the side wall panels. This measurement is how far apart the ends of the trusses must be when they are assembled.

Lay out a pair of the truss halves. Butt the upper ends together. Spread the bottom ends apart to the necessary measurement. Nail or screw one of the the gussets to the faces of the truss halves, linking the halves together *(See Photo 4:1).* Turn the truss over and attach the second gusset. Repeat this assembly process until all five trusses are assembled.

Set up the trusses. The trusses stand on the sidewall plates. In the *Handy Home* line, the trusses are

always set on 2-ft. centers, but the base point for the layout varies according to the shed size. For our 10 × 12-ft. shed, the base point is the center truss (of five). It's back face is positioned 70⁵⁄₁₆ in. from the inside of the front wall. The other trusses are placed 2-ft. on-center, measured from the center truss.

Rather than struggle to align each truss with a tape measure, measure and mark the locations for them on the plates. Then simply lift each truss into place, align it with its marks, and toenail it to the plate with 16d common nails *(See Photo 4:2).*

Build the soffits. The soffits are built onto the shed at the tops of the side walls and project out from the side. Rainwater shed by the roof won't run directly down the walls, thanks to the soffits. This will prolong the life of the shed.

You've already installed the soffit end caps. Now you must mount the soffit nailers. One nailer is attached to the wall at the end of each truss. Because

Photo 4:1 The roof trusses arrive in two sections that must be joined together with gussets at the top. Attach a gusset to each side of each truss assembly. Make all the roof trusses.

Photo 4:2 Set the trusses in position, beginning with the center truss. Toenail the trusses to the top wall plates with 16d common nails.

in the 10 × 12-ft. shed the trusses are positioned just off the wall studs, mounting the soffit nailers is relatively easy. Hold the nailer in place against the sidewall, ¼ in. below the wall's top edge. From inside the shed, drive a couple of screws through the wall into the ends of the nailers *(See Photo 4:3).*

With the nailers mounted, install the fascia next. This trim piece fits into the rabbets in the ends of the soffit caps. Drive finish nails through the end caps into the ends of the fascia, then nail through the fascia into the ends of the nailers.

The soffit roof panels go on next. Two panels are used on each side of the shed. Set each panel in position and nail it to the end cap and the nailers. We used a pneumatic nailer for this job *(See Photo 4:4),* but a plain old hammer will do just as well.

Sheathe the roof. All the panels used in sheathing the roof are pre-

cut. Installing them is a simple matter of setting them into place, one at a time, and nailing them to the trusses and the edges of the front and back walls. As you do this, it is important to keep the trusses from shifting out of correct position.

Start with the lower roof sections. Set the large panel in place, with one end aligned on the centerline of the fourth truss from the back and the other end held ³/₁₆ in. back from the face of the back wall trim. Nail it to the shed only at its corners for now, in case you must adjust the position or trim the panel to get the correct fit of both lower roof panels on that side. Position the smaller panel next. It should butt tightly against the large panel over the truss and be back ³/₁₆ in. from the face of the trim. Nail it at the corners.

If both panels fit correctly—the setback from the trim is critical—

then nail the panels to the roof trusses and the edges of the front and back walls. Use the same 8-in. spacing you've used everywhere else. The first nails you drive should be close to the upper edges of the panels, and before driving one of these nails, double-check the truss spacing to ensure that none of the trusses shifted or distorted slightly as you placed the panels *(See Photo 4:5).* Once you have a nail through the panels into each truss, you can finish nailing. Install the two lower panels on the other side of the roof.

Position the panels on the upper roof next. Here, you want to reverse the positions of the large and small panels, and you need to shift the setbacks as well. At the front of the shed, the edges of the roof panels should be set back ³/₈ in. At the back, the panel edges should be flush with the wall trim. The panels need to be tight at the

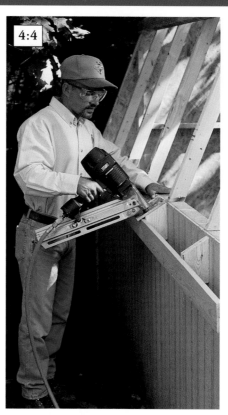

Photo 4:3 Attach soffit nailers to the sidewalls by driving screws through the wall panels and into the inside edges of the nailers.

Photo 4:4 After attaching the soffit fascia boards, nail the soffit sheathing panels to the soffit nailers.

Photo 4:5 Install the lower roof panels on each side of the roof. Tack them at the corners first in case you need to trim them slightly. Once they fit, nail them to the trusses.

Photo 4:6 Install the roof sheathing on the upper roof sections.

Photo 4:7 Construct the two gable overhang sections, then attach them to the front wall trim boards.

roof peak, which will leave a slight gap between the panels of the lower and upper roofs.

Place a panel and nail its corners. When all four panels are in place, nail them to the trusses and wall trim *(See Photo 4:6)*.

Install the gable overhang. There should be four parts left: the parts that make up the gable overhang. Two are triangular pieces of the roof sheathing material, while the others are 2 × 3 supports. Lay one of the roof pieces atop the appropriate support and nail it in place. Assemble the second half of the overhang in the same way.

To install the overhang, set the edge of one of the units on top of the front wall, back against the edge of the roof panel. Drive nails down through the triangular roof piece into the wall trim. Drive a couple of nails through the support into the trim as well.

Attach the second piece in the same way *(See Photo 4:7)*. Then, toenail though one triangular roof piece into the adjacent unit's support. Toenail in the opposite direction as well.

FIVE: Shingle the roof

Materials required for actually weatherproofing the roof are not included in the kit. For the 10 × 12 shed we built, we needed to buy seven bundles of shingles, drip edge molding and building paper.

Cut and install the drip edge molding on the bottom edges of the sheathing. Any joints between individual strips should be positioned somewhere other than a corner. The end of one strip should overlap the its neighbor by about 1 in.

With the drip edge nailed in place, apply building paper (we used 15-pound). This can be cut into strips as necessary and stretched out in horizontal courses beginning at the bottom edge *(See Photo 5:1)*. You want the building paper to overlay the seams

Photo 5:1 Attach drip-edge molding along the bottom edges of the soffit sheathing, then apply 15-pound building paper over the roof. Start stapling the building paper at the low end of each roof side. After the building paper is installed, attach drip edge to the side edges of the sheathing.

Photo 5:2 Install the starter course of shingles upside down. Use the lines printed on the building paper for reference.

between sheathing panels to forestall leaks. The first course should overlap the drip edge, and the second and third courses as you work toward the peak should each overlay the previous course.

Install drip edge at the side edges of the roof, overlapping the building paper. At the corners, the drip-edge should follow around. The proper approach here is to cut wedges out of the flange that overlays the sheathing so you can bend the material to follow the roof-edge contour.

Start shingling the roof at the bottom edges on each side of the shed. Peel the cellophane strip off the back of each shingle before you apply it. Align the first course of shingles across the soffit projection, orienting the edge with the slots facing up the roof slope. Nail the shingles in place with roofing nails *(See Photo 5:2)*, positioning them along the line marked across the center of the shingle.

Apply the second course directly over the first course, orienting the edges of the shingles with the

Photo 5:3 Work your way up toward the ridge when installing the shingles. Be sure to stagger the shingle tabs so they are not aligned.

Photo 5:4 Shingle up over the ridge from each direction. Trim the overhanging shingles with a utility knife or aviator snips.

Photo 5:5 Cut and trim the shingle tabs from whole shingles and use them for the ridge cap shingles. Start nailing at one end — generally, the end that's less exposed to the prevailing wind direction.

Photo 5:6 Since the last ridge cap shingle will not be overlapped by another to cover the nail heads, apply plastic roof cement to the nails heads to seal the nail holes.

slots down *(See Photo 5:3)*. All subsequent courses are oriented tab-edge down, and must overlap the preceding course by half the width of the shingle. The slots should be staggered from course to course. To keep the courses straight, follow the lines printed on the paper. Shingle both sides all the way up and over the peak *(See Photo 5:4)*, making sure the final course on each side has enough "good" surface to cover.

At the peak of the roof, install "ridge caps" to seal the seam. To make a ridge cap, cut a shingle into thirds and trim off the top corners of the tab (non-mineralized) at a 30° angle. Starting at the back of the shed, fold a ridge cap across the ridge and nail it in place. Follow that with another ridge cap, then another *(See Photo 5:5)*. Work your way along the ridge to the front of the shed. The last cap is made from a one-third shingle that's had the un-mineralized material cut off. The roofing nails used to fasten this cap will be exposed. Cover each nail head with roofing cement *(See Photo 5:6)*.

SIX: Finishing touches

If you haven't done it already, mount the barrel bolt to the side of the door containing the weatherstripping. The bolt should be attached to the door and the catch to the gable wall. The assembly should be positioned close to the weatherstrip. Also attach the four door stiffeners *(See Photo 6:1)*. These turnbuckles are used to adjust the door alignment and to keep the door panels from warping.

Paint the shed. Don't delay in priming and painting the shed. Paint will significantly improve the life of your shed by deterring damage caused by the sun's ultra-violet radiation and by moisture. The design of the trim suggests that you use a two-color paint job, although obviously that is a bit more work.

Photo 6:1 Attach any remaining hardware, including the metal stiffeners that are attached to the inside of the door panels. The stiffeners are essentially turnbuckles that can be adjusted to bring the doors into alignment in the door frames.

Photo 6:2 Prime the entire shed. Because we planned to use a relatively light-colored paint, we chose a white, stain-killing primer product.

Photo 6:3 Paint the shed. Typically, the shed is painted in the same color scheme as your house (some neighborhood covenants require that out-buildings be the same color as the main structure). If you are painting the trim a contrasting color, paint the walls first, then mask the walls and paint the trim.

But suit yourself. Begin the job by caulking all the seams with good-quality caulk. Hit all the seams between walls and trim and between the wall panels on the front and back.

Prime the whole shed—trim, wall panels, and doors *(See Photo 6:2).* Either latex or oil-based primer can be used. You may hear a lot of opinions about which type of primer and/or paint is better. Some will recommend priming with latex then top-coating with oil-based paint. Others will recommend doing it the other way around—latex paint over an oil-based primer. However, most coatings specialists will tell you that latex coating keeps getting better, and that using latex paint over a latex primer will give you the longest-lasting coating. Moreover, the job will get done more quickly (because latex dries faster) and clean-up will be easier.

Primer typically is white, but it can be difficult to conceal it under a single top-coat of a dark color. You can save yourself some work and some paint if you have the primer tinted. You don't necessarily have to match the paint color; tinting it a medium gray is enough to make it easier to cover with a color.

Read the paint manufacturer's directions printed on the can. Prime the shed and allow it to dry as long as the manufacturer stipulates. Top-coat the shed with at least two coats of quality paint *(See Photo 6:3).*

Build a driveway. To make it easier to get rolling equipment (in our case, a lawn tractor) in and out of the shed, we built a "driveway." We simply staked a pair of short pressure-treated 2 × 4s to the ground so their tops were level with the top of the slab at the shed end and at grade on the open end. We filled the space between the 2 × 4s with compactible gravel, then tamped it down with a hand tamper. *(See Photo 6:4).* For a decorative touch, we installed landscape edging from the front of the driveway back to the edges of the shed in a semicircular pattern, creating a pair of symmetrical planting beds.

6:4

Photo 6:4 Install a driveway feature and do a little landscaping to dress up your new shed and make it easier to use. We created a compactible gravel "driveway" set into a semicircular planting bed.

VENTILATION

Ventilation is a very important feature to include in your shed. The best way to go about it is simply to cut a vent hole or two at the top of your back wall. Cover the vent holes with louvered soffit vent covers. Make sure the covers are equipped with insect mesh.

Tool Shed

The basic tool shed is a must for any handyman or gardener.
Building one is an unbeatable way to create practical storage for garden and lawn
maintenance tools; and building it from scratch will help your tool shed
stand out from the sameness of kit sheds and yard barns.
The construction is simple, the price tag is low and building your own shed
is a highly satisfying backyard project.

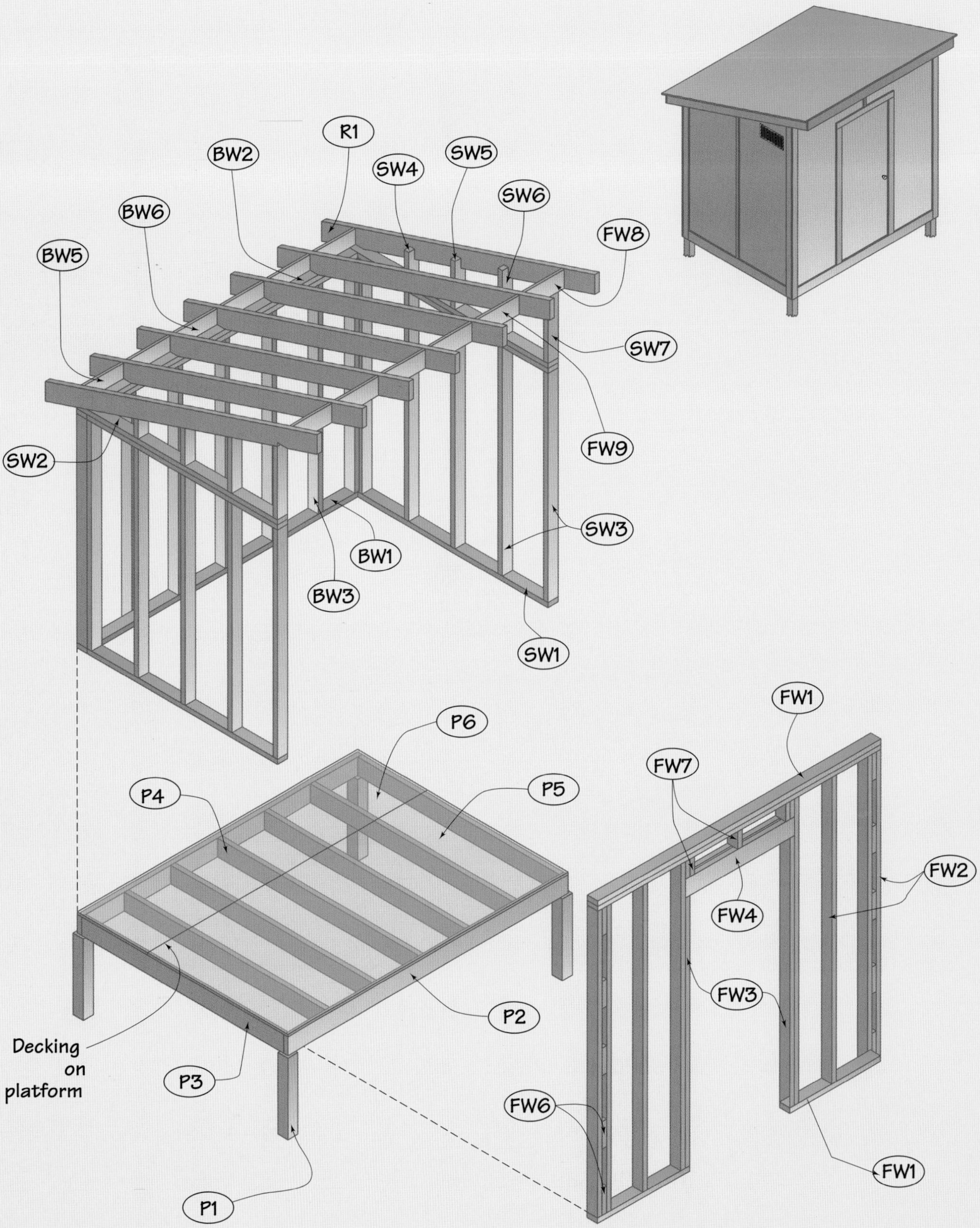
R1
BW2
SW4
SW5
SW6
BW6
FW8
BW5
SW7
SW2
FW9
SW3
BW1
BW3
SW1
FW1
P6
FW7
P4
P5
FW2
FW4
FW3
P2
Decking on platform
P3
FW6
FW1
P1

OVERALL DIMENSIONS (99"W × 103"L × 111¾"H)

KEY	PART NAME	QTY.	SIZE	MATERIAL
PLATFORM				
P1	POST	4	3½ × 3½ × 24"	PRESSURE TREATED
P2	RIM JOIST - FRONT/BACK	2	1½ × 5½ × 96"	DIMENSIONAL LUMBER (2x6)
P3	RIM JOIST - SIDE	2	1½ × 5½ × 69"	DIMENSIONAL LUMBER (2x6)
P4	FLOOR JOIST	5	1½ × 5½ × 69"	DIMENSIONAL LUMBER (2x6)
P5	FLOOR DECKING	1	¾ × 48 × 96"	CDX PLYWOOD
P6	FLOOR DECKING	1	¾ × 24 × 96"	CDX PLYWOOD
P7	EXT. SHEATHING - SIDE	2	¾ × 5¼ × 73½"	CDX PLYWOOD
P8	EXT. SHEATHING - FRONT/BACK	2	¾ × 5¼ × 96"	CDX PLYWOOD
BACK WALL				
BW1	SOLE/TOP PLATE	2	1½ × 3½ × 96"	DIMENSIONAL LUMBER (2x4)
BW2	CAP PLATE	1	1½ × 3½ × 89"	DIMENSIONAL LUMBER (2x4)
BW3	STUDS	9	1½ × 3½ × 67⅜"	DIMENSIONAL LUMBER (2x4)
BW4	CORNER BLOCKING	8	1½ × 3½ × 8"	DIMENSIONAL LUMBER (2x4)
BW5	RAFTER BLOCKING	2	¾ × 4⅝ × 13¾"	DIMENSIONAL LUMBER (1x6)
BW6	RAFTER BLOCKING	4	¾ × 4⅝ × 14½"	DIMENSIONAL LUMBER (1x6)
BW7	SHEATHING	2	¾ × 48 × 71½"	TEXTURED PLYWOOD
SIDE WALL (QUANTITY IS FOR TWO WALLS)				
SW1	SOLE/TOP PLATE	4	1½ × 3½ × 65"	DIMENSIONAL LUMBER (2x4)
SW2	CAP PLATE	2	1½ × 3½ × 68½"	DIMENSIONAL LUMBER (2x4)
SW3	STUDS	10	1½ × 3½ × 67⅜"	DIMENSIONAL LUMBER (2x4)
SW4	CRIPPLE	2	1½ × 3½ × "8⅞"	DIMENSIONAL LUMBER (2x4)
SW5	CRIPPLE	2	1½ × 3½ × 14¼"	DIMENSIONAL LUMBER (2x4)
SW6	CRIPPLE	2	1½ × 3½ × 19½"	DIMENSIONAL LUMBER (2x4)
SW7	CRIPPLE	2	1½ × 3½ × 24¾"	DIMENSIONAL LUMBER (2x4)
SW8	SHEATHING	2	¼ × 36¾ × 83¾"	TEXTURED PLYWOOD
SW9	SHEATHING	2	¾ × 36¾ × 96"	TEXTURED PLYWOOD
FRONT WALL				
FW1	SOLE/TOP PLATE	3	1½ × 3½ × 96"	DIMENSIONAL LUMBER (2x4)
FW2	STUDS	8	1½ × 3½ × 90¼"	DIMENSIONAL LUMBER (2x4)
FW3	TRIMMER STUDS	2	1½ × 3½ × 79½"	DIMENSIONAL LUMBER (2x4)
FW4	HEADER	2	1½ × 5½ × 37"	DIMENSIONAL LUMBER (2x6)
FW5	HEADER BLOCKING	1	½ × 5 × 37"	SCRAP PLYWOOD
FW6	CORNER BLOCKING	10	1½ × 3½ × 8"	DIMENSIONAL LUMBER (2x4)
FW7	CRIPPLES	5	1½ × 3½ × 5¼"	DIMENSIONAL LUMBER (2x4)
FW8	RAFTER BLOCKING	2	¾ × 5½ × 13¾"	DIMENSIONAL LUMBER (1x6)
FW9	RAFTER BLOCKING	4	¾ × 5½ × 14½"	DIMENSIONAL LUMBER (1x6)
FW10	SHEATHING	2	¾ × 48 × 96"	TEXTURED PLYWOOD
ROOF				
R1	RAFTERS	7	1½ × 5½ × 99⅞"	DIMENSIONAL LUMBER (2x6)
R2	SHEATHING	2	¾ × 48 × 83½"	CDX PLYWOOD
R3	SHEATHING	2	¾ × 19½ × 48"	CDX PLYWOOD
R4	SHEATHING	1	¾ × 7 × 83½"	CDX PLYWOOD
R5	SHEATHING	1	¾ × 7 × 19½"	CDX PLYWOOD
TRIM				
T1	SKIRT BOARD - SIDE	2	¾ × 5½ × 66½"	DIMENSIONAL LUMBER (1x6)
T2	SKIRT BOARD - FRONT & BACK	2	¾ × 5½ × 92"	DIMENSIONAL LUMBER (1x6)
T3	CORNER BOARD - SIDE/BACK	2	¾ × 3½ × 78"	DIMENSIONAL LUMBER (1x4)
T4	CORNER BOARD - SIDE/FRONT	2	¾ × 3½ × 10¼"	DIMENSIONAL LUMBER (1x4)
T5	CORNER BOARD - BACK	2	¾ × 3½ × 76½"	DIMENSIONAL LUMBER (1x4)
T6	CORNER BOARD - FRONT	2	¾ × 3½ × 10½"	DIMENSIONAL LUMBER (1x4)
T7	DOOR CASING - STILE	2	¾ × 3½ × 80"	DIMENSIONAL LUMBER (1x4)
T8	DOOR CASING - RAIL	1	¾ × 3½ × 39½"	DIMENSIONAL LUMBER (1x4)
T9	SIDE BATTEN	2	¾ × 1½ × 83¾"	DIMENSIONAL LUMBER (1x2)
T10	FRONT BATTEN	1	¾ × 1½ × 12½"	DIMENSIONAL LUMBER (1x2)
T11	FASCIA BOARD - SIDE	2	¾ × 5½ × 101¾"	DIMENSIONAL LUMBER (1x6)
T12	FASCIA BOARD - FRONT/BACK	2	¾ × 6¹/₁₆ × 99"	DIMENSIONAL LUMBER (1x8)
HARDWARE REQUIRED				
VENT COVERS		2	8 × 16"	
PREHUNG DOOR		1	1⅜ × 32 × 80"	EXTERIOR
BUILDING PAPER		100 sq. ft.		
ROOFING MATERIAL			100 sq. ft.	YOUR CHOICE
NAILS				
SCREWS			#8 × 1½"	

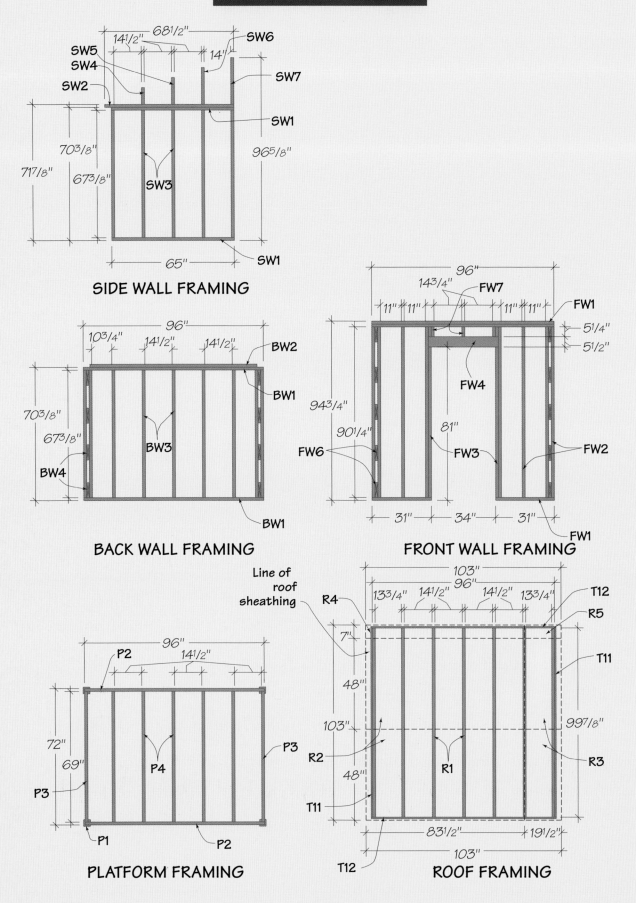

SIDE WALL FRAMING

BACK WALL FRAMING

FRONT WALL FRAMING

PLATFORM FRAMING

ROOF FRAMING

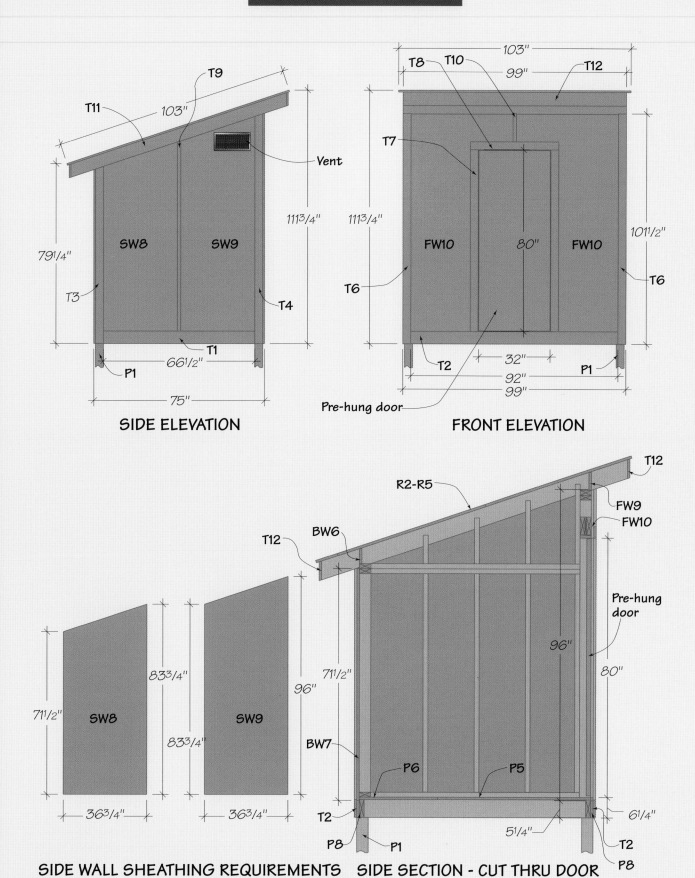

SIDE ELEVATION

FRONT ELEVATION

SIDE WALL SHEATHING REQUIREMENTS   SIDE SECTION - CUT THRU DOOR

Shed kits like the one shown on pages 282 to 302 can be great time and money savers that are virtually foolproof to assemble. But the sizes and styles are somewhat limited, causing them to be easily identifiable as kit-built yard structures. For maximum versatility and to avoid the sameness of kit sheds, design and build your shed from scratch. Among yard structures, they are relatively simple to plan and to build in most cases.

The "stick-built" shed plan shown here is for a small, simple shed. It can be modified easily to reflect your particular size and style needs. It does not require an elaborate foundation—indeed, in some parts of the country it may be practical to simply set out four concrete blocks and construct the shed on top of them (as always, check with your local building department to determine structural requirements in your area).

Build the undercarriage

To create the undercarriage (post-and-joist structure) for a small structure such as a shed, you have several options. The traditional method is to use strings and batter boards to lay out the post hole locations, dig the holes, set the posts in concrete, then trim the tops off so they are level and at the correct height (See pages 185 to 187). But because the framework for the undercarriage in this case is relatively small and light (especially if you choose to use 2 × 4s instead of 2 × 6s), you can use a slightly less conventional method that is virtually foolproof: build the post-and-joist framework first, making sure it is square, use it as a guide for digging post holes, then set the assembly into the post holes. Before you

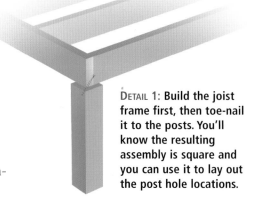

DETAIL 1: **Build the joist frame first, then toe-nail it to the posts. You'll know the resulting assembly is square and you can use it to lay out the post hole locations.**

begin, grade the shed site so it is level and well packed.

Construct the joist frame assembly from pressure-treated lumber (we used 2 × 6, but for smaller sheds you can usually get by with 2 × 4). Cut the joists to length, then join them using 16d common nails (galvanized) driven through the rim joists and into the ends of the interior joist members (nails have much greater sheer strength than deck screws). Or, you may use joist hangers with joist hanger nails instead. Check to make sure the assembly is square by measuring the diagonals.

Cut the posts to length (we used 4 × 4 treated lumber). To determine post length, add 2 inches to the depth of the post holes you plan to dig, allowing for a 4-in.-deep layer of rocks and gravel at the bottom of each hole. The posts normally should be long enough to extend beyond the frost line, but you may be able to get around this restriction in some cases.

Attach the posts to the joist frame. The frame should be positioned on the posts to create ledges on the outer edges the same thickness as your wall sheathing (½ to ¾ in. in most cases). Toe-nail through the frame and into the post on all sides, using galvanized nails *(See Detail 1)*.

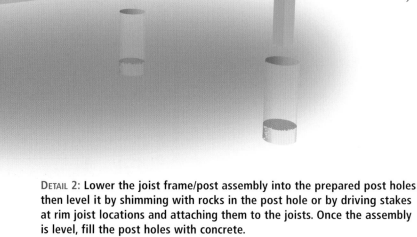

DETAIL 2: **Lower the joist frame/post assembly into the prepared post holes then level it by shimming with rocks in the post hole or by driving stakes at rim joist locations and attaching them to the joists. Once the assembly is level, fill the post holes with concrete.**

With a helper, set the undercarriage assembly (posts and joists) on the building site in the planned orientation and mark the post locations onto the ground. Remove the assembly and excavate the post holes — the diameter of each hole should be two to three times the post thickness. Use a story pole to gauge the hole depths. Add a 4-in.-thick layer of rock and gravel into each hole and tamp with a 2 × 4.

Again with a helper, lift the undercarriage assembly and set it in place with the posts in the post holes *(See Detail 2)*. Check with a level and adjust the position of the assembly by adding or removing subbase material from the holes or by lifting the assembly at low sides and securing it with stakes (attach the stakes with deck screws so they can be removed easily).

With the assembly secured in a level position, mix concrete (See pages 172 to 173) and shovel it into each post hole. Use a 2 × 4 to work the concrete down into the hole. Crown the concrete slightly with a

trowel to shed water. Let the concrete cure overnight.

Cut floor sheathing to fit, making sure seams fall midway over the floor joists. Leave a gap of ⅛ in. or so between sheathing panels. We used ¾ in. exterior plywood for the floor. The edges of the floor should align with the outside edges of the joist frame. Apply construction adhesive to the tops of the joists before attaching the sheathing with 1½-in. deck screws.

Frame the walls & roof

You'll find it easier to build and square up each of the four stud wall frames, then attach them to

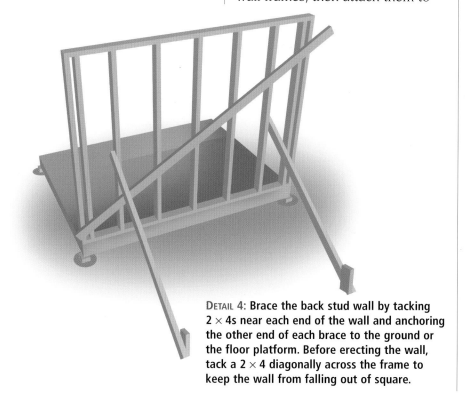

DETAIL 3: **Gang the cap and sole plates for the top and bottom together then lay out common stud locations using a framing square as a guide.**

the floor platform.

Build the front and back wall frames. Begin by cutting the sole and cap plates to length, then clamping them together edge-to-edge with ends aligned. Gang-mark the stud positions on the sole and top plates *(See Detail 3)*, using the layout diagrams on page 306 as a guide. Use a framing square to outline the stud locations. Designate one of the sole plates as the front and lay out the door jamb locations. NOTE: *The front wall layout shown on page 148 includes nailers near each corner of the shed for installing the interior wall coverings. If you do not plan to install interior wall coverings, you can eliminate these studs.*

Cut the full-height wall studs to length and nail the plates to the ends of the studs with 12d common nails. Cut the jack studs for the door opening to length, then fashion a header from 2× stock and ½ in. plywood (See *Tip*, next page). Nail the jack studs and header in position, then fill in above the header with shorter cripple studs. Once the entire wall frame is done, measure the diagonals to ensure that the walls are square. Tack a temporary diagonal brace across it to hold it in alignment while you position it on the floor platform.

Erect the walls. Move the newly framed walls onto the floor platform, beginning with the back wall. Have a couple of long 2 × 4 studs handy to brace the wall. With a helper, raise the wall into posi-

DETAIL 4: **Brace the back stud wall by tacking 2 × 4s near each end of the wall and anchoring the other end of each brace to the ground or the floor platform. Before erecting the wall, tack a 2 × 4 diagonally across the frame to keep the wall from falling out of square.**

tion. Align it flush with the edges of the floor platform. With a 4-foot level, bring the wall into rough plumb. Attach (temporarily) one end of a 2 × 4 brace to a wall stud, and nail the other end to a short 2 × 4 stake driven into the ground or cleat nailed to the floor. Add a brace near each end of the wall *(See Detail 4)*.

Double-check to make sure the back wall frame is level and plumb, then nail or screw the wall to the floor platform.

DETAIL 5: The doubled cap plates are interlocked at the back wall to stiffen the frame structure.

Fasten through the sole plate into the header joist in each stud bay.

Before installing the front wall, build and erect the side wall frames. Build the frames one at a time. Lay out the stud positions on the sole and top plates, and crosscut the necessary studs to length. Lay out the parts on a flat surface, nail them together and square the frame.

Move the first of the frames to the shed and lay it on the floor platform. Raise the frame into place and check the wall for plumb with a 4-foot level. When the wall is lined up properly, attach it to the back wall with 3 in. deck screws (nailing may throw the back wall out of position), then attach it to the floor platform. Attach the other side wall, then remove the braces

from the back wall.

Double the top plates *(See Detail 5)*. This ties the separate wall frames together. Measure from the front of the sidewall to the back of the back wall. Cut a 2 × 4 to that length. Lay it atop the top plate and screw it in place. Do the same at the other side. Then measure and cut a doubler for the back wall. This 2 × 4 will be shorter than the wall's top plate, since it must fit between the doublers already nailed to the sidewalls, which overlap the back wall top plate.

Erect the front wall frame. Plumb it up and screw it to the adjoining walls and to the floor platform. Finally, use a hand saw to cut the sole plate out of the rough opening for the door *(See Detail 6)*.

Install the rafters

This tool shed is capped, quite appropriately, by a *shed roof.* It features seven rafters nailed to the top plates. The eave end of each rafter is cut with a birdsmouth: a triangular cutout that allows the sloping rafter to rest solidly on the horizontal top plate. The ends of the rafters are trimmed with plumb cuts so they will form a line perpendicular to the ground when installed at a slope. This shed is made with 2 × 6 rafters, but for smaller sheds built in areas with minimal snow load,

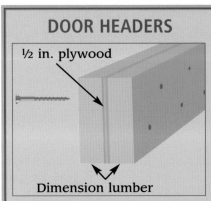

DOOR HEADERS

½ in. plywood

Dimension lumber

Door headers are made by sandwiching a piece of ½ in. plywood between two lengths of dimensional lumber (2 × 6 is shown, but many sheds may require only 2 × 4). Join the elements with construction adhesive and 3 in. deck screws driven through both outer faces.

2 × 4s might be allowed, as long as the slope of the roof does not require you to cut the birdsmouth more than halfway into the rafter. Use 10-ft.-long pieces of dimension lumber to make the rafters.

To begin making a rafter, *plumb cut* one end. The pitch of the roof is 4-in-12, meaning the roof rises 4 in. for each foot of run. Use a framing square to mark cutting lines for the plumb cuts *(See Detail 7)*. Begin by aligning the 4-in. mark on the square's tongue and the 12-in. mark on the blade with the edge of the rafter, near one end. Draw a line along the tongue. This is the line for the plumb cut. Make the

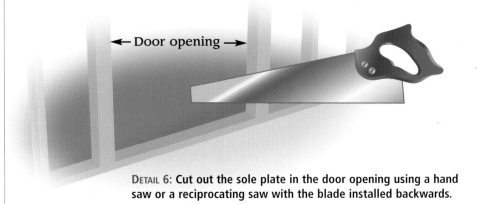

← Door opening →

DETAIL 6: Cut out the sole plate in the door opening using a hand saw or a reciprocating saw with the blade installed backwards.

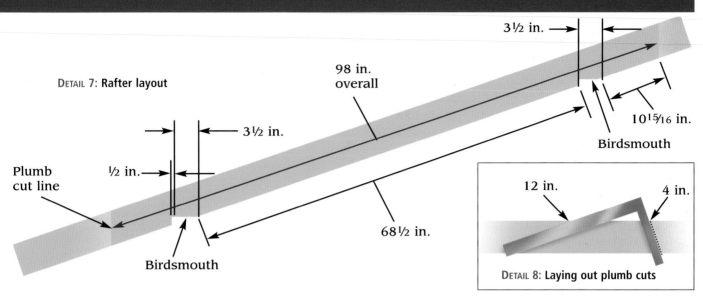

DETAIL 7: Rafter layout

3½ in.

98 in. overall

Plumb cut line

½ in.

3½ in.

68½ in.

Birdsmouth

10¹⁵/₁₆ in.

Birdsmouth

12 in.

4 in.

DETAIL 8: Laying out plumb cuts

plumb cut using a circular saw and straightedge cutting guide. Measure 98 in. along the top edge of the rafter and at that point lay out a second plumb cut, parallel to the first. Make the second cut to trim the rafter to length.

(See Detail 8) Now, measure 10¹⁵/₁₆ in. from each plumb cut along the bottom edge of the rafter and scribe building lines parallel to the plumb cuts to mark the outer surface of the shed's framing. To lay out the first birdsmouth, set the outside corner of your framing square dead on the edge of the rafter at the building line. Align the blade on that line. Scribe a 3½ in. line along the tongue of the square. This marks the seat cut. Shift the square around and mark another line parallel to the plumb cut (this is the inside building line), which establishes the back of the birdsmouth. Cut the birdsmouth with a jig saw.

Measure along the bottom edge of the rafter and lay out the second birdsmouth in much the same way. Note on the layout that the back birdsmouth has a 4-in. seat cut (compared to 3½ in. on the front), to accommodate the sheathing. Cut this birdsmouth. Lay out and cut all the rafters.

Install the outer rafters. With a helper, position them so the seat

cuts rest flush on the cap plates (the ½ in. gap should be at the outside edge of the rear cap plate). The outer faces of the rafters should be aligned with the outside edges of the wall frame. Attach the rafters by toenailing them to the cap plates with 16d common nails (See Detail 9).

Attach the interior rafters according to the spacing layout shown on page 306.

Cut and install cripple studs between the top plates on the side walls and the outer rafters. NOTE: *The traditional way to build shed side walls is to cut full-height studs that span all the way from the sole plate to the rafters and are cut at the top to follow the rafter line. We designed the shed shown here using "platform" type construction because it is easier to square up and is generally less vulnerable to errors in construction.* The best way to produce the cripples is to take a rough measurement from plate to rafter above each regular stud in the side wall. Add about 10 in. to each measurement and cut pieces of

2 × 4 to that length. One by one, set the cripples in place, level them and scribe the edges of each cripple along the bottom edge of the rafter, marking the shoulder of the lap. Also scribe each cripple along the top edge of the rafter to mark it for cutting to length. Cut the cripples to length, then lay out 1¾-in.-deep lap cuts on each cripple, extending between the rafter lines. Trim each cripple to length by cutting along the top rafter line. Make the *shoulder* portion on each lap cut with your circular saw set to 1¾ in. cut-

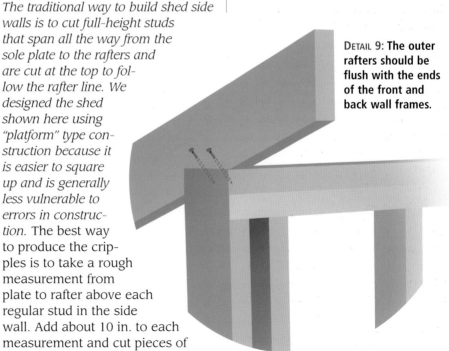

DETAIL 9: The outer rafters should be flush with the ends of the front and back wall frames.

ting depth. Use a reciprocating saw or hand saw to make the *cheek cuts*.

Install the cripples by toe-nailing them to the cap plate and face-nailing them through the lap joint and into the rafter *(See Detail 10)*.

Install the wall & roof coverings

When selecting materials for sheathing and siding your shed, consider several factors: the type of siding used on nearby structures and your house; the amount of exposure the shed will receive; the difficulty of installing the siding; and whether or not you intend to install interior wall coverings. The fastest (and usually cheapest) product for cladding shed walls is plywood siding. It is sold in 4 × 8 sheets with either a smooth or rough-textured surface. For a shed, ⅜-in.-thick stock generally is adequate, but we suggest ⅝ in. siding for added stability and durability.

Cut and install the roof sheathing. We used ¾-in. exterior ply-wood sheathing. Make sure the seams fall along rafters. The edges of the sheathing panels should overhang the rafter frame by 3 in. on all sides. Use 1½-in. deck screws or ring shank nails to attach the sheathing. The seams and edges of the siding will be trimmed later.

Trim out the roof frame *(See Detail 11)* by cutting and attaching 1 × 6 furring boards to the outside faces of the outer rafters (the ends should be cut at the same plumb cut angle as the rafters). Then, cut and attach fascia boards to the front and back so the ends cover the edges of the furring strips. To make these parts, the best method is to bevel-rip 1 × 8 stock at the slope angle (4-in-12). This way, the bottom and top of each fascia board will continue the line of the roof. Nail the fascia to the ends of the rafters.

Cut and attach side panels to the wall frames, according to the sheathing pattern shown on page 307 (but double-check your measurements first for dimension and to make sure the seam between panels will fall over the middle of a stud). Use galvanized siding nails driven at 8 in. intervals along each stud and along the cap plate and sole plate. Don't butt the sheets of plywood tightly together; leave a gap of about ¹⁄₁₆ in. at seams.

Attach the front siding panels. The framework for the shed is sized so you should be able to cover the wall with two full-length sheets of siding that are flush with the top of the doubled cap plate and the top edge of the rim joist. The siding should cover the door opening.

Before installing siding on the back wall, cut out the door opening in the front wall sheathing. Drive a nail at each corner of the opening,

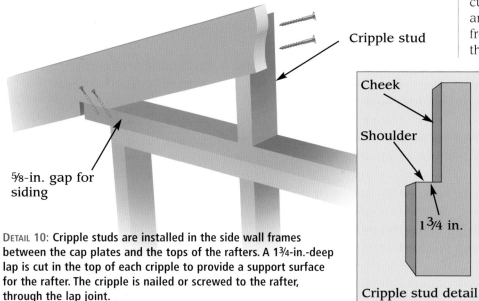

DETAIL 10: Cripple studs are installed in the side wall frames between the cap plates and the tops of the rafters. A 1¾-in.-deep lap is cut in the top of each cripple to provide a support surface for the rafter. The cripple is nailed or screwed to the rafter, through the lap joint.

Cripple stud

⅝-in. gap for siding

Cheek

Shoulder

1 ¾ in.

Cripple stud detail

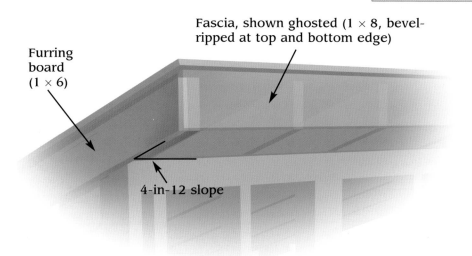

Fascia, shown ghosted (1 × 8, bevel-ripped at top and bottom edge)

Furring board (1 × 6)

4-in-12 slope

DETAIL 11: Cut two 1 × 6 furring boards with the same plumb cut angles as the rafters and tack one board to the outside face of each rafter. Then, bevel-rip 1 × 8s along the top and bottom edge to produce fascia boards that follow the roof slope and completely cover the ends of the rafters.

then connect the nail heads with chalklines to outline the door opening *(See Detail 12).* Cut the opening with a circular saw, using a straightedge if you need to. Stop the cuts short of the corners and finish them with a hand saw or reciprocating saw. Clean up the cut edges with a handsaw so the cutout is smooth and even with the 2 × 4s that frame the opening.

Cut and install siding for the back wall, slipping the top edge of each piece into the gaps at the backs of the rafter birdsmouths.

Install the roof covering. Begin by tacking metal or vinyl drip edge to the back (low) edge and sides of the roof. If you are installing regular tab-style shingles, you'll need to staple strips of building paper to the sheathing, laid with 6-in. overlaps beginning at the low end of the roof. After the last piece of building paper is installed, tack drip edge along the high edge of the roof, overlapping the drip edge, then install the shingles (See pages 201 to 203 for more information on shingling). If you're using roll roofing to cover the shed, no underlayment is required. See *Roll Roofing,* page 314, for instructions.

Install *bird blocking* cut from scrap siding or 1 × 6 pieces in the gap between the double cap plates and the underside of the roof sheathing at the front and back of the shed *(See Detail 13).* Measure and cut each piece to fit. Tack nailing strips around each opening so the blocking pieces will be flush with the siding.

TIP: To minimize mess and avoid masking, apply paint or wood protectant to the siding before installing the trim. Also prime and paint the trim pieces after cutting them to size, but before installation.

DETAIL 12: **Install sheathing over the door framing, then cut out around the framed opening to create the opening for the door. To mark the opening on the sheathing, drive a nail through the sheathing at each corner of the framed opening, then connect the nail points with chalklines.**

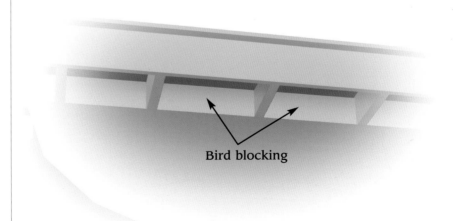

Bird blocking

DETAIL 13: **Cut pieces of 1 × 6 or siding material (called *bird blocking*) and fit them into the gaps between the tops of the front and back walls and the underside of the sheathing.**

Hang the door & install siding trim

The shed design is sized to accept a standard 32-in.-wide by 80-in.-high prehung exterior door. The door opening should be 34 in. wide and 81 in. high to allow for the door jambs and shims.

Hang the door in the door opening, according to the manufacturer's installation instructions.

Before installing the 1 × 4 casing, cut strips of scrap siding to fur out the rim joists, then attach 1 × 6 skirt boards to cover the rim joist areas. Install the side skirting first, flush with the furred-out faces of the front and back rim joists. Then cut the front and back skirt boards long enough to cover the ends of the side skirts. Attach the skirt boards with 6d galvanized finish nails.

Cut and attach 1 × 4 door casing pieces *(See Detail 14).* Cut the side casing strips to fit between the skirt board and the bottom of the door head jamb. The ends of the top casing should be flush with the outside edges of the side casing.

Cut and install 1 × 4 corner boards, beginning at the sides

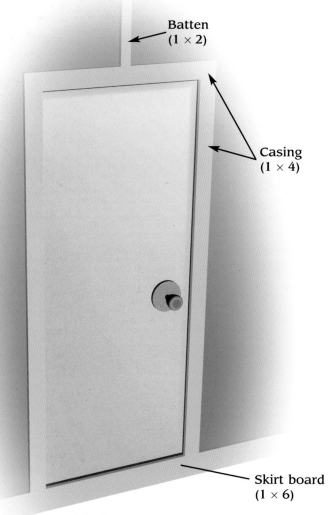

Batten
(1 × 2)

Casing
(1 × 4)

Skirt board
(1 × 6)

DETAIL 14: Trim around the door opening with 1 × 4 casing, butted at the header joints, and a 1 × 6 skirt board to cover the rim joist. 1 × 2 battens are attached to conceal vertical seams.

ROLL ROOFING

Roll roofing is a fiberglass-based roof covering product made in 36-in.-wide strips that are designed for either *single coverage* or *double coverage* installation —in most cases, single coverage rolls will be adequate for a shed. It can be installed directly to the roof sheathing in most areas, requiring no building-paper underlayment. It is designed for flat roofs or roofs with a pitch of 4-in-12 or less. Because it doesn't require underlayment and can be rolled out in long strips, it is generally faster to install than other roofing products.

To install single coverage roll roofing, begin by cutting 12-in.-wide starter strips of roofing and attaching them around the perimeter of the roof. Attach the starter strip at the low end first by bonding it to the sheathing with fibrous roof cement, then driving roofing nails at 4 in. intervals around all edges. The starter strip should stop about ¼ in. before reaching the edges of the drip edge. Cut and attach starter strips along both sides (the rake edges) in the same fashion as the front edge starter strip. Then attach a starter strip at the high edge of the roof.

After the starter strips are all in place, begin to install the full-width strips. Starting at the low end of the roof, cover the starter strips with roof cement. Lay the first strip so it is flush with the edges of the front and side starter strips and seat it in the roof cement. Drive roofing nails along the top edge of the strip according to the nail-spacing requirement recommended by the roofing manufacturer. After the first strip is installed, apply a 3-in.-wide layer of roof cement along the top edge and to the side starter strips in the coverage area. Roll out the second strip so it overlaps the first strip by 3 inches, concealing the nail heads and resulting in a 33-in. reveal. Nail the second strip in place, and work your way up toward the top of the roof. Trim the last strip as needed to neatly cover the top starter strip, fully bonding it with roof cement as you did at the low end and sides. Apply a dab of roof cement over all the exposed nailheads at the top edge, then tack drip edge molding over the roofing at the top edge.

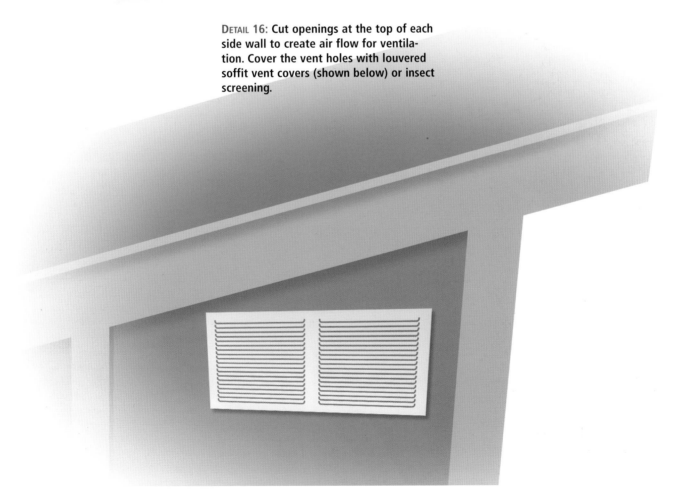

Corner boards (1 × 4)

DETAIL 15: Finish trimming out the siding by installing 1 × 4 corner boards. The boards on the front and back walls should overlap the edges of the side corner boards.

(See Detail 15). The side corner boards should extend from the bottom of the the skirt board to the underside of the roof sheathing. Cut the top edge at an angle to match the slope of the roof so it will fit tightly against the sheathing. The front and back corner boards should cover the edges of the side corner boards and also should be trimmed (beveled) at the top to match the roof slope.

Cut and install strips of 1 × 2 to make battens for covering the vertical seams between siding panels.

DETAIL 16: Cut openings at the top of each side wall to create air flow for ventilation. Cover the vent holes with louvered soffit vent covers (shown below) or insect screening.

Finishing touches

To create ventilation in the shed, cut a hole near the top of each side wall, over a stud cavity. Cover the openings with louvered soffit vent covers after you paint the shed *(See Detail 16).*

Finish the interior (optional). The doubled corner posts shown here provide nailing surfaces for installing interior wall coverings. Many sheds, however, do not need interior walls. If you choose to install them, ⅜-in.-thick oriented strand board (OSB) is a good material choice.

To prolong its life, paint the floor with enamel floor paint.

Caulk around all the exterior trim pieces and between the roof sheathing and the walls.

Part 3
Backyard Woodworking Projects

Introduction

Wood projects designed for outdoor use tend to be rugged and sturdy, utilizing simple joinery techniques and able to withstand extreme changes in temperature and humidity. Building outdoor projects can be a great way to develop and practice woodworking skills, while at the same time creating attractive pieces that you and your family will use for years to come.

In *Part 3—Backyard Woodworking Projects*, you'll find 15 outdoor projects that cover a diverse range of styles and levels of complexity. Some projects are quite basic, and well within the capability of all woodworkers; others are more refined (meant for sheltered spaces like porches and breezeways) and require a higher level of woodworking skills for successful completion.

Each project here includes a beautiful photograph of the finished piece, complete cutting and shopping lists, detailed plan drawings, clear color photographs of key points in the building process and straightforward step-by-step instructions.

Outdoor wood furniture can survive for many years in the elements, but the kind of wood you use will influence the longevity of your project. Good weather-resistant woods include Western red cedar, white oak and Honduras mahogany. Other excellent wood choices for outdoor projects include redwood, teak and cypress, but these varieties are harder to find in many areas of the United States and can be quite expensive.

Other less weather-durable woods, like red oak and pine, can be used for outdoor projects as well, but these woods must be topcoated thoroughly with primer and paint or other UV-protective sealers.

Refine the look of outdoor furniture by concealing screw heads with wood plugs. Wood plugs also keep galvanized screws sealed from moisture, which can otherwise cause them to react with woods like white oak and cedar over time, producing black stains. Counterboring and plugging are used on several projects in this book. We show you how to install wood plugs below.

It's a good idea to topcoat even weather-resistant woods as a final project step, especially if you want to retain the wood's natural color. Without a UV-protective finish, woods like cedar and mahogany will turn a harmless silvery gray color, which may not achieve the look you're after for your project. Apply several coats of a clear or tinted penetrating water-repellent preservative with ultraviolet inhibitors and a mildewcide, or use marine-grade spar varnish, a favorite of boat builders. Plan to recoat annually for projects that are kept outside all the time. The other route to take for exterior finishes is to use a premium-quality latex primer followed by multiple coats of exterior latex paint.

HOW TO INSTALL WOOD PLUGS

STEP 1: Drill a counterbored pilot hole deep enough into the wood so the counterbored portion of the hole can accommodate both the screw head and a plug.

STEP 2: Drive the screw into the hole until it stops at the bottom of the counterbore. Glue and insert a wood plug cut from the same wood species or from a piece of dowel.

STEP 3: Trim any protruding portion of the wood plug flush with the surrounding wood using a flush-trimming handsaw. Then sand the plug area smooth.

Basic Adirondack Chair

No piece of outdoor furniture conjures up an image of elegance and rugged outdoor comfort quite like the Adirondack chair. There are many variations of this American classic. This design features a straightforward concept and easy-to-work materials for a satisfying project that can be built in a day, yet provide years of enjoyment.

Vital Statistics: Basic Adirondack Chair

TYPE: Adirondack chair

OVERALL SIZE: 36½W by 37D by 37½H

MATERIAL: Cedar

JOINERY: Butt joints reinforced with galvanized deck screws

CONSTRUCTION DETAILS:
· Largely square, straight cuts can be made with
  simple hand or power tools
· Chair made entirely from dimension lumber
· Exposed screws throughout to enhance rustic appearance

FINISHING OPTIONS: Penetrating UV protectant sealer,
exterior paint or leave unfinished to weather naturally to gray

Building time

 PREPARING STOCK
0 hours

 LAYOUT
1-2 hours

 CUTTING PARTS
2-4 hours

 ASSEMBLY
2-4 hours

 FINISHING
2-4 hours

TOTAL: 7-14 hours

Tools you'll use

· Jig saw or circular saw

· Drill/driver

· Tape measure

· Combination square

· Clamps

Shopping list

☐ (4) 1 × 4 in. × 8 ft. cedar

☐ (2) 1 × 8 in. × 6 ft. cedar

☐ (1) 2 × 4 in. × 10 ft. cedar

☐ Galvanized deck screws
   (1¼-, 2-in.)

☐ Finishing materials

Basic Adirondack Chair

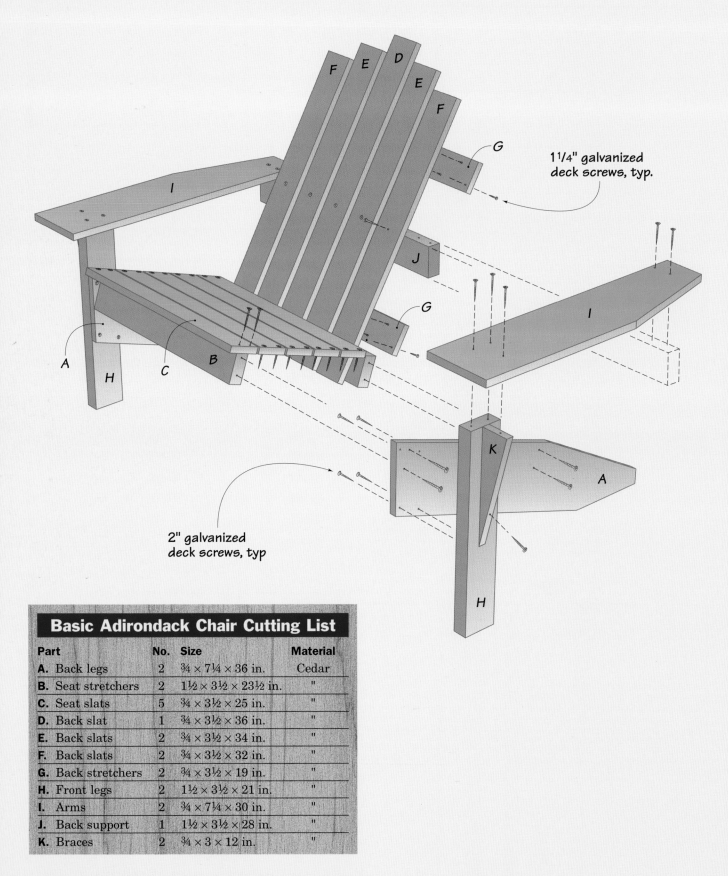

1¼" galvanized deck screws, typ.

2" galvanized deck screws, typ

Part	No.	Size	Material
A. Back legs	2	¾ × 7¼ × 36 in.	Cedar
B. Seat stretchers	2	1½ × 3½ × 23½ in.	"
C. Seat slats	5	¾ × 3½ × 25 in.	"
D. Back slat	1	¾ × 3½ × 36 in.	"
E. Back slats	2	¾ × 3½ × 34 in.	"
F. Back slats	2	¾ × 3½ × 32 in.	"
G. Back stretchers	2	¾ × 3½ × 19 in.	"
H. Front legs	2	1½ × 3½ × 21 in.	"
I. Arms	2	¾ × 7¼ × 30 in.	"
J. Back support	1	1½ × 3½ × 28 in.	"
K. Braces	2	¾ × 3 × 12 in.	"

Basic Adirondack Chair Cutting List

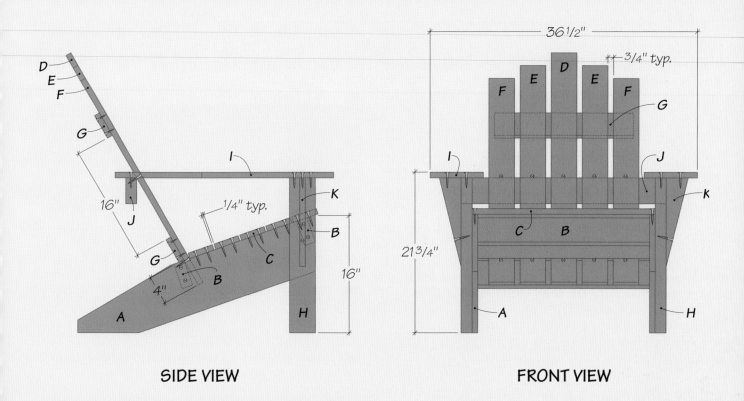

SIDE VIEW

FRONT VIEW

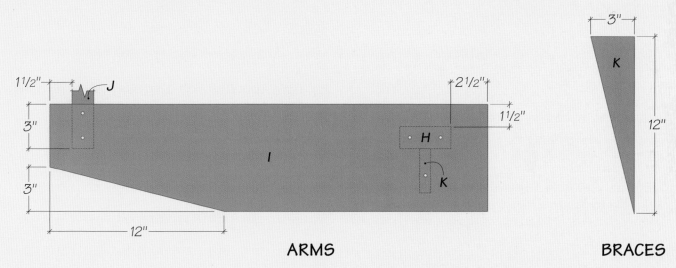

ARMS

BRACES

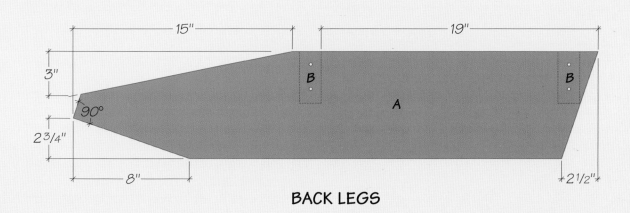

BACK LEGS

Basic Adirondack Chair: Step-by-step

BUILD THE SEAT ASSEMBLY

❶ Cut the back legs to length from 1 × 8 stock. Follow the *Back Legs* drawing, page 11, to mark the angle cuts on the legs. Cut the leg angles with a jig saw or circular saw using a straightedge guide. Then cut the two seat stretchers to length.

❷ Attach the back legs to the seat stretchers. Position the face of the back stretcher 19 in. from the front ends of the legs and the leading edge of the front stretcher flush with the front ends of the legs. Mark the stretcher locations with a square, drill countersunk pilot holes through the legs and the stretchers, and fasten the parts with 2-in. galvanized deck screws **(See Photo A)**.

BUILD THE ARM ASSEMBLY

❸ Cut the front legs and the back support to length.

❹ Cut the arms and braces to size and shape. Mark for the angle cut on the back corner of each arm by measuring 12 in. along one long edge and 3 in. along the adjacent short end. Draw a line between these two points, and cut the angles with a jig saw guided by a straightedge. Save the triangular cutoff pieces; they'll become the arm braces.

❺ Measure and mark the positions of the front legs, braces, and back support on the arms (See *Arms* drawing, page 11). With the arms face down on your workbench, use a combination square to mark the position of the front legs 2½ in. from the front of each arm and 1½ in. from the inside edges. Center and mark for a brace on the outside face of each leg. Then position the back support. It overlaps the inside edge of each arm by 3 in. and is inset 1½ in. from the ends.

❻ Build the arm assembly. Turn the arms face up and drill countersunk pilot holes through the arms for attaching the legs and back support. Attach the front legs and back support with 2-in. deck screws driven through the arms. Attach the braces to the arms and legs with countersunk 2-in. deck screws **(See Photo B)**.

PHOTO A: Attach the back legs to the seat stretchers with 2-in. galvanized deck screws. Countersink the screw heads.

PHOTO B: Attach the back support, front legs and arm braces to the arm workpieces with 2-in. galvanized screws.

ATTACH THE ARM & SEAT ASSEMBLIES

Fastening the arm and seat assemblies together will require the use of temporary braces and clamps. Cut two 21-in. lengths of scrap for the temporary braces.

❼ Stand up the arm assembly and set the temporary braces beneath the arms to hold the arm assembly level. Position the seat assembly between the front legs so the front ends of the back legs are flush with the front edges of the front legs. Clamp the two assemblies together. The top corner of the back legs should be 16 in. up from the bottom of the front legs.

PHOTO C: Install the seat. Clamp the seat assembly between the front legs. You'll need to set temporary braces beneath the arms to hold them level. Attach the seat assembly to the front legs with deck screws.

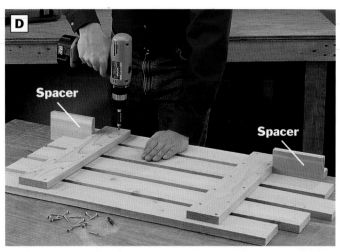

PHOTO D: Arrange the back slats face down on the bench, and fasten the back stretchers to the slats with 1¼-in. galvanized deck screws. Insert ¾-in. scrap spacers between the slats to make alignment easy.

8 Fasten the seat assembly to the front legs with countersunk 2-in. deck screws. Drive the screws through the back legs into the front legs **(See Photo C)**. Remove the temporary braces.

BUILD & ATTACH THE BACK

9 Cut the back slats and the back stretchers to length. Assemble the back by laying the slats face down on your workbench with the bottom edges flush. Position the stretchers so the lower stretcher is 4 in. from the bottom ends of the back slats, and there is 16 in. between the top and bottom stretchers. Drill countersunk pilot holes, and drive 1¼-in. deck screws through the stretchers into the slats **(See Photo D)**.

10 Install the chair back. Attach the chair back by sliding it into position with the lower back stretcher resting on the rear seat stretcher. Drill countersunk pilot holes through the back slats into the rear seat stretcher and the back support. Attach the back with 2-in. deck screws.

ATTACH THE SEAT SLATS

11 Cut the five seat slats to length, and attach them to the back legs with 2-in. deck screws. Countersink the screw holes, and use ¼-in. hardboard spacers to hold the slats evenly apart as you fasten the slats **(See Photo E)**. NOTE: *You'll need to remove the chair arms one at a time to fasten the slats. Drive all the screws on one side of the seat, replace the arm, then remove the other arm and attach the slats.*

FINISHING TOUCHES

12 Smooth all exposed chair surfaces and ease the corners with a sanding block. Apply the exterior sealer, stain or paint of your choice. Or leave the chair unfinished so it weathers naturally to gray.

PHOTO E: Set the seat slats in place and insert ¼-in.-thick hardboard spacers between the slats. Remove one chair arm for drill clearance and fasten the seat slats to the back leg. Once the slats are attached on one side, reinstall the arm, remove the other arm and fasten the slats to the other back leg. Then reinstall the arm.

Cedar Bird Feeder

Invite songbirds into your yard or garden with this aromatic cedar bird feeder. Our design features a wide, protective roof to keep the feed dry, along with narrow perches to discourage larger predator birds. The feeder can be mounted to a post or hung from a branch, and you can build one in an afternoon.

Vital Statistics: Cedar Bird Feeder

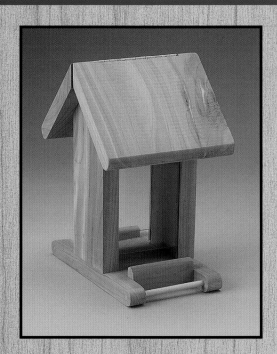

TYPE: Bird feeder

OVERALL SIZE: 6W by 9¾H by 8L

MATERIAL: Aromatic cedar

JOINERY: Miters, screwed butt joints

CONSTRUCTION DETAILS:

· Lid hinges open on one side for cleaning and filling
· Plexiglas end panels are epoxied into shallow grooves in the sides
· Perches made of ¼-in. doweling
· Part ends are rounded over for finished look

FINISH: None

Building time

PREPARING STOCK
1 hour

LAYOUT
1 hour

CUTTING PARTS
2 hours

ASSEMBLY
2 hours

FINISHING
None

TOTAL: 6 hours

Tools you'll use

· Table saw
· Drill/driver
· Power miter saw (optional)
· Clamps
· Router table with ⅜-in. roundover bit
· Belt sander (optional)
· Drill press
· Hammer and nailset

Shopping list

☐ (1) ¾ × 6 in. × 4 ft. aromatic cedar

☐ (2) ⅛ × 3½ × 5⅞ in. Plexiglas

☐ ¼-in.-dia. hardwood dowel

☐ Two-part epoxy

☐ 4d galvanized finish nails

☐ ¾ × 4-in. brass jewelry box hinge

☐ Polyurethane glue

Cedar Bird Feeder

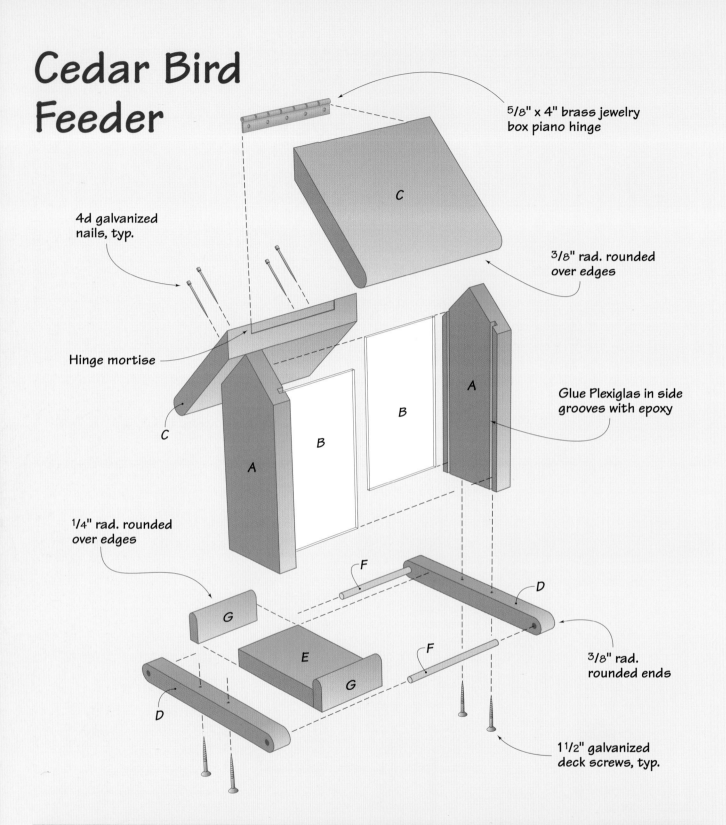

5/8" x 4" brass jewelry box piano hinge

3/8" rad. rounded over edges

4d galvanized nails, typ.

Hinge mortise

Glue Plexiglas in side grooves with epoxy

1/4" rad. rounded over edges

3/8" rad. rounded ends

1 1/2" galvanized deck screws, typ.

Cedar Bird Feeder Cutting List

Part	No.	Size	Material	Part	No.	Size	Material
A. Sides	2	¾ × 3 × 8 in.	Cedar	E. Base plate	1	¾ × 3 × 4½ in.	Cedar
B. Ends	2	⅛ × 3½ × 5⅞ in.	Plexiglas	F. Perches	2	¼ dia. × 4½ in.	Hardwood dowel
C. Roof panels	2	¾ × 6 × 5⅛ in.	Cedar	G. Feed dams	2	½ × 1¼ × 3 in.	Cedar
D. Base strips	2	¾ × ¾ × 8 in.	"				

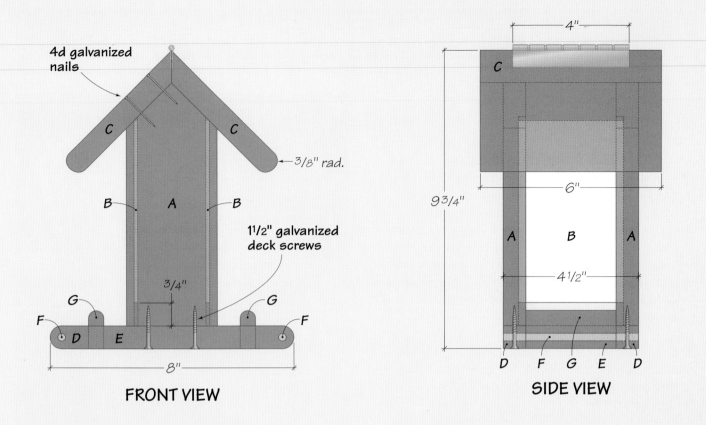

4d galvanized nails

3/8" rad.

1 1/2" galvanized deck screws

3/4"

FRONT VIEW

4"

9 3/4"

6"

4 1/2"

SIDE VIEW

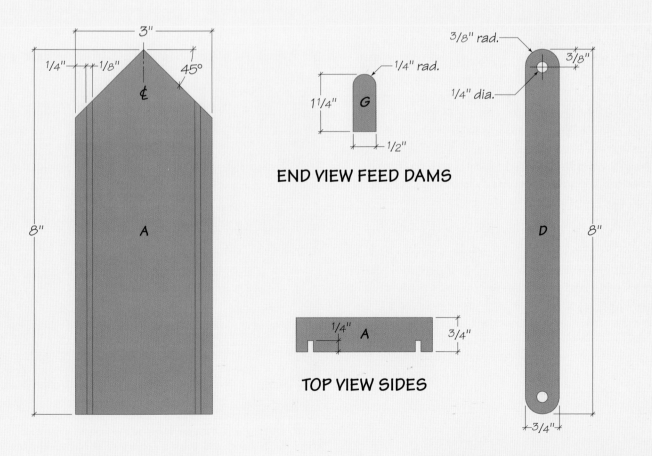

3"

1/4" · 1/8"

45°

¢

8"

FRONT VIEW SIDES

1/4" rad.

1 1/4"

1/2"

END VIEW FEED DAMS

1/4" A

3/4"

TOP VIEW SIDES

3/8" rad.

3/8"

1/4" dia.

8"

3/4"

FRONT VIEW BASE STRIPS

MAKE THE SIDES & ENDS

❶ Lay out and cut the two sides to shape: Rip stock for the sides to 3 in. wide, and crosscut the workpieces to 8 in. long. Form gables on one end of each side panel at the power miter saw with the blade turned 45° to the right or left (**See Photo A**). You can also make these gable cuts on the table saw with each workpiece held against the miter gauge, set at 45°. Align the cuts so the tip of the gable is centered on the width of the sides.

❷ Cut grooves in the sides for the Plexiglas end panels. See the *Front View Sides* drawing on page 67 for positioning the grooves on the sides. Plow these ¼-in.-deep grooves on the table saw with a ⅛-in. kerf blade and the fence set ¼ in. from the blade.

❸ Cut the Plexiglas end panels to size: To avoid scratching the panels, don't remove the clear film that covers the plastic for marking or cutting. Lay out the part shapes and cut the Plexiglas to size on the band saw with a fined-toothed blade (**See Photo B**). You can cut Plexiglas on the table saw also, but use a fine-toothed plywood-cutting blade or a blade intended to cut plastic and laminate. Otherwise, the Plexiglas will tend to chip as you cut. Gently sand the edges of each panel, then dry-fit them into the grooves in the cedar side pieces to be sure they fit. Widen the grooves if necessary on the table saw.

MAKE THE ROOF SECTIONS

❹ Start by making a blank for both roof sections from one piece of stock. The board dimensions should be 6 in. wide and 10⅜ in. long. Round over both ends of the blank on the router table with a ⅜-in. roundover bit. NOTE: *Be careful when the router bit exits the board. Aromatic cedar is soft, and the end grain will tear out on the edges of the boards. Rout these bullnose profiles in several passes of increasing depth, which will also help minimize chipping and tearout.*

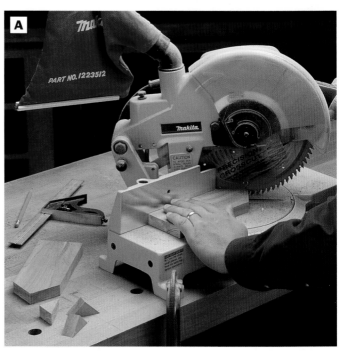

PHOTO A: Trim the gable ends of the sides on a power miter saw with the blade swiveled to 45°. Center the gable peaks across the width of the workpieces.

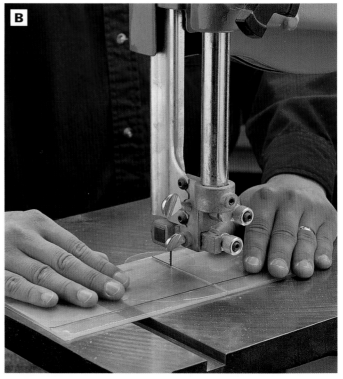

PHOTO B: Measure and cut the Plexiglas end panels on the band saw with a fine-toothed blade. Leave the protective film on the plastic as you machine it, to minimize scratching.

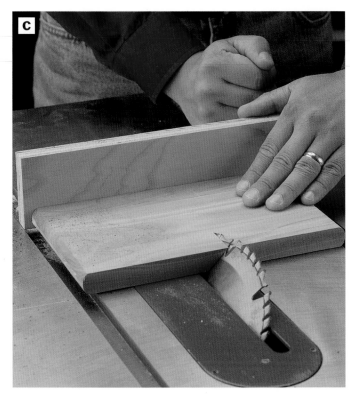

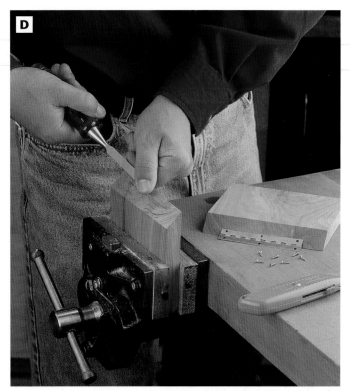

PHOTO C: Tilt the table saw blade to 45° and cut the roof blank in half to form two roof sections. Take time to set up this cut accurately. Otherwise the roof section lengths won't match. One cut both trims the parts to length and forms the roof miter joint.

PHOTO D: Mark and cut the shallow hinge mortises into the beveled edges of the roof sections. Score along your mortise layout lines first with a utility knife, then pare out the mortise with a sharp chisel. Keep the mortise depth the same as the hinge leaf thickness.

5 Split the roof blank in half to form the two roof sections. Since the roof sections meet at a 45° angle at the bird feeder peak, you'll crosscut the roof blank in half at the table saw with the blade set at a 45° bevel angle **(See Photo C).** Be careful when setting up this cut so you'll divide the roof blank equally.

6 Cut hinge mortises into the top bevels of the roof sections: The roof halves will be joined together with a single brass jewelry box hinge. In order to form a relatively tight miter joint at the bird feeder peak, you'll need to recess the hinge leaves into shallow mortises cut into the roof sections. Lay out the hinge location on each roof section by outlining the shape of the hinge leaves along the top edge of the roof bevels. Keep the knuckle of the hinge above the bevel edge, as shown in the *Side View* drawing, page 67. Clamp each roof section in a vise, and score along your mortise layout lines with a utility knife. Then pare away the material within your layout lines with a sharp chisel **(See Photo D).** The mortises shouldn't be deeper than the hinge leaves are thick.

BUILD THE BASE

7 Make the base strips: Rip a ¾-in.-wide stick of cedar to 16⅛ in. long on the table saw. Crosscut the workpiece in half to form two 8-in.-long base strips. Round over the ends of the strips with a wood rasp and random-orbit sander or on a stationary disk sander. NOTE: *These ends are too narrow to round over with a router without tearing out the wood.*

8 Drill holes through the ends of the base strips for the perches: Lay out the centerpoints for these perch holes on one base strip, ⅜ in. in from each end. Stack the marked base strip on top of the other strip, and clamp them to your drill press table. Use a backer board beneath the base strips to keep from drilling into the drill press table. Chuck a ¼-in.-dia. bit in the drill press, and drill holes completely through both base strips **(See Photo E).** Dry-fit the perch doweling into the base strip holes to be sure it fits.

9 Make the remaining base parts: Rip and crosscut the base plate to size. Measure and cut the perch dowels to length at this time as well.

10 Assemble the base. Install the perches in one of the base strips, using a dab of polyurethane glue in

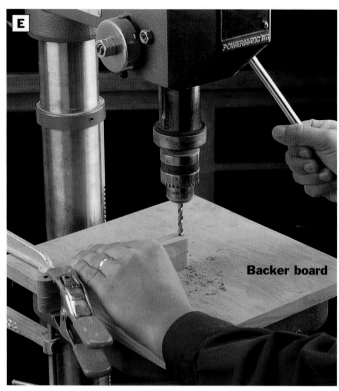

Backer board

PHOTO E: Bore ¼-in.-dia. holes for the perches through both ends of the base strips. We stacked these parts and drilled both strips at once on the drill press.

PHOTO F: Assemble the base plate, base strips and perches with polyurethane glue. Clamp the parts together to keep the glue from forcing the joints open as it cures.

each dowel hole. Apply a coat of polyurethane glue to the long edges of the base plate, and wet the mating surfaces of the base strips with a water-dampened rag. Squeeze a drop of glue into the dowel holes of the other base strip and assemble the base parts together, making sure the perches are properly seated in their holes **(See Photo F).** Tap them gently, if needed, with a mallet. Polyurethane glue will foam and expand as it cures, so hold the base strips against the base plate with a couple of short bar clamps or large C-clamps until the glue cures. Clean up excess glue immediately with mineral spirits.

⓫ Make the feed dams: Since these parts are small, and one long edge of each receives a bullnosed profile, start from a piece of wide stock (6 in. wide or wider) and rout the bullnoses first before ripping and cross-cutting the dams to size. Routing wider stock will keep your hands a safe distance from the router bit. Round over one long edge of the workpiece on the router table with a ⅜-in.-dia. roundover bit. Then rip and crosscut the feed dams to size.

⓬ Install the feed dams on the bird feeder base. Attach the dams to the short ends of the base plate in between the base strips with polyurethane glue.

Use a clamp to hold the dams in position until the glue cures. Again, clean up excess glue before it sets.

ASSEMBLE THE BIRD FEEDER

⓭ Install the clear end panels in the grooves in the cedar sides: Spread a thin coat of two-part epoxy into each of the grooves in the sides, keeping the adhesive about 1 in. shy of the top and bottom of each groove. (Two-part epoxy is a good adhesive for bonding Plexi-glas.) Remove the protective film from the Plexiglas, and slip the two end panels into their respective grooves, aligning them so they're approximately ¾ in. up from the bottoms of the sides **(See Photo G).**

⓮ Fasten the base to the sides: Apply a bead of polyurethane glue along the bottom edge of each side, then center the sides on the base strips. Drill counter-sunk pilot holes up through the bottom of the base strips and into the sides, and drive 1½-in. galvanized wood screws into the holes **(See Photo H).** Then drill a few 1⁄16-in.-dia. weep holes through the base, which will help keep the feed dry.

⓯ Assemble the roof: Mark and drill pilot holes for the brass screws that will attach the hinge to the roof sections. Install the hinge.

PHOTO G: Spread two-part epoxy into the grooves in the side panels, remove the protective film from the Plexiglas end pieces, and slide the end pieces into the grooves. The end pieces should stop ¾ in. from the bottoms of the sides.

PHOTO H: Attach the base to the sides with polyurethane glue and 1½-in. countersunk galvanized wood screws. Then drill a few small weep holes (smaller than the seed you'll put in the feeder) to allow any moisture to drain away, keeping the bird seed dry.

⓰ Fasten the roof to the side panels. Spread a bead of polyurethane glue along one gable edge of each side panel. Wet the mating surfaces of one of the roof sections and set the roof in place over the sides. Be careful to align the roof so it overhangs the sides evenly. Drive a few galvanized 4d finish nails down through the glued roof section to fasten it to the sides **(See Photo I)**. It's a good idea to drill pilot holes for these nails first, to keep the nails from splitting the sides. Then countersink the nailheads with a nailset.

PHOTO I: Attach one half of the roof to the body of the bird feeder with polyurethane glue and galvanized 4d nails. The other roof section hinges open to allow easy access for filling and cleaning the feeder.

Feeding songbirds

The type of food you provide in the feeder will in large part determine the bird species you attract. Dark-eyed juncos, for example, love millet, especially when it falls on the ground below the feeder. Sunflower seeds are a sure bet for bluejays, chickadees, cardinals, gold and purple finches, nuthatches, the tufted titmouse and pine siskens. Downy woodpeckers and blue jays also like an occasional meal of shelled peanuts. Regardless of the type of feed you use, experts agree that the feeder must be cleaned out regularly to keep the contents from molding. If the birds should consume molded seed, it can cause aspergillosis, a fatal illness for songbirds.

Garden Bench

Made from dimensional cedar, this garden bench has a rustic quality that lets it blend into a casual, country-style garden. But the graceful curve of the top rail on the backrest gives this bench just enough style to fit into a formal garden as well. With its sloped back and contoured seat, it offers a comfortable resting spot where you can while away the hours in the great outdoors.

Vital Statistics: Garden Bench

TYPE: Outdoor bench

OVERALL SIZE: 50W by 34H by 24D

MATERIAL: Cedar (1× and 2×)

JOINERY: Dowel joints, butt joints reinforced with screws

CONSTRUCTION DETAILS:
- Sloped back rest and contoured seat for comfort
- All wood parts made from standard dimensional cedar available at building centers
- Decorative contour on top back rail
- Seats three adults

FINISHING OPTIONS: Clear coat UV-inhibiting wood sealant to prevent graying of wood. Apply redwood-tinted stain for richer wood color.

Building time

PREPARING STOCK
1 hour

LAYOUT
2-4 hours

CUTTING PARTS
4-6 hours

ASSEMBLY
2-4 hours

FINISHING
1-2 hours

TOTAL: 10-17 hours

Tools you'll use

- Table saw or circular saw
- Drill/driver
- Straightedge cutting guide
- C-clamps
- Bar or pipe clamps
- Jig saw or band saw
- Hammer
- Combination square
- Tape measure
- Doweling jig

Shopping list

- ☐ (1) 2 × 8 in. × 8 ft. cedar dimension lumber
- ☐ (1) 2 × 6 in. × 8 ft. cedar dimension lumber
- ☐ (3) 2 × 4 in. × 8 ft. cedar dimension lumber
- ☐ (6) 1 × 4 in. × 8 ft. cedar dimension lumber
- ☐ (60) ¼-in.-dia. × 1½ in. fluted wood dowels
- ☐ Finishing materials
- ☐ Galvanized deck screws (2 in. and 3 in.)
- ☐ Exterior wood glue

Garden Bench

2" gap (typ)

Garden Bench Cutting List

Part	No.	Size	Material
A. Back legs	2	$1\frac{1}{2} \times 7 \times 34$ in.	Cedar
B. Front legs	2	$1\frac{1}{2} \times 3\frac{1}{2} \times 22$ in.	"
C. Back rail (top)	1	$1\frac{1}{2} \times 5 \times 46$ in.	"
D. Back rail (bottom)	1	$1\frac{1}{2} \times 2\frac{1}{2} \times 46$ in.	"
E. Seat support (front/back)	2	$1\frac{1}{2} \times 3\frac{1}{2} \times 46$ in.	"
F. Seat support (side/center)	3	$1\frac{1}{2} \times 3\frac{1}{2} \times 14$ in.	"
G. Stretchers	2	$1\frac{1}{2} \times 2 \times 14$ in.	"
H. Arms	2	$\frac{3}{4} \times 3\frac{1}{2} \times 23$ in.	"
I. Seat slats (center)	4	$\frac{3}{4} \times 3 \times 49$ in.	"
J. Seat slats (front/back)	2	$\frac{3}{4} \times 3 \times 46$ in.	"
K. Back slats	11	$\frac{3}{4} \times 2 \times 10$ in.	"

Each square equals 1"

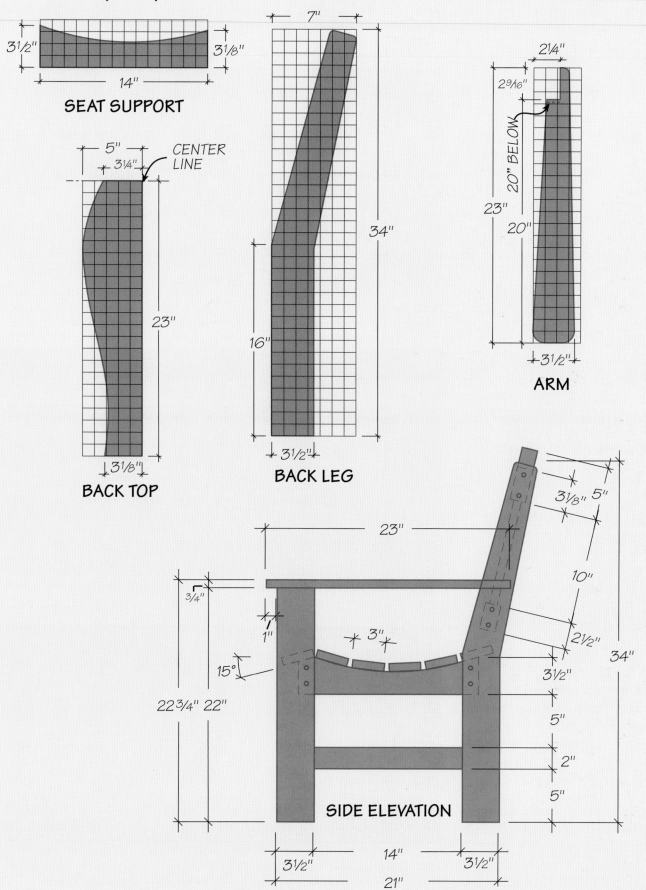

SEAT SUPPORT

3½"

3⅛"

14"

5"

3¼"

CENTER LINE

23"

3⅛"

BACK TOP

7"

34"

16"

3½"

BACK LEG

2¼"

2⁹⁄₁₆"

20" BELOW

23"

20"

3½"

ARM

23"

3⅛" 5"

10"

2½"

3½"

34"

3/4"

1"

3"

15°

22¾" 22"

5"

2"

5"

SIDE ELEVATION

3½"

14"

3½"

21"

Garden Bench: Step-by-step

Since a garden bench is designed for use outdoors, the wood type options are fairly limited. Cedar and redwood are two exterior woods that traditionally have been cheaper than other wood types suitable for outdoor use, like white oak or teak. But diminishing supply has driven up the price of cedar and redwood in some regions of the country. The most cost-effective wood for building any exterior project is usually pressure-treated pine. The drawbacks are that treated pine doesn't stain well (you'll probably want to paint the project), and it releases dangerous irritants when cut. Wear gloves when handling treated pine, and wear a particle mask when machining it.

CUT THE CONTOURED PARTS

The top back rail, back legs, arms and side/center seat supports all feature contours. The patterns for the shapes can be found on page 153. The pattern for the top back rail is a half pattern. Reverse the template on the centerline shown to draw the other half.

❶ Cut the top back rail, back legs, arms and side/center seat supports to length and width, according to the dimensions in the *Cutting List* on page 152. Transfer the patterns for each part to the workpiece. For the arms, seat supports and rear legs, draw the pattern on one workpiece only, then use that workpiece as a template for marking the other similar pieces after the part is cut to

PHOTO A: Cut the contoured bench parts with a jig saw or a band saw. Make sure to transfer the patterns accurately and secure each workpiece to your worksurface if cutting with a jig saw.

PHOTO B: Label the back slats with numbers that correspond to their positions on the top and bottom back rails, then drill dowel holes at each joint using a doweling jig.

PHOTO C: Glue and dowel the back slats into the bottom back rail, then glue the dowels into the dowel holes on the top end of each slat. Glue the dowels into the top rail, then clamp.

PHOTO D: Make sure the bevels on the front and back seat supports are facing up and pointing toward the back of the bench, then attach the center seat support with glue and 3-in. deck screws.

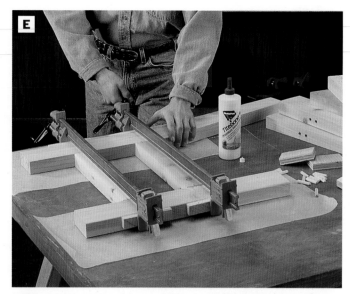

PHOTO E: Make bench side assemblies by joining a front leg to a back leg with a side seat support and a stretcher. Reinforce the glue joints with dowels.

shape. Cut the contours with a jig saw or band saw **(See Photo A)**. Smooth out all cuts with a file or sander. Use a file or a chisel to smooth the top center V-point of the shape. Do not cut out the rear-leg notches on the arms yet.

MAKE THE BACK REST

2 Rip-cut a piece of 1× cedar to 2 in. wide, then cross-cut the eleven 10-in.-long back slats.

3 Lay out all the rails and slats on a flat surface. Allow 2-in. spacing between slats and at the ends (you can cut 2-in. spacer blocks if this will help). Number the slats in sequence and note the numbers on the back rails so you know how the parts go together.

4 Lay out and drill two ¼-in.-dia. × ¾-in.-deep dowel holes at each slat location and in both ends of each slat. We used a doweling jig **(See Photo B)**.

5 Finish-sand all the parts of the back with 150-grit sandpaper.

6 Assemble the back, using exterior (moisture-resistant) wood

glue. Apply glue to each dowel end and pound the dowels home with a wood mallet **(See Photo C)**. Put the parts together and clamp up the assembly. Be careful to pad the clamps so the parts don't get marred. Clean up any squeeze-out and leave the clamps on until the glue sets.

MAKE THE BENCH FRAME

The frame for the garden bench consists of the front and back legs, the seat supports, and the stretchers that fit between the front and back legs near the bottom.

7 Cut the front and back seat supports to size. Set the table saw blade to 15° and rip a bevel along the top edge of each. Finish-sand the front, back, and center seat supports.

8 Mark a centerpoint along the length of each seat support. Measure ¾ in. to each side of the centerpoint and draw square lines down the faces of the boards. Attach the center seat support on these lines with glue and 3-in. galvanized deck screws (two per

joint). Drill clearance holes for the shanks before driving the screws, and make sure the bevels on the tops of the seat supports are both facing up and pointed toward the back of the bench. Use a bar clamp or pipe clamp on each side of the center seat support **(See Photo D)**.

9 Cut the two front legs and the two leg stretchers to size. Finish-sand the front and back legs, the stretchers, and the side seat supports.

10 The next step is to put together the two end assemblies. Lay out dowel joints on the front and back legs so the leg stretchers are 5 in. up from the bottom ends, and the side seat supports are 5 in. up from the stretchers. *Note: the shorter ends of the seat supports go against the back legs.*

11 Mark out and drill two dowel holes per joint. Glue and clamp the front and back legs, the stretchers, and the side seat supports into two pairs **(See Photo E)**. Use clamp pads to protect the wood.

PHOTO F: Drive 3-in. deck screws through the rear legs and into the ends of the rear and front seat supports to complete the rough assembly of the bench frame. Clamp braces to the front and back seat supports so they stand 12 in. above the worksurface.

PHOTO G: Fit the backrest assembly between the rear legs so it's centered and the top rail of the back rest is ⅜ in. below the tops of the rear legs. Clamp the assembly in position, then attach the backrest by driving 3-in. deck screws through the rear legs and into the rails.

⑫ Attach one side assembly to the end of the center seat support assembly. Use glue and two 3-in. deck screws per joint. Drive the screws through the legs and into the ends of the seat supports. (The seat section needs to be held at 12 in. off the floor and level while you're working, so cut four pieces of scrap 2 × 4 to about 16 in. long and clamp them near the ends of the front and back seat supports to hold them at the right height.) Glue and screw the remaining side assembly to the seat section **(See Photo F).**

INSTALL THE BACK REST

⑬ Mark placement lines for the ends of the backrest assembly on the upper inside faces of the rear legs. The top and bottom rails should be centered on the width of the legs, with the ends of the top rail located ⅜ in. down from the top of the legs.

⑭ Clamp angled scrap support blocks under the back assembly to hold it up at the right height, and start by drilling and screwing the tops of the legs to the top rail— two screws per joint. Then check for alignment, and drill and screw through the legs into the bottom rail **(See Photo G).**

ATTACH THE SEAT SLATS

⑮ Rip-cut the six ¾-in.-thick seat slats to 3 in. wide. Cross-cut the four center slats to 49 in. long and the front and back slats to 46 in. Finish-sand all the slats.

⑯ Glue and screw the front and back seat slats to the front and back seat supports. Use 2-in. deck screws. Align the inside edges of the slats with the inside edges of the seat support bevels. Use one screw near each end and a third screw in the center (so it will line up with the screws attaching the slats to the center seat support).

⑰ Screw the center seat slats to the side and center seat supports. Butt the first one up to the front seat slat, and use ½-in. spacers between the others to ensure even gaps. The ends of the center seat

PHOTO H: Attach the seat slats to the seat supports by driving one 2-in. deck screw through each slat at the ends and at the center of slat. Use ½-in. spacers to set the distance between the slats.

PHOTO I: The arms are notched to fit around the rear legs. After laying out the notches, set each arm in position and trace the line of the rear leg onto the arm to mark the cutting angle for the front of the notch.

slats should be flush with the side seat supports. Use one screw per joint **(See Photo H).**

ATTACH THE ARMS

18 Mark cutting lines for a notch in the back of each arm where it will meet a rear leg (See *Grid Pattern,* page 153). Position each arm so it's centered on the front leg and the front cutting line of the notch aligns with the front edge of the rear leg. Make sure the arm is level. Mark the angle of the front of the rear leg onto the edge of the arm **(See Photo I).** Mark both arms, then use a small back saw or a dovetail saw to cut out the notches (make sure to follow the bevel at the front of each notch).

19 Attach the arms to the front legs with glue and 2-in. deck screws **(See Photo J).** At the rear leg joints, drive the screws through the outside edges of the arms and into the rear legs.

APPLY FINISHING TOUCHES

20 Touch up any remaining rough surfaces with sandpaper and ease all sharp edges. Apply the exterior finish of your choice, or leave the bench to weather naturally to a rustic silver-gray.

PHOTO J: Attach the arms to the tops of the front legs with 2-in. deck screws driven into countersunk pilot holes in the arms. Use two screws per joint. Attach the arms to the rear legs by driving screws through the side edges of the arms and into the rear legs. Glue all joints.

Planters

Deck plants provide a graceful transition from the distinctly indoor space of your home to the distinctly outdoor space of your yard. Attractive planters filled with flowers, herbs and shrubs can transform your deck into a cozy and inviting outdoor "room." These planters are designed to be used either as enclosures for potted plants or to be lined with landscape fabric and filled with dirt. We built these planters for a cedar deck; for best results, build yours from the same material as your deck.

Vital Statistics: Planters

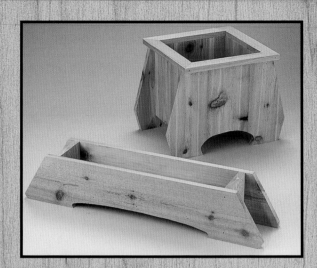

TYPE: Deck and railing planters

OVERALL SIZE: Railing planter: 7¼W by 35¼L by 7¼H
Deck planter: 16W by 20½L by 15⅛H

MATERIAL: Cedar, exterior plywood

JOINERY: Butt joints reinforced with galvanized finish nails and screws

CONSTRUCTION DETAILS:
· Railing planter fits over standard 2 × 6 railing cap
· Recessed bottoms and weep holes improve air circulation and drainage on both planters

FINISHING OPTIONS: UV protectant sealer, exterior paint or leave unfinished to weather naturally to gray

Building time

PREPARING STOCK
0 hours

LAYOUT
1-2 hours

CUTTING PARTS
1-2 hours

ASSEMBLY
2-3 hours

FINISHING
1-2 hours

TOTAL: 5-9 hours

Tools you'll use

· Circular saw
· Jig saw
· Drill/driver
· Clamps
· Hammer
· Nailset

Shopping list

☐ (3) 1 × 8 in. × 8 ft. cedar
☐ (1) ¾ × 12 × 12 in. exterior plywood
☐ Galvanized deck screws (1¼-in.)
☐ Galvanized finish nails (2-in.)
☐ UV protectant sealer

Planters

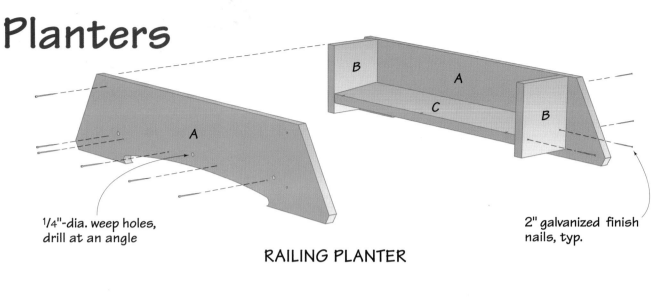

1/4"-dia. weep holes,
drill at an angle

2" galvanized finish
nails, typ.

RAILING PLANTER

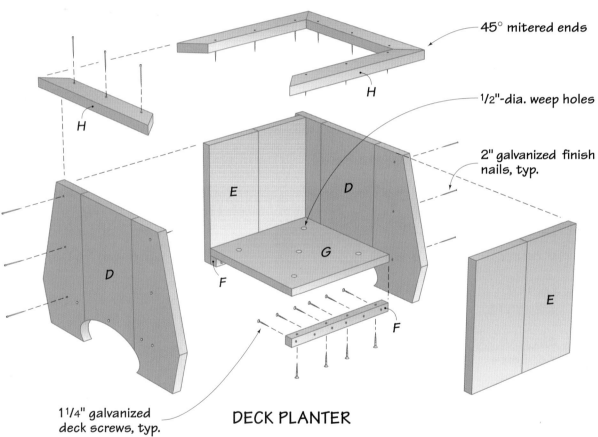

45° mitered ends

1/2"-dia. weep holes

2" galvanized finish
nails, typ.

1 1/4" galvanized
deck screws, typ.

DECK PLANTER

Planters Cutting List

Part	No.	Size	Material	Part	No.	Size	Material
Railing Planter				**Deck Planter**			
A. Sides	2	7/8 x 7 1/4 x 35 1/4 in.	Cedar	**D.** Sides	2	7/8 × 20 1/2 × 14 1/4 in.	Cedar
B. Ends	2	7/8 x 5 1/2 x 6 1/2 in.	"	**E.** Ends	2	7/8 × 12 × 12 in.	"
C. Bottom	1	7/8 x 5 7/16 x 24 in.	"	**F.** Cleats	2	7/8 × 7/8 × 12 in.	"
				G. Bottom	1	3/4 × 12 × 12 in.	Exterior plywood
				H. Crown	4	7/8 × 2 × 16 in.	Cedar

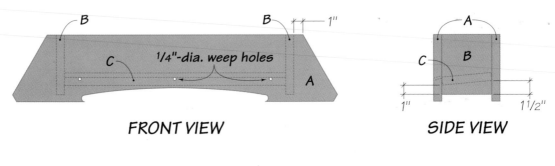

FRONT VIEW

SIDE VIEW

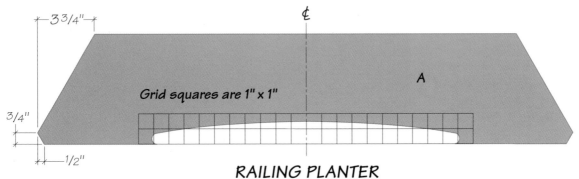

Grid squares are 1" x 1"

RAILING PLANTER

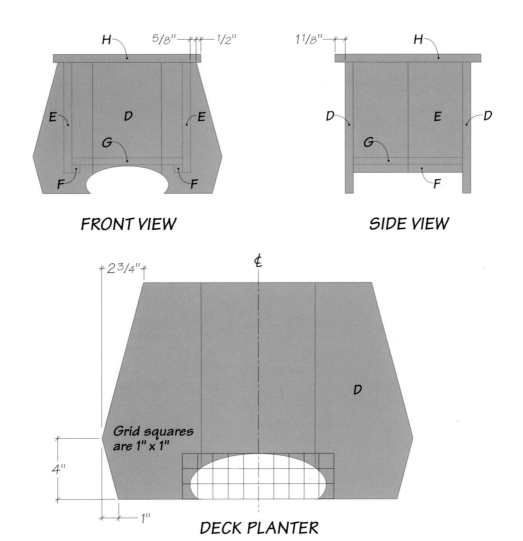

FRONT VIEW

SIDE VIEW

Grid squares are 1" x 1"

DECK PLANTER

Cedar lumber is typically sold with one side rough and one side smooth. This feature provides you the opportunity to choose which surface to emphasize in the finished planters. For these planters, we held the rough side out because we wanted a casual, rustic look. If you prefer, you can achieve a more refined look simply by building your planters with the smooth surface out. If you intend to paint your finished planters, we recommend building with the smooth side out.

RAILING PLANTER
CUT OUT THE PARTS

❶ Make a template for marking the two side profiles. Cut a piece of hardboard or stiff cardboard to size, 7¼ in. by 35¼ in., for use as a pattern. Following the *Railing Planter* drawing on page 394, mark the angles on the ends and the curved cut-out profile on the bottom edge. Cut the template to shape with a jig saw and sand the cuts smooth.

❷ Trace the profile from the template onto the side workpieces.

❸ Cut out the sides. Clamp the blanks securely to your workbench and cut the profiles with your jig saw (**See Photo A**).

❹ Cut the ends and bottom to size, according to the dimensions in the *Cutting List* on page 394.

PHOTO A: Lay out and cut a template for making the sides of the railing planter, then use this template to draw the shapes on the side workpieces. Cut out the shapes with a jig saw.

ASSEMBLE THE PLANTER

❺ Attach the ends to the bottom. The bottom is sloped to route seepage water away from your deck railing cap. Refer to the *Side View* drawing, page 395, and mark the slope of the bottom piece on the inside faces of the ends. Drill pilot holes in the ends. Clamp the bottom in place between the ends, and attach the parts with 2-in. galvanized finish nails (**See Photo B**).

❻ Attach the sides. Lay the end/bottom assembly on your workbench. Center the first side piece on the assembly left-to-right with all top edges flush. Clamp it in place. Note that the lower edges of the end pieces are ¾ in. above

the lower edges of the sides; this allows the planter to rest on the railing cap while the sides overlap it for stability. Attach the side by driving galvanized finish nails through the side into the ends and the bottom. Use a nailset to recess the nailheads. Follow the same procedure to position and attach the remaining side.

❼ Drill the weep holes. Clamp the assembled planter to your worksurface with the deeper side of the compartment facing up. Drill three angled ¼-in.-dia. weep holes through the side of the planter into the deepest corner of the compartment (**See Photo C**). Position the weep holes so they

PHOTO B: Mark the slope of the bottom piece on the planter end pieces, then attach the ends to the bottom with galvanized finish nails. Clamp the pieces to help hold them steady during assembly.

PHOTO C: Fasten the planter sides to the ends and bottom with nails, then drill three angled ¼-in.-dia. weep holes through the side where the bottom of the planter slopes to its lowest point.

are just above the bottom piece inside the planter.

DECK PLANTER

MAKE THE SIDE PANELS

Each side panel is composed of three boards, which are held together during the construction process by a temporary cleat.

❶ Cut six pieces of 1 × 8 cedar to 14½ in. long (you'll need three pieces for each side).

❷ Cut two temporary cleats (not shown on the *Cutting List*) 13½ in. long from scrap wood.

❸ Build the sides. Lay groups of three boards facedown on your workbench in two groups. Center a temporary cleat left-to-right along the top edge of each group of boards, and fasten each panel together by driving 1¼-in. wood screws through the cleat into the

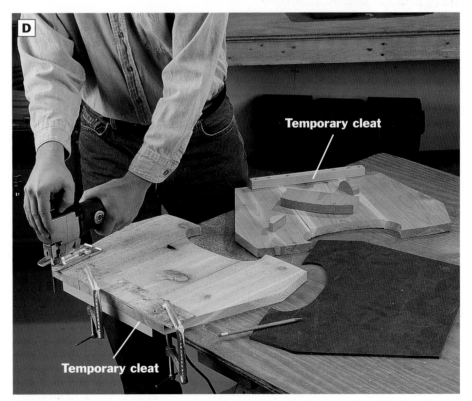

Temporary cleat

Temporary cleat

PHOTO D: Assemble two blanks for the deck planter sides using three lengths of 1 × 8 cedar per blank, fastened together with a temporary cleat. Mark the profiles on the side pieces with a template, then cut the sides to shape. You'll remove the temporary cleats later.

PHOTO E: Clamp pairs of 6-in.-wide boards for the end panels and fasten each panel together with a cleat. Use 1¼-in. galvanized screws to join the parts. These two cleats are permanent parts of the planter.

PHOTO F: Cut the bottom piece to size, drill five weep holes through the bottom for drainage, and fasten it to the cleats on the end pieces with countersunk screws. Attach the bottom so it will rest on the cleats when the planter is finished.

boards.

4 Make a template for marking the profiles of the two sides. Cut a piece of hardboard or stiff cardboard 14¼ in. wide by 20½ in. long. Following the *Deck Planter* drawing on page 395, mark the angles on the ends and the shape of the curved cutout along the bottom edge. Cut the template to shape with a jig saw and sand the cut edges smooth.

5 Trace the profile from the template onto the side panels. Draw on the face of the panels that does not have the cleats. Clamp each panel securely to your workbench and cut the parts with a jig saw **(See Photo D)**.

MAKE THE ENDS & BOTTOM

The end panels are each composed of two boards fastened together with a permanent cleat.

6 Rip a 4 ft. 1 in. length of 1 × 8 cedar to 6 in. wide. Cut the ripped board into four 12-in. lengths. Lay each pair of boards facedown on your workbench and clamp them together with the ends flush.

7 Cut two pieces of scrap left over from Step 6 to ⅞ × ⅞ × 12 in. to form two cleats. Drill countersunk pilot holes in the cleats.

8 Assemble the end panels by positioning a cleat flush with the bottom edges of each pair of boards and fastening the parts with 1¼-in. galvanized deck screws, screwing through the cleats into the end panels **(See Photo E)**.

9 Cut the bottom to size from ¾-in. exterior plywood. Draw intersecting lines from corner to corner to use as a guide for locating and drilling five ½-in.-dia. weep holes.

ASSEMBLE THE PLANTER

10 Attach the end panels to the bottom. Clamp the bottom in place between the ends so it will rest on top of the cleats when the planter is right-side up. Drill through the cleats from below to fasten the bottom (**See Photo F**).

11 Attach the sides. Position the first side panel on the end/bottom assembly so it is centered left-to-right and the top edges are all flush. Drive 2-in. galvanized finish nails through the side panel into the ends and the bottom, using a nailset to drive the nails below the surface of the wood. Attach the remaining side in the same fashion (**See Photo G**).

12 Unscrew and remove the temporary cleats from the side panels.

13 Cut the four crown pieces. Rip cedar stock to 2 in. wide. Measure your planter to verify the length of the crown pieces. The inside edges of the crown should sit flush with the inside of the planter when installed. Cut the pieces to length with the ends mitered at 45˚.

14 Attach the crown pieces to the planter with finish nails (**See Photo H**).

FINISHING TOUCHES FOR BOTH PLANTERS

15 Break all edges with sandpaper and check that all nailheads are set. You may choose to leave the planters unfinished, apply the same finish as you have on your deck or topcoat with paint.

PHOTO G: Fasten the sides to the end/bottom assembly by nailing through the sides and into the ends and bottom. Drill pilot holes before you drive the nails to keep the cedar from splitting. Once both sides are attached, remove the temporary cleats.

PHOTO H: Install the four crown pieces around the top of the planter with nails. Lay out and cut the crown pieces so they are mitered on the ends and fit flush with the inside of the planter.

Part 4
Perfect Yard

Introduction

If you want to track down a handyman, the first place to look is the workshop. If he's not there, check the garage. Still no luck? Then he must be out working on the yard.

Whether we see it as a passion or a chore, yard care is a major part of a do-it-yourselfers world. We're no more likely to hire a lawn service company to mow the grass than we are to pay a "professional interior surfaces technician" $75 an hour to paint the utility room. In fact, for many of us, the condition and appearance of our yard is real source of pride, and knowing that we we're the ones who keep it looking great is a genuine source of satisfaction. We understand that our lawn makes a statement to our neighbors and anyone else who sees it.

Creating a beautiful, fully functional yard takes work, patience, good ideas and sound information. In this section you'll find all the information you need, along with some very good ideas (we'll leave the work and patience up to you). From laying sod to installing lawn edging to eliminating those chinch bugs once and for all, just about everything you need to know to make the perfect yard your own is covered.

You'll find a wealth of information about grass. How to identify it, how to choose it, how to plant it, how to cut it, how to fertilize it, how to heal it, even how to kill it. But a yard is not just grass. In these pages, you'll discover many useful tips and techniques for creating planting beds that both define and unite all the elements of your yard. And plenty of straightforward advice on yard maintenance is included as well.

The Perfect Yard wouldn't be a proper book for our club members if it didn't mention tools. Which are the most useful? Which can be rented? What do you need to do to keep them running smoothly? What's the difference between a riding lawnmower and a garden tractor? Again, you'll find the answers to all these question, and so many more, right here.

At its most basic level, a yard is a community of plants that fulfill a purpose or purposes. You can stroll through it and feel the morning dew on your feet. You can watch your children or grandchildren frolic across it. You can host party guests on it. You can throw down a lawn chair and read a good book on it. There is plenty that a nicely designed, well-tended yard can do to improve your quality of life.

So take some time and thumb through this colorful, information-packed section. We think you'll find it to be rich with new and interesting information that will help make your yard more attractive and your yard work more efficient. And who knows, maybe next time the phone rings and your spouse or kid goes out to find you, the first place they'll check is the yard.

A Gallery of Yard Ideas

Make coming home an aesthetic experience. A rich variety of colors and textures in the landscape are a beautiful complement to your home, adding to its value and providing a welcome that extends beyond your front door.

Name your desire: an inviting path meandering through flowering shrubs, a broad park-like lawn on a summer evening, or the secret-garden atmosphere of old-fashioned perennial beds and specimen trees.

Whether creating the rustic simplicity of a woodland theme, or cultivating a cottage garden filled with an abundance of flowers and fragrance, keep an eye on the harmonious balance of landscape elements. A lawn may be a site for play and recreation, but it is also a major design feature in the home landscape and merits consideration beyond simple utility. The gently curving contours of these two lawns set up pleasing rhythms to the border plantings, directing the viewer through the garden and enhancing the aesthetics of the whole.

Attention to detail enhances every area of the yard. A utilitarian path is made beautiful with a few well-chosen plantings. A backyard flower bed abandons conventional rectilinearity to stunning effect. Even the traditional broad lawn becomes a private retreat when bordered by hedges and a screen of specimen trees.

DESIGNING A NEW YARD:
An Exercise in Practical Imagination

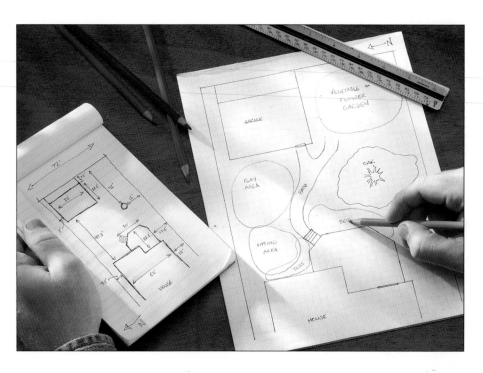

Have you ever tried to imagine a brand new yard? It's sometimes hard to see past the forty-foot oak and the barbeque pit that are already there. But you can still see that there is room for improvement. So, where do you start?

The secret to visualizing new yard features is to do it on paper in a spot where you can't look at the real thing. This is useful even if you aren't intending to do a whole yard makeover, because it allows you to make small advances towards a bigger goal, rather than an assortment of individual projects that don't work together.

First, put the permanent features of your yard on graph paper. Measure off the house and lot lines first, and then corroborate measurements by checking distances between other features. Decide on a scale and transfer all the measurements to the graph paper with pencil, so you can erase. Observe the yard for a day and indicate the approximate hours of sun each area gets. Be aware of how this will change if trees will be coming down and as the angle of the sun changes with the seasons.

Forget about your existing yard and visualize the "stage" you have on paper. Think about your needs and the needs of your family. What effect do you want to create? Where are the best places to meet the various needs of the yard's users? Don't worry about specifics yet, just get the general features down. For example, block in the play area, the utility area, the nature/retreat area, the vegetable garden—you decide how you want to set the space up. After drawing things in on paper, go back to the yard with some flags or marking paint to see if your ideas still make sense at life size.

Using the actual space and your map as a reference, figure out in broad terms how those general areas will be defined. Pencil in the tall hedge, drop in the groundcover under the tree, draw the curves for the border plantings. Try not to create numerous small islands of lawn that will be difficult to mow, but don't be afraid to reduce the size of a lawn; it will save you time in the long run. Remember that even "shade-tolerant" grasses like to have three or four hours of direct sun a day. Be prepared to sacrifice grass to a low light groundcover, pavers, or mulch in shady areas.

Now, decide what to plant. Your plan may indicate broadly that you need a hedge here, a tree there, and a low bed of flowering plants there, but which species do you select from these broad categories? How many of each will you need? Go to a reputable garden center and get help. Importantly, know the square footage of each planting area you intend to fill, be conscious of the colors of existing plants and structures, and know how much direct sunlight each area gets. You may want to get design advice from an expert at the garden center or a hired landscape architect. Once you've got a plan you like in your mind and on paper, you're halfway home.

Taking accurate measurements and experimenting with shapes, sizes and ideas are important parts of planning you new yard.

US Grass Zone Map

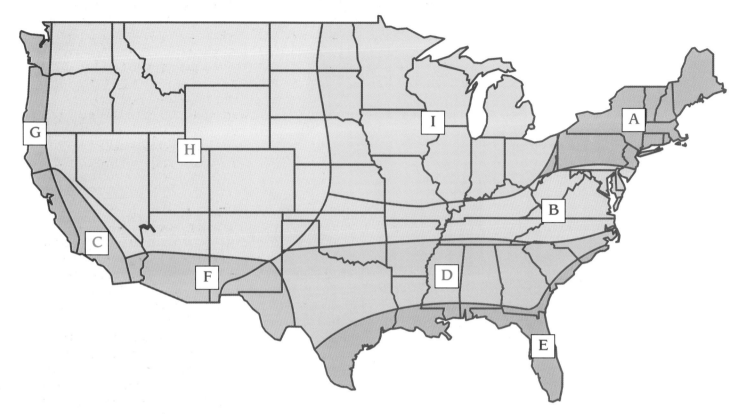

The lawn zone map above can help you figure out which grasses to grow and how to keep them healthy. The lawn zones take winter and summer temperatures into account, and also soils, rainfall patterns, and wind. Keep in mind that weather patterns can vary dramatically within each zone, and your local climate may differ from the norm for your region. Typically, areas close to large bodies of water are wetter and experience more moderate temperature swings. Areas at higher elevations are colder. On a finer scale, sunny areas, south slopes, and areas south of buildings are warmer, and sandy soil and sloped land is dryer. It's always a good idea to ask a local Cooperative Extension Agent or another lawn expert for lawn-care and grass-variety advice specific to your lawn and local climate.

Climate Zones for Lawns

Northeast (A)

Cold winters and generally good precipitation allow cool-season grasses to flourish in the Northeast.

Popular lawn grasses: Cool-season mixes of bluegrasses, perennial ryegrass, and the fine fescues are very common. In the coastal south of the zone, zoysia-grass (warm season) handles summer well but will brown-out in the winter.

Planting considerations: Plant from seed in August or September (after the heat breaks) so the grass has fall and spring to establish before summer heat. As a second choice, plant as soon as you can in the spring. Cool-season sods may be laid anytime from April to October, but establishment is easiest during the cool fall months. Northeast soils tend to be acid so lime may need be added to them.

Transition Zone East (B)

What you plant depends on your local climate and what kind of lawn you want. The warm-season grasses will brown out in winter. The cool-season grasses will need a lot of water if you want them to stay green in the summer.

Popular lawn grasses: Tall fescue (cool-season), zoysiagrass (warm-season), bermudagrass (warm-season for mild winter areas).

Planting considerations: Sow cool-season grasses in September or October or early spring (less ideal). Cool-season sod can be laid any time during the growing season with enough watering, but establishment is easiest in the fall. Plant warm-season grasses from when the soil has warmed in May or June right through the summer, with earlier planting helping you avoid lots of watering and later planting helping you avoid spring weeds. Warm-season sods can be laid anytime during the growing season with adequate water.

Transition Zone West (C)

This transition zone does not get as cold as the eastern transition zone, but neither does it get very hot. For this reason, many cool-season and warm-season grasses can be grown here. Water shortages can influence grass choices in this zone.

Popular lawn grasses: Tall fescue (a cool-season grass); bermudagrass (warm-season). Overseeding with ryegrass in the winter; plant buffalograss (warm-season) for the driest areas; use drought-hardy groundcovers.

Planting considerations: Same as Transition Zone East.

Middle South (D)

The middle South has hot humid summers with good and sometimes excessive rainfall. The eastern part of the zone is wetter and the soils are more likely to be sandy, acidic, and infertile. If you live in the western part of this zone, read about zones F and H, too.

Popular lawn grasses: Cooler and drier parts favor tall fescue (cool-season grass) and zoysiagrass (warm-season). Warmer and wetter parts favor bermudagrass, centipedegrass, and bahiagrass (all warm-season grasses). Overseed with ryegrass for winter green.

Planting considerations: Plant warm-season grasses starting April or May through the middle of the summer. Plant from sprigs, plugs, or seed when the soil has warmed to at least 65°F. Plant too early and the grass becomes overrun with weeds and doesn't grow well. Plant in the heat of summer and the grass grows well but requires a lot of irrigation or rain. Lay warm-season sod in the spring, summer, or early fall. Seed cool-season grasses in the fall. Lay cool-season sod in fall for best results.

Coastal Deep South (E) (includes Hawaii)

Use warm-season grasses exclusively. Lawn disease is a problem due to the wetness of the region.

Popular lawn grasses: Carpetgrass and centipedegrass (for wet, low maintenance lawns); St. Augustinegrass, bermudagrass and zoysiagrass.

Planting considerations: Plant when the soils warms in the spring or during or just before your summer rainy season. Warm-season sods can be laid all year round in most of this zone with irrigation.

Southwest (F)

Because of water restrictions in the Southwest, many explore ways to minimize the size of lawns using drought-tolerant ground covers.

Popular lawn grasses: Grow drought-tolerant Bermudagrass and zoysiagrass at low elevations. Overseeded bermudagrass with rye for a green winter lawn. Grow native, drought tolerant species like buffalograss and blue gramagrass. At high elevations and in the northern part of the zone, grow natives or tall fescue blends, which stay green through the winter.

Planting considerations: Gypsum, sulfur, or iron may be called for by a soil test. Cool-season grasses are best planted in March, April, or early fall. Warm-season grasses can be planted in spring when the soil has warmed, which could be anytime from March to May. Plant before or during seasonal rains if possible. Contact your county Cooperative Extension Service for planting advice specific to your area.

Pacific Coastal (G)

This moderate climate favors cool-season grasses. Soils may be acid in the northern part of the zone, and could require lime.

Popular lawn grasses: The deep roots of tall fescues can carry a lawn through periods of low moisture. You may also grow bermudagrass and zoysiagrass where it is warm enough. In Oregon and Washington the bluegrasses, ryegrasses and fine fescues work well. Colonial bentgrass is popular on the northern coast also.

Planting considerations: Sow cool-season grasses in September or October or in the spring (second choice) when the ground can be worked. Lay cool-season sod March to October, with the fall being preferable, especially in warmer, dryer areas. Dry areas will require an inch per week of water when it doesn't rain, unless you want to let the grasses go dormant.

West (H)

This zone is often dry and cold.

Popular lawn grasses: Grow zoysiagrass and bermuda-grass in the south, tall fescue everywhere, fine fescues and bluegrass where water is available, buffalograss where water is scarce and traffic on the lawn light.

Planting considerations: Sow cool-season grasses after the heat breaks in late summer or early fall, or as soon as you can in the spring (second best). Plant warm-season grasses from late spring to mid summer. Your soils are alkaline and salty in places, and may require special amendments like gypsum and sulfur.

Midwest (I)

This zone has generally good soils, a real winter with authentic snow, and a hot humid summer. Read also about zone H if you live toward the west of this zone and Zone B if you live in the south.

Popular lawn grasses: Plant Kentucky bluegrass, ryegrass and fine fescues throughout; tall fescue in all but the extreme north; and zoysiagrass and bermudagrass in the lower part of the zone.

Planting considerations: Sow cool-season grasses in August or September. Sod can be laid any time during the growing season, but fall sodding makes establishment easier, since you won't need to water quite so frequently.

Bermudagrass Tip: When starting a new lawn in the fall, plant a mixture of unhulled bermudagrass seed and ryegrass. The ryegrass will cover the ground in the winter and the bermudagrass will germinate in the spring.

| A | B | C | D | E | F | G | H | I |

Zone suitability

= Acceptable

= Borderline/risky

= Not suitable

Advantages: Fine, even, rapidly spreading lawn cover; heat and drought resistant.

Disadvantages: Requires heavy watering & fertilizing and frequent mowing for optimal appearance. Does not tolerate shade. Aggressive weed in beds.

Bermudagrass, Common *(Cynodon dactylon)* and Hybrid *(Cynodon dactylon x C. transvalensis)*

Where to Plant: Prefers full sun in zones (D), (E), (F), (C) and parts of (H) and (B). Tolerates many kinds of soil, traffic and salt.

Planting: Sow hulled common bermudagrass seed at two pounds per 1,000 sq. ft. in late spring or early summer after the soil temperature has reached at least 65°F. Mix seed thoroughly with sand for easier planting. Expect germination in 7 to 21 days, with faster germination happening between 85 and 100°. Plant 5 to 15 bushels of sprigs per 1000 sq. ft. if you broadcast, or less than a bushel if planted in rows 12 in. apart spaced 12 in. in the row. One sq. yard of sod provides about a bushel of sprigs. Plant plugs 12 in. apart.

Care:
Hybrid: Takes more care than common bermudagrass. Mow to ¾ in. with a power reel mower. Fertilize with 3 to 5 pounds of nitrogen per 1000 sq. ft. per year. Water deeply and infrequently. Use a dethatcher, a plug aerator or both if thatch-buildup is excessive.
Common: Same, but power reel mower is not needed. Fertilize with one to four pounds nitrogen per 1000 sq. ft. per year.

BERMUDAGRASS

Characteristics for identification:

- Leaves folded in bud
- Ligule short, hairy
- Collar narrow with long hairs
- Sheath flat
- Blades short, rough edged, sharp pointed
- Seedhead 3 to 5 narrow spikes

St. Augustinegrass Tip:
Older varieties are susceptible to St. Augustine Decline (SAD) virus. Prolonged temperatures below 25° F kill St. Augustinegrass.

Advantages: A springy, luxurious grass that will tolerate shade and salt spray as long as water is ample. Recovers quickly from rough use.

Disadvantages: Does not tolerate drought, cold temperatures or disease well. High maintenance.

A	B	C	D	E	F	G	H	I

Zone suitability

= Acceptable

= Borderline/risky

= Not suitable

St. Augustinegrass, Common
(Stenotaphrum secundatum)

ST. AUGUSTINEGRASS

Characteristics for identification:

- Leaves folded in bud
- Ligule short, hairy
- Collar wide
- Sheath very flat
- Blade wide, short, boat-shaped
- Seedhead a single narrow spike

Where to Plant: Prefers the warm, wet areas of the Deep Coastal South. Will grow in southern California with enough irrigation. St. Augustinegrass is the most shade tolerant of warm-season grasses.

Planting: Plant plugs (preferable) or sprigs 6 to 12 in. apart in early spring. Requires 3 to 6 sq. yards of sod per 1000 sq. ft. if you cut your own 2-in. plugs. Requires 1 to 2 sq. yards of sod per 1000 sq. ft. if you make your own sprigs. Keep sprigs especially well watered, since St. Augustine sprigs are stolons and are less hardy than bermudagrass rhizomes.

Care: Water in the mornings to reduce disease. Fertilize in spring and fall with 2 to 5 pounds of nitrogen per 1000 sq. ft. per year. Mow to 1 to 3 in. high. High mowing discourages weeds but may encourage thatch and disease. Use a dethatcher, a plug aerator, or both if thatch-buildup is excessive. Test soil for iron deficiency if grass is yellowish.

Zoysiagrass

Zoysiagrass Tip: In the transition zones, zoysiagrass goes dormant early and greens up late, leaving a brown lawn while cool-season grass owners have green. It does not take well to overseeding of cool season grasses.

| A | B | C | D | E | F | G | H | I |

Zone suitability

█ = Acceptable

█ = Borderline/risky

█ = Not suitable

Advantages: Tolerates shade, salt, and high levels of traffic well; can go partly dormant in drought.

Disadvantages: Can't be planted from seed in many areas; takes a long time to establish from sprigs or plugs; spiky feel under foot.

Zoysiagrass, (*Zoysiagrass japonica, Z. matrella, Z. tenuifolia*)

Where to Plant: Broadly, zoysiagrass is planted in zones B, C, D, E, and F and southern parts of other zones where drought tolerance and some cold tolerance is desired. Zoysiagrass's cold tolerance (for a warm-season grass) makes it popular in the Eastern Transition Zone. Shade tolerance favors zoysiagrass on dry southern sites where other shade-tolerant warm-season grasses can't grow.

Planting: Sow 1 to 2 pounds of seed per 1000 sq. ft. in late spring or early summer when soil has warmed to at least 65°F. You may mix the seed thoroughly with sand to make planting easier. Plant sprigs 2 in. apart in rows 6 in. apart (3 to 6 bushels of sprigs per 1000 sq. ft.) or plugs 6 in. apart in all directions when the soil has warmed in mid to late spring. Sprigs should have one node left above the soil. Sprigs and plugs of zoysiagrass can take two years to fill in, so weed control is important. Monthly light fertilizing can help it fill in faster.

Care: After established, water zoysiagrass deeply and infrequently. Fertilize with 1 to 3 pounds of nitrogen per 1000 sq. ft. per year. Mow 1 to 2 in. high. Use a dethatcher, a plug aerator or both if thatch-buildup is excessive.

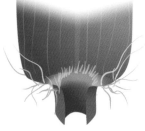

ZOYSIAGRASS

Characteristics for identification:

- Leaves rolled in bud
- Ligule hairy
- Collar with long hairs
- Blade short, pointed, stiff
- Seedhead a single spike

Buffalograss

Buffalograss Tip: Its tolerance of dry, alkaline, compacted, and clay soils make it a perfect native-grass choice for low-maintenance Western lawns.

Advantages: Fine blades, sod-forming, compact growth well suited for lawns; slow-growing; tolerates imperfect soil conditions.

Disadvantages: Turns brown in dry summer if not watered frequently; recovers slowly from damage; seed is expensive.

A	B	C	D	E	F	G	H	I

Zone suitability

= Acceptable

= Borderline/risky

= Not suitable

BUFFALOGRASS

Characteristics for identification:

- Leaves rolled in bud
- Ligule with longer hairs at sides
- Collar wide and hairy
- Blade flat, fine, dull green, sparsely hairy
- Female seedhead burrs on stem above leaf collars
- Male flowers on curved branches at top

Buffalograss *(Buchloe dactyloides)*

Where to Plant: Plant this tough, warm-season native grass in full sun in the West (Zone H), the Southwest (Zone F) and other areas that receive less than 25 in. of rain a year. Buffalograss is tolerant of cold and heat extremes. Do not plant in soils that stay wet.

Planting: Sow in the late summer, early fall, or spring. Spring-planted seeds will need to be soaked and chilled first to break dormancy. Recommended seeding rates vary widely (consult your Extension Agent). Plant sprigs or plugs one foot apart. Keep watered and weeded until established.

Care: Buffalograss prefers to be left alone, as water and fertilizer favor weeds over buffalograss. Don't fertilize or fertilize sparingly (1 pound or less of nitrogen per 1000 sq. ft. per year) in the spring. Mow to 2 or 3 in. high infrequently, or just once in the spring after the grass greens. To keep green, you may water deeply and infrequently during times of drought.

Tip: Can't find buffalograss? Blue gramagrass and western wheatgrass are two other drought-hardy low-maintenance natives more suited to some Western States.

Seashore Paspalum

Seashore Paspalum

Tip: Called "the environmental grass," it can be watered with pure sea water or residential waste water. If water with salts is used, the soil must be well drained so salt-buildup can be flushed out with periodic heavy watering. Seashore Paspalum protects natural water supplies by filtering heavy metals from water.

Advantages: Environmentally friendly; tolerates both drought and complete submersion in water.

Disadvantages: Does not tolerate much shade or cold.

Zone suitability

	= Acceptable
	= Borderline/risky
	= Not suitable

Seashore Paspalum (*Paspalum vaginatum*)

Where to Plant: Grows in the Deep Coastal South and Southern California. Tolerates high-salt, alkaline, acidic, and polluted conditions.

Planting: Grow from sod or sprigs. Broadcast 5 to 14 bushels of sprigs per 1000 sq. ft. and cover thinly with soil or compost. Fertilize with 1:2:3 or 1:3:4 NPK starter fertilizer. The herbicide granular *Ronstar* is safe to use at planting.

Care: Mow ½ to 1 in. high, preferably with a sharp mulching rotary mower. Fertilize lightly with nitrogen in the fall and spring only. Fertilize with 1 to 2 pounds of potassium per 1000 sq. ft. in the fall to enhance winter hardiness.

SEASHORE PASPALUM

Characteristics for identification:

- Leaves rolled in bud
- Ligule a jagged membrane
- Collar wide, hairy
- Sheath compressed
- Blade wide, prominent mid-vein
- Seedhead three or more spikes

WARM SEASON GRASSES
BAHIAGRASS *(Paspalum notatum)*

Bahiagrass prefers sun or light shade in eastern parts of the Middle South (Zone D) and in the Coastal Deep South (Zone E) but is not often found west of East Texas. Tolerates slightly acid, sandy soils but will not tolerate salt or dry, alkaline soils. Deep roots make this species good for erosion control. Bahiagrass stays green longer than most warm-season grasses in the winter and is easy to overseed with rye. It requires less fertilizer and less frequent watering than bermudagrass and St. Augustinegrass to stay green. It can be mowed high (4 in.) to control weeds, and it takes traffic well and is resistant to disease.

On the downside, bahiagrass needs fairly frequent mowing to stay looking lawn-like and the tough leaves require a sharp blade. Though it maintains its green well, it's only moderately drought-hardy. Bahiagrass lawns appear rough. Sow seed at 7 to 10 pounds per 1,000 sq. ft. if it's scarified (preferable) and up to 14 pounds if it's not. Sow in spring and expect germination in 2 to 4 weeks. Bahiagrass may be overseeded with rye or tall fescue in the winter. Water deeply and infrequently, fertilize moderately (1 to 4 pounds nitrogen per 1000 sq. ft. per year). Mow 2 to 4 in. high.

WARM SEASON GRASSES
CENTIPEDEGRASS *(Eremochloa ophiuroides)*

Centipedegrass prefers sun or light shade in the Middle South and Coastal Deep South (Zones D and E). It tolerates somewhat acid and poor soils, but will not tolerate salt or dry, alkaline soils. Centipedegrass is an aggressive, creeping grass resistant to cinch bugs and brown spot and a number of other diseases. It requires less mowing and fertilizer than bermudagrass. Centipedegrass is shallow-rooted and turns brown quickly in dry weather and with cold. It does not tolerate heavy traffic.

Sow seed at ¼ to 1 pound per 1,000 sq. ft. and expect germination in 20 days. Mix fine seed thoroughly with sand for easier planting. Buy 4 to 6 bushels of sprigs per 1,000 sq. ft. and plant in rows 6 in. apart, or plant plugs 6 in. apart. Keep sprigs and seed especially well watered. Plant in spring when recommended by a local Cooperative Extension Agent. The lawn will be slow to fill in.

Keep established centipedegrass watered in times of drought and fertilize lightly (1 to 2 pounds nitrogen per 1000 sq. ft. per year). Apply iron and/or sulfur (acidifier) if soil test indicates a need. This can make the grass greener, but it will never be as green as bermudagrass. Mow when needed to 1 to 2 in. high.

Rating the Warm-season Grasses

The ratings below can help you pick the grass that's right for you. For example, you can see by the chart that ryegrass is going to make a tougher play surface (through wear resistance) than bentgrass. But be aware that plant properties tend to be difficult to pin down in general terms. A species that needs a lot of additional nitrogen in one area may get by on very little in another. Note, also, that the ratings only compare species within each table. So even though zoysiagrass has a 'high' cold tolerance rating in the Warm-Season chart, it's more tender than fine fescue, which has a 'medium' rating in the Cool-Season chart.

	Bahiagrass	Bermudagrass, Common	Bermudagrass, hybrid	Blue gramagrass	Buffalograss	Carpetgrass	Centipedegrass	St. Augustinegrass	Zoysiagrass
Cold tolerance	Very low	Medium	Low	Very high	Very high	Very low	Very low	Very low	High
Drought Tolerance	Medium	High	High	Very high	Very high	Very low	Very low	Low	High
Shade tolerance	Medium	Very low	Very low	Low	Low	Medium	Medium	Very high	High
Low "N" Tolerance	Very good	Medium	Very poor	Good	Good	Very good	Very good	Poor	Medium
Disease resistance	Very good	Medium	Medium to good	Very good	Very good	Good	Very good	Very poor	Medium
Salt Tolerance	Very low	Very high	Very high	Good	Good	No info.	Very low	Very high	Very high
Wear resistance	Medium	Good	Very good	Medium	Medium	Good	Very poor	Poor	Very good
Thatch Resistance	Very good	Very poor	Very poor	Very good	Very good	No Info.	Good	Poor	Poor
Establishment Rate	Medium	Very fast	Medium	Slow	Very slow	Fast	Very slow	Medium	Very slow
Recovery Rate	Fast	Very fast	Very fast	No info.	No Info.	Fast	Very Slow	Fast	Slow

Kentucky Bluegrass

Kentucky Bluegrass
Tip: The bluegrass family is extremely large, and includes rough bluegrass *(P. trivialis),* which tolerates shade and wet soils, but does not tolerate drought, hot sun, or wear. Some newer varieties are highly disease resistant.

A	B	C	D	E	F	G	H	I

Zone suitability

- = Acceptable
- = Borderline/risky
- = Not suitable

Advantages: Makes a fine, soft lawn with a rich green color; hundreds of varieties available.

Disadvantages: Requires a lot of water, fertilizer and mowing; does not tolerate shade; slow to germinate from seed.

Bluegrass, Kentucky *(Poa pratensis)*

Where to plant: Plant in the sun in the northern and transitional zones (A, B, C, G, I) or in cooler parts of the south. Plant in dry western states only with ample irrigation. Kentucky bluegrass is often planted with one or more of the fine fescues, which colonize the shady and dry parts of the lawn, and perennial ryegrass, which takes over in high-wear areas.

Planting: Sow 1 to 2 pounds of seed per 1,000 sq. ft. Expect germination in 2 to 4 weeks. Kentucky bluegrass is best planted in the early fall, but early spring is a good

second choice. Sod may be planted any time during the growing season, if you can provide daily water afterwards. Sod establishment is easiest in the fall.

Care: Apply 1 to 3 pounds of nitrogen per 1000 sq. ft. per year for bluegrass mixed with fescues. Water when the grass becomes dull and holds footprints, unless you want the grass to go dormant. Mow to 1½ to 3 in. high, using the greater height to suppress spring weeds and to carry the lawn through drought and hot summer weather.

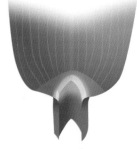

KENTUCKY BLUEGRASS

Characteristics for identification:
- Leaves folded in bud
- Ligule a short membrane
- Collar narrow
- Sheath green, flattened
- Blades long, narrow, with boat-shaped tip
- Seedhead branched and open, like a conifer tree.

Ryegrass Tip: New varieties of perennial ryegrass are less coarse and shaggy than their ancestors. Many varieties have endophytes against insects.

Advantages: quick germination, fast establishment, and endurance under traffic make it popular on well-used lawns.

Disadvantages: Does not tolerate deep shade or extreme cold or heat.

A	B	C	D	E	F	G	H	I

Zone suitability

▨	= Acceptable
▨	= Borderline/risky
■	= Not suitable

RYEGRASS

Characteristics for identification:

- Leaves folded in bud
- Ligule a long membrane
- Collar narrow
- Blades clearly veined
- Seedhead a spike bearing short spikelets along length.

Ryegrass, Perennial *(Lolium perenne)*

Where to Plant: Plant alone or mixed with bluegrass and fescues in all northern zones in areas that receive heavy traffic. Use also where quick cover is desired. Use to overseed southern lawns for winter green.

Planting: Sow at rates recommended for individual varieties, usually 4 to 8 pounds of seed per 1000 sq. ft. When overseeding, spread at double the rate for cleared ground.

Care: Mow 2 to 3 in. high, using the greater height to suppress weed competition in the spring or to help the lawn stay green during drought. Fertilize with 1 to 3 pounds of nitrogen per 1000 sq. ft. per year. High maintenance lawns with very long growing seasons may need more fertilizer. Water regularly.

Related Species: Annual ryegrass *(L. multiflorum)* is also used for annual overseeding in the South. It grows quickly but dies after one year. Northern mixes should contain little or no annual rye.

Tall Fescue

Tall Fescue Tip: Tall fescue is tough underfoot, making in useful for athletic fields and play areas.

A	B	C	D	E	F	G	H	I

Zone suitability

■ = Acceptable

■ = Borderline/risky

■ = Not suitable

Advantages: Great wearability and low fertilizer need; tolerant of shade, disease, and drought.

Disadvantages: Intolerant of humid, wet heat; relatively coarse.

Fescue, Tall *(Festuca arundinaciea)*

Where to Plant: Deep-rooted tall fescue is tolerant of warm, dry climates in sun and shade. Grow in zones B, C, and F; in the dryer parts of zone D; and in warmer parts of zone H. Tall fescue is used to overseed southern lawns for winter green.

Planting: Look for blends of two or more cultivars. Sow 4 to 10 pounds of tall fescue seed per 1000 sq. ft., depending on variety. It should germinate in 7 to 12 days. Plant in the early fall or early spring. Tall fescue may also be purchased as sod.

Care: Apply 1 to 4 pounds of nitrogen per 1000 sq. ft. per year using the higher rate when the grass is irrigated over a long growing season. Mow 2 to 3 in. high, using the greater height for suppressing weeds, for drought conditions, and for shady sites. Water infrequently and deeply.

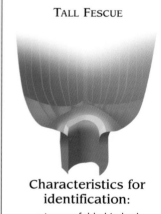

TALL FESCUE

Characteristics for identification:

- Leaves folded in bud
- Ligule a short membrane
- Collar narrow
- Sheath green, flattened
- Blades long, narrow, with boat-shaped tip
- Seedhead branched and open, like a conifer tree.

Red Fescue

Fine Fescue Tip:
The other fine fescues are bunch grasses and are more tolerant of heat than red fescue. Sheep fescue *(F. ovina)* is good for out-of-the way, dry, and shady nooks with little traffic Hard fescue *(F. longifolia)* is well-suited for stabilizing banks under dry conditions at high elevations. Chewings fescue *(F. rubra commutata)* can tolerate poor acidic soil and is fast-growing enough to compete with weeds in the shade.

Advantages: Does well in shade; thin, fine texture.

Disadvantages: Does not wear well; susceptible to disease; does poorly in high heat.

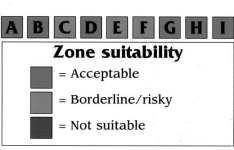

A	B	C	D	E	F	G	H	I

Zone suitability
- = Acceptable
- = Borderline/risky
- = Not suitable

RED FESCUE

Characteristics for identification:

- Leaves folded in bud
- Ligule a short membrane
- Collar narrow
- Sheath round and wider than blade
- Blade very narrow
- Seedhead narrowly branched with spikelets

Fescue, Red *(Festuca rubra)*

Where to plant: Red fescue is the most widely planted fine-fescue. Plant with bluegrass to colonize dry and shady parts of the lawn. Red fescue is sometimes used on slopes in pure stands, where it can be mowed for a lawn or left unmown for an attractive ground-cover effect. Red fescue is used most around the Great Lakes, in the Northeast, and in the Pacific Northwest. In contrast to other fine fescues, red fescue is a creeping grass and is considered the most refined.

Planting: When planted alone, sow 3 to 5 pounds of seed per 1000 sq. ft. Follow seeding recommendations for blends. Expect germination in 1 to 3 weeks. In the north, the fine fescues are best planted in the early fall or the cool part of spring.

Care: The fine fescues suffer from disease and weed competition if watered and fertilized too much. In the fall, apply compost or 1 to 2 pounds slow-release nitrogen per 1000 sq. ft. Water infrequently but deeply. Mow 2 to 3 in. high. Use the greater height in shade; when annual weeds are germinating in the spring; and before, during, and after drought.

Bentgrass

Colonial Bentgrass
Tip: In damp parts of the Pacific Northwest, you may grow colonial bentgrass without much fertilizer and care, especially if you see your neighbors growing it successfully or are advised to grow it by a local expert.

Zone suitability (Colonial)

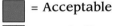

= Acceptable

= Borderline/risky

= Not suitable

Advantages: Colonial variety is an attractive, tight-knit sod that makes a nice, even lawn surface.

Disadvantages: Colonial damages easily and is fairly high maintenance; creeping is very high maintenance and not recommended for homes.

Bentgrass, Colonial *(Agrostis tenuis)* and Creeping *(A. stolonifera)* (shown above)

Where to Plant: Colonial bentgrass is well adapted to full sun or light shade in the Pacific Northwest, but is very difficult to grow anywhere else. In the Northwest it coexists with various bluegrasses and weed grasses. Creeping bentgrass is very high maintenance and is only appropriate on putting greens, lawn bowling greens, grass tennis courts and the like.

Planting (Colonial): Sow ½ to 2 pounds of colonial bentgrass seed per 1000 sq. ft. and expect germination in 1 to 3 weeks, or plant plugs according to your supplier's instructions. Seed is usually sown in the early spring.

Care: In naturally damp and cool areas, apply compost or 1 or 2 pounds of slow-release nitrogen per 1000 sq. ft. per year, in the fall. Where the grass is irrigated over a long season, apply 4 pounds or more of nitrogen per 1000 sq.ft., distributed in 1-pound doses in fall and spring. Bentgrass needs frequent irrigation to stay green if rain and fog is insufficient, or it may be allowed to go dormant. Aerate and dethatch annually if needed. Mow colonial bentgrass ½ to 1 in. high.

CREEPING BENTGRASS

Characteristics for identification:

- Leaves rolled in bud
- Ligule a tall membrane
- Collar narrow
- Sheath round
- Blade narrow and veined
- Seedhead narrowly branched with spikelets

The Ecolawn

Creeping bentgrass is the most-often used grass for golf course putting greens. It is a beautiful but high-maintenance grass that is better avoided in residential yards.

Oregon turf scientist Tom Cook was after the perfect lawn—one that would require no fertilizer, little water, and infrequent mowing. Cook soon realized that grass alone wasn't going to cut it, so he turned from the American concept of "lawn" to the medieval concept of "flowery mead," a sward of grasses and other low growing flowering plants developed in Europe for the recreation of lords and ladies. After years of research the *Ecolawn* was born, a combination of grasses, clover, yarrow, English daisies and chamomile.

The *Ecolawn* is low, drought tolerant, and a delight to look at and walk barefoot upon. While the *Ecolawn* itself is available from Nichols Garden Nursery in Albany, Oregon, Cook encourages lawn growers everywhere to not worry too much about "weeds" but allow the toughest, best adapted grasses and plants to step up to the plate for a durable, low maintenance ground cover. "A good lawn," says Cook, "is one that looks good from across the street."

Cool Season Grasses (values relative to species within table only)

	Bentgrass, colonial	Bentgrass, creeping	Bluegrass, Kentucky	Fescue, fine (including red, hard, sheep, and chewings)	Fescue, tall	Ryegrass, Perennial
Heat tolerance	Low	High	Medium	Medium	Very high	Low
Cold Tolerance	High	Very high	High	Medium	Medium	Medium
Drought Tolerance	Very low	Very low	Medium	High	High	Low
Shade tolerance	Medium	Medium	Low	Very high	High	Medium
Low N Tolerance	Usually poor	Very poor	Poor	Very good	Good	Poor
Disease resistance	Poor	Very poor	Good	Medium	Very good	Medium
Salt Tolerance	Very low	Good	Low	Low	Good	Medium
Wear resistance	Low	Low	Medium	Low-Medium	Very Good	Good
Thatch Resistance	Poor	Very poor	Medium	Medium	Good	Good
Establishment Rate (from seed)	Medium	Medium	Very Slow	Fast	Fast	Very Fast
Recovery Rate	No info.	Very fast	Very fast	Very slow	Fast	Fast

Yard Maintenance

Like any other kind of maintenance, taking care of a yard is mostly a matter of diligence. Performing routine, timely chores, like mowing and sprinkling, and seasonal procedures like dethatching and topdressing, is the surest way to keep your lawn healthy and avoid the need for "emergency" procedures.

Fertilizing

Of all routine lawn maintenance procedures, fertilizing requires the greatest precision. Over-fertilizing a lawn can burn the grass, kill beneficial soil organisms, promote thatch development, and even damage the structure of the soil. Under-fertilized turf grasses may appear thin and pale and have difficulty competing against broadleaf weeds better adapted to low-fertility conditions. It's a very good idea to get a soil test as the starting point of a successful fertilizing regimen (See page 49). A test will determine if you need to add high phosphorous or potassium fertilizers. The test will alert you to the need for any micronutrients, like iron, or the need to adjust the pH with lime or an acidifier. Tests let you know if you need to add organic matter, too.

Nitrogen determines rate

Nitrogen is the queen of lawn maintenance fertilizers, and is the element that determines maintenance fertilizer application rates. That is, you calculate how much fertilizer to spread based on a yearly nitrogen budget for your lawn, letting the other elements be slightly over- or under-applied. You usually won't get a nitrogen analysis on a soil test, because nitrogen compounds can travel quickly out of the root zone in water. A high nitrogen reading could therefore be temporary. Instead, nitrogen appli-

A soil test can alert you to fundamental imbalances in your soil. Lime, sulfur, high phosphorous and potassium fertilizers and micronutrients can make big differences in the health of your lawn, but only if scientifically applied based on the recommendations of a soil lab. See page 49.

Fertilizer Calculation Table Based on Nitrogen Net Weight*	
4 pounds per 1000 square feet per year (Very high)	Apply if you regularly irrigate your bentgrass, bahiagrass, bermudagrass, or St. Augustinegrass lawn, remove your clippings, and your grasses are actively growing for eight or more months of the year. Do not apply these high fertilizer rates to grasses with fungal diseases, insect problems, or thatch buildup.
3 pounds per 1000 square feet per year (High)	Apply if conditions above apply, but you leave your clippings to rot. Apply if you irrigate and remove clippings on most blue grasses, rye grasses, tall fescue, carpetgrass and zoysiagrass. Apply a lower rate if thatch, disease, or insect problems exist.
2 pounds per 1000 square feet per year (Medium)	Apply if you irrigate and remove clippings on low-maintenance grasses like the fine fescues, centipedegrass, blue gramagrass, and buffalograss. High maintenance grasses get two pounds if clippings are left to rot and they are not irrigated regularly.
1 pound per 1000 square feet per year (Low)	Apply to non-irrigated grasses when the clippings are left in place. Apply to low maintenance grasses immediately if they are irrigated but the clippings are left in place. Apply to otherwise high maintenance lawns that are dormant for much of the year due to winter cold, drought, or summer heat.
0 pounds per 1000 square feet per year	Low maintenance grasses may be left unfertilized or fertilized infrequently if clippings are returned to the soil and if the lawn is not irrigated. The existence (and acceptance) of clovers and medics in any lawn can reduce or eliminate the need for fertilizer, especially nitrogen. The regular addition of compost to a lawn can reduce or eliminate the need for fertilizer.

*Lawns in shade should receive 1/2 these rates to avoid disease problems. Adjust rates up on well irrigated lawns and down on dry lawns.

cations are based on what kind of lawn you are after. Lawns fed more nitrogen will be greener but will need to be watered and mowed more. Lawns not fed at all may do fine, but they will have a higher percentage of non-grass plants in them.

NOTE: Plant-usable nitrogen enters soil naturally from three main sources: decaying plant and animal matter (including grass clippings) that return nitrogen and other elements to the soil; lightning in thunderstorms; and bacteria in the roots of pea and clover family plants that convert elemental nitrogen from the air into plant-usable forms.

Phosphorous, potassium and other elements

Phosphorous and potassium (sometimes called "potash") are less mobile in the soil than nitrogen and therefore may not need to be added at all. In the Deep South, some apply a complete fertilizer containing nitrogen, phosphorous, and potassium in the spring and fall and just slow release nitrogen in the summer. Get advice from local garden center experts or Extension Agents to see what's appropriate for your area. Soil tests give you phosphorous and potassium recom-

CORRECT pH

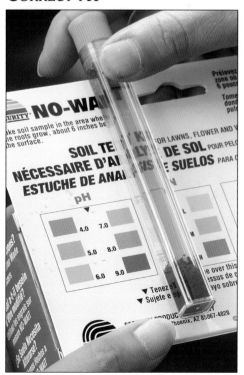

Correct pH (around seven or a little below) is needed so that grass can access nutrients already in the soil. If you have acid (low pH) or alkaline (high pH) soil, a soil test will determine how much limestone to add to raise the pH or how much of an acidifier (such as sulfur) to add to bring down the pH. pH meters and simple testing kits are also available from garden centers.

mendations specific to your yard, letting you know if you should be using a maintenance fertilizer high in one or both of these elements. A soil test may also recommend the addition of one of the secondary elements, or "micronutrients." Adding micronutrients without the recommendation of a soil test is risky, since many are toxic to plants at relatively low concentrations. However, in some parts of the country adding micronutrients like iron can be essential for achieving a healthy lawn. For soils with special problems, special soil conditioners are recommended by soil labs. For example, on high-salt soils of the west, gypsum is often added.

Buying fertilizer and other amendments; calculating quantities

By convention, fertilizer bags always give the weight percentages of nitrogen (N), phosphorous (P), and potassium (K), in that order. This allows you to adjust the application rate of a particular fertilizer to a recommended rate of application. For example, say you want to apply two pounds of nitrogen per thousand square feet per year in two applications. That means at each application you will spread one pound of nitrogen per 1000 square feet. Say that, because of a soil test, you know you don't need any phosphorous. You should buy a 50 pound bag of fertilizer with an analysis of 10:5:0. Fifty pounds times 10% (.10) nitrogen equals five pounds of nitrogen.

Let's say that earlier, you determined that your lawn was about 1,500 sq. ft. 1,500 sq. ft. times the recommended rate of 1 pound/1000 sq ft. (per application) equals 1.5 pounds of nitrogen. 1.5 divided by five pounds (the total nitrogen in the bag), gives you 0.3, meaning you need to spread three tenths, or a little less than one third, of the bag onto your lawn. If you like formulas, we've provided the one used here below. Incidentally, compost usually has a fertilizer value around 1-1-1.

Buy a fertilizer with at least half its nitrogen in slow release form. Slow release nitrogen includes IBDU, sulfur-coated urea,urea-formaldehyde (Nitroform, for example), and natural organics such as Milorganite or composted cow manure. Slow release and natural products last longer, are less likely to burn your grass, and will leach less nitrate into surface waters or the ground water.

FERTILIZER RATE TO AMOUNT OF BAG FORMULA:

Pounds Recommended/1000 sq. ft. × size of lawn in sq. ft. = pounds of nitrogen (N) needed

Pounds N in bag = Percentage N/100 × net weight of bag.

Pounds N needed/Pounds N in bag = numbers of bags (or fraction of bag) needed.

READING FERTILIZER BAGS

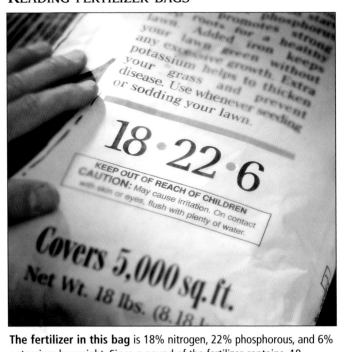

The fertilizer in this bag is 18% nitrogen, 22% phosphorous, and 6% potassium by weight. Since a pound of the fertilizer contains .18 pounds of nitrogen, you would need about five and a half pounds of the fertilizer to give you one pound of nitrogen. The whole 18 pound bag contains about 3¼ pounds of nitrogen.

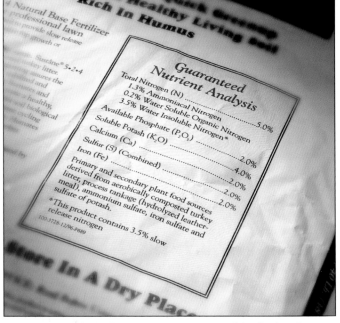

This analysis label tells us that nitrogen is 5% of the fertilizer by weight. Importantly, it also tells us that 3.5% of the fertilizer, or more than two-thirds of the nitrogen, is slow release nitrogen.

Gurus of Good Management

Even golf course managers are figuring out ways to use fewer chemicals. Glenn Smickley, a manager of a golf course on a water reservoir in Virginia, won the Environmental Stewardship Award from the Golf Course Superintendents Association of America. He reduced fertilizer application to 1 pound nitrogen per 1000 sq. ft. per year and switched entirely to slow-release organic fertilizers. He found that these stimulated microbial activity in the soil, which cycled nutrients from the grass clippings more efficiently and cut his pesticide expense by more than 60%.

Topdressing makes a little fertilizer go a long way. Chemical fertilizers and some pesticides can reduce microorganism populations, making elements in the soil unavailable for plant uptake. Topdressing with compost, composted manure or rich topsoil provides nitrogen, phosphorous and potassium (NPK) and carbon compounds. The carbon compounds feed the soil microorganisms. Soil organisms not only make NPK available to plants, they keep disease organisms in check. If you topdress yearly, you may reduce or eliminate fertilizer applications. Apply ½ to 1 cubic yard of well-composted material or topsoil per 1000 sq.ft. of lawn with a rake or peat spreader.

How often, how much, & when to fertilize

Quick-release fertilizers should be applied at a rate of no more than 1 pound of nitrogen per 1000 sq. ft. at one time, and slow-release fertilizers should be applied no heavier than 2 pounds of nitrogen per 1000 sq. ft. at a time. If you employ multiple fertilizer applications in one year, it is best to decide ahead of time the total quantity of nitrogen you will spread in the year. This will enable you to determine how much nitrogen should be applied at each application. Naturally, with multiple applications you may be applying fertilizer rates in a single application that are below those recommended on the bag.

Apply fertilizer in the afternoon when the grass is completely dry. The best time of year to fertilize warm-season grasses is during their growing season in the late spring and summer. Use only slow-release fertilizer on warm-season lawns in the summer to prevent burn. In the Coastal Deep South (Zone E on our Grass Climate Map, page 34), you may fertilize in the spring and fall before considering a summer application, since fall fertilization can help warm-season grasses build up reserves for winter. Fall fertilization of warm-season grasses is dangerous too far north, since frost damage of over-stimulated grasses can occur. Ideally, a fall fertilizer application should be low in phosphorous and relatively high in nitrogen and potassium.

The best time to fertilize cool-season grasses is when they are actively growing in the fall. High maintenance grasses may receive a late spring application, but avoid early spring applications. Also, never apply fertilizer close to or during summer dormancy. The grass should not be encouraged to grow lush top growth just before the heat of the summer, and nitrogen that does not get used by grass will only help fertilize summer weeds.

Important: Only fertilize dry grass. Fertilizer will stick to damp grass and burn the blades.

Watch your pH balance

You may need to adjust the pH over the period of a year with two or three lime or acidifier applications. Apply no more than 50 pounds of ground dolomite or calcitic limestone or 5 pounds of elemental sulfur per 1000 sq. ft. of established lawn at one time.

Applying Fertilizers and other Amendments.

Fertilizers, limestone, gypsum, and other substances must be spread as evenly as possible to achieve optimal results and to avoid damaging the lawn. You probably don't need a scale, but do take the time to pour the fertilizer you will use into a clean bucket or another bag. Be sure to write on the bag how much unused fertilizer is left. By dividing a bag of fertilizer with a known net weight ahead of time, your application weights will be more precise.

Once you've got the quantity you want to spread, divide it into two approximately equal portions. Load one of the portions into your drop or broadcast spreader. If your spreader is calibrated for the brand of fertilizer you're using, that's great. Set the spreader to disperse the fertilizer at half the rate you'll be applying. Otherwise, aim low. It's better to spread too thin and have to take another pass than to spread too heavily. Disperse your first load in one of the patterns shown in the illustrations to the left, as it's easier to cover the edges first. This way you can spread up to, but not beyond, the borders of the lawn. When you fill in the middle, you'll want to release the spread lever or button before U-turning over the edges you've already fertilized.

Now, load in the other half of the fertilizer. Adjust the calibration as needed, and begin spreading in a pattern perpendicular to the first. You may need to do the edges as you did them the first time, but the criss-cross pattern in the middle will help even out the application and prevent striping. When you're done, wash out your spreader well, particularly if it's made of metal, since fertilizer is corrosive.

Use the two-batch method to spread fertilizer. Divide the total volume of fertilizer you'll be applying into two equal parts. Adjust your spreader to provide coverage that's half of the recommended coverage rate. Fill the spreader with half of the fertilizer and spread it evenly onto the entire area. Add the other half and spread it over the first pass, operating the spreader at perpendicular angles to the first run. This helps ensure very even fertilizer coverage.

SPREADING PATTERNS

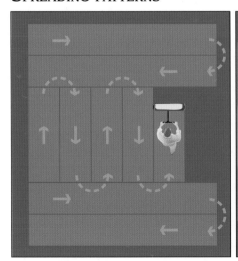
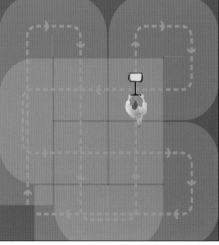

Use one of the patterns shown above as a model for spreading fertilizer with a drop spreader. The best approach is to start at the edges of the area being fertilized, then fill in the middle area. When using the two-batch method described above, you may need to retrace your steps at the edges when you make the second pass, but work at perpendicular angles to the original pattern whenever possible.

When to Fertilize Your Lawn

Cool-season grasses (northern climate)

Annual rate of nitrogen

Spread one pound at a time (complete fertilizer)	Divide evenly for application on these dates
4 pounds N/1000 ft^2	4 applications: August, September, October-November, May-June
3 pounds N/1000 ft^2	3 applications: August, October-November, May-June
2 pounds N/1000 ft^2	2 applications: August, October-November
1 pound N/1000 ft^2	1 application: September

This fertilizer timing chart for Minnesota illustrates that cool-season grasses prefer to be fed before periods of cool, wet weather.

Warm season grasses (southern climate)

Note: summer applications are not recommended when disease or insects are a problem.

Annual rate of nitrogen

Spread one pound of total N at a time. Use a complete fertilizer (NPK) in the spring; Slow release N only in the heat of late spring and summer; and a complete fertilizer low in P in the late summer or fall (where fall fertilizer is appropriate).	Total nitrogen divided evenly for application at these dates
4 pounds N/1000 ft^2 (common bermudagrass, Gulf Coast)	April 1, May 1, June 1, August 1
3 pounds N/1000 ft^2 (common bermudagrass, Central Miss.)	May 1, June 1, August 1
2 pounds N/1000 ft^2 (centipedegrass, Gulf)	April 1, August 1
1 pound N/1000 ft^2 (centipedegrass, Central Miss.)	May 1

This fertilizer timing chart for Mississippi illustrates that warm-season grasses prefer to receive most of their fertilizer prior to the hot months. It also cautions that phosphorous, potassium, and quick release nitrogen can harm grass if applied in hot weather.

Cool-season Grasses

Soluble nitrogen produces a burst of top-growth in grass plants. Rampant growth can work against the long-term health of the lawn, particularly if it comes at the wrong time. A common (but ill-advised) practice is to apply fertilizer to cool-season grasses at the first signs of greening in the spring. This over-stimulates growth, which depletes carbohydrate reserves in the roots. The overgrown blades are soft and susceptible to disease, late frost and insects. As the weakened grasses come under attack, the same fertilizer used to plush-up the grass is raising a healthy crop of annual weeds that are well adapted to use the excess nitrogen. Disappointed homeowners finally put on herbicides and more fertilizer come summer. Now it has become too hot for the cool-season grasses to benefit from the nitrogen. Instead, warm-season weed grasses like crabgrass take the fertilizer and run.

The correct way to fertilize cool-season grasses is with an early fall application of a balanced, slow-release fertilizer. This allows the grass to soak up solar energy and stock their roots with carbohydrates and other fertilizer elements before winter. Come spring, the grass is ready for sustained, even grown, and nothing is left for the weeds.

Warm-season Grasses

Fertilizing warm-season grasses too much and too early can cause the same problems described above for their northern cousins, especially if quick-release nitrogen is used. The tops of the grass grow too lushly and too fast while the roots languish in cool soil, inviting disease, insect, and late-frost destruction of leaves. Since the roots are low on carbohydrate reserves, they cannot push up replacement leaves indefinitely. Instead, a well-fertilized crop of weeds takes over. That's why southern Extension Agents usually recommend waiting three or four weeks into the growing season before fertilizing warm-season grasses. Since the warm-season grasses like heat, you might apply fertilizer during the summer on a high maintenance lawn. Summer fertilization becomes unnecessary or harmful if the grass goes dormant or if a summer disease or insect problem exists. There is nothing pests and disease like more than soft, overfed grass. The application of a late-summer or early-fall fertilizer that's low in phosphorous and high in potassium and slow-release nitrogen (e.g. a 2-1-2 ratio) can promote root development and carbohydrate storage during a long, mild fall growing season. This puts the grass in good position to come back strong in the spring. Do not fertilize too close to winter weather, since nitrogen inhibits dormancy. Ask a local expert when the last safe date to apply fertilizer in your area is.

Watering

As a rule, lawns stay healthiest with infrequent but deep watering. Frequent shallow watering promotes thatch build-up, annual-weed growth, and disease, and "spoils" the lawn by concentrating all the feeder roots in the top inch of soil. Deep watering builds resilient, deep-rooted lawns that survive cold, heat, drought and insects better. Here are some tips for watering your lawn effectively:

Don't water by hand. A deep watering can take an hour or more. Select a sprinkler or sprinklers that can be set up to deliver an even spray to all parts of your lawn. For time efficiency, position multiple sprinklers around an area, and use Y-connectors and extra hoses to run them simultaneously. Try to use the same kind of sprinkler everywhere for consistent coverage, and avoid inconsistent overlaps of sprinkler patterns.

The ideal sprinkler has a distribution pattern that matches or can be matched to the shape you are trying to water. The flow rate should not exceed the ability of your lawn to absorb the water, and the sprinkler should deliver water uniformly, without creating overly wet areas near the base of the sprinkler.

Soak the soil six to eight inches down. Typically, this will take about an inch of water, although very sandy soils may take half that and a heavy clay can take twice that. For heavy clay soils, you may need to apply water in short 10-minute sessions, spaced 10 minutes apart to avoid run-off. This is only practical with a programmable water timer. If you have thatch or compaction problems in your yard, your lawn may absorb less than 5 minutes of water at a time from a high-flow sprinkler or irrigation system. Adjust your watering schedule accordingly, but deal with the thatch as soon as possible.

GAUGING WATER AMOUNTS

To gauge how much water you've applied to your lawn, arrange tuna-fish cans or other straight-sided cans at incremental distances from the sprinkler and monitor the depth of the water as the sprinkler runs. Better sprinklers will fill all the cans evenly, but you'll probably need to average between the cans. Overlapping multiple sprinklers will provide more even coverage.

Let the lawn completely dry before watering again. Constant damp conditions encourage weed, disease, and insect problems. Probe the soil with a screwdriver or use an earth auger or a moisture meter to see if the soil has dried to a 6 to 8 in. depth. Drying could take two or three weeks for a heavy clay soil or a matter of days for a sandy soil.

Important: New lawns and sod should be watered more frequently and for shorter times until the roots are well established. A new lawn in hot weather may need to be watered briefly three or four times a day.

Water conservation

Deep-rooted grasses like tall fescue, bermudagrass, zoysiagrass and buffalograss can be watered so that the ground is moist 12 in. down 24 hours after watering, and then not watered again until the soil dries to that depth. This will train your grass to root deeply, taking better advantage of deep rainfalls and stored water.

In dry areas, your water utility service, the Cooperative Extension Agency, or even the newspaper can provide average evapotranspiration (ET) figures for grass in your area for any particular month. If your rate is ".2," that means your grass (in full sun) must receive .2 in. of rain or irrigation water per day (1.4 in. per week). Notice that the frequency of watering will still depend on how many inches of water your lawn can absorb at one time. Be aware that lawn ET rates are 20 to 40% less than the generic, base ET rates that are averaged out for all plants. If your newspaper's ET is not specifically for grass, contact your Cooperative Extension Service to determine the conversion factor.

The Freedom Lawn

Assuming it's acceptable in your neighborhood, any lawn can be treated as a "freedom lawn," a term coined by the authors of the classic book *Redesigning the American Lawn*. Rather than water a freedom lawn, one lets it adapt to dry conditions by going brown and dormant. This works in most parts of the country for the most prevalent grass species; however, some species of grass, such as Kentucky bluegrass and St. Augustinegrass, may actually die under prolonged drought conditions. Even drought-tolerant grasses like zoysiagrass and bermudagrass can die if a drought is long enough. Your local Cooperative Extension Service can recommend grass and groundcover mixes adapted to a low maintenance regimen for your climate and soil conditions.

TESTING FOR MOISTURE

Moisture meters provide an easy, non-destructive way to test soil moisture at varying depths. They can be found at any garden center.

CHECKING DEPTH OF WATER PENETRATION

Probe your soil with a spade, trowel or an earth auger (with a cut-away window) before, then 12 hours after watering to see how far the water has penetrated. Waiting 12 or even 24 hours before probing clay soil is needed because water moves very slowly through clay soil. This is a reliable method, but obviously is more disruptive to the lawn than a moisture meter (top of page).

HOSE ACCESSORIES

A Y-connector with dual shutoff valves allows you to turn one hose bib into two, each with a shut-off. Brass Y-connectors are more durable than plastic Y-connectors, which can spring leaks under high pressure.

Quick connectors are two-part assemblies that allow you to change sprinklers in a hurry. One connector part is screwed onto the end of a hose or a hosebib; the other end is screwed onto the port on a sprinkler or hose. The two parts snap together in the same fashion as air compressor hose connectors, and create a reliably leak-free connection.

SPRINKLING TIMERS

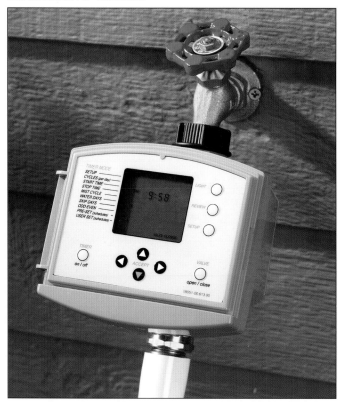

Sillcock timers. The better water timers attach directly to your sillcock, so the hose isn't left under pressure when the automatic valve shuts. Programmable electronic timers can be set to water in repeating cycles, which is useful if your soil absorbs water slowly.

On-board sprinkler timers. The oscillating sprinkler above has an integral water timer. Such a timer requires a sturdy, leak free hose, and even then, you may not want to leave it unattended. But they are a cost-effective option to sillcock timers (left).

A rolling cart/hose reel simplifies garden hose management.

Hoses, carts & reels

If you ever need to deliver a constant flow of water more than 50 ft. away from your primary sillcock, you have a decision to make when it comes to garden hose. Decent quality garden hoses are sold in lengths of 50, 75 and 100 ft. You'll want to consider purchasing the 75 or 100-foot hose for maximum reach without joining multiple hoses together (and creating the inevitable leaks at the connections). If you go with the longer hose, consider a hose reel or hose cart to keep it organized. But if the bulk of the watering you do is within the 50 ft. range, or reachable with a sprinkler from a point 50 ft. away from the sillcock, consider the shorter hose. You may need to attach an extension hose to it occasionally, but you'll avoid the constant battle that comes with trying to manage all that extra hose. In either case, ⅝ -in. dia. hose is a better choice than ½ in., because it's less likely to restrict water flow. Five-ply is better than 4-ply when purchasing rubber/vinyl combination hoses. All-rubber hoses tend to be high quality, but they're more expensive and a bit heavy to lug around. Better quality garden hoses have brass fittings, not plastic or vinyl.

Repairing a garden hose

Pierced hose or leaking connector? Don't throw away an otherwise perfectly-good garden hose: Repair it instead.

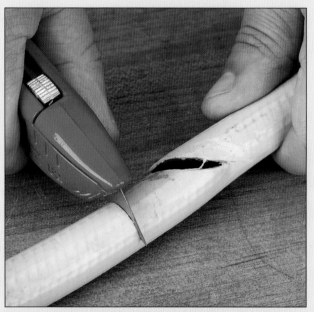

1 Cut out the damaged section of hose with a utility knife. Measure the inside diameter of your hose so you can purchase a repair coupling of the correct size. Hardware stores carry a variety of easy-to-use repair products for damaged hoses, including male and female ends and hose to hose connectors. Most employ a barbed coupling (brass are better than nylon) that slips into each cut end of the hose to make the repair joint.

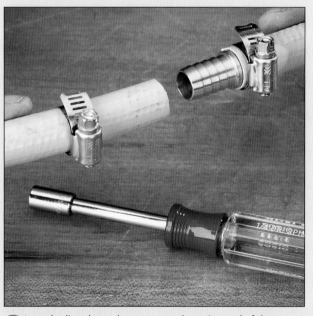

2 Loosely slip a hose clamp onto each mating end of the cut hose, then insert an end of the barbed coupling into each hose section. Position the hose clamps over the coupling in each section and tighten the clamps.

A. Spinning Style

D. Oscillating Style

B. Adjustable Style

C. Sprinkler Hose

E. Impulse Style

F. Soaker Hose

G. Self-propelled

Sprinklers

Spinning sprinklers **(A)** have uneven distribution and low throw radius, making these a generally poor choice. Inexpensive adjustable sprinklers **(B)** that offer a choice of spray patterns can work for small areas if you don't water much, and they can work with low water pressure. But these are not a good solution for regular waterers, since they often leak and have uneven distribution patterns. Sprinkler hoses **(C)** work well for long, awkward shapes and on slopes, since their low flow rate does not exceed the ability of the soil to absorb water. They are difficult to set up for even coverage. The better quality oscillating sprinklers **(D)** allow you to adjust the width and sweep of the rectangular-shaped spray pattern, and the gentle spray is good for newly seeded areas and clay soils that absorb water slowly. However, they lose more water to evaporation than other sprinklers. Quality metal impulse sprinklers **(E)** are durable and lay down a lot of water in a large circular or semi-circular pattern. Distribution is uniform. Their high flow rate can cause runoff on high-clay soils if watering isn't broken up into short sessions. Soaker hose **(F)** is normally installed semi-permanently in planting beds under a layer of mulch. Self-propelled sprinklers **(G)** use water pressure to move slowly along a track formed by your hose. These can be perfect for oblong alleys of lawn (plus, they're kind of fun to watch). Don't make them take sharp corners or travel over rough terrain.

In-ground sprinkler systems

In-ground sprinkler systems are gaining popularity as a labor-saving tool that rigorously maintains a watering schedule. Even if you have no intention of installing a system yourself (it's really not that hard to do), if you have an in-ground system you'd be well advised to understand its basic components and how they work.

Well-attended in-ground sprinkler systems can maintain an even, green lawn with as little water (and labor) as possible. They can be programmed for zone watering, so areas that require less water, such as perennial planting beds, are watered less frequently than thirstier areas. Because they water your yard automatically, you can head to the spa for a few days of recovery after laying sod, and be confident that the new sod will get the water it needs in your absence. They can even improve the resale value of your house—especially if you have a very large yard. There are plenty of good reasons these up-and-coming mechanical systems are gathering a lot of interest.

Traditionally, installing and maintaining in-ground sprinkler systems has been left to contractors. But in case you're feeling ambitious (and a little thrifty), you can also purchase the components and install a system yourself. System distributors even offer free system design services.

Measuring your water flow rate

Before you can choose and design an in-ground sprinkler system, you'll need to determine the rate and pressure at which water flows through your plumbing. If you can't locate a gauge like the one shown to the right, test this way:

• Attach an ordinary water pressure gauge to a faucet inside your house and open the faucet all the way.

• Turn on your exterior sillcock full-blast. Check the pressure on the gauge inside the house. If it's less than 35 PSI, turn down the sillcock until the pressure climbs up to 35 PSI.

• Without changing the rate of flow from the sillcock, time how long (in seconds) it

Available water flow and pressure will impact how many heads, and of what type, you can install in each "valve zone." You can measure both water pressure and flow with a gauge like the one shown above—you may be able to borrow one from your irrigation system distributor.

takes to fill a 5-gallon bucket. Divide 300 by the number of seconds to calculate your rate of flow in gallons per minute (GPM).

Sprinkler Heads

The type of sprinkler head you choose should be determined by the size and nature of the watering zones in your yard, as well as your budget.

Pop-up height. Lawn sprinkler heads pop-up out of the ground under water pressure. Even in landscaping borders, these are preferable to shrub-style heads, which stay up all the time. Pop-up models come in different heights. Professionals usually install heads that pop up 4 in. Anything less than a 3-in. pop-up is not recommended. Heads for garden or shrub borders should pop-up higher: as much as 12 in.

Material. Brass sprinkler heads will last longer than plastic, and they may provide a more even flow, but the good ones cost much more than good plastic heads, which are more than adequate for just about any residential installation. Plastic or brass, look for heads with a spring for retracting the nozzle (some rely on gravity), and a separate, well-fitting wiper seal to keep water from running out between the riser and housing.

Rotor or fixed?

Lastly, you need to choose between a rotor-style head and a fixed head. The rotor style sends rotating streams of water out from the head in about a 30 ft. radius. They cover more ground per head, but they are more expensive, and they require at least 40 pounds per square inch (PSI) of water pressure. Fixed heads usually spray a

A typical plastic, pop-up sprinkler.

15-ft. radius. If you have a small lot, you're better off going with the fixed head. These are easier to adjust and maintain. Whatever kind of heads you get, they will demand a minimum amount of water flow, which will figure into how you set up the system: specifically, whether you can feed the system from the sillcock, or will need to tie directly into your water supply system to get sufficient water pressure.

The Timer

The timer is a programmable control panel that is wired directly to the valves controlling the flow of water into the irrigation system. Through electronic impulses it opens and closes the valves according to the multi-zone watering schedule you plug in.

Tubing & Fittings

The sprinkler heads are connected to the supply valves with a network of flexible poly tubing and PVC pipe fittings. Most of the joints between tubing and fittings are secured with pipe clamps.

The Valve Manifold

The valve manifold is the cluster of automatic or manual valves that distribute water to each of the individual watering zones. It is usually located in an underground box next to the foundation of the house. The manifold is connected directly to the main water supply for the house (the supply line to the system needs to be fitted with a backflow prevention device). Each valve in the manifold controls one specific zone, called a "valve zone." Supply tubing runs from the valve in a branch supply line. At each sprinkler head, tubing that supplies the head is connected to the branch originating at the valve.

When running supply "branch lines" from the manifold, try to come up with an efficient path that minimizes trenching—sharing a trench with another branch line is a good way to obtain this goal.

It's a good idea to put filters downstream of the valves. These can save you the headache of replacing clogged sprinkler nozzles, since the high flow of irrigation systems tend to carry sand and other particles from the water supply into the system.

Note to Northerners: Even if your valve manifold is at a high point among the branch lines to the sprinkler heads, you may still need a drain valve in the manifold that is accessible through the valve box opening—it depends on the type and manufacturer of your irrigation system. The drain valve is opened to drain the system before winter, and is often attached to a drain pipe.

The Valve Box

The valve box contains and protects the valve manifold. It is usually heavy plastic with a removable, bolt-on cover that's kept level with the ground. The box should rest on a bed of gravel.

Parts of an in-ground sprinkling system

Miscellaneous fittings include: *Replacement flow nozzles (left)* inserted to change the pattern of an in-ground sprinkler head; *Saddle fitting (middle)* used to locate sprinklers directly over supply lines or to provide a tap for flexible tubing extensions; *Flexible extension tubing (right)* used to locate sprinklers off of main lines without having to extend main supply lines off of their direct path.

SYSTEM VARIATION: Automatic Drip Lines

Drip lines utilize an additional pressure reducer after the valve.

Drip lines are staked in planting beds and covered with mulch.

In-ground watering systems can be equipped with drip lines instead of sprinkler heads. Drip lines provide a slow, constant supply of water to confined areas, like small planting beds, or around specimen trees. They are run as dedicated lines from the valve manifold, not tacked onto sprinkler lines.

Designing your in-ground sprinkler system

To build a successful irrigation system, you need to know exactly what you are irrigating. Draw the area to be irrigated to scale on graph paper. It's best to put parts of buildings in first and develop the rest of the map by measuring off them. When the broad outlines of fences, garden beds, buildings and pavement are noted, sketch in objects like trees, bushes, grills, and play areas.

Draw a scale map of your yard, including planting beds, that notes any special watering requirements. Then, after choosing a sprinkler head type and determining how many sprinkler heads can be supported by each system of heads, plot out possible watering patterns that effectively divide your yard into watering zones.

Map the sprinkler circuits

Before you can proceed with any drawings of the sprinkler system layout, you'll have to decide which type of sprinkler heads you want your system to have—this is actually kind of a back-and-forth process of trying to reconcile the shapes and ranges of the sprinkler heads that are available with the shapes and sizes of the areas in your yard. You'll want to have a complete catalog of options from the manufacturer during this process. Here are some tips:

• You want as many of the heads as possible to be up against the borders and corners of the lawn, where they are out of harm's way.

• At borders, you'll want heads that spray in 180° patterns. At corners, a 90° pattern is preferred.

• Once you've established the perimeter, fill in the middle, staggering the heads in a triangle pattern for greatest efficiency.

• Sprinklers should spray head-to-head, which means each head is separated from its neighbors by the radius of its spray. More widely spaced heads will produce an uneven watering pattern. Manufacturers provide different ways of reducing the spraying radius of individual heads when necessary, and most also provide a head for long, narrow spaces.

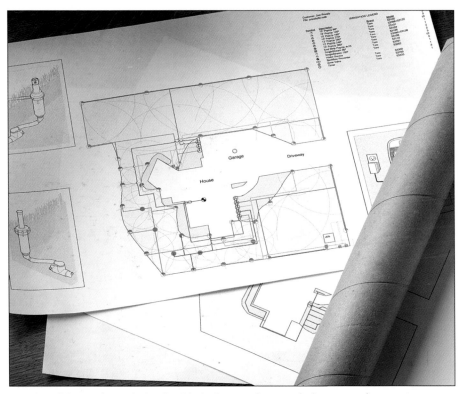

TIP: For tricky yards, work closely with the in-ground system dealer or manufacturer. Some suppliers will generate sprinkler-head patterns for you on a computer if you provide them with a scaled map of your yard.

Watering zones

One of the benefits of zone irrigation is the ability to provide different levels of water to different parts of the yard, depending on how much water each area needs. You could create a low-water hydro-zone for your shrubs, for example, a medium-water zone for your perennials, and a high-water zone for your lawn. Shady parts of the lawn can receive less water, as long as a thirsty tree isn't responsible for the shade. You could even set up a zone of drip emitters to conserve on water. Factor these watering zones into your master plan drawing.

Valve zones

A valve zone includes all the sprinkler heads that lead back to a particular control valve. You can have more than one valve zone in a watering zone, but you can't have a single valve zone cross between two watering zones. The size of the valve zone is determined by the number of gallons per minute (GPM) your water supply system can provide, as well as the operating water pressure available to the irrigation system (See page 82): these system capacities will dictate how many heads can be installed per valve zone, since all the heads in a valve zone go on at the same time. Usually, the GPM demand load within a valve zone should be no more than 75% of the GPM flow your supply system can provide. Valves, pipe, and elevation impact the actual GPM available at the sprinkler heads. Use the sprinkler head manufacturer's charts to figuring out how many heads can go in one valve zone. It's safer to err on the side of caution and stay safely below the GPM rate that's (theoretically) available.

Maintaining an Underground Sprinkler System

Test the laterals and heads

Hit the bleeder valve or turn on your manual knob to see a valve's sprinkler heads. Most likely they'll come telescoping out of the ground and start rotating, or they will spray water in a fixed pattern. Notice that the heads are arranged to provide complete coverage within the station. Does it look like all the heads came up? Are the heads distributing water evenly? Is water spraying on a surface it shouldn't? If you leave the water on for a while, do you get a muddy spot or water coming out of the ground anywhere? Mark problem areas before turning off the station and moving on to the next.

Unclogging or replacing a sprinkler-head nozzle or drip emitter

Sometimes you need only to unclog the nozzle or reposition the spray head to get it to work right. Clogged sprinkler nozzles can be flushed or replaced. Drip emitter heads can also be removed and cleaned if they become clogged. While nozzles and emitter heads are off, flush out the system's pipes by running the water. You may need to protect the sprinkler heads with pieces of hose, so dirty water doesn't get sucked into the openings when you turn their valves off.

Replacing Heads or Risers

Leaks near or at a head that won't pop up may require that you replace the sprinkler head or the riser. The riser is the length of tubing that connects the head to the lateral line.

Fixing a Broken Pipe

Broken or leaking pipes show up as muddy spots or bubbling springs that appear when the station is on. Dig down to the problem area using the bleeder valve to reveal the leak if necessary. Dig around and below the damage so you have plenty of room to work without getting dirt in the line. With PVC, you may cut out the damaged area squarely with a hack saw and purchase a piece of pipe of the same size, two repair couplers, sandpaper, PVC solvent cement and primer (for one repair, you may get by with just the cement, but the primer will form a more solid weld). Sand the rough-cut pipe ends, apply the primer and cement as directed on the labels, and stick everything together. You'll need to wait a day for the solvent weld to cure before you can turn the water back on to test your fix. If you have black polyethylene supply tubing (PE), you'll cut the pipe at the leak and make the repair with a brass coupling that inserts into the pipe ends and is held on to the pipe with hose clamps.

Resetting the Control Box Using 'Soil Based' Watering

The control box will be found in a garage, basement, or utility room. It houses the timers for putting water on the different zones. Figure out the timing by manually operating the zones first, monitoring soil moisture levels before and the day after watering. Most lawn grasses should be watered when the soil dries below 6 in. More drought-adapted plants tolerate or even prefer periods of dry soil between rain or irrigation. When you do water, though, it should be deeply.

Your lawn or garden soil may be unable to absorb all the water it needs at one time without runoff and puddling. With your control box, you can set the system to cycle through the zones repeatedly, allowing each area to receive its full "dose" of water in a series of short waterings. This gives the water time to sink in. If you need to apply less than five minutes of water at a time, your lawn is probably ready for dethatching or aeration.

Push reel mowers are a joy on smaller, flatter, lawns and a workout on large or hilly lawns. This old classic has charm, but high quality modern push reel mowers are lighter, lower in maintenance, and more effective.

Mowing

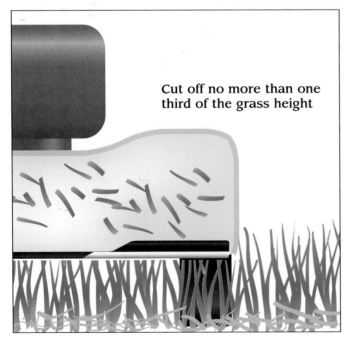

Cut off no more than one third of the grass height

Cut your grass frequently enough that you don't need to remove more than ⅓ of the total plant height to trim it back into its recommended height range.

Grass evolved with grazing animals and still depends upon regular cutting to stay healthy and thick. Attentive mowing promotes development of new grass and helps control certain weeds. Mowing too short can be just as much of a problem as not mowing frequently enough. Below are the five rules for proper mowing.

1. Mow high. Mow to the maximum recommended mowing height for your grass species (listed in "Grass Types," pages 34 to 46) when the grass is stressed. Stresses include drought, shade, and emergence of annual weeds. Annual weeds germinate in the spring in the north and in the spring and late summer/early fall in the south. Certain creeping warm-season grasses, like bermudagrass, centipedegrass, and carpetgrass, are kept competitive by short mowing. Lastly, it's a good idea to mow before weeds go to seed to prevent their spread.

2. Take one-third of the leaf blade at a mowing. This could mean weekly or more frequent mowing during high-growth periods for the faster growing grasses and much longer intervals between mowing when the grass is not growing fast or the species is a slow grower. Note that you'll mow less frequently when you cut grass high, since ⅓ of a longer blade takes more time to grow. Taking more than ⅓ of the leaf blade stresses the plant by reducing the supply of sugars to the roots and by exposing the previously shaded lower part of the plants to sunburn.

TIP: If your grass gets too high, mow at your highest mower setting on the first mowing, wait three days, then mow to the preferred height.

3. Leave grass clippings to rot, whether you use a mulching mower or not. You should not rake clippings or use a mower with a bag unless special circumstances exist. The clippings return nitrogen to the soil, reducing the need to fertilize; they add organic matter to the soil, which feeds valuable microorganisms and increases the resilience of the lawn to disease and drought. Contrary to popular belief, grass clippings do not contribute to thatch buildup. Remove and compost clippings if they contain many weed seedheads or rooting runners of weeds. Also, remove or disperse rows, piles, or clumps of grass clippings.

4. Don't mow a wet lawn, as it leaves clumps of grass and can foster the spread of disease.

5. Keep your lawnmower blade sharp to prevent injury to grass and spread of disease. Sharp blades are critical on newly seeded grass, which may be uprooted by a dull rotary blade.

Mulching mowers speed up the decomposition of clippings in your lawn, serving the two-fold purpose of fertilizing and eliminating unsightly clipping clumps.

Never mow a wet lawn. It creates clumps of grass that are strewn throughout the yard, where they can damage living plants if left for more than a day; it leaves the cut grass very vulnerable to disease; it causes stress on your mower engine, and makes a mess of the mower deck, too.

A sharp blade does a neater job of mowing grass and is much less likely to damage the grass plants than a dull blade.

Mower Safety

Danger: Please be careful with lawnmowers, which in sheer numbers of accidents are one of the most dangerous machines to users and bystanders. They can take the use of a hand, an eye or seriously injure or kill a child. Importantly:

1. Keep hands, feet, and clothing away from cutting blades.
2. Motor should be off and spark plug disconnected before attempting service that will put your hand near the blade.
3. Keep children inside when mowing.
4. Mow across slopes, not up and down.
5. Do not leave a running mower unattended.
6. Look down and behind before mowing backwards.
7. Remove objects from lawn before mowing and do not mow over gravel or stones.
8. Do not mow wet grass.
9. Mow sober and alert and wear shoes with good traction.

MORE MOWING TIPS

Power reel mowers can cut lower than rotary mowers without scalping because they conform to uneven ground. While rotary mowers can leave blade ends ragged and brown, reels produce an even scissor-action cut. Power reel mowers are by far the best tools for cutting hybrid bermudagrass, creeping bentgrass, and St. Augustinegrass.

Generally, it's better not to bag lawn clippings; however, if the grass has become very long or if weed grasses and broadleafs are in seed, bag the clippings.

One of the advantages of owning a garden tractor is that you can find a host of useful accessories, from trailers, like the one shown above, to tillers, broadcast spreaders and even grading attachments.

Edging

Visually, humans focus on edges. Practically, this means that if you make the borders of your lawn sharp and clean, you can relax a little about imperfections in the middle. There are a number of tools out there that can help you maintain the lawn's edge on an ongoing basis. These include grass shears, long-handled edging shears, string trimmers, and manual rotary edgers that can be pushed along the edge. Use these whenever the grass starts creeping beyond the lawn area.

If your edge is allowed to run wild for a while, the more mild-mannered of these tools will not be able to pull the grass back, however. It's then that you'll want to rent a power edger to chop back the spreading grasses. For information on establishing a new edge or laying edging, see pages 130 to 131. For a tidy border effect, chop a clean vertical edge on the lawn and clip back any vegetation coming in the other direction from the garden. Don't be afraid to reach back under larger creeping plants like junipers to clip them closer to the source. That way all the cutting doesn't happen in a single plane.

Power edgers (available at most rental centers) make short work of badly overgrown lawn borders. A flat-edge spade also works well for cutting back sod to the edge of a paved surface.

A manual roll edger works for regularly maintained edges, but may meet its match on long-neglected lawn borders.

Create an unplanted area 6 to 12 in. wide between garden and lawn. As an added effect, lay mulch in the cleared area—this will help slow the invasion of grass, garden plants, and weeds, and it will create a striking visual border.

Adjust the pH of acidic or alkaline soil to help control moss and other weeds. Correct pH also helps your grass grow better, controlling the weeds indirectly. Lime pellets and hydrated lime are applied to a lawn to help neutralize acidic soil.

Weeds & Weed Control

Weeds are a little bit like vegetables—you know one when you see one, but they tend to defy hard, scientific definitions. A weed to one person is a valued plant to somebody else, and may not even show up on the radar screen of yet a third person. But the only person whose opinion really matters is yours. If there is a plant in your yard that you wish to get rid of, there are ample ways it can be accomplished.

But to editorialize for a moment, think twice before you automatically attack any intruding plant in your yard. Allowing a lawn to include non-grass plants does have some advantages. Ecological diversity in your

WEED OR NOT-WEED? The case for clover

Ultimately, a weed is a plant you don't want. Clover, henbit, violets, daisies and other low-growing broad-leaf plants may be weeds or turf plants, depending on your point of view. Pure grass lawns are more even, but mixtures of grass and other plants may be easier to maintain and more insect and disease resistant.

White clover fertilizes grass by fixing nitrogen from the air, and clover impedes the spread of grass diseases. But some don't like the rustic look of lawns with clover, its attraction to bees, or its tendency to stain clothes green when played on. Is clover a weed or turf plant? You decide.

White clover

yard makes disease and insect problems less likely. Many turf plants have low, attractive flowers and are more tolerant of poor soil, drought and neglect than grass. Finally, maintaining an all-grass lawn in an area that favors another plant type means that you will need to work that much harder to keep the grass there and the "weed" out.

However, keeping certain plants out, whether "weed" species of grass or non-grass plants, can make sense for aesthetic and practical reasons. Annual plants, whether grasses or non-grasses, die after one year, leaving ugly dead spots in the yard. Some plants send up large, ragged seed heads or spikes and others have coarse, unsightly leaves that break up the evenness of the turf. Finally, plants that spread aggressively when your main turf species are dormant can leave a lawn patchy and uneven when the invader is dormant.

Decide for yourself which and how many non-turf grass plants you will tolerate before establishing a weed control regimen. Determine if a particular plant is adding to your dissatisfaction with your lawn, or if the weed is incidental to larger lawn-health problems that could be mitigated with a better watering, fertilizing, composting, aerating, or dethatching program.

Weed Control

Turf grasses are naturally aggressive, and if the conditions are right, they will out-compete other plants. Below are cultural practices that favor grass over weeds.

Keep grass the right height. Regular mowing controls taller perennial weeds and keeps weeds from seeding. But mowing high when you do mow helps many grasses out-compete germinating weeds. Tall grass will smother the competition from newly germinating annual weeds. Higher mowing in shade and during dry periods also give these grasses an advantage over weeds. Low creeping grasses like bermudagrass, centipedegrass and creeping bentgrass usually don't benefit from high mowing.

Nitrogen fertilizer generally benefits grass more than broad leaf plants, helping your grass win the battle for turf. Do not add fertilizer when the weeds will benefit more than the grass, such as when warm season-grasses are dormant in the fall and winter or cool-season grasses are dormant in the summer. Adding too much fertilizer can damage the soil and the grass, opening up a window for weeds that tolerate compaction and fertilizer salts. See pages 70 to 75 for more information on the correct timing and application of fertilizers.

Provide drainage for waterlogged soils, provide aeration for compacted soils, and provide a path in soils that undergo heavy foot traffic. Alternately, switch to a grass species that will tolerate your existing soil conditions.

Give grass a competitive edge. Thin out crowded trees and tree branches to allow underlying grass to out-compete shade- and dry-soil-tolerant weeds. Even so-called "shade tolerant" grasses need some sun. Plus, tree roots draw a lot of water from the soil.

Tall Grass As Weed Control

Studies at the University of Rhode Island found that after five years there was more than 700% more crabgrass in plots that were mowed to 1¼ in. than in plots that were mowed to 2¼ in. At the University of Maryland, scientists found almost seven times as many kinds of weeds in a plot mowed to 1½ in. than in a plot mowed to 2½ in.

Direct weed control methods

Direct weed control is the process of taking your battle right to the weed, through a variety of methods, rather than attempting to resolve the underlying reasons for the weed's presence. It is sometimes the only alternative if invading plants are on the verge of becoming established. In the long run, you'll need to implement the cultural fixes that will make the lawn environment less hospitable for weeds.

There are basically two ways to attack a weed directly: dig it out, or kill it with herbicide. Once the weeds are gone, look into aerating, dethatching, sensible fertilizing, and proper watering as long-term cures to keep them at bay so your turf grasses can thrive.

Use a dandelion digger or other appropriate weeding tool to remove deep-rooted perennial weeds by hand. This is best done a day after rain or a thorough watering, when the soil is soft. Get as much of the root as possible, since large pieces of tap root will come back more often and with more vigor than small pieces will.

CONTROLLING WEEDS BY HAND

Rake and mow early in the season before spreading weeds get the upper hand. Weeds, like ground ivy (creeping Charlie to some) and perennial speedwell, can have their rooting stems dislodged from the ground with a thatch rake or a stiff garden rake. Mow low after raking, then rake up and dispose of the stems (severed stems can re-root).

Specially designed weeding tools like this dandelion digger can get deep into the soil and slice the weed root, leaving virtually no tap root behind to reestablish.

Pre-emergent herbicide

Pre-emergent herbicides kill broad leaf and grass weeds (like crab grass) just as they are germinating from seed. If the weed is already growing, pre-emergent herbicides will not work, and they will not control perennial weeds coming back from established roots and rhizomes. Apply in early spring. In the south, pre-emergent herbicides may also be spread in the late summer or early fall, before winter weeds germinate. Identify your grass species (See page 34 to 36) and check herbicide labels for grass sensitivities. Even "non-sensitive" grasses can be injured by herbicides if they are stressed by drought. Most herbicides should not be applied to new lawns, though siduron and simazine are two pre-emergent herbicides that control crab grass in new lawns. Carefully follow the container instructions when applying pre-emergents. They should be watered-in after application. Be extremely careful to sweep up any herbicide that spills onto pavement. Keep pets and children off treated areas for the specified amount of time.

Post-emergent herbicide

Post emergent herbicides for lawns usually contain 2,4-D and related chemicals that kill broadleaf plants such as dandelions, clover, and chickweed, but don't harm grass or grass-like weeds. The spray-on kind work much better against the weeds than granular postemergent herbicides, but sprays pose a real risk to the environment from drift and the most common ones have known toxicity to humans and animals. Instead of broadly spraying these herbicides with a hose end sprayer, spot-apply smaller quantities with a tank sprayer or a ready-mixed sprayer. That way, you can target weeds without risk of damaging non-target plants, like ornamental trees and perennials. Spot-application is also safer for children, pets, and the environment, since not as much product is applied. Apply post-emergent herbicides when soil moisture is plentiful, weeds are actively growing, and temperatures are below 90°. Weeds are particularly vulnerable after they're done flowering but before they go dormant in late summer or early fall. At this time, sugars are traveling from leaves to root and the herbicide can hitch a ride. Bentgrass, St. Augustinegrass, and centipedegrass may be injured by post-emergent herbicides for broadleaf weeds.

Apply post-emergent, spot weed killers for broadleafs when soil moisture is plentiful and weeds are growing vigorously. Avoid spraying in very hot weather and before rain. Wear protective clothing when spraying and keep pets and children away for the recommended time. Products for broadleafs do not kill grass weeds, but some turf grasses may be slightly injured by these herbicides.

Common Weeds & How to Control Them

Weeds are divided roughly into categories: broadleaf or grass, perennial or annual, and warm-season or cool-season. This gives you eight possible categories in which a weed can fall (e.g. cool-season broadleaf annual, cool-season broadleaf perennial, warm-season broadleaf annual, etc...). Even if you just figure out what category your problem weed falls into, you're a long way toward figuring out how to control it. That's because weed control depends heavily on these variables. Weeds also tell you when something is wrong with your lawn. You may kill the messenger, but if you don't address the underlying problem, the health of your turf grass will not improve and weeds will invade again. Below we look at some representative weeds from each of the categories, see how they are best controlled, and look at underlying conditions that may have allowed these weeds to become established to begin with.

What's wrong with weed-and-feed products?

Pre-emergent weed-and-feed products for the spring have a timing problem. The pre-emergent needs to be applied early, before the weed seeds germinate. Fertilizing grass at this time can over-stimulate top growth, making the grass susceptible to disease and a late frost damage.

The timing of post-emergent weed-and-feed products is perfect when used in the early fall on cool-season grasses, but they have a delivery problem. Granular products do a poor job of coating leaves with herbicide, thus granular weed-and-feed products with post-emergent herbicides are not very effective.

Defining Weed Categories

Grasses: The grass family is huge and includes many important flowering plants including sugarcane, bamboo, corn, wheat, and rice. All emerge from the ground as a single cotyledon (they are "monocots") and all have parallel veined and relatively long narrow leaves. Grasses are distinguished from broadleaf plants for weed control because certain classes of herbicides kill grasses and others kill broadleaf plants. That's why it's possible to broadcast some post-emergent herbicides over the whole lawn and have only the broadleaf plants die.

Broadleaf Plants: Broadleafs include many families of flowering plants. All emerge from the ground as two cotyledons, which is why broadleaf plants are called "dicots". Leaves on broadleaf plants have veins that branch from a single point or off a central rib. Broadleaf plants include most trees, bushes, and annual and perennial plants, but not things that look like grass, such as tulips, daffodils, onions, and irises. Some broadleaf plants, like dandelions, don't have very broad leaves, but if you examine their leaves, you will see the branching vein pattern that puts them in the group.

Perennials: Perennial plants live from year to year. Herbaceous perennials, like the kind that become weeds in lawns, die down to the ground each year but store carbohydrates for next years growth in swollen underground roots, rhizomes, corms and bulbs. Whether monocots or broadleaf plants, perennials often survive when cut down to the ground since they grow from underground buds.

Annuals: Annuals die after a season of growth, but before they do, they put all their energy into producing as many seeds as they can. Some annuals, like lambsquarters, can produce more than one million seeds per plant. Mowing your grass high keeps annual species under control because it leaves no room for the delicate young plants to sprout and grow. Pre-emergent herbicides work well against annuals because they prevent seeds from germinating—the only way an annual can carry on from year to year.

Warm-season and cool-season plants: All of the plants discussed above may be either a warm-season or a cool-season plants. Warm-season plants like bermudagrass do most of their growing in the summer when soil temperatures are over 70°F. Cool-season plants grow better in cool fall and spring weather. They even grow in the winter in the south.

Cool-season perennials are a tough class of weeds from north to south. They weather cold winters and hot summers with reserves stored underground, and come on strong in spring and fall (and winter in the south). Many of the broadleafs of this category stay close to the ground and root as they spread. It's best to catch these early in the spring—raking up the runners, mowing low, and removing the debris, which could otherwise re-root. The grasses of this category need to be dug up or spot-killed with herbicide specifically formulated for grass weeds or all weeds (herbicides that can also kill your turfgrass). Do not fertilize and water in the cooler parts of the year in the south if you have a cool-season weed problem.

Cool-Season Perennial Grass & Grass-Like Weeds:

Quackgrass. *Agropyron repens.*

The wide, coarse leaves of this perennial can grow up to three feet high if unmown. Quackgrass spreads by long, fast-growing, white rhizomes and may turn brown in summer. Keep grass mowed and fertilized to help crowd out quackgrass. Chop into the runners with a spade. Spot treat with a non-selective herbicide like glyphosate, but realize that this will also kill lawn grass.

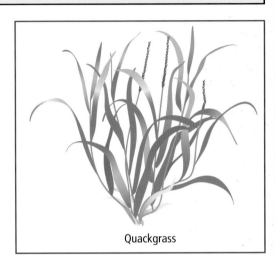
Quackgrass

Wild garlic and onion. *Allium vineale and A. canadense.*

Wild Garlic

Early to green in the spring, these weeds have hollow (garlic) or solid (onion), narrow round leaves that smell like onions and garlic when crushed. An early low mowing before the grass has started to grow will remove old dead grass tips, knock back the onions and garlic, and prevent these from spreading by seed, which develop from purple and white flowers on the tops. (Garlic also forms bulblets). To eliminate these plants, their bulbs must be dug up or a broad-spectrum herbicide containing glyphosate or a spot weeder that controls this genus must be applied to each plant when they are growing in early spring. Late fall herbicide applications are also effective since sugars from the leaves are being transported to the bulbs and the herbicide can hitch a ride. Avoid getting these herbicides on your lawn grass.

Cool Season Perennial Broad-leaf Weeds:

Canada Thistle. *Cirsium arvense.*

Leaves are lobed with margins prickling with spines. Numerous purple or white composite flowers are borne on one-to five-foot tall stems that branch near the top. A network of roots sends up new shoots around one established plant, creating dense clumps of thistles, which are very difficult to eradicate. Eliminate by pulling the plants or by regularly treating them with a spot herbicide. Complete elimination can take years. Keep a lawn with thistle well mowed; never allow the plant to go to seed. They usually establish in lawns that have been allowed to get too long and sparse.

Canada Thistle

Cool Season Perennial Broad-leaf Weeds (cont.):

Dandelion. *Taraxacum officinale.*

A low rosette of basal leaves lets dandelions survive the mower, and a puffball of parachuted seeds after spring and fall blooming keep the species colonizing new turf. But contrary to popular belief, dandelion is not the toughest weed on the planet. A little persistence with any of the control methods outlined below will eliminate dandelions from a healthy lawn.

Method 1) When dandelions are blooming, their root reserves of carbohydrate are at their lowest. Dig as much of the root out as you can at this time with a dandelion weeder, weed popper, or any other tool designed to uproot tap-rooted weeds. Try to get at least 4 or 5 in. of root. The remaining root tip will rarely have enough energy to send up another plant.

Dandelion

Method 2) Use long-handled shears to cut the dandelion leaves and stem off as low as possible. Do this repeatedly, perhaps 5 or 6 times during the growing season, and the roots will run out of energy.

Method 3) Spot-treat dandelions with an herbicide advertised to kill dandelions. Herbicides are most effective on dandelions before blooming in early spring and again in late summer or early fall, when the leaves are sending starches to the root.

Creeping Charlie

Ground Ivy, Creeping Charlie. *Glechoma hederacea.*

This mint blooms in late spring and early summer and has the square stem and trumpet-like, two-lipped purple flowers typical of the family. Round, deeply veined, scalloped-edged leaves are opposite each other on the stem. The plant spreads rapidly with running stems that can root where they contact soil. Control is most effective in early spring, before the plants have gotten too big. Use a garden rake to uproot the runners, then mow the plants close for control, or pull them up to eliminate. Either way, make sure you rake up the stems so they don't root again. Ground ivy responds slowly to spot treatment of herbicides.

Plantain. *Plantago major.*

Broad leaves grow in a rosette from a ground-level growing point that also sends up narrow spikes of inconspicuous flowers that become seeds. Plantain likes thin grass and compacted soil. Aerating, adding compost, and fertilizing can all help a struggling turf grass overcome plantain. Dig plantain up by the root to remove.

Plantain

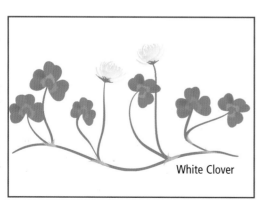

White Clover

White clover. *Trifolium repens.*

White clover has three-leaflets and white pom-pom flowers. In the first part of the twentieth century, white clover was planted purposefully in lawns. It was considered attractive and the symbiosis it carries out with nitrogen-fixing bacteria allowed clover to derive usable nitrogen from the air, thus fertilizing the lawn. Some still choose to plant clover with cool-season grasses. If you wish to eliminate or reduce your clover, increase nitrogen fertilizer rates and reduce phosphorous fertilization to give grass the competitive edge.

Many cool-season annuals are not considered weeds by northern lawnsmiths. In the south, cool-season annual weeds germinate and grow in the fall, winter and spring, making brown, winter lawns look particularly unkempt. Southern lawn owners can fight annual weeds by mowing turfgrasses high in the late summer and fall, which discourages the germination of cool-season weeds. This only works with tall grasses like bahiagrass and St. Augustinegrass. Otherwise, overseed with annual or perennial ryegrass in the fall for a green mowable winter lawn. Prevent the germination of cool-season annuals in the south with an application of pre-emergent granular herbicide in late summer and early spring.

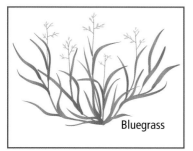

Bluegrass

Annual bluegrass. *Poa annua.*

This annual resembles perennial bluegrass but goes to seed more quickly, giving lawns a whitish cast. Annual bluegrass usually turns brown in the summer, causing northern owners to suspect disease. This grass likes compacted, moist soils. Aerate the soil and mow with the blade high to smother annual bluegrass, but mow often to keep seeds from forming. Remove the grass by pulling. Control in the winter in the south by overseeding with an annual rye.

Common Chickweed. *Stellaria media.*

Chickweed is a low annual with small, smooth, pointed leaves and small white flowers that bloom almost continuously. Seeds germinate in late fall and early spring. Chickweed spreads with rooting branches on wet, shady, or too frequently watered lawns. Pull or cut chickweed and rake up the stems, which can continue to ripen seeds even when uprooted.

Chickweed

Henbit

Henbit. *Lamium amplexicaule.*

Square stems give henbit away as a member of the mint family. Opposite-paired, roundish, ruffled leaves clasp the stem and are stalkless near the tops of upturned stems, though the lowest leaves have long stalks. Purple flowers are trumpet-shaped. Henbit grows on new or thin lawns in soils that are rich and well-watered, and it grows as a vigorous winter annual in the South. Before seeding a new lawn, eliminate henbit with a season of regular tillage or herbicide application. In established lawns, pull henbit and correct fertility, drainage, or aeration problems that are keeping the grass from filling in thickly. In the south, vigorous, thick grass mown high in late summer and early fall will discourage fall germination of henbit.

Prostrate Knotweed. *Polygonum aviculare.*

Wiry stems spread from a central taproot and form a mat of foliage, but the branches do not root. Tiny white flowers emerge at the base of oblong leaves. Knotweed appears in early spring on compacted soils, looking like grass at first. Knotweed can be pulled, cut back, or spot killed with an herbicide at the three-leaf stage in mid to late spring. Correct the pavement-like conditions that favor knotweed by aerating the soil and adding compost.

Knotweed

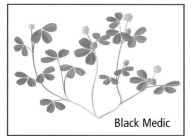

Black Medic

Black Medic. *Medicago lupulina*

The three-leaflet clover-like leaves of medic have shallow teeth at the tips of the leaflets, and center leaflets that sit on a little stalk. The yellow flowers give rise to kidney-shaped, one-seeded pods that become black with age. Like clover, medic derives its own nitrogen from the air with the help of a symbiotic bacteria. This puts them at an advantage on nitrogen-poor soils. Applying compost and nitrogen fertilizer and reducing or eliminating phosphorous fertilizer will help grass get the upper hand.

The bane of the North, warm-season annual weeds thrive under conditions unwittingly created by many cool-season lawn enthusiasts. Frequent shallow watering favors their germination and shallow-rooted growth. Summer fertilization keeps them growing when cool-season grasses are too hot and dry to put up a fight. Southern lawn owners may find themselves up against warm-season broadleaf weeds on thin grass over poor or dry soils. Compacted soils from heavy traffic make life difficult for deep-rooted perennials, letting these undesirable annuals jump into the openings. The best way to control warm-season annuals is by fertilizing at the appropriate times, watering infrequently but deeply, aerating compacted soils, mowing high, and by pulling the offending weeds and removing clippings when these plants are in seed. Below are a sampling of the weeds, what they tell you about your lawn, and what you can do to control them.

Warm Season Annual Grass Weeds:

Crabgrass. *Digitaria ischaemum and D. sanguinalis.*

These light-green, annual grasses with prostrate stems and short hairy leaves can take over thin cool-season lawns when the turf-grasses slow down in the summer. The spreading plants will root at the stem nodes, expanding "crablike". Setting the mower high and fertilizing at the right time allows turfgrass to take control in one to five seasons. Mow high in the spring and summer. Fertilize cool-season grasses once in the fall, twice in the fall, or twice in the fall and once in late spring, but never in the summer.

Crabgrass

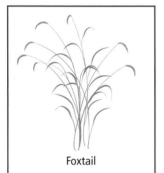
Foxtail

Foxtail (green and yellow). *Setaria viridis and S. glauca.*

Green foxtail has hairy leaf-tops. Both green and yellow foxtail produce dense, bristly seedheads. Mow the lawn high and avoid summer fertilization on northern lawns. Dig up plants and remove clippings when the foxtail is in seed. Foxtails can indicate a need for soil aeration and compost, which will favor your turfgrass over foxtail.

Sandbur. *Cenchrus pauciflorus.*

Sandbur is a low spreading annual grass with spiked seed burrs. It does best on poor sandy soil, so if you've got it, it's probably not your only problem. Rake half an inch of a fine compost or composted manure into your lawn every year until your thickened turf grass drowns out the sandbur. Mow high.

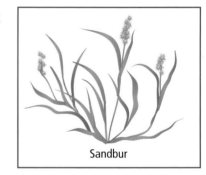
Sandbur

Warm Season Annual Broadleaf Weeds:

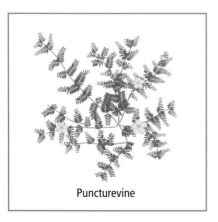
Puncturevine

Puncturevine. *Tribulus terrestris.*

Prostrate branching stems spread up to 5 ft. Two-inch long leaves are hairy and divided into tiny leaflets along a central rib. Yellow flowers in summer turn to sharp-spined seedpods from July into fall. This is mainly a southern weed on poor compacted soils. Eliminate puncturevine by digging and by spot applications of herbicide, but more importantly, by aerating your soil, topdressing with compost, and by keeping off your lawn when it's wet and you're likely to cause soil compaction.

Warm-season Annual Broadleaf Weeds (cont.):

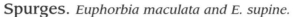

Purslane. *Portulaca oleracea.*

Thick, reddish stems with small oblong or egg-shaped fleshy leaves spread low over dry ground. Small yellow flowers turn to pods full of small black seeds in summer. The sap of this plant is clear. Purslane tolerates dry, hot soils and readily invades new or thin grass. Pull and remove plants, which will re-root if left in place. Regular deep watering of new grass will favor your turf over purslane.

Purslane

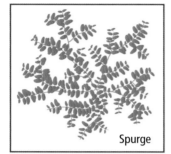

Spurge

Spurges. *Euphorbia maculata and E. supine.*

These spurges (spotted and prostrate), a relative of the poinsettia, are found in lawns and in the cracks of sidewalks as very flat plants, with low stems that radiate out from a central tap root. Tiny pale pink or white flowers grow at the bases of small, smooth, oval leaves that may be tinted red or have reddish spots. If you break the stem, milky fluid will come out. Spurges are found in thin, drought-stressed northern lawns. Deep, regular irrigation, the addition of compost and fall fertilization will help keep lawns free of spurges.

Warm-season perennials are those overgrown, sometimes creeping, things with lots of roots that come back in the same place, in the heat of the summer, year in and year out. Most of them are grasses or grass-like. Though they are tough, they create more headaches when pampered in summer, especially in cool season lawns where the desirable grasses can't benefit from summer fertilization due to heat. To control, fertilize and water in spring and fall, not in the summer, and mow high in summer. If you do water in the summer, water deeply and infrequently. Dig up warm-season perennials by hand and reseed or sod with your grass species. Many of the warm-season weeds are themselves warm-season turf grasses out of place in northern lawns.

Yellow nutsedge. *Cyperus esculentus.*

Nutsedge has triangular stems, a sure giveaway that it's a sedge and not a grass. The leaves are light green to yellow. Nutsedge has shallow roots and doesn't like dry soil, so water infrequently and deeply in the summer. High mowing also gives your grass an advantage over sedge.

Yellow Nutsedge

Bermudagrass. *Cynodon dactylon.*

(See page 356 for identification information). Bermudagrass spreads underground by rhizome and above ground by stolons and can take over cool-season lawns during summer in the transition zone. As a warm-season grass, it will turn brown in the winter. Bermudagrass tolerates compacted soils and likes high fertility, so fertilize only in the fall to help your cool-season turf win out, and while you're at it, aerate the soil. For serious infestations, you can kill bermudagrass with Roundup, Kleenup, or some other glyphosate-containing herbicide and then plant a new cool-season lawn in the fall, preferably with a more competitive species. Warning: leave a month or more to kill off bermudagrass, you'll probably need repeated applications.

Zoysiagrass. *Zoysia japonica*

(See page 358 for identification information). Zoysia is more cold-hardy than other southern turfgrasses, and so makes a natural weed in cool-season grasses as far north as southern New England. Zoysiagrass spreads by stolons and rhizomes and tolerates traffic. It browns out in fall until warm weather returns in mid spring. To contain, avoid summer watering and fertilization. To eliminate, kill it with repeated applications of glyphosate or dig up zoysiagrass and reseed a cool season grass in the fall.

Rust. Lawns infested with rust should be kept growing with adequate water and fertilization. Mow frequently, bagging and discarding clippings diligently.

Lawn disease

Diseases of grass are almost all caused by fungi. Even more than insects and weeds, fungi require conditions to be just right. Golf course managers create those conditions by fertilizing, mowing and watering frequently, which is why many managers regularly spread fungicides against fungal diseases. The use of herbicides and insecticides also make grass susceptible to disease by reducing populations of soil organisms that compete with or consume the fungi. The practices below reduce the vulnerability of your lawn to fungal disease.

1. Water deeply and infrequently. Water early in the morning, since night watering leaves grass blades wet. Fungi require a certain minimum length of time when the leaves are wet to establish.

2. Fertilize occasionally with compost or a slow release fertilizer, but do not over-fertilize. Too much nitrogen increases the susceptibility of grass to disease. Undernourished grass is susceptible to disease as well.

3. Topdress yearly with ¼ to ½ in. of compost or activated sewage sludge. Aerobically decomposed organic matter fertilizes the grass, while reducing the incidence and severity of turf diseases. This documented effect may be due to increased activity of soil organisms that feed on fungi and their spores.

4. Aerate, and dethatch yearly. This increases the vigor of the grass and permits air to circulate and dry out areas that would otherwise remain moist and anaerobic.

5. Mow to the correct height for the species, specifically avoid scalping your lawn. Use a sharp blade. Bag and discard clippings if infected with fungi.

6. Take a soil test and act on the recommendations. Soil outside the normal pH range is prone to fungal disease. Deficiencies of nutrients can make grass more susceptible to disease. NOTE: The over-application of one element can lead to deficiencies of other elements by displacement, which is another reason soil testing is important.

Common Grass Diseases

NOTE: The following discussion contains information on chemical controls of specific disease fungi. These fungicides should be used cautiously and as a last resort, after fully reading safety and environmental information.

Brown Patch/ Rhizoctonia Blight

Hits hardest when temperatures are in the low 80s and humidity is high, making it common in spring and fall in the south and in the summer in the north. High available nitrogen and a thick thatch layer favor the disease. Brown patch manifests as large spreading patches that start out as wilting grass and turn brown. Recovering grass in the middle may turn the patches into donut shapes. To control, use only slow-release fertilizers and avoid excessive nitrogen fertilization. Irrigate deeply when needed and in the morning only. Avoid traffic on affected areas. Mow affected areas last and collect the clippings. Spray with *Iprodione,* thiram, or triadimefon. Resistant tall fescue *(Rebel II, Wrangler)* and perennial ryegrass *(Manhattan II, Pennant)* varieties are available.

Dollar Spot

Dollar spot usually appears as small spots (2 to 4 in.wide) on the lawn (See photo, next page) that may later grow together. The spots eventually dry and bleach to a pale brown. In the morning, you may see fluffy strands of the mycelium. This disease usually hits between 60 and 80°, under low nitrogen and potassium conditions. Fog, dew, or light irrigation may start the disease, even if the soil is dry. Water deeply when needed early in the morning and apply a light dose of fertilizer high in nitrogen. Sewage sludge (like *Milorganite)* works better than chemical sources of fertilizer according to university research. Mow high and frequently and remove the clippings. Dethatch if needed. Spray with *Iprodione* or thiram. Resistant varieties of fine fescues *(Biljart, Scaldis),* perennial ryegrass *(Manhattan II),* and Kentucky bluegrass *(Adelphi, Midnight)* are available.

Powdery Mildew

Appears as light patches of gray or white during cool damp weather in early summer to fall. Powdery mildew attacks Kentucky bluegrass, zoysiagrass, and bermudagrass, especially when over-fertilized with nitrogen. Shade, temperatures between 60 and 70°F, and high humidity favor its growth. Avoid over-watering and over-fertilizing. Spray with *Iprodione* or triadimenfon. Resistant varieties of Kentucky bluegrass *(America, Chateau)* and red fescue *(Cindy, Flyer)* are available.

Red Thread

Starts out as water-soaked spots, like other diseases, but this fungus eventually forms red threads of mycelium between the grass blades. Red thread hits cool-season grasses in the spring and fall when temperatures are between 68 and 75° and humidity is high. Spray with triadimefon. Resistant varieties of Kentucky bluegrass *(Chateau),* perennial ryegrass *(Pennant),* and the fine fescues *(Biljart, Claudia)* are available.

Rust

Causes most damage to Kentucky bluegrass in summer and fall. Leaves will develop spots of rust-colored spores (See photo, previous page). Develops under moderately warm, humid conditions. Keep grass growing with morning watering and adequate fertilization, and mow frequently to remove spore spots. Spray with triadimefon. Resistant varieties include *America* and *Eclipse* Kentucky bluegrass and *Manhattan II* perennial ryegrass.

Stripe Smut

Susceptible varieties of bentgrass and Kentucky bluegrass will appear pale and stunted in the cool weather of spring and fall, developing stripes that start light and turn to black spore masses along the blades. Blades or the ends of blades die and become shredded as the disease advances. Dethatch and avoid over-watering and over-fertilizing to control stripe smut. Hot and dry weather will slow or even eliminate the disease. Resistant Kentucky bluegrass varieties include *America, Eclipse,* and *Midnight.*

Pythium Blight

Mostly affects cool-season grasses in hot, moist weather. It requires fourteen hours of rain, fog, or high humidity to get going. Small spots appear slimy and water soaked at first, then infected blades turn light brown. Smaller spots converge into larger blighted areas eventually. The white cotton of the mycelium may be visible on top of infected patches in the early morning. Water deeply and infrequently and avoid watering in the evening. Avoid walking on turf when

Dollar spot. Deep, infrequent morning irrigation, high mowing, and adequate slow-release nitrogen help control dollar spot.

Necrotic ring is a common disease of newly sodded bluegrass lawns. Water and fertilize adequately to keep infected grass alive.

wet. Reduce frequency of mowing. Spray *Ethazole* or *Chloroneb. Amigo* tall fescue is resistant to the disease.

Necrotic Ring Spot

Attacks Kentucky bluegrass and to a lesser extent bentgrass and fine fescue. Starts in spring but causes rings of dead grass to appear in summer (See photo above). Rings may be green in the center. Keep grass properly watered, mowed, and fertilized, with more frequent, morning watering needed to keep infected grass alive. Aerate if needed. Spray fenarimol or *Iprodione.*

Raking is part and parcel of just about any lawn renovation or repair project. If you haven't done it already, invest in some high-quality rakes.

disease, and frost damage or just plain kill your grass outright.

Repairing the lawn

Fortunately, planting, leveling, aerating, and dethatching doesn't always need to happen on a grand scale. Often a lawn will be great except for those spots where the dog urinated or the gas spilled or that buried tree trunk rotted away. Dealing with these small-scale ills is not different in principal than correcting large-scale problems, but you don't need all the expensive rental tools, and you don't need to call in a lot of IOUs for help. Below we cover leveling and planting small areas.

Core aerating

Power-core aerators require some physical strength and practice to control. Practice using them away from obstacles.

Use a core aerator once or twice yearly on compacted clay soils or soils with thatch problems. If you overseed a southern lawn in the fall, and it needs aerating, you might as well kill two birds with one stone and aerate before

Renovating & repairing

A tired lawn with thin grass, bare patches, and/or a thick layer of thatch can be revived with rental tools. A power-core aerator lets air and water into compacted soil and speeds the decomposition of the thatch layer. A power rake tears out thatch and scratches the soil to let the roots and stems breathe and allows wet havens of disease and insects to dry out. Both tools expose soil so new seed may be planted. See page 21.

These tools can be used in conjunction with herbicides to completely replace a sick, weedy lawn without tilling or exposing the soil to erosion. Power-raking is harder on grass and should generally be done at the beginning of the peak of the growing season, when the lawns will have the ability and time to recover—September for cool-season grasses and May or June for warm-season grasses. Power raking at other times can invite weeds,

Aerating tips:

- Consider hiring a lawn service to perform this strenuous task.
- Don't rent a solid-spike aerator.
- Haul the machine home in a trailer, truck, or van when empty of water.
- Practice aerating on an open area of your lawn.
- Go up and down, not across slopes.
- Raise tines when approaching stone or cement.
- Fertilize and seed after aerating, if desired.

preparing to overseed, as this will help the winter grass establish. Seeds that fall into the holes grow well since they are protected from drying. Aerating before fertilizing, adding lime, or adding sulfur helps these amendments penetrate. Avoid aerating in hot dry weather since the holes can dry out the soil, and avoid aerating when weeds like dandelions are in seed, since the weeds will root in the holes.

How to aerate

Water a dry, hard lawn thoroughly a couple of days before aerating to soften the soil. Rent a heavy aerator with hollow tines that pull plugs of soil from your lawn. Solid-tine aerators are not as good. Often, aerators have a place to put water to make them heavier. Don't try to transport them full of water, but do fill them before using them. Ask the rental center to demonstrate how to use the machine and, if needed, how to adjust any weights for use on hills. At home, flag obstacles like sprinkler heads and shallow pipes or wires. Set the tines at maximum depth and begin aerating an open

Aerate to let oxygen, water, nutrients, and even grass seed into compacted, heavy, or thatchy soil. You may also aerate before amending soil or before overseeding grass seed. Don't aerate a hot dry lawn, and don't aerate when lots of weeds are in seed.

part of your lawn. Aerate once in a parallel line pattern, then again perpendicular to the first pattern. Ultimately, you want holes every 2 or 3 in. Leave the soil plugs on the surface; they will help break down the thatch layer. If you want to get

rid of the plugs more quickly, you may break the plugs up with the back of a rake or by dragging a piece of chain link fencing over the lawn. This may work better after the plugs have dried out.

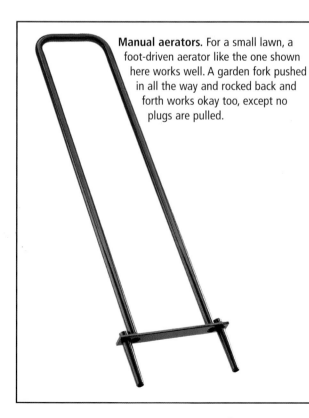

Manual aerators. For a small lawn, a foot-driven aerator like the one shown here works well. A garden fork pushed in all the way and rocked back and forth works okay too, except no plugs are pulled.

Dethatching rakes are handy for smaller areas, but for most folks they're too labor-intensive for use dethatching an entire yard.

Dethatching

Thatch is the buildup of dead plant matter that collects around the crowns of grass plants in a yard. By itself it isn't harmful, but it does make an excellent home for pests and fungi, and can prevent nutrients from reaching the living plant roots if it gets extremely heavy. The process of getting rid of thatch, called *dethatching,* can be done either with a heavy, sharp-tined dethatching rake or a rented power dethatcher.

Bermudagrass, bluegrass and zoysiagrass are good candidates for power raking, since they build up thatch and become choked, but other grasses can also develop the problem. A layer of thatch more than ½ in. thick is considered too much, and even small amounts of thatch buildup should be removed if you want to overseed your lawn.

Power raking will damage the grass in the short run. With warm-season grasses, power rake in late spring or early summer. With cool-season grasses, August or September is best. If you are power raking to overseed winter grass on a southern lawn, then do so in October or November, but not as aggressively as you would in the spring.

Rent a verticutter for thick thatch, especially on tough southern grasses, or if you are replanting a lawn and are not too concerned about damaging the existing grass. Rent a power rake for cool-season lawn maintenance.

What is thatch?

Thatch is a soft, spongy layer between the soil and the grass blades made up of roots, stems, and runners. It is not caused by leaving clippings on the lawn. You can't see thatch unless you dig a wedge out of your lawn, and then look for a peaty layer between the soil and where the grass emerges. Less than ½ in. of thatch is not a problem, and can actually protect the lawn against drying and frost damage. More than ½ in. can lead to an uneven, unmanageable lawn susceptible to lawn mower scalping, drought, cold, heat stress, and insects. Simply speaking, water, nutrients and the grass roots stay matted in the thatch layer instead of moving down into the soil where temperature and moisture levels are more constant. Zoysiagrass, bluegrass, and bermudagrass are all highly susceptible to thatch formation.

Causes of Thatch:
• Frequent, shallow watering
• Too much nitrogen fertilizer
• Infrequent mowing
• Overuse of pesticides

How to dethatch by power-raking

Set the tine depth. Lower the tines of a power rake to the pavement to adjust the depth the flails will penetrate.

Aggressive power raking will damage grass, and should be done prior to optimal growing conditions—early September for cool-season northern grasses and late spring for warm-season southern grasses. Exposure of dirt makes seeding possible.

Dethatching Options: Power rake tines vs. slit seeder (verticutter) blades

Power rakes. Flexible flails are used on power rakes. These are more popular on the softer, less thatchy, cool-season grasses of the north.

Slit seeders and verticutters use moving blades for a more aggressive cut. These are used for dethatching purposes on tough, southern grasses and for direct seeding everywhere.

Slit seeders are verticutters fitted with a hopper that accepts seed then injects it into the slits as it cuts. Load the hopper with seed and set it for the recommended spread rate for the species of grass you're planting (See pages 36 to 46).

Set the cutters so they rip into the ground about ¼ in. deep, then make parallel passes across the area to be overseeded. Keep an eye on the hopper to make sure you don't run out of seed.

Overseeding

Thin or damaged lawns often can be improved simply by doing some minor preparation, then adding fresh grass seed—called "overseeding." Exclusive of any soil amendments that may be needed, the primary preparation involves getting rid of thatch and roughening or scarifying the soil so the seed has somewhere safe to settle.

For overseeding an entire lawn, there's no better tool than a slit seeder or a verticutter. The first order of business is to set the cutters so they rip into the ground to the correct depth for seeding. To set the cutters, first put the machine on a hard surface. For a living lawn, set the blades to cut ⅛ to ¼ in. into the soil. You may go deeper on a lawn that's been killed with herbicides and will be completely reseeded. First, zero the blades by seeing where they just touch the pavement, and then add the necessary depth using the gauge as a guide.

Overseeding with a verticutter or a slit seeder

Using a verticutter. First mow the lawn as low as possible with your lawn mower. This low mowing is critical if you intend to seed. Run the machine over the yard in a parallel-line pattern. If you don't have a bagger, rake up the lawn after this first pass. If more dethatching is needed, run perpendicular to the first pattern and rake again. If you will be seeding, you must expose dirt between existing grass plants. For a very dense thatch, you might need to tackle dethatching over two sessions spaced months apart.

Using a slit seeder. If you will be planting with a slit seeder, less preparation is needed since the seed is injected into a furrow cut by the machine. You should still address a serious thatch problem prior to planting. You may compost the thatch if you maintain a hot pile; otherwise, throw out thatch that is infested with stolons and rhizomes from aggressive warm-season grasses that could become weeds in your garden.

Planting bare spots

For best results, repair bare spots in the late spring and early summer for warm-season grasses and in the early fall (preferable) or early spring for the cool-season grasses. This will save you the headache of trying to keep new grass alive when the weather and weeds are not in your favor.

Clear a bare spot of all weeds and straggling grass right out to where the grass is thick and healthy. If needed, correct problems that led to grass's decline. This may mean adjusting the spray patterns on a sprinkler system, removing a rock or other object from under the damaged area, or removing oil- or chemical-saturated soil and replacing it with fresh.

Prepare the ground as you would for a full lawn. Cover ground planted with sprigs or plugs with a thin layer of straw, compost or peat to keep the soil moist. If you use seed, you will either need to rake the seed and soil lightly until most of the seeds are covered, then cover it with a thin layer of straw; or, cover seed with ¼ in. of compost or peat without raking. Water the area thoroughly. Water only intermittently if runoff is a problem, particularly with seed, which is easily dislodged. Then, keep the area from drying out until the grass emerges, watering gradually more deeply and less frequently after that. Keep sprigged or plugged areas weeded.

1 Remove any weed roots, then incorporate compost or peat moss and starter fertilizer into the soil using a fork or shovel. Smooth the ground with a garden rake, tamp it down with a shovel, a roller, a hand tamper, or your feet. Smooth again.

2 When the soil is graded and tamped correctly, your feet will sink in no more that ½ in. If you will plant sod, the grade needs to be a little lower than the surrounding grass. Rough-up tamped soil with a rake then plant seeds, sprigs or plugs.

3 Topdress the unraked, broadcast seed—peatmoss is used above. Rake in seed that will be covered only with straw to provide better soil contact. Grass seed should never be buried more than ¼ in. Finally, lightly tamp down or roll planted area.

Accent Plantings & Border Treatments

Border treatments define your yard by creating shapes, adding colors and texture, and even introducing entirely new functions. If you want a lawn with relaxed curving edges, for example, you can achieve it by building border beds to establish those curves. For a quiet, shady spot to kick back with the newspaper, carefully selected, strategically planted trees, shrubs and perennials hold the key by providing shade and muffling noise—something that the grass lawn just can't do by itself.

In this section, we'll look at some fundamentals of creating and maintaining your lawn accent plantings—including the planning of non-grass areas; the establishment of edged beds; the planting and care of annuals and perennials, trees and shrubs, and groundcovers; and the use of mulches.

Planning & Design

In "An Exercise in Practical Imagination" on pages 00 to 00, we suggest a strategy for planning your yard so it will look and function as you'd like. Please take the time to review this section as you consider ways to embellish your yard with accent and border plantings in planting beds.

To begin, you need to be able to answer the following questions:

1) How much sunlight does the area get? Half a day of direct sun or a full day of dappled sun is usually enough for sun-loving and partial-sun-requiring plants. If your yard area doesn't get these minimum amounts of sun, you'll have to limit your plant selections to shade and part-shade plants. Keep in mind though, that while many shade plants can tolerate some morning sun, they may dry and burn in hot afternoon sun. So just as you shouldn't plant sun-loving plants in deep shade, neither should you plant shade plants in areas that receive more than a half-day of sunlight. Remember also that the north sides of buildings cast a longer shadow as summer progresses.

2) Are your growing seasons dry and will you irrigate regularly? Good garden centers and plant tags provide information on the moisture requirements of plants.

3) How tall and wide do the plant varieties you are considering become? Ignore the current size of plant material you are buying; rather, situate plant material with an eye to how it will look when it reaches its full size. Space plants according to recommendations on tags.

Once you've made these preliminary assessments, map out your planting beds on graph paper, paying close attention to make sure the dimensions and symbols are to scale. In the illustration below, we used a scale of one square equals one square foot. An accurate rendering such as this allows you to plan the bed completely before making any plant purchases or turning any dirt. Armed with a good plan, you'll know exactly how many plants of each species you need. Use information from your local garden center catalogs to select plants that will work with the size, the zone, and the light conditions of your planting area.

Design tips for accent planting

Know your square footage and light. Measure and record the spaces you're buying plants for, and note the light zone of each: sun, part-sun, shade or deep shade.

Work from back to front. When planting border beds, keep tall plants to the back and move forward with progressively smaller plants. Shrubs work well against the foundations of houses; short annuals and perennials make colorful accents in the foreground of a bed.

Be conscious of scale. Little plants at the nursery can get very big with time. Small yards need smaller beds, trees and shrubs. Big spaces need big trees and shrubs and/or wide masses of annuals or perennials.

Keep it simple, repeat masses. Too many different plants lead to chaos. Select a few species that work together, then plant each species in masses of three, five, seven or more (odd numbers work better). Repeat these masses to unify the landscape.

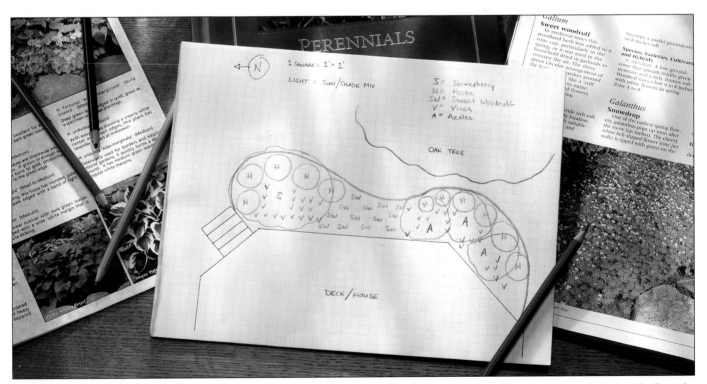

The plan shown above uses a one-foot-per-square scale. Each plant is allowed approximately the room it will require at maturity. Larger shrubs and trees may share space with smaller, shade-tolerant plants. You may even plant sun-loving varieties near young trees and shrubs that will take years to overgrow these underplantings.

Ornamentals: The meanings of the terms

Annuals: Ornamental annuals, by definition, die after one growing season. They are planted for intense, prolonged periods of bloom or showy foliage. A number of "annuals," such as the red *Pelargonium* geraniums in the photo above, are actually tender perennials that are grown in areas where they're killed by winter cold.

Perennials: Perennials die down to the ground after the growing season in temperate climates and, under favorable growing conditions, regrow from surviving underground parts. In the photo to the right, sweet woodruff (flowering), hostas (big, variegated leaves), and *Epimedium* (upper right of photo) complement one another in a shade garden.

PERENNIALS

Woody Plants: Shrubs, trees, and woody vines all have above-ground parts that do not die back and can survive periods of dormancy. This characteristic allows woody plants to get bigger every year, sometimes for many years. Spring-flowering trees (like the ornamental pears pictured to the right) use sugars stored from the previous year to put out early, stunning floral displays.

Groundcovers: Groundcovers are perennial or woody plants used in masses to form a mat of a single species over the ground. Most plants used as groundcovers may also be used individually or in smaller numbers in mixed planting beds; hence, "groundcover" describes a particular plant only when it is used in masses. *Pachysandra,* the groundcover featured below, thrives in moist, acid soils beneath trees.

NOTE: Contrary to a popular misconception, "groundcover" does not refer only to very low plants, such as Creeping Charlie, that have the general look and feel of a lawn and can even withstand light foot traffic.

WOODY PLANTS

GROUNDCOVERS

Preparing a Planting Bed

Plan to plant perennials, shrubs or trees in the spring, late summer, or early fall, when at least a month of mild temperatures (neither hot nor freezing) follows. Use your scale plan drawing as a reference for laying out the planting area. Ground-marking paint, a hose or a rope can be used to outline the area.

First, turn the soil with a garden fork to ten inches deep. Amend the forked soil with a three-inch layer of compost, composted manure, peat or other organic material (See "Estimating Quantities," page 00, for calculating volumes of materials in cubic yards). Add a complete fertilizer, following the label directions for application and coverage. If you are incorporating quantities of un-decomposed organic matter, like leaves or sawdust, add extra fertilizer to help the material decompose without robbing the plants of nitrogen. A soil test can alert you to to the need for micronutrients, sulfur, or lime (see page 00), but it's best not to use these unless you're positive they're needed—they can harm plants if added indiscriminately. Roto-till to mix the soil, compost, and amendments.

If you are using a sod kicker on grass, cut just inside your bed line with the kicker to establish the border. Next, slice along your bed border with a flat-nosed garden spade, cutting a vertical edge eight to ten inches deep. Toss the dirt to the middle or back of your bed and remove the sod chunks and weeds. Your edge may seem deep, but you'll lose most of this height after grading the bed later. Dig an edge trench along pavement as well to make grading easier. Once the dirt is removed in this manner, lay any edging material you intend to use around the perimeter of the planting bed.

Next, shape the soft, turned soil of the planting bed with the back of a garden rake. Avoid creating steep slopes near the edges of the bed, as steep slopes are more prone to erosion of soil and loss of any mulch or loose topping. It's best to start the slope at the back of the bed and distribute the drop-off as evenly as possible across the bed. In the process of grading, the level of the amended soil in the planting bed area may approach or even surpass the surrounding lawn area. If you find this is happening, don't compact the soil, remove it. Ideally, the surface of the soil in the graded bed should be two to four inches below ground level. If you'll be adding mulch, you'll need three or four inches of lip at lawn and pavement edges to keep the mulch from washing out of the bed—generally, landscape edging is installed to provide the lip. For an un-mulched bed, leave an open border of an inch or two at pavement edges and three inches next to lawns to keep the grass from growing into the bed.

CLEARING THE PLANTING AREA

Kill vegetation in the planting area. Water a day or two in advance of spraying vegetation with glyphosate (Roundup, Kleenup, GLYPHOS). Repeat procedure two weeks later for tough weeds and wait for herbicide to fully kill the plants. Roots and stumps of dead plants may be left in place if they do not interfere with planting. Dig up woody plants and large perennials that will grow back or interfere with planting. Use a spade, mattock, and axe. Kill living stumps left in place with concentrated glyphosate painted on the fresh cut.

CAUTION: Does this scene look familiar? Using the old truck and a towing chain to pull out a stubborn stump or woody shrub is an idea that many of us have had at one time or another, and perhaps even attempted once. But not twice. Under the right conditions it can work, but more likely than not, you'll experience one or more of the following outcomes: damage to your vehicle or anything else that's in the path of the stump or trunk when it catapults out of the ground under force; deep furrows in your lawn created by spinning tires; damage from chain snapback if the object being pulled snaps. In short, it's very dangerous. You're much better off using saws and shovels for the extraction.

EXCAVATING & PREPARING THE SOIL

Peel out sod in the planting area. Simplify and the job by renting a sod kicker (shown here) from a garden center or hardware store. If you've used an herbicide to kill the grass, the sod may be tilled under instead of removed. If your planting bed is on a steep slope, it is sometimes necessary to forego proper bed preparation and plant directly into sod that's been killed with herbicide. The roots systems of the dead sod hold the soil in place.

TIP: If you're careful removing the sod, you can often re-lay it in another part of the yard. Or, you can re-use it by composting it. Turn the sod upside down and layer it into a compost pile that's dish-shaped on top to collect water. In a year, the compost from the sod may be sifted and used as a lawn topdressing.

Clear out debris. Buried building debris, old pavers, edgings, gravel, cypress mulches, plastic sheeting, large rocks and all other debris that could potentially interfere with the growth of your new plants must be removed and disposed of before preparing and amending the soil for a new planting bed.

Amend soil with specific fertilizer elements and lime or sulfur, according to the results of a soil test. Fork and then till in 3 or 4 in. of organic matter. Even if no soil test is done, a balanced fertilizer may also be tilled in at this time. A roto-tiller will make quick work of the soil blending and turning task.

Edging

A well-defined edge is necessary for a planting bed to look neat and "intentional." Without one, the plants will sprawl out into the lawn, the lawn grass will migrate into the bed, and the effectiveness of the planting bed will be reduced. In most cases, edging is used to define the border. It may be just the raw, spade-cut side of the sod, or it can be any of a number of edging materials.

Edging is not needed if the planting bed abuts a paved surface. If material from the planting bed does wash onto the paved surface, you'll need to excavate material from the planting bed to lower its surface.

Edging Options

• *The Spade Edge.* Many gardeners prefer to take a laid-back approach to edging, simply relying on the sharp edges of the cut sod to create a border for their planting bed. This method does have some advantages that make it worth considering. It's very easy to make; just cut the sod off vertically at the side of the lawn, leaving a short "cliff." Rhizomes that grow out of this edge will be discouraged when they encounter only air, although some will certainly find their way into the bed. The impermanence of the spade edge is something you may find desirable; there will be nothing to dig up if you decide to move the boundary of the bed.

A spade-cut edge will need to be recut at least once a year to keep creeping grasses (or creeping garden plants) in check.

• *Plastic Band Edging.* Easily the most common edging product, plastic band edging (also called landscaper's edging) is inexpensive and easy to install on straight or curved beds. It helps keep grasses that spread by rhizomes, like bluegrass and bermudagrass, from spreading into beds. Don't try to use plastic edging to contain raised beds or to keep mulch off a path—they are too flexible for aboveground use. If you live in the north, get plastic edges that are staked in place to resist frost heave. You'll find quite a range of qualities in plastic edging. The more expensive plastic edging is thicker and more rigid, which makes it easier to install and longer-lasting.

• *Brick Edging.* In addition to contributing attractive color and new texture to your yard, brick edging provides a mowing strip so you can mow right up to the edge of the grass. You can use just about any kind of brick product to make edging. Concrete landscaping pavers tend to be the most durable, and you'll find them in many sizes, colors and shapes that offer a number of layout options. But ordinary building bricks will work just fine, too. If you have any leftover or reclaimed bricks laying around, put them to work as edging, and feel free to mix and match as you please.

THE SPADE EDGE

Slice the sod. After outlining the planting bed, use a spade (a flat spade works best) to make deep, perpendicular slices all around the border. Remove all weeds and plants to create a gap between the cut edge and the border plants. Avoid stepping on the sod too close to the border area.

Create a buffer zone. A band of mulch between grass and bed plants enhances the border effect and suppresses migration. The mulch should be just below ground level. In the photo above, cypress mulch is used, mostly because of its ability to mat and resist spill-over into the lawn. Avoid stone mulches—they'll mix with the soil and never decompose.

PLASTIC BAND EDGING

Use plenty of stakes. The spade-cut edge can be made impervious to aggressive grass rhizomes with plastic edging. The tubular crown of the edging should be set so half of the crown is below ground level to keep the edging clear of lawn mower blades. Generous use of metal edging stakes helps keep the edging safe from movement caused by ground forces, including frost heave. Make sure to use the correct connectors to join the mating ends of edging strips (higher quality plastic edging comes in shorter rolls that require more joints).

Backfill with soil. Using an inverted garden rake, rake the soil in the planting bed right up to the edging. The pressure of the soil against it helps keep the edging stationary. Move or remove soil as needed to provide room for mulch or other top dressing materials.

BRICK EDGING

Prepare a base for the bricks. Dig a trench for bricks or pavers. The trench should be about ½ in. deeper than the thickness of your bricks. Bury a strip of landscape fabric at the bottom of the trench, then cover the strip with a ½-to-1-in.-thick layer of coarse sand. Lay the bricks or pavers onto the sand base. The top of each brick should be at or slightly above ground level to create a mowing strip. Press down on each brick to set it into the base.

Fill in with soil. Cut back any overhanging landscape fabric that will be visible, then back-fill up to the bricks so the soil covers roughly half the thickness. Backfill with soil between the bricks and the lawn, as well.

Mulch

Mulch is any material that covers the ground between plants. Mulch keeps the ground moist and suppresses the new growth of weeds. Loose mulches let air, and water through. Perennial weeds that already have roots can usually push through loose mulch. Organic loose mulches, like shredded and chipped wood products, improve the soil as they rot. Barrier mulches and products suppress growth of all weeds, not just seedlings, but plastic and fabric barrier mulches prevent organic mulches on top from adding organic matter to the soil. Barrier mulches need to be covered with loose mulch to keep them from degrading in the sun or blowing away. Thick mulches used only during the winter protect tender plants from winter kill.

Typical Loose Mulches

Chipped mulches. Bark and wood chips look nice, but do not hold together well on slopes or in other areas where they are not easily contained. Chips generally last longer than shredded products. Do not turn cypress chips into the soil—they decompose very slowly and cause drainage problems. If you are renovating a bed, remove chipped mulch first, work the soil, then replace the mulch with fresh product.

Shredded mulches. Shredded bark and wood hold together better on slopes than chips, they can be purchased in bulk (as opposed to bagged), and they look good. Mulches like the shredded cypress bark shown here are expensive, though, and need to be replenished yearly.

Chipped mulches decompose slowly but do not stick together well.

Shredded mulches hold to slopes better. They rot more quickly than chipped mulches.

Shredder/chipper wastes are often free, and have a higher nutrient content than most commercial mulches.

Cocoa mulch is expensive, but is darker and more refined than some of the other organic mulches.

Stone mulches are low maintenance at first, but they can burn plants in hot sun and eventually become contaminated with dirt and debris.

Winter mulches completely cover cut back perennials. They prevent thawing and re-freezing and winter drying of tender plants.

Landscape fabric lets water and air through but keeps weeds down. Use under mineral mulches.

Newspaper blocks grass and other perennial weeds and then rots away after these weeds die.

Black plastic is not good for plants but may be needed near buildings to keep water away from the foundation.

Shredder/chipper wastes.

Municipalities and yard waste collection facilities often give shredder/chipper wastes away free or for a very low cost. They are the ground-up remains of branches, leaves and logs. These mulches vary in quality, but after a month or so exposed to the elements, it becomes more difficult to distinguish shredder/chipper wastes from more expensive, commercial shredded mulches.

Organic byproducts. Marsh hay, cocoa shells, buckwheat hulls, partially composted farm animal bedding, and other byproducts of agriculture and forestry make fine mulches. Avoid products that may contain weed seeds, such as hay.

Mineral Mulches. Stone mulches laid on landscape fabric create a distinct design effect, but do have some disadvantages. Vegetation that falls on the mulch eventually rots and, along with dust and dirt, forms a layer of compost within the mulch that supports weeds. Removal and replacement of a stone mulch that has bonded with dirt and compost is difficult. Reserve mineral mulches for accessible, cleanable areas with few plants.

Winterizing Mulches. These are thick, fluffy mulches applied to newly planted areas or to plants that may be susceptible to winter kill. Winter mulches include straw, leaves, and pine branches, which are applied six to 12 inches thick after the ground freezes or is close to freezing. They are left in place until spring.

Weed Barriers

Newspapers and cardboard. When layered on the soil or sod around plants, wet newspapers or cardboard present a temporary barrier to tough perennial weeds. Use newspapers with predominantly black ink. Cover newspaper and cardboard with soil or another mulch to hold it in place. The paper, cardboard, and mulch will rot in place, improving the soil structure after suppressing weeds.

Landscaping Fabric. Used mostly in exterior construction projects, such as installing patios, landscape fabric can be installed under rock mulches to prevent perennial weeds from sprouting. It does allow water and air to get through, so it may be used around plants. Though landscaping fabric is permanent, weeds eventually colonize the compost and dirt that settles on top of the fabric. When covered with loose organic mulches, fabric will prevent those organic materials from improving the soil beneath.

Black plastic. Not considered appropriate for gardening purposes by most professionals, black plastic is often used as a weed barrier by homeowners. Unlike landscape fabric, it does not permit air and water to get through, and it will degrade more rapidly than you might think, creating a mess that deteriorates the general condition of the soil.

Tips for applying mulch:

• Fine, dense mulches should be spread in 1-in.-thick layers; medium-density mulches, like shredded bark, should be spread two or three inches thick; very airy mulches, like salt marsh hay, need to be spread at least 6 in. deep; winter mulches must be at least 6 to 12-in. thick to be successful insulators.

• Do not pile mulches (except winter mulches) right up against plants unless you know that the plant tolerates close mulching. Instead, form basins or "donuts" around plants with the mulch.

• Avoid applying mulch to slopes. A mulch may be temporarily held to a slope with course netting and stakes, however, until a permanent ground cover takes over.

NOTE: The information in this section presumes that you are planting in a new planting bed that has been prepared and amended according to the information on the previous pages. For standalone accent plants, prepare the planting area as if it were a tiny planting bed, according to the information on pages 128 to 133.

Experiment with layouts while the plants are still in their containers. Allow the recommended distance between plants, since the plants will get much bigger—although it may take perennials two or three growing seasons, or even longer, to fill in completely.

Adding plants to a new planting bed

Once your soil is amended and tilled you are ready to plant. With small plants that come in cell trays or pots, you may wish to lay the mulch before planting. For larger potted plants, plant before mulching. Either way, lay out the plants, while still in their containers, prior to planting. The goal is to find a natural-looking arrangement that allows each plant its approximate recommended space. Experiment a bit until you find a layout that pleases you.

How to plant your plants

Remove plants from the pots, unless the pots are made of peat. Break roots free with your hands, or use a knife if the roots are growing in a tight circle. Take care to keep the root system or ball intact. You may plant in a slight depression to facilitate watering, but the soil should not run over the stem, as this can cause rot. Dig the hole a bit shallow if you will be laying thick mulch that would otherwise run high on the stem. The majority of the pot ball of even small cell-tray plants needs to be embedded in dirt, however.

Do not force the plant into a hole that's too small or too shallow. When the plant is in place, backfill around it with loose soil (don't pack it) then cover the area around the plant with two or three inches of mulch.

TIPS FOR PLANTING ACCENT & BORDER PLANTS

Provide irrigation. Lay soaker hoses or drip irrigation lines before you begin planting.

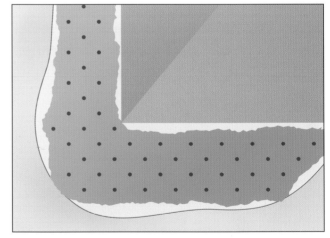

Plant single-species beds in intersecting diagonal rows. Plants are best spaced in roughly triangular patterns. This allows equidistant planting and prevents the "garden row" effect. When planting a single plant species as a groundcover, as in the illustration above, the plants may be set out in intersecting diagonal rows. Spacing of plants in mixed gardens varies with species and is looser and more natural.

HOW TO PLANT LARGE ACCENT PLANTS

1 Support the root ball with one hand while pulling off the pot. Make three vertical cuts in the rootball and peel out some roots if the rootball is tightly circled with roots (the hosta shown above does not require that roots be peeled free).

2 Plant annuals and perennials to the same depth they were growing in their container. Set the plant in the hole, positioned so it is perfectly upright. Fill in around it with soil, taking care not to cover up any part of the stem. Do not overpack the soil.

3 Larger plants are most easily mulched after planting. Keep the mulch thick between plants and thin near the stems. Heavy mulch piled against a plant stem can promote disease.

TIPS FOR PLANTING

Small plants. Lay mulch before planting small plants that come in cell trays, like many ground-covers and the annuals shown above. If the soil is soft, you may push aside the mulch and press the root ball into the soil with only a little digging. Again, you want the top of the root ball at about soil level, but with small plants you'll sometimes plant a little high so the plant stem is not buried too deeply in mulch.

Extricating stubborn plants. To remove a jammed plastic pot from the root ball, slice the pot in a couple of spots with a utility knife. Do not use the stem as a handle to try to get the plant out of the pot.

Tips for Planting on Slopes

Cut soil from up-slope to build a solid berm down-slope, creating a mini terrace that collects water for the plant.

• **Use the no-till method** of planting by spraying old vegetation with glyphosate herbicide and planting without turning the soil. As an alternative to broadcast fertilizing, put a little time-release balanced fertilizer in the bottom of each planting hole. This prevents fertilizer run-off.

• **If sloped ground is tilled,** it's useful to shape the soil into a series of ridges and troughs that run across the slope. These contour ridges keep water from running down the slope and creating erosion gullies. In the tillage process, you may incorporate organic matter and any amendments called for by a soil test, which is one reason to use this method instead of no-till. Make ridges by tilling across the slope or by forming the troughs and crests with a shovel.

DIVIDING OLD PLANTS:
Why and When to Do It

Most overgrown perennials may be divided to increase the size of flowers, improve the health of the plants, and as a cost-free way to acquire new plants for your yard. Divide fall-blooming plants in the spring, leaving time for the plants to establish before hot weather. Divide spring- and summer-flowering plants in late summer or early fall, at least six weeks before the ground freezes.

Tip: *Water dry ground well a day or more before dividing; the ground should be moist but not muddy when you divide the plants.*

HOW TO DIVIDE PLANTS

1 Cut the top foliage down to six inches, or by two-thirds, to reduce evaporation and to make working with the plants easier. Then, dig up the plants to be divided, preserving as much of the root system as is practical.

2 Plants with multiple stems may be pulled apart so that each new plant has three to five stems. Plants with thick, fleshy central crowns (like the hosta above) should be divided with a spade or knife so each section has some of the crown. Plants that grow by rhizome, such as irises, can be cut or broken apart. Each piece of rhizome should have a fan of leaves and some roots.

3 Discard any rotten or dead plant material and remove all weeds and weed roots. Keep the uprooted plants moist and plant at the same level they were growing at previously. Leave plenty of room for the new plants to grow to their full size, as crowding usually reduces flowering. Keep plants watered until established.

Remove spent flowers or flower stalks. This is called "deadheading." With many plants, deadheading encourages new blooms. With the hostas shown here, it simply neatens up the plants.

Topdress annually. A yearly topdressing of compost and fertilizer followed by a fresh layer of mulch supplies nutrients and valuable organic matter to your garden plants while keeping weeds down.

Winterize. Perennials that are growing a zone too far north, as well as new or recently transplanted perennials, benefit from the protection of a winter mulch. Wait until the ground is frozen or almost frozen to apply the mulch. Remove it gradually when the ground starts to thaw in the spring.

Caring for Plants, New and Old

Your new planting will need a little extra care at first. Importantly, you'll need to water as soon as the plants begin to wilt, possibly every day in hot weather. Gradually move to deep, infrequent watering as the roots establish. Most mature perennials prefer that the ground dries to a depth of 8 to 12 inches between waterings. If you have a zoned in-ground watering system (See page 00), set the controls so mulched perennial beds and groundcover zones receive less frequent watering than the lawn once the plants are established. But when you do water, water deeply.

Hand-pull weeds that push through the mulch. Deadhead to encourage flowering. Fertilize yearly with a slow-release balanced fertilizer for flowering plants. Alternatively or additionally, spread an inch or two of compost or composted manure on top of the old mulch yearly, and replenish the mulch on top of that.

Cut back perennials to two or three inches when they start to go dormant in the fall. Uproot annuals. Apply a layer of mulch around recently planted or winter-tender perennials.

GROUNDCOVER OPTIONS: The Moss Lawn

If you can't beat it, join it. Rather than battle moss to get grass to grow in a shady area, take pride in a lawn of moss. To encourage moss, remove weeds and leaves diligently. A light application of an acid-balance fertilizer is beneficial to moss, but too much fertilizer will burn the moss and encourage weeds. To increase the size of a moss lawn, remove other plants from the expansion area, save any pieces of moss, and till in plenty of peat moss and compost. Transplant plugs of moss every two or three inches into the new area. Keep the area watered and weeded until the moss takes over.

GROUNDCOVER OPTIONS: Sweet Woodruff

Sweet woodruff thrives in moist shade where grass languishes, and adds a touch of the woodland to this backyard suburban tree base.

GROUNDCOVERS: Choosing Alternatives to a Grass Lawn

Nothing compares to grass for sunbathing, tag football, or for providing a fun, safe surface for toddlers and children to frolic upon on a mild summer afternoon. But grass doesn't grow well everywhere, and in some places it's more trouble than it's worth.

Rather than fighting constantly to keep moss and weeds out of a shady area, or living your life in dread of that weekly mowing of a steep, dangerous slope, why not minimize your worries by shrinking your lawn and planting groundcover? Groundcovers are perennials and vines that often require less maintenance than grass, while looking great. They usually don't need to be fertilized or mowed and often require less water than lawns to stay green.

You can get a sense for which groundcovers thrive in your area by observing (and, if possible, getting leaf samples from) nicely landscaped homes in your area. A good garden center should provide more information on groundcovers. But because *groundcovers* is not actually a botanical category, you may not find a groundcover area at your local garden center.

Areas planted to groundcovers described as 'invasive' should have physical barriers between them and other garden areas. Barriers include masonry paths, drives, houses, and regularly mowed lawns. Edging material may or may not block ground covers that spread underground and definitely will not block plants that spread above ground by stolons or rooting branches.

Here's a little exercise to help you decide which areas of your yard should remain planted in grass, and which might be good candidates for groundcover instead.

English Ivy aggressively covers humus-rich slopes, stabilizing the soil and eliminating the need for dangerous lawn maintenance. Keep it weeded and trimmed away from areas where it's not wanted. ***NOTE:*** *Ivy and other groundcovers labeled "invasive" may spread uncontrollably if not contained or regularly pruned.*

The Lawn Audit

Walk around your property with a critical eye. Look for places where grass is hard to water or mow, or seems to take extra care to keep healthy and weed free. Narrow strips and islands of grass, dry shady areas, slopes, and areas immediately around the trunks of trees are places that may be candidates for ground-covers or mulch. An area of heavy foot traffic may need a walkway of stone or another durable material.

Trace out the lawn you want to save by cutting its outline with your lawn mower. When possible, avoid sharp angles and isolated peninsulas of lawn, opting for graceful curving lines that are easy to follow with the mower and simple to divide into convenient water-ing zones.

Make a new lawn plan based on your lawn audit and your needs and desires. Consider mowing time and watering schedules. Ask yourself if the new grass area(s) accommodate the needs of your family. If you are satisfied, it's time to decide how to cover the area that will no longer be lawn.

Pachysandra is easy on the eye in the shady spaces below trees and requires a fraction of the maintenance of grass once it's established.

Blue fescue or sheep fescue, *Festuca ovina glauca*, grows from zone 5 to 8. Plant blue fescue in full to part sun. This 4 to 12-in. high bunch grass has blue-gray, spiky, bunched foliage and is drought tolerant. Plant 6 to 12 in. apart. Divides well.

Bugleweed or ajuga (ah-joo-guh), *Ajuga reptans*, grows from zones 3 to 9. Most varieties like part shade, but bronze and purple-leafed varieties thrive in sun. Bugleweed, about 8 in. tall, forms a dense, rapidly spreading mat and develops spikes of blue to violet flowers. This invasive groundcover prefers moist, rich soil. Plant 6 to 12 in. apart. Divides easily.

Chamomile, *Chamaemelum nobile*, grows from zones 3 to 8 in full sun (preferable) to part shade. It grows 6 to 12 in. high with fine, fragrant foliage and yellow flowers. Chamomile tolerates hot dry conditions and can be mowed and even endures light, occasional foot traffic. It does well between stepping-stones. Plant 6 to 12 in. apart. Divides well.

Creeping thyme (time), *Thymus praecox arcticus*, is hardy to zone 3. This fine-leafed spreading plant prefers full sun. Creeping thyme grows just 3 to 6 in. tall, with aromatic foliage, small leaves, and pink, red, purple, or white flowers. It prefers dry, infertile soils and may be stepped on and mowed like a lawn. Creeping thyme is often used between pavers or in the stones of a retaining wall. Plant 6 to 10 in. inches apart. Divide to propagate.

Leadwort, *Ceratostigma plumbaginoides,* grows in zones 5 to 9 in full sun to part shade. The 8 to 12 in. plants with shiny green foliage fill in after the soil warms in late spring. Foliage turns reddish in the fall. Half-inch blue flowers bloom from late summer through fall. Tolerates poor, dry soil. Plant 8 to 12 in. apart. Propagate by division in the spring.

Junipers, *Juniperus chinensis, J. horizontalis,* grow in zones 3 to 9 in full sun. They are low (6 in. to 2 ft., depending on species and variety), spreading, coniferous shrubs with blue-green to gray-green evergreen needles and blue berries. Junipers prefer well-drained, dry soil once established and are very useful for slopes. They are low maintenance. Plant 2 to 5 ft. apart, depending on variety.

Kinnikinnick, manzanita or bearberry, *Arctostaphylus uva-ursi*, grows in full sun in zones 2 to 10. This is a shrubby plant that grows just 6 to 12 in. high. Kinnikinnick has shiny evergreen foliage, white flowers in spring, and red fruit later. It prefers acid soil and is suited to slopes and windy, dry locations. Deer won't eat it. Plant 1 to 2 ft. apart in late fall or early spring.

Stonecrop sedums, *Sedum spurium, S. kamtschaticum, S. ternatum* and others, grow in zones 3 to 10 in sun to shade, depending on species and variety. The sedums range from 2 to 24 in. high, but the short, mat-forming varieties like goldmoss stonecrop are most suitable for groundcover. Most spread along the ground with rooting runners. Fleshy evergreen or deciduous (depending on zone) foliage may have red tips and the plants bear yellow or pink flowers. They will grow on poor, rocky, and dry soil, tolerating drought. They spread very rapidly under the right conditions and may be invasive. Plant 9 to 12 in. apart. Propagates easily by division.

Creeping lilyturf, *Liriope spicata*, grows from zone 4 to 10 in sun or shade. The plant spreads underground, forming mounds of grassy leaves 6 to 12 in. high and spikes of lavender to white flowers in summer. Creeping lilyturf tolerates poor soil but not traffic. It is grown mostly in the south. Cut off and compost old growth in spring. Plant 12 in. apart. Divide to propagate.

English Ivy, *Hedera helix*, includes varieties hardy to zone 5, but more are available in zones 7 to 9. Plant in deep shade or sun. This spreading, mat-forming vine will cover the ground and any other horizontal or vertical surface. The lobed leaves of English ivy are dark green, yellow, variegated, purple, or light green, depending on the variety. Ivy has insignificant flowers. Slow to establish, ivy grows rapidly after the first year. Ivy is very invasive, and can damage the siding of buildings. Plant 12 to 18 in. apart for rapid infill.

Native meadows

An attractive alternative to traditional lawns and planting beds is the meadow of native species. Like native prairies, such plantings comprise a mix of grasses, broadleaf perennials and legumes, a beneficial family of plants that fix nitrogen from the air, thus fertilizing the plant community. The native grasses, like buffalograss and wheatgrass, can be mowed like any other lawn grass and endure foot traffic.

There is a wide variety of plants native to any given area in the United States, so gardeners who wish to create alternative, ecologically-sensitive landscapes have a fine range of cultural options from which to choose.

Native meadow and prairie plants require little water and no fertilizer once they are established. Fertilizing a native planting with nitrogen tends to drive out the legumes and invites weedy species to invade. At first natives need to be kept weeded, but eventually they will hold their own against weeds.

The prairie planting above is suited to full sun locations in the midwest and plains states. It includes switchgrass, Indiangrass, little bluestem, purple prairie clover, Illinois bundle flower, partridge pea and Maximilian sunflower.

Ferns include various species and genera in a division of plants that once predominated on Earth, and that predates plants that make flowers and seeds. Ferns make neither. Ferns come in sizes from small to gigantic and spread by rhizomes. Each zone has adapted fern species. Most grow well in the deep to part shade of trees. Most prefer humus-rich, acid soils. Ferns mix well with bulbs and many ground covers. Visit a nursery for adapted species in your area.

Goutweed or bishop's weed, *Aegopodium podagraria,* is hardy to zone 3 and grows in sun to shade. Goutweed foliage is light green or green and white (variegated) and 12 in. high. Flower stalks shoot up above the foliage in early summer bearing umbels of tiny flowers. The plant spreads aggressively in practically any soil by underground rhizomes. Goutweed responds well to two or three mowings in a year, especially in sun, where old leaves may become brown. The plant is very invasive. Plant 6 to 12 in. apart. Propagate by division.

Hostas or plantain lilies, *Hosta crispula, H. plantaginea* and others, grow in zones 3 to 9 in part shade and shade, with darker varieties preferring more shade. The plants grow 8 to 24 in. high, depending on variety. Hundreds of varieties are planted mainly for their foliage. Leaves are large to very large and from deep blue-green to yellow-green to variegated. Lavender or white flowers are borne singly on tall stalks, and are relatively small. Some varieties have fragrant flowers and/or flowers that are a little larger and more interesting. Hostas are tolerant of dry soil, but they will look better in rich, moist, well-drained soil. They are easy to divide. Spacing varies.

Lily-of-the-valley, *Convallaria majalis*, grows in zones 2 to 7 in part shade and shade. Lily-of-the-valley grows 12 in. tall and spreads aggressively by underground rhizomes. Broad, pointed, dark-green leaves accompany arching stems lined with white, fragrant, bell-shaped flowers in late spring. This woodland lily is easily propagated by division. It requires little maintenance but is at its best in rich, moist, well-drained soil. Plant 4 in. apart.

Mondo grasses, *Ophiopogon japonicus* and *O. planiscalpus*, are found mainly in zones 8 to 10, though some *O. planiscalpus* varieties are hardy to zone 6. This popular southern groundcover thrives in part sun and shade, but needs protection from midday sun in hot areas. Mondo grass grows 6 to 12 in. tall, depending on species and variety. Leaves are dark green to purple and grass-like. Look for small blue flowers and blue berries, which may be hidden by the foliage. Prefers rich, well-drained soil. May be divided in spring and fall. Space 6 to 12 in. apart, depending on variety.

Pachysandra, *Pachysandra terminalis*, grows in zones 5 to 8 in the shade. The 8-to-12-in. high plants grow in spreading clumps. Green and variegated foliage varieties are available; the flowers are insignificant. Likes rich, moist, acid soil. Plant 6 to 8 in. apart in soil amended with peat moss and compost. Apply a mulch. Grows well with other acid-loving woodland plants like azaleas and rhododendrons. Plant 6 in. apart.

Creeping Phlox, *Phlox stolonifera*, grows in zones 2 through 8 in part to full shade. The 3-to-5-in. plants mix well with other low groundcovers (it is pictured here with *Vinca*). Masses of pink, blue or white flowers bloom in late spring. Prefers moist, fertile soil. Plant 12 to 24 in apart. Propagate by division after flowering.

Green-and-gold or Golden star, *Chrysogonum virginianum*, grows in zones 5 through 8 in part to full shade (full shade in southern climates). The 8-to-12-in. plants spread by rooting stems and rhizomes. They are evergreen in the south. In the spring, 2-in.-wide yellow flowers bloom heavily, then sporadically all summer. Plant 12 to 18 in. apart in rich, moist soil. Propagate by division in the fall.

Periwinkle or myrtle, *Vinca minor* and *V. major*, is a different species in the north than in the south, though both will grow in zones 7 and 8. *V. minor* grows from zones 4 to 8, *V. major* from 7 to 9. *V. minor* is 6 to 12 in. tall, *V. major* can grow up to 2 ft. tall. Both spread above ground in light to moderate shade, tolerating more sun in the north. Both have shiny smallish green or variegated leaves and lilac-blue or white blossoms. The plants cover wet and dry areas, with *V. major* more tolerant of dry soil. Both are invasive. Plant 12 to 18 in. apart.

Spotted lamium or spotted dead nettle, *Lamium maculatum*, grows in zones 3 through 8 in part sun to deep shade. The plant is 12 to 14 in. high with white or silver and green leaves and pink, lavender, or white flowers. It prefers rich, moist soil, but tolerates dry soil in the shade. Lamium is invasive, spreading aggressively underground by rhizomes. Contain with an edging. Plant 12 to 14 in. apart. May be cut down to 2 to 6 in. once or twice a season to stimulate fresh growth.

Sweet woodruff, *Galium odoratum,* grows from zones 4 to 8 in part to full shade. Grows 6 to 8 in. tall. Leaves are light green, divided and whorled around the stem. Small, fragrant white flowers grow in open clusters in the spring. Sweet woodruff does best in rich, moist soil. It is aggressive against weeds but compatible with shrubs. Plant 6 in. apart. For a dense, low carpet, trim back mature plants in spring, leaving some growth near the soil.

Winter creeper, *Euonymus fortunei*, grows north to zone 4 or 5. The plant likes full sun to deep shade, depending on variety. This low-spreading shrub covers the ground with waxy green foliage that turns dark purple in winter, offsetting the pink fruit. Wintercreeper is a slow-growing, non-invasive groundcover that will cover slopes and require minimal maintenance. Needs no fertilizer and prefers dry soils once established. Plant 1 to 3 ft. apart.

Planting trees and shrubs

Trees and shrubs establish the vertical lines of your yard, along with providing many practical benefits (and a few annoyances, depending on how you feel about raking). For best results, plant them right away in the spring so they have a chance to establish before the dormant season.

Balled-and-burlapped plants should be handled by the ball as much as possible to avoid breaking roots near the stem. Only remove twine and pins after positioning the tree or shrub. Remove pots before planting. You may need to cut off a plastic pot with shears or a utility knife. If the roots are densely circled, make three quarter-inch-deep vertical cuts in the pot-ball roots and peel out some of the roots. It is better to plant a little high than a little deep, since deep planting will kill many trees.

Aftercare of Trees and Shrubs

New trees and shrubs should be watered deeply from the start. Leave a soaker hose curled outside the root ball, position a slowly-trickling hose end under the tree for an hour, or fill the basin around the tree one or two times. At first, water once a week or when the soil dries at the surface. Over the season, move to deeper, less frequent watering.

HOW TO PLANT A TREE OR WOODY SHRUB

1 Measure from the ground to the point where the stem emerges from the root ball or pot ball. Dig your hole this deep, or a bit shallower. The diameter of the hole should be a third larger than the diameter of the ball. In heavy soils or if you will be mulching, you may plant the root or pot ball a little high, but do not bury the base of the stem.

2 Handle balled-and-burlapped plants by the ball, not the stem, as much as is practical. When the ball is in the hole and positioned correctly, cut off the twine and pull the pins out of the top of the burlap. Fold back the burlap and bend the metal cage off the top of the ball.

3 Fill the space around balled-and-burlapped plants with water before backfilling with dirt. When backfilling, use the water stream from a hose to work dirt into hollow spaces around large root or pot balls. Build a wide berm around the stem of trees and shrubs, using the soil displaced for the hole.

4 Unstable trees should be securely staked with three stakes and tight cords positioned so their directions of force are counter-posed. Run the cord though pieces of old garden hose where they contact the plant and allow room in these loops for the tree to grow.

5 Cover the soil within the berm with three inches of organic mulch, leaving it thinner near the stem. You may want to wrap soaker hose within the berm before laying mulch for more efficient watering.

Pruning Shrubs

Correct pruning improves the health, appearance and performance of woody plants. Pruning can help shrubs develop more and larger flowers. Fruit trees can be induced to grow larger fruit. All woody plants can be aided in attaining a more pleasing shape, and a more appropriate size. By removing misplaced, dead, and oversized branches, storm damage and disease can be reduced, resulting in a healthier, longer-living plant.

Why and When to Thin Shrubs

Thinning, or cutting back, is good for sheared and natural-form shrubs because it allows air and light into the central area of the plant, reduces insect and disease problems. It also removes branches that have been sheared at the same level for years, which can cause them to carry ugly and unhealthy tufts of branchlets. Overgrown deciduous shrubs and some evergreens, whether alone or in hedges, can be completely renovated by clearing out one third of the wood each year. The best time to thin shrubs is in the early spring, after the wood has thawed but before the buds have broken. You may thin spring-flowering shrubs after they have finished blooming. You may remove dead branches and do very light thinning any time.

How to Thin Shrubs

First, cut dead or damaged branches back to strong living shoots or buds that aim away from the center of the plant. For a major renovation, cut some of the oldest branches on single-trunk shrubs back to the trunk or back to where a branchlet or bud departs from the branch. If the shrub has multiple stems from the ground, you may remove some of the very oldest and almost all of the very youngest right down to the ground. Young stems shooting from roots in the ground are called *suckers,* and should be completely removed, unless you're saving some on a multi-stem plant to replace older stems. Remove any branches that rub and any water sprouts, which are young sprouts that shoot straight up from larger branches. Remove "bottle-brushes" (where numerous branchlets depart from a single stem) at a convenient fork below the bottlebrush. Small gaps left in the foliage will fill in quickly, but try not to create large gaps or remove too much at once—instead plan to prune a little bit each year. Your pile of cuttings should generally not exceed one third of the shrub's mass, and if you prune lightly on an annual basis, you will need to take much less.

Regular Pruning for Spring Flowering Shrubs

Spring-flowering shrubs may be cut back hard when the flowers begin to fade, to contain the shrub and to increase the size or numbers of flowers that will bloom

1 In general, undertake major pruning in early spring before leaves are out. Your local County Extension Agent or Master Gardner will know when it's safe to prune specific shrubs in your locality. Though in full leaf, this overgrown lilac may be pruned safely in Minnesota.

2 Dead, very small, and overgrown stems may be removed to the ground, leaving a balanced assemblage of healthy, midsized stems.

3 We have removed from 1/3 to 1/2 the biomass of this clump by pruning out conflicting and dead branches as well as whole stems, leaving a graceful stand that affords a view of the yard and reveals the lamp post.

the following year. Forsythia, flowering currant, mock orange, kerria, beauty bush, weigela, and spring flowering spirea are some examples of shrubs that benefit from this post-flowering pruning. Cut off a combination of large and small branches and/or stems to remove about one-third of the total growth. Try to cut branches that are just above another living branch.

NOTE: *Flowering dogwood, potentilla, barberry, magnolias, most viburnum and most lilac prefer to be left alone most years. Hard pruning may result in a year or two with few or no flowers.*

Regular Pruning for Summer-and-winter Flowering Shrubs

Summer-and-winter-flowering shrubs produce a lot of growth quickly, then flower from the new growth. You can tell, since the flowers are coming from fresh green or pinkish wood rather than darker, older wood. Examples include peegee hydrangea, crape myrtle, lippia, buddleia, deciduous ceanthus, indigo, summer-flowering spirea, and winter-flowering jasmine. Cut all the branches down in early spring to a low framework of branches two or three buds or forks from the ground. This will keep the plants small and the flowers big. Remember not to leave stubs; cut branches in spots where other branches or buds can replace the removed branch.

Prune spring-flowering shrubs, like this spirea, back by one-third when the flowers begin to fade.

Shearing hedges

Shearing with hand shears or electric hedge trimmers cuts back all new growth evenly, producing a dense outer layer. This layer casts shade on the interior of the plant, inhibiting new growth. Consequently, the hedge that is sheared, but not thinned, can only undergo growth in its outer "shell" and is also more vulnerable to disease. To avoid this problem, thin hedges after shearing, taking branches just above points where other buds or branches can replace them.

Shearing is done on an as-needed basis, usually once or twice a year for evergreens and two or three times a year for deciduous shrubs. Do not shear within two months of the first fall frost, since shearing promotes fresh growth that's vulnerable to frost damage.

1 Shear the outer branches to shape the hedge. It's best to shear large-leaf hedges with hand pruners only, since shears will cut many leaves in two, giving the plant a ravaged appearance. Encourage the hedge to grow in a flattened "A" shape, with a slight slope inward from bottom to top. This lets light get to the bottom branches, preventing dieback at the bottom of the hedge.

2 Now, take out dead branches and a few of the bottlebrushes. Leave small gaps in the foliage so light and air can get in to the middle of the plant and promote new growth. Do this only a little bit at each shearing; small gaps will fill in quickly, but large gaps may be difficult to eliminate.

Accent Plantings & Border Treatments   433

Pruning Trees

Young, growing trees should be pruned a little each year in the late winter or early spring before leaves emerge. Never take too much in a single year, since too much pruning when the tree is dormant will lead to rampant, unhealthy spring growth. Also, the bark of many smooth-barked species is susceptible to sun

(LEFT) The pole tree trimmer lets you saw and lop high branches while keeping your feet on the ground.

scald if too much of the canopy is removed. Birches and maples should be pruned in late summer, since they will bleed if pruned in early spring. Generally, prune in the following order:

1) Prune off all dead branches. **2)** Cut off water sprouts and suckers (rapidly growing branches that shoot straight up from much larger branches, the trunk or roots) flush with the branch or root they grow from. It may be necessary to dig down a little to cut a sucker off flush with the root. **3)** If the leader on a small tree or branch forks narrowly, cut off one side of the fork. A narrow fork will make a weak crotch when the two sides become large. Branches that form wide angles with the branch or trunk will be stronger. **4)** Prune branches that grow inward, and remove one of two branches that rub. Prune so the new lead bud or branch is growing away from the center of the tree. **5)** Remove small branches that crowd other branches and branches that are too low on the trunk. Pruning is an on-going process; so don't try to finish the job in one year. Taking too much at once can kill some trees.

Mature trees should be pruned for several reasons:

MAKING THE CUT

Use sharp pruners to make a clean cut that slants slightly away from the branch or bud that is not being removed.

A correct cut is made about 1/4-in. above a living branch or bud—close enough to heal over, but not so close that the strength of the crotch is compromised.

to remove dead, injured or rubbing branches; to keep the tree from catching too much wind and toppling; to eliminate branches that threaten wires, buildings or other property; and to increase sunlight to lawns and gardens. Suckers and water shoots should continue to be removed on adult trees. High and large branches should be pruned professionally for safety reasons.

The Don'ts of Pruning

Don't use tree paint. It interferes with healing. If diseases of your tree species are common in your area, cover the cut with thick paper and masking tape.

Don't "head" a tree. Cutting off the top of a mature tree to keep it small looks like vandalism. Better remove the tree and plant a species of a more appropriate size.

Don't leave stubs. Always try to make cuts where another bud or branch can take over so the wound can heal properly.

THE RIGHT WAY TO CUT OFF A BRANCH

WRONG: Too Long. A branch cut too long will never heal over, which permits rot and disease to enter the tree through the exposed wood.

WRONG: Too close. Here, the ring is cut away, leaving a gash that could take years to scab over and may introduce disease and rot to the heartwood of the limb.

JUST RIGHT. This cut will allow the injury to heal. Notice the thick ring of living wood that will form the scar tissue.

HOW TO CUT HEAVY BRANCHES

1 Heavy branches need to be cut three times to avoid tearing bark and wood from a tree. Under-cut the branch 6 to 12 in. outside the planned cutting line.

2 Over-cut a little to the outside of the undercut to drop the branch.

3 Cut the remainder of the branch off close to the branch that will remain (See photos, above).

Seasonal Guide to Yard Care

Don't think of spring, summer, fall, and winter as being defined purely by their assigned calendar months. These "seasons" are tied to different months in different parts of the country, and can even change from year to year in a single place. Perform lawn and garden chores when the plants are ready for them: not just because the calendar tells you it's March or October. In the following pages, we'll describe each season to help you perform garden chores at the right time. But look over the guide for the subseason immediately prior to and following the on you're in. You might find chores that need to be done right now in your yard.

Seasonal Guide to Yard Care

Late Winter, Early Spring

Late winter or early spring is marked by melting snow (if you get it), softening earth, swelling buds, and the return of early songbirds. This season starts in January or February in the south and may not start until April or May in the far north.

Trees and Shrubs: Prune dead branches from any woody plant. Prune living wood of evergreens, trees, vines, summer-flowering shrubs, and winter-flowering shrubs after the wood thaws but before new growth. Do not prune bleeding trees, like birches and maples, and don't prune spring flowering shrubs now. Wait to prune tropicals like hibiscus to avoid stimulating early growth. Feed with compost or a slow-release fertilizer if needed, but wait until late spring to spread a thick mulch. Plant bare-root trees and shrubs as soon as you can.

Perennials: Remove winter mulch. In places where the ground freezes solid under winter mulch, gradually remove the mulch as it thaws. In places where the mulch keeps the ground from freezing, gradually remove the mulch when the plants under it begin to grow. Cut down and remove dead plant material. Evergreen ground-covers may be mowed or cut back and raked to remove dead or old growth. Divide perennials if the ground can be worked. In areas with mild and rainy winters such as the Pacific West, fall may be a better time to divide perennials, though a wet early spring is a good second choice.

Lawns: You may overseed cool-season grass seed in the north. If you will be working the soil, however, wait until mid-spring when the soil is dry enough to till. Pull or spot-treat cool-season weeds in the south. Apply pre-emergent herbicides only if needed to dormant, warm-season lawns before the spring flush of annual weeds, but not if you will be dethatching or aerating later, since these procedures will eliminate the effects of the herbicide. If you will be planting a warm-season lawn, begin taking soil samples.

Mid-spring

Daffodils are blooming, cool-season grasses are growing, and some early leaves and the flowers of early shrubs are emerging. You may still have a late frost in northern areas.

Shrubs, Vines and Trees: Plant bare-root trees and shrubs in areas where it's still moist and cool, and plant balled-and-burlapped and containered trees, shrubs, and hardy vines anywhere, although fall and winter is a better choice in mild areas with a winter rainy season. Begin shearing hedges as needed in the south. Keep newly planted woody plants watered.

Perennials: Remove mulch, cut back old dead growth, and rake debris. Divide perennials where cool, moist conditions will prevail for a month or more. Fertilize and/or spread compost or rotted manure, but wait to mulch until the soil warms up. Plant containered perennials anywhere, although fall is preferable in mild areas with a winter rainy season. Keep new perennials watered. Begin weeding.

Lawn: Sharpen your lawnmower if it was not done in fall; buy new gas; service your lawnmower if it was not done in fall. Raking, pulling, and digging young perennial weeds will save a lot of work later. Check for grub infestations, if this has been a problem, and apply biological controls if needed.

Mow warm-season grasses low the first time and rake for the first time to remove old brown growth. Aerate and dethatch warm-season grasses after the third mowing. If you will be planting a new warm-season lawn, eliminate weeds with glyphosate when temperatures allow. If the ground is prepared, you may lay sod, or plant sprigs or plugs for a warm-season lawn, but it's still too early for seeding in most of the south.

Begin mowing cool season grasses, but mow high to discourage germinating weeds. Aerate cool-season grasses, if needed, and apply compost. Fertilize cool-season grasses if needed, though fall is a better time if you only fertilize once or twice. Continue to work on bare spots and uneven spots on a cool-season lawn. Apply pre-emergent herbicides only if needed to cool-season grasses now, or a bit later before warm-season weeds like crabgrass germinate (but after performing any mechanical treatment, like aerating or dethatching, which will deactivate the herbicide).

Late Spring

Leaves are almost fully expanded, spring-blooming trees and shrubs are in full flower and may be starting to fades. Evergreens are sprouting new growth. Lawns are growing full tilt.

Shrubs, Vines and Trees: Prune early-flowering shrubs when the flowers fade. Deadhead rhododendrons and azaleas for better blossoms next year. Shear evergreens and deciduous shrubs if needed, leaving some new growth on the plants. Continue to water newly planted shrubs, vines, and trees. Spread mulch.

Perennials: Shear faded flowers that bloom in masses and deadhead larger, faded flowers. Continue to plant containered perennials if you can keep them moist. Plant cold-sensitive annuals now also, when you are sure you are past the last frost date. Divide daffodils. Cultivate and pull weeds. Keep new plants watered. Spread mulch.

Lawns: Warm season grasses are growing now and may be dethatched, aerated, and fertilized or spread with compost. Late spring is a good time to plant or make repairs to warm-season lawns using sod, plugs, or sprigs. In warmer parts of the south you can seed warm-season grasses now. Keep new cool-season and new warm-season grasses watered. Established grass should be watered deeply and allowed to dry between waterings. Mow when lawn grass grows one-third higher than its optimal height. Most cool-season grasses may continue to be mowed high to fight weeds. Control caterpillar worms and grubs if levels are unacceptable.

Early Summer

Gardens, lawns and weeds grow vigorously in the warm, often wet weather of early summer. Nights are warm. This is a good time to start a compost pile.

Shrubs, Vines and Trees: Prune early flowering shrubs when the flowers fade. Remove suckers and water sprouts from the roots and stems of trees and shrubs. Shear evergreens and deciduous shrubs if needed. Continue to water newly-planted shrubs, vines and trees. Pick and destroy pest beetles.

Perennials: Shear faded flowers that bloom in masses and deadhead larger, faded flowers. Cultivate and pull weeds. Keep new plants watered and water established plants deeply if needed. Apply mulch.

Lawns: Warm season grasses may be dethatched, aerated, top dressed and fertilized if needed and you have not done this yet. Keep new cool season and new warm season grasses watered. Established grass should be watered deeply and allowed to dry between waterings. Continue to mow when lawn grass grows one-third taller than its optimal height. Plant warm-season grasses by any method now, since it's warm enough for the seed (although new seed will require watering multiple times during the day when it doesn't rain). Most cool-season grasses may continue to be mowed high to resist drought or shade-out stress. Spray for caterpillar worms and grubs if needed. Take soil samples if you will be planting a cool-season lawn in late summer.

Mid-summer

Mid-summer is often hot and dry in much of the country, slowing growth and browning grass. Parts of the deep south have a mid-summer rainy season, where it's a good time for establishing new lawns.

Shrubs, Vines and Trees: Prune early-flowering shrubs that are now finishing flowering. Shear evergreens and deciduous shrubs if needed. Continue to water newly-planted shrubs, vines and trees. Deadhead flowering vines. Prune suckers and water sprouts as needed.

Perennials: Deadhead faded flowers on perennials and annuals. Cultivate and pull weeds. Keep new plants watered, and water established plants deeply, if needed. A diseased or ragged groundcover may be sheared to the ground and allowed to re-grow).

Lawns: Keep new warm-season grasses watered; established grass should be watered deeply and allowed to dry between waterings. Continue to mow when lawn grass grows one-third taller than its optimal height. You may provide a slow-release, high-nitrogen or only-nitrogen fertilizer to actively-growing grass in the south. Plant warm-season grasses, especially if you have a mid-summer rainy season that is conducive to starting lawns at this time. Cool-season grasses may continue to be mowed high to resist drought, summer weeds, or to shade-out sun stress. Take soil samples if you will be planting a cool-season lawn in the fall. Kill old grass with an herbicide if you will be planting in late summer. Control caterpillar worms and grubs as necessary.

Late Summer

Days are getting shorter and the sun is less intense, but some hot days are still in store. Now is a good time for lawn and garden work because cooler weather is just around the corner.

Shrubs, Vines and Trees: Early August is the last safe time to shear evergreens and deciduous shrubs in much of the north, since shearing stimulates tender growth that may be damaged by frost. Continue to water newly-planted shrubs, vines, and trees. Prune maples, birches and other deciduous trees that tend to bleed if pruned in early spring. Oaks, elms and other disease-susceptible trees should only be pruned in the winter or early spring. New woody plants are easy to plant and establish now.

Perennials: Deadhead faded flowers on perennials and annuals. Keep new plants watered, and water established plants deeply if needed. Begin cutting back spent plants. Divide perennials that are done blooming in short-season northern areas to give them plenty of time to take root before winter (fall-blooming perennials should be divided in the spring). Plant containered perennials.

Lawns: Grass should be watered deeply and allowed to dry between waterings. Continue to mow when lawn grass grows one-third taller than its optimal height. Most cool-season grasses may continue to be mowed high. Plant warm-season grasses in hot parts of the Southwest that experience a rainy season now or in early fall. Pre-emergent herbicides may be applied in the middle south and transition zones to control germination of winter weeds in warm season grass (but only if these are a problem and not if you will be over-seeding in the fall). Consult local authorities to learn the best time to apply pre-emergent herbicides in your area. Begin killing the old grass if you will be planting a new cool-season lawn. Where winters come early, this is the best time for planting a new cool-season lawn or repairing an old one, and also for aerating, dethatching, over-seeding, and topdressing a cool-season lawn.

Early Fall

Early fall is gentle with plants, making it a popular time for working with perennials and cool-season lawns.

Trees, Vines and Shrubs: In temperate climates, prune maples, birches and other deciduous trees that tend to bleed if pruned in the spring. Early fall is a good time to plant woody plants in most of the country, though you might hold off until the winter rains in California.

Perennials: This is a good time to plant spring-flowering bulbs and containered plants of all kinds almost everywhere. Divide early-blooming perennials in the south as you get a break from the heat, but still have two or three months for the plants to establish before winter. In the southwest, a break from summer heat and a little more rain make this a good time to plant and divide a wide range of perennials. You may wait for the rainy season to divide plants in the Pacific west. Keep any transplants watered. Fall-blooming perennials will be showing their colors and may be planted for immediate gratification north and south.

Lawns: Wherever cool-season grasses are the primary lawn type, this is the best time to: plant a new cool-season lawn or make repairs to an old one; fertilize cool-season lawns; and aerate, dethatch, overseed, and topdress a cool-season lawn.

Apply pre-emergent herbicides for winter weeds on warm-season lawns in the south if this is needed and if you will not be overseeding with a winter grass. You may overseed for a green winter lawn in early fall in the mid-south, the transition zones, and some other parts of the south. Begin mowing a warm-season grass to the maximum height for the species. You may apply a complete fall fertilizer high in nitrogen and potassium in the deep south.

Middle Fall

The cleanup season is upon us in most of the country. Fall color is in full swing and leaves are falling.

Trees, Shrubs and Vines: Plant containered woody plants in most areas.

Perennials: When herbaceous plants die back, chop them back a few inches from the ground and rake out the debris. Fall-blooming perennials may be kept going. You may still plant bulbs and containered plants, which go on sale in the north. Water new transplants if they are still growing. Outdoor clay flowerpots should be emptied of soil and stored.

Lawns: You may overseed for a green winter lawn in the south; this may happen as late as November in Southern California and other very mild areas. Reduce mowing height for the last mowing in the north if fungal disease is a problem. Increase mowing height in the south to the maximum for your warm-season species or for the recommended height for an overseeded cool-season grass.

In the north, drain irrigation systems and water features. Shut down and drain outside water spigots and pipes. Winterize your lawnmower. Clean out any sprayers and note which chemical they were used to apply. Drain and hang hoses for the winter. Rake and compost leaves.

Late Fall

Leaves have fallen. Perhaps an early snow has blanketed a northern state. In the temperate south, most plants have entered winter dormancy. In Southern California and the Gulf States winter plants are coming into their own.

Trees, Vines and Shrubs: In the north, evergreen shrubs may be protected from winter drying with burlap or anti-desiccant sprays. Protect the trunks of young trees against rodents and sunscald with plastic tree wraps. Any delicate woody plant may be protected from heavy loads of snow with a protective structure. In the Pacific Northwest, you may prune summer-flowering trees and shrubs in late fall. In southern California and other areas with mild, wet winters, plant bare-root trees, shrubs, and vines now, as well as any containered woody plants.

Perennials: Finish cutting and removing dead growth from beds, but you may wish to leave any that look good in the winter. Apply mulch to tender or new plants after a few hard freezes. If you apply mulch too early, rodents may build nests in it. In areas with mild, wet winters, such as in the Pacific West, you may divide perennials in November and December.

Lawns: Rake any leaves off the grass. Finish winterizing chores. Sharpen and oil all tools. Fertilize with NPK (nitrogen, phosphorous, potassium) in the north if you normally fertilize twice and have already fertilized in late summer: it gives the grass a good start in the spring without assisting spring weeds. In the south, mow overseeded cool-season grasses to the correct height for the species.

Winter

Much of California and parts of the Southwest experience a rainy season in the winter, and enjoy lush growth of winter plants. If you live elsewhere, try not to think about this.

Shrubs, Vines and Trees: Shovel heavy snow from hedges. Prune woody plants in the south, including southern California, but wait until the wood thaws in early spring in the north. Do not prune spring-flowering plants anywhere now, since this would remove the flower buds. In Southern California, plant shrubs, vines, and trees in December or early January so these may establish in the rainy season.

Lawns: Mow overseeded southern lawns to the height recommended for the cool-season grass used. Pull or spot-apply herbicides for winter weeds.

Index

A

A. canadense (See Garlic)
A. stolonifera (See Creeping Bent-grass)
Accent plantings, designing, 408-409
Aegopodium podagraria (See Goutweed)
Aerating, 402-403
Aerator, manual, 403
  power core, 402
Aggregates, 171
Air compressor, 169
Agropyron repens (See Quack-grass)
Agrostis tenuis (See Colonial Bent-grass)
Ajuga reptans (See Bugleweed)
Allium vineale (See Garlic)
Angle brackets, 107
Angled joist hangers, 107, 137
Annual Bluegrass, 397
Annual Ryegrass, 363
Aquatic plants, 56-57
Arbor/Trellis project, 243-251
  cutting list for, 245
  lay out for, 248
  plans for, 244-247
Arc,
  laying out, 329, 342, 370
  positioning slats with, 330, 331
Arch, creating with wood, 218-221
Arctostaphylus uva-ursi (See Kinnikinnick)
Ashlar (See Cut-stone)
Auger, gas-powered (See Gas-powered auger)
Aviator snips, 168

B

Backer board on drill press, 329, 330, 370
Backfilling, 33, 39, 65-68, 75
Bahiagrass, 361
Balusters, types of, 153
Balusters, use for rails, 240-242
Bamboo, 394
Bare spots, planting, 407
Bark, as a loose-fill, 171
Basketweave pattern,
  for decking, 107
  for pavers, 25
Batter (See Setbacks)
Battens, 195-199, 200, 204-205, 209, 295
Batterboards,
  foundation form creation and, 285-287

in deck layout, 112-116
  lay out and, 185-188, 229, 284
  positioning posts with, 187
Beam saddle, 128
Beam size, for decks, 103
Bearberry (See Kinnikinnick)
Benches, built-in, for decks, 98, 99, 159
Benches, posts for, 141
Bermudagrass, 356, 361, 399
Birdsmouth, 310-311
Bishop's weed (See Goutweed)
Black Medic, 397
Blue Fescue, 424
Blue Gramagrass, 359, 361
Bog plants, 56-57
Braces as temporary assembly aids, 322, 323
Branches, cutting, 435
Brick edging, 414-415
Bricklaying, technique for creating wood arch, 218-221
Brickset, 64
Bridge project, 233
Brown Patch, 400
Bt (See Bacillus thuringiensis)
Buchloe dactyloides (See Buffalo-grass)
Buffalograss, 359, 361
Bugleweed, 424
Building codes, 19, 165, 166
  for deck stairs, 142-143
  for decks, 117
  for fences, 76
  for railings, 150, 153
  for water gardens, 47
Building inspection, 164-165
Building materials,
  shopping for, 165, 170, 172, 174
Building paper, 299-300
  attaching, 200-202
Building permit, 284
Built-in benches, 151
Bull float, 288
Buried lines, 19, 118, 166

C

Canada Thistle, 395
Cantilevered decks, 127
Cap blocks, 67
Cap rails, 204-226
Cattails, 56
Caulk gun, 168
Cave molding, 250
Cedar bark chips, 41
Cedar deck boards, 106
Cenchrus pauciflorus (See Sandbur)
Centipedegrass, 361
Ceratostigma plumbaginoides (See Leadwort)
Chamaemelum nobile (See Chamomile)
Chamfer,
  on hand rail, 240-241, 250-251

Chamfering,
  on router table, 338
  with hand-held router, 338
Chamomile, 424
Chewings Fescue, 365, 367
Chisel,
  mortising for hinges with, 329
Chrysogonum virginianum (See Green-and-gold)
Circular saw, 168
  angled cuts with, 136
  cutting notches with, 134-135
  cutting siding with, 124
  masonry blades for, 39, 64
  trimming deck boards with, 140
  trimming posts with, 86
Cirsium arvense (See Canada Thistle)
Clamping taper jig,
  building, 328
  using, 329
Clamshell, 169, 248
Clover (See White Clover)
Coastal deep south lawn zone, 354-355
Cobblestones, 13, 25
Codes (See Building codes)
Cold frame project, 262-267
  cutting list, 263
  kit, 262
  plans for, 263
Colonial Bentgrass, 366-367
Combination square, 141, 168
Common Chickweed, 397
Compactible gravel, 18, 23, 36-37, 60, 63, 70-71, 75, 85, 119-120, 171
Compass, shop-built, 329
Composite deck boards, 106
Composting pen project, 254-261
  cutting list, 254
  instructions for building, 257-261
  plans for, 255-256
  use of, 260
Compressor, air, 269
Concentric square pattern, for decking, 109
Concrete,
  buying options, 173
  curing, 290
  estimating need, 172
  mixing yourself, 173
  ready-mix, 173
  uses for in structures, 172
Concrete blocks, hollow core, in landscape building, 58
Concrete footings, crowning, 121
Concrete forms, tubular, 106, 117, 187, 188
  installing, 118-121
Concrete piers, precast, 170
Concrete slab,
  as a foundation, 284
  pouring, 287-290
Concrete tube forms, 170, 172
Concrete water gardens, 44